THE SHOW BUSINESS
NOBODY KNOWS

THE
SHOW
BUSINESS
NOBODY
KNOWS

Earl
Wilson

COWLES BOOK COMPANY, INC.
A subsidiary of Henry Regnery Co.
CHICAGO · NEW YORK

DEDICATION

Upon thinking over the title of this book, I realize it is preposterous. Today almost everybody knows almost everything about Show Business. The possible exception is my mother, Mrs. Cloe Wilson, who at near 85 is pretty busy with her grandchildren and her gardening in Fort Wayne, Indiana. I dedicate this work to her for the additional reason that she was shrewd enough when I was a young man to hint to me that it would be agriculture's gain, and not loss, if I left farming to farmers.

Contents

Prologue

The Golden Age of Show Business started at about the end of
World War II. This column, which I wrote on the night of the death
of Franklin Delano Roosevelt, describes something of the mood
of that time:

Broadway, Tough and Hard,
Weeps Openly for FDR

April 13, 1945

Broadway cried.

On the world's hardest-boiled street you don't expect tears. Yells
and laughter and beefs, but no tears. Last night the waiters in Lindy's
wept openly, the Broadway sharpies in their slick sports jackets
dropped tears onto their loud ties. A prostitute cracked under her
hard veneer and called to sob over the phone. Franklin D. Roosevelt's
tragic death stabbed Broadway to the soul.

Frank Sinatra cried long distance. The Voice was at Columbia records when he heard, and he slipped out wordlessly to St. Patrick's Cathedral. Seven or eight bobby-soxers followed almost to the pew. He lit a candle. Then he called his wife Nancy in California, and they both cried a little. I saw a cluster of people in front of Jack Dempsey's Broadway restaurant staring into a window, some of them crying, others looking misty-eyed. I pushed closer.

It was the way it was done. A placard in the window said, "Closed on account of the death of our beloved President." Close to the placard I saw a picture of the handsome, somewhat younger Franklin D. Roosevelt. And under it flickered four candles—the sad touch.

"That's what all night clubs and restaurants ought to do," a man said. He was half crying. As a matter of fact, nearly all the clubs did close, including those on 52nd Street, which by ten P.M. was as lonely as a grave.

So FDR even in death set a precedent. Certainly nobody ever made so much of The Street cry before. Never was there such an outpouring of emotions, not when Will Rogers died, not when Charles A. Lindbergh flew the Atlantic and crowds rose at a fight in Madison Square Garden to pray for him. FDR has become a part of everybody's family. One odd fact I picked up was a remarkable statement that Donald Nelson made only night before last to Jim Moriarity, owner of the swank Barberry Room.

"It'll be the greatest miracle in this world," Nelson said, "if Roosevelt lives two months."

He said this hardly fifteen hours before the president's death.

So the insiders knew, but the outsiders never did. Yet tears came to those who must have expected it. Bob Hannegan, the National Democratic Chairman, was sobbing when Toots Shor got him in Washington. Mark Hellinger wept cross-country when he phoned from Hollywood, and so did the Andrews Sisters. Belle Baker, the onetime speakeasy queen, who is considered by some to be incapable of tears, gave me the news of the president's death with her crying.

I was calling her about something else. She was weeping, having just heard the flash.

But not to make this story too idyllic, it must be admitted that some of the swank East Side night clubs were mobbed with customers— some of whom couldn't understand why there wasn't any dance music and said so. And there was one great industrialist at an expensive night club who was so upset by the news that he forgot himself and ordered domestic champagne.

The boor we have always with us.

Broadway loved FDR for many reasons—but especially because he was a colossal showman with a wondrous sense of humor.

Only three weeks ago at the correspondents' dinner, Danny Kaye led the crowd in a song and begged everybody present to bark like a dog. FDR's loud, spirited "Arf, Arf!" could be clearly heard around the main table. At the Washington radio correspondents' dinner in January, FDR almost fell out of his chair laughing at Jack Benny, who had apologized for his informal appearance by saying, "I'm wearing a Hart, Schaffner and Marx suit, and this shirt and tie—I got them at Montgomery, Roosevelt and Ward."

It will not be sacrilegious, I hope, to recall that upon the occasion of one of FDR's illnesses, a Washington newspaper perpetrated a typographical error and ran a story headlined: "FDR Kept In Bed With Slight Coed." He howled over that and sent over for several copies.

FDR's contempt for the hypocritical prohibition amendment also endeared him to the people of New York and Broadway. I was one of the young legmen at the Democratic National Convention in Chicago in 1932, at which he was nominated for the first time. The platform makers thought several hours per day about whether to come out for repeal.

We of the press were getting liquored up meanwhile on bootleg stuff in our rooms, favoring a potion known as rye and ginger ale.

I can still see FDR arriving there by plane to accept the nomination and the wild delegates greeting him with "Happy Days Are Here Again." I can also see the return of beer and liquor not long afterward. His bitterness toward the dry law was sincere.

When he campaigned in a heavy rain here last fall, it was necessary for his physician to prescribe some brandy and tea for him at the end of a long auto ride.

"Don't forget, Mr. President," some friend said, "you have a speech to deliver tonight."

"Yes," said FDR, winking, "and the subject is not prohibition."

So passeth the Eleanor gags. We are entering, no doubt, an era about President Truman's piano playing—or whatever else the gag writers will be able to concoct—and probably they will discover soon enough that Chopin rhymes with Tin Pan. Truman is not known to have any New York intimates. He, his wife, and his daughter came to New York about two weeks ago to shop and to see *The Barretts of Wimpole Street*. They allowed no fuss to be made over them. The Sherry Netherland has been his stopping place. And he has usually requested a piano for relaxation.

"He'll do a good job," one self-confessed Republican said last night, and he added, "He's got to!" That is the sentiment of about everybody except the worst Tories.

As for FDR, I like this epitaph, written by Broadway guy Irving Hoffman: "FDR—May He Rest in Peace—He Fought and Died for It!"

Introduction

AT the age of sixteen, I was driving a team of horses that pulled a water wagon for a threshing rig in rural Ohio. It was my summer vacation from high school, and I got $1 a day and board. It was hard, hot work, and since I had to get up at five, I often went to bed at seven or eight—never later than nine. Rockford, the biggest town in this farming area, had fewer than 1,000 people. Nobody was more of a rube, or hick, or country Jake, than I was in the 1920s.

Today I reside and work in the Times Square area, stay up all night, sleep till noon, and go in a dinner jacket to Broadway first nights, movie premieres, and café openings. I fly to hotel openings in Las Vegas, Los Angeles, and even overseas, and I am supposed to be something of an expert on show business because I have been covering it with my notebooks, tape recorders, cameras, and typewriters for thirty years.

Rockford didn't have a saloon, let alone a café or a night club. It was "dry." Every summer Harry Shannon's Famous Shows from nearby St. Mary's pitched a tent there for a week or two. The town boasted an opera house, but I never remember hearing of an opera being performed in it. There was just no show business in my home town. Consequently, when I began reporting show business in New York, I was literally popeyed at the wonders I saw.

Fortunately for me, I began reporting show business at what now must be recognized as the dawn of its Golden Age. None of us quite realized it then. Radio was just reaching its peak. Jack Benny and Fred Allen were the great masters, coining fortunes with jokes. Television wasn't taken seriously. Many big stars laughed it off and vowed they'd never be seen on it.

The managing editor of the *New York Post* had a television set in his office, but it stood silent and untouched. There were no programs.

Suddenly, in one great rush, the situation changed in the middle 1940s. The few people who owned television sets became the most popular tenants in the apartment building. Everybody stopped by to see them—usually when the wrestling matches were on.

"They're going to spend $25,000 a week on just one program!" we heard. The stars who had shrugged off television as a trivial affair began to view it differently. "Fifty thousand dollars for one program!" we heard later. These figures were incredible, and we were certain that they would never go higher than that.

There was "Howdy Doody," "Lucky Pup," "Kukla, Fran, and Ollie," and all the other children's shows. There was a lot of slapstick and occasionally some good drama originating in New York, and individuals with real insight discerned the beginnings of variety.

I had long been a friend of a young comedian named Milton Berle, who had become a millionaire in his middle thirties by stealing other comedians' jokes and retelling them in theaters and night clubs. Berle called himself "the thief of bad gags" and never denied the larceny.

Before television, Berle and I used to troop around to the night clubs, where he would find a way to insinuate himself into somebody else's show by either heckling or actually getting up on the stage. The action was always—or almost always—welcomed by the other stars.

Then, one morning Berle awoke to find his picture on the covers of both *Time* and *Newsweek* the same week: "Mr. Television"— "Uncle Miltie"—the entertainer for whom shopkeepers closed up on Tuesday nights so they could watch his variety show on NBC; and those without television sets visited their favorite bars to watch him. Up to that time only Winston Churchill and FDR had been on the covers of the two leading news magazines on the same week.

Meanwhile, there was a very fat comedian who everybody said was "the best table comedian" in New York but the worst on the floor or on the stage. If he could only get paid for the gags he flung across the tables when he was drinking at night, he'd be in clover. In fact, a couple of gag writers kept assuring me that they had found a medium that would make this man great and they begged me to look at the film. Three or four years later, Jackie Gleason was making television deals that paid him even more than Milton Berle was getting.

The new era in show business was starting. By coincidence, the new leisure was also about to begin. They were to go hand in hand.

When I first went to Las Vegas in 1946 to have a look at the incredible town, I didn't consider it a show business outpost. To me it was just a place to watch legalized gambling.

Bugsy Siegel, the mobster who was later to be assassinated in Los Angeles, was just then building the Flamingo Hotel in Vegas. We stayed at El Rancho Vegas, which has since burned down in a fire that has never been explained.

A strange trick of fate worked in my favor on that trip to Las Vegas. As we were flying back with a test pilot in a private plane, we heard a flash that Howard Hughes had crashed in a superfast XF-12 experimental reconnaissance plane, destroying one home, rocking much of Beverly Hills, and injuring himself. He was being treated in Good Samaritan Hospital, where he was given only a fifty per cent chance to survive.

I was to have been his passenger that week.

The crash occurred during the long Fourth of July weekend in 1946. Hughes was out of the hospital August 12th. None of us—except possibly Hughes—suspected that he was going to own an enormous part of Nevada one day and to control some of the most luxurious hotels and casinos in the world.

Liberace played the piano in the Raleigh Room at the Hotel Warwick in New York without any outstanding financial success, yet in April, 1955, he was to open the new Riviera Hotel in Las Vegas for an unheard of $50,000 a week. Yet the figure suited one of the biggest stars on television, beloved by middle-aged women everywhere in the country.

Those were the days of Sophie Tucker, Ted Lewis, Joe E. Lewis, the Ritz Brothers, and Harry Richman—and of the shy and reticent high roller Nick the Greek, all of whom I got to know very well.

I haven't counted the trips I've made to Las Vegas since then.

But no one could have envisioned the world of show business that animates Las Vegas now—with two "strips," two main streets, lined with luxury hotels and casinos making $1,000,000 deals with superstars such as Barbra Streisand.

Recently Caesar's Palace was sold for $60,000,000. One of the departing owners went back to gamble after he had sold out. He stayed at the tables for thirty-six hours and lost more than half a million.

Las Vegas pays the stars so much now that they can and do tell everybody else to go to hell from time to time. Vegas has created a colony of temporary millionaires who are colorful, zany, and full of idiosyncrasies.

Then there was Europe, where I traveled almost as many times as I did to Las Vegas, chasing Ingrid Bergman when she was having her famous romance with Roberto Rossellini and again when she broke up with Rossellini, pursuing Rita Hayworth when she was being captivated by Aly Khan, and laying pipelines to get the first word on Grace Kelly's baby by Prince Rainier.

And of course there was New York, where such stars as Marilyn Monroe arrived unknown but eventually became the focal point of American entertainment. I interviewed her for the first time because I needed a feature story for the following Saturday. And from then on I was a spectator of her amazing life drama, which climaxed when her ex-husband Joe DiMaggio barred her Hollywood friends from her funeral.

My constant wanderings about New York, Las Vegas, Hollywood, Europe, and other places where the action was concentrated plunged me into the orbits of the greats and near-greats of the entertainment scene and into the middle of key events and changing phenomena. I interviewed Jayne Mansfield because we were both interested in the same commodity—bosoms. Then there was Carroll Baker and the beginning of nudity. And the list goes on indefinitely.

In fact, I have been in the thick of show business since the 1940s, when, in its modern guise, the Golden Age of Show Business began—unfolding before the eyes of a boy from the farm as he sat in hundreds of aisle seats and ringside tables. And to think that when I went out to "see the sights" on my first night in Manhattan, I was such a hayseed that I headed downtown instead of uptown, and I plunged into the darkness of the garment district. I had just ar-

rived from Ohio, and, as I looked around the dimly lit section for
some action, I said, "Akron's livelier than this!" It was just about
then that I started learning a few things about New York and the
world of show business.

Today's show business has become cynical and acquisitive—due
to the revolution in sex, morals, language, and ethics it has undergone—and much of the sentiment has gone from the period of the
early 1940s, when I began covering this particular zoo.

The show business revolution has introduced a world of entertainment that then would have seemed not only impossible but
undesirable.

Sometimes the new show business appears to be a great sex-for-
sale bazaar. The new sexiness, the new and now nudity, the new
sliminess, the old dirty words, the lack of censorship, and the permissiveness occasionally make you wonder if you're glad you came.
Maybe I should have "stood" on the farm.

I see it daily on Broadway.

"Nude Live Models," screams a sign above a storeroom.

"Beautiful Nude Girls Available For Body Painting . . . Rub-
down—Massages—Photographs—Open 10 A.M. to Midnight. Ama-
teurs Welcome. We Can Supply Cameras and Film."

Girls can be seen wiggling in and out of the store, and men sneak
inside furtively. The girls sit on couches in the front room, waiting
to be chosen by the customer, ready to make backroom deals for
various forms of sexual gratification.

Across the street there's another "Nude Live Model" sign, and a
man peers out from behind a curtain and beckons to passersby.

This is not show business, strictly speaking, but it is associated
with the total nudity and candid sex that have revolutionized the
once proud profession. The adjunct is extensive. It includes Las
Vegas computers that prevent the bosses from stealing the gambling
winnings from the owners and the waitresses who sell sex as well
as cocktails; Broadway, with its copulation on stage, its dialogue
written by playwrights trying to outdo each other in obscene language and sexual candor; Hollywood producers who outbid each
other for the masturbation masterpieces; *Playboy's* models now
showing their pubic hair; women who can now see nude men on the
screen, on stage, and in magazines; and acid rock music, distorted
by the drugs used freely by the listeners and the musicians.

"God, no, I don't want it!" we would have said in 1945.

Yet show business, for all its aberrations, remains the most exciting of all worlds, a veritable hell to live and love through but probably more fun than heaven. As an incurable optimist, I foresee the depression being cleared away, the dirt and vulgarity being sifted out, and show business being left cleansed and profitable once again. That I believe.

Broadway, New York City

June 30, 1971

EARL WILSON

1
Las Vegas—Battle for the Stars

THE story of show business of the late 1960s and early 1970s is the story of how it became a great Sexorama. But it is not possible to understand how that happened without surveying the entire scene. Sometimes, sex wasn't obvious at all; sometimes it sneaked in like a thief in the night. It's nearing eleven o'clock at night during Christmas Week when your limousine rolls away from McCarran International Airport, just outside Las Vegas, and you approach the "Strip," now blazing with more bright lights than have ever illuminated Times Square in New York. Out here in what used to be a desert you have come to Star City, the playground of the richest, handsomest, prettiest, wittiest, screwiest, weirdest, wildest, sexiest—and probably the meanest and wickedest—folks in Show Business. You have come to the Hedonists' Heaven. But don't ever say "Hedonists' Heaven" out loud or somebody will build a new hotel just to use that name.

Leaning forward, you gawk at the lighted signs fronting the highway, enticing you into the legalized gambling dens that are more numerous than those in Monte Carlo, Cannes, Nice, Deauville, Estoril, London, the Bahamas, and old-time Havana combined. The truth is that the only place in the world that even approaches Las Vegas in the number of its alleged sin palaces is Reno, Nevada.

You spot one sign that reads, rather demurely:

The Riviera
BARBRA STREISAND

You are wondering if you will be able to get a reservation to see Miss Streisand, when you behold another sign:

Barbra Streisand
Is at the
Las Vegas International.

"She can't be at both," you're thinking, and then you remember. Miss Streisand, currently the greatest female night club, concert and "personal appearance" attraction on earth, winner of the Oscar, Tony, and Emmy Awards, is finishing a two-week engagement she had owed the Riviera from an old contract. After a four-day rest, she is starting at the International on a new contract. For five weeks, she will receive $525,000. There is no other city in the world that can afford to pay performers such a salary. Even Reno can hardly pay it. And as nearly everybody knows, Las Vegas can pay it only because Miss Streisand's remarkable voice and wondrous nose attract people who will dump enormous sums into the hotels' coffers while gambling either before or after they've seen Miss Streisand's shows. That she may be a shill for the gambler-bosses who have a sure thing going for them has probably never occurred to Barbra. The gambling public knows it can't win, yet seemingly because it knows, it stubbornly keeps trying. Barbra Streisand as a performer is likely to rationalize that she is the biggest attraction and should be paid the most money. What's wrong with that? It only makes sense.

As your limousine rolls on, you realize that, although this is a Christmas Week—supposedly a slow season—you have access to a staggering array of stars, not much less renowned than Barbra Streisand, at the other hotels. For example:

The Sands
SAMMY DAVIS, JR.
MEL TORME

***

Louis Prima
Celebrity Lounge

***

RIVIERA
Dean Martin Presents
BURT BACHARACH
The Establishment

***

SILVER SLIPPER
Girls
Girls
Girls
No Cover

The highway signs continue to reveal Las Vegas's abundance of talent:

FLAMINGO
Marty Allen
Kaye Stevens

A sedate oblong sign modestly states:

ELVIS
Christmas Greetings.

Elvis Presley is not currently appearing in Las Vegas, but he will be soon, and he has placed his Christmas card on the highway for his fans. He will appear at the International, where he is rated as the male equivalent of Barbra Streisand.

And there are more neon signs leaping through the night at you:

Frank Sennes Presents
BOB NEWHART

Extra Added Attraction
EDIE ADAMS
in the Crystal Room
DESERT INN

The Sahara Hotel advertises the name *"Buddy Hackett"* across the entire width of its top story. Caesar's Palace, probably the most affluent of the hotels, seems rather modest in boasting only the *"Smothers Brothers"* and the *"Everly Brothers."*

The Landmark, the hotel with a tower, reminds you that it has the highest casino in the world and that it is bringing Nashville to Las Vegas: in the form of the famous Grand Ole Opry. The Frontier presents: "Mr. Excitement, Wayne Newton." The Tropicana has *"The Follies Bergère"* in the Theater restaurant, *"Julie London"* with *"Bobby Troup"* and *"Dick Lord"* in the Blue Room, and *"The Red Norvo Trio"* in the Casino Lounge. The Dunes has *"Casino de Paris."* The girls of the *"Bottoms Up"* company at the International are getting their bottoms punctured for a trip to Australia. The Desert Inn's Lady Luck Lounge announces, in a separate sign, *"Billy Daniels, Irish Pixies, St. Paul's Sisters, and Jody's Four."*

And that is outside downtown Las Vegas—Glitter Gulch.

The dozen mighty gambling halls each pay an average of $100,000 a week for entertainment, which means that the stars can leave with more than $1,000,000 a week—if they can lick the tables. The great salaries gave birth years ago to the expression, "that Las Vegas fuck you money"—which must be clear in meaning.

The first person I heard utter the vulgarism "Las Vegas fuck you money" was Red Buttons. Then a television star with writers' troubles that eventually cost him his show, he was sitting in Sardi's one night explaining that he'd found a solution.

What were his plans? I asked.

He told me simply, "I'm going to work in Las Vegas and get some of that 'fuck you' money."

In its days of glory, Broadway never offered such an assemblage of stars nor such a pile of money. Nor, of course, did it have legalized gambling. When you have arrived in Vegas, Broadway's successor, the odds are good that you won't proceed immediately to your hotel room. Almost anywhere else in the world, yes, but in Las Vegas you are overcome by an itch to see whether the roulette wheel, the dice, the slot machines, or the blackjack tables are friendly. While checking in, you might glance at a paper called *Vegas Visitor* and be intrigued by the following:

There's also an ad for "Talk of the Town," an adult book store at 2232 E. Charleston that proclaims it's open twenty-four hours a day and that it sells "marital items."

With several weeks of that a year—the least important acts get $25,000 a week—an actor can defy the world the rest of the time. And that's what lured all the stars there—and still does. They, in turn, bring in the crowds of gamblers.

It's the big name stars who bring in the "traffic" to the casinos, and the casino with the biggest name usually gets the most traffic. That's how salaries skyrocket from Danny Thomas's $10,000 a week at the Sands in 1952 to Barbra Streisand's $1,000,000 deal in 1970 (that figure will be disputed—but read on).

The hoodlums, the racket guys, "the boys," were in control in the beginning. There was an unwritten but well understood rule that nobody was supposed to murder anybody on the premises, or leave any bodies lying around. Preferably, they shouldn't murder anybody even within the city limits. Be a good kid and have them find the body outside of town or, if possible, across the Nevada line was the general idea.

The opening of the Sands, on December 16, 1952, introduced an era of big name entertainment that has continued until this minute. The late Jack Entratter, long the manager of the Copacabana night club in New York, became the purchaser of entertainment at the Sands, and he immediately began bringing into play the connections he'd used to book the biggest stars into the Copa to sign them up for the Sands. He had an extra advantage: thanks to the gambling riches pouring in, he had more money at his disposal.

Just before Christmas, 1952, we junketed out.

Except for the war in Korea, it was a generally carefree time. Dwight D. Eisenhower would soon be sworn in as president, and Elizabeth would be crowned Queen of England. Eleanor Roosevelt visited backstage at *Seven Year Itch* and had no transportation home, so Vanessa Brown, the former Quiz Kid who became a stage star, flagged down a cab for her.

Vincent Impellitteri, New York's mayor, angered the newspapers because he wouldn't tell them where he was going on his vacation in Florida. Perle Mesta was the Minister to Luxembourg and was serving "Eisenhower potato salad" to the GIs at her parties. I was deploring the increase in smut and sermonizing against the "Filthy Fifties."

New York had twice as many newspapers as it has today, and each one had invitations to send somebody to cover the Sands opening. There was a little teaser added to the invitations that had a fascinating importance: each of those invited was to be given $25 in silver dollars to use for gambling.

Now $25 was a big chunk of money in 1952. But having somebody hand it to you, saying "Here, be my guest—squander it," was much better than your saying to yourself "I'm going to throw $25 away" and actually tossing away that much money of your own. We ladies and gentlemen of the press couldn't wait to give that $25 back to the house, just as the house managers knew we would. It was a good conversation starter, and I would guess that the reporters of the Sands opening remember those silver dollars more than anything. And one and all of us loved Jack Entratter and publicity director Al Freeman for dreaming up the gimmick.

It was a night that split the ears and blinded the eyes. Danny Thomas was the first headliner. Because Jack Entratter was from New York with a title of a vice-president, some of the locals were resentful. The rival hotel owners—some of them wild, crazy gamblers—rushed in to give the Sands what they called "a friendly play." That meant they hoped to clean out the new place, bust it, ruin it before it got started.

That very first night the high rollers hit the Sands for a quarter of a million dollars.

With the winners yelling and the losers moaning, the celebrity-hungry crowd gawked at Humphrey Bogart and Lauren Bacall, Dick Powell and June Allyson, and Lucille Ball and Desi Arnaz. Louella Parsons, the most illustrious member of the Hollywood press present, watched the gambling action with the stars.

Swashbuckling through the casino in a Western outfit, Jake Friedman, the Sands' bankroller, kept mopping his brow with a bandana and bellowing, "The house is a $250,000 loser."

The gambling elite were there. Ray Ryan from Texas, Pennsylvania, Acapulco, Palm Springs, and later Nairobi—"the fastest gambler in America"—was rolling the dice wildly. Aging, wrinkled Nick the Greek was studying the picture, deciding how to risk his sponsor's money. Terry Moore, a beautiful young actress who had hopes of marrying Howard Hughes, looked on from the sidelines with Spike Jones, Jimmy Durante, and the Ritz Brothers, who at the opening ceremony took off their pants and threw them into the time capsule. (Years later the executives wanted to open the time capsule but couldn't remember where they'd put it.)

Jack Entratter looked haggard as he saw the "friendly rivals" from the other hotels standing in line to cash in their winnings.

"It's a great story—about people winning," publicist Al Freeman insisted. "It's good advertising."

An hour later when they were still cashing in, Entratter gazed down at Freeman a little anxiously.

"How long is this advertising campaign going to go on?" he asked.

By six A.M the gambling tide turned; and the house began to win. Jake Friedman, with a fresh bandana in his fist, was buying drinks and ordering a steak breakfast.

Thus was launched the hotel that was for a long time as important to Las Vegas as the Palace Theater had been to Broadway.

I never ceased to be amazed by the experience of seeing the sun rise while people were still shooting craps indoors. Most of them were so immersed in their labors with the dice that they didn't realize the night was over. It is an old observation but a true one that it is as hard to find a clock in Las Vegas as it is to find a virgin. Barbra Streisand said in her act, "Have you noticed that in Las Vegas the Bibles only have five commandments and the television sets in your rooms never work?

"They want you in *there!*" She pointed toward the gambling casino.

"Glitter Gulch" downtown was a place you went to gamble between gambling sessions. Once I saw some garbage cans on the street brimming with silver dollars.

"Don't throw those away," I said to the man pushing the garbage can. "If you're finished with them, I'll take them off your hands."

The man explained that he was merely making a bank deposit. Silver dollars were the popular coins then. Silver dollars were dumped freely into garbage cans and pushed onto hand trucks to be taken to the banks. Later the banks loaded them into other garbage cans and pushed them back to the casinos.

"Using silver dollars takes care of the robbery problem," someone explained to me. "If a holdup man has a hundred silver dollars on him, he's not going to be able to run very fast."

There are very few dumpy, squat little buildings in downtown Las Vegas nowadays. "Glitter Gulch" has given way to high-rises in the building expansion. The phrase "high-rise," meaning tall building, probably originated in Las Vegas. A decade ago the hotel owners began boasting of building plans for their new high-rises, which usually were additions to their original setups. The high-rises were first built on the Strip; then downtown Las Vegas felt it too had to have high-rises.

"You can read a newspaper at midnight on a street corner in downtown Las Vegas," somebody told me recently.

There was a time that Times Square was so brightly lit that you could read a paper at night, but now between the illuminated areas there are dark blobs and shadows that strain your eyes. However, in downtown Las Vegas, I saw a newsdealer sitting on a street corner at three A.M. contentedly reading his paper. The lights around him made it almost as bright as day.

Tourists often hunt out casinos in downtown Las Vegas, where they believe the slot machines will be "looser." But usually the word "looser" changes to "loser," and those people return to the Strip. Johnny Carson (who bought a home in Las Vegas "to be near his money," according to one of the jokes) claims that Las Vegas is the only place in the world "where you can see women in Cadillacs counting the nickels they're carrying in a Dixie cup."

The battle for the stars—and that's what it was—began back in the early fifties when Lena Horne and Martin and Lewis were getting $6,000 a week or maybe $7,500, and Dennis Day was raking in $10,000. The Sands, newly opened and needing to attract attention, captured Johnny Ray, who had been a sensational enticement for customers at the Copacabana in New York, for about $10,000. The Desert Inn plunged in and outbid the Sands for Johnny's services, paying him $20,000, the top money at the time.

Frank Sennes, the entertainment booker for the Desert Inn, then snared the great woman movie star of the period, Betty Hutton, for $25,000 a week, and Betty jitterbugged all the way to the bank, happy in the fact that she had topped Johnny Ray by $5,000 per week.

Bill Miller had been running Bill Miller's Riviera in New Jersey, attracting large New York City audiences, but a highway project forced the demolition of his club. Very popular with the entertainers and acquainted with most of them through the Riviera, he went to the Las Vegas Sahara in 1953. One of the first things he did was create "lounge entertainment"—putting acts in what they called "the little room." He hired Louis Prima for $3,500 a week, and Louis played five shows a night.

Jack Entratter, Bill Miller, and Frank Sennes were trying to bring stars to Vegas who had never played there before and, in fact, had never even considered the idea.

"How about Tallulah Bankhead?" Jack Entratter wondered. He got Tallulah at the Sands at a period when she thought $10,000 was a lot of money.

"They call those things *crap* tables," Tallulah said in her act and seemed to strike a nerve with her audience, judging by the laughs that greeted the line.

Later, Marlene Dietrich came out to look things over. Jack tried to sign her up to do an act with Tallulah, but it didn't work out.

"The girls got into some kind of thing," Entratter told me. "Marlene wanted more than Tallulah, even if it was only $1 more. Finally, she got a better offer from the Sahara."

Bill Miller doesn't remember the battle between the girls. "I told Marlene that if she was going to work Vegas, she should work the Sahara. I gave her $25,000 a week. I got Red Skelton for $25,000 and Sonja Henie and her ice show for $25,000. The big money was then $25,000."

Ezio Pinza, Robert Merrill, Kathryn Grayson, Jose Greco, and other big names were being lured out to the desert. For entertainers who had considered $10,000 to be more than they were worth, getting $25,000 a week was some kind of a miracle, and they must have thanked God that there was a gambling streak in the general public, whose losses at the slots and tables enabled the hotels to overpay them so much.

"It's just to get that traffic in the casino . . . traffic is the name of the game in Las Vegas," Bill Miller declares. It's an expression you'll hear echoed by every booker and hotel executive.

To get that traffic a casino must have big, exciting names who are drawn there to see the show or to see other stars who have been drawn there. That's the appeal of Dean Martin, for example. Wherever Dean is, there's action, and players go where the action is.

In April, 1955, the stars cracked the $50,000 barrier. The new Hotel Riviera—the first "skyscraper" hotel (nine stories)—announced it was paying that enormous sum to Liberace.

This was always the pattern. A new hotel has to offer something spectacular or sensational, and it's usually a star who's paid an unheard-of sum.

Liberace was the darling of middle-aged television viewers. Though these middle-aged mothers weren't powerful crapshooters, they adored "Lee," his clothes, his mother, his brother George, his piano, and his candelabra. They would talk about him and they would goad and cajole their husbands into taking them to the Riviera. Thus, he would bring out the traffic in the casino.

But soon somebody else appeared, to pay $50,000 a week: the New Frontier, whose booker John Goldman guaranteed that salary to Mario Lanza, the sex symbol who believed he had inherited Enrico Caruso's vocal cords.

Liberace gave them a show for their money. Lanza did not. Lanza didn't show up.

Lee stands out as a landmark in my many visits to the Nevada mirage. He appeared on that April night wearing a silver-colored tailcoat created by Dior. His teeth were the pearliest examples of the art of dentistry. He sat down on the stage—carefully lifting the tail of his coat first—and discovered, not exactly to his surprise, that his mother was there.

He bent down and kissed his mother. He flashed his teeth at Sonja Henie, allegedly his latest romance, who was at the ringside, and at Constance Bennett, who had flown out from New York with her husband. In this carnival-like atmosphere, he remarked apologetically to the audience that he had made a mistake.

"I feel sort of selfish calling her 'my mother' because she's George's mother, too. Isn't she, George?"

George nodded vigorously that she certainly was.

Lee paused in his entertainment to comment upon the significance of his salary of $50,000 a week.

"It wasn't very long ago," he said, "that George and I went with our grocery wagon to get county relief. And now I'm the first one to get $50,000 a week, who *opened*, you know . . ."—a reference, understood by all, to the fact that Mario Lanza hadn't made his appearance, because of one of his illnesses. Laryngitis was the authorized reason.

Lee could honestly consider himself just as big a hit as his mother wanted him to be. It was so crowded that night in the new $8.5 million skyscraper that we representatives of the press had to go through the kitchen to push our way into the jam-packed Hickory Room.

Despite their keen rivalry, the Las Vegas hotels have always aided each other in emergencies. Lacking Lanza, the New Frontier sent an SOS to Bill Miller at the Sahara for help from Ray Bolger, his star.

"I'll do it if you'll dance with me," Bolger told Miller, an ex-hoofer who hadn't danced in years. They sent a plea to Jimmy Durante at the Desert Inn, who likewise responded gallantly.

An intriguing point about the exorbitant Las Vegas salaries is that there is always some cynic who claims they never existed at all, that the figures are phony. These skeptics contend they're exaggerated, that Liberace's $50,000 was really $40,000, and that he had to pay for the entire show out of his salary.

Some say there's a conspiracy of silence among the bookers about how much they pay. This silence is observed especially when you try to draw one out on the story of the "under the table" payoffs to avoid income taxes.

The hoodlum influence has always figured in Las Vegas and there's nothing a hood likes to tamper with more than income taxes. They would sit up days—they were up nights anyway—trying to concoct under-the-table payoff schemes to cheat on taxes.

"I swear on my mother's life I never saw or knew of any under-the-table stuff," one booker told me.

"Sure it happened, but who's ever gonna talk about it?" stated another booker.

Very coyly, another one said, "Oh, we give them *gifts*—maybe a car or something—but it's out in the open . . . nothing under the table."

Nevertheless, when the salaries leaped beyond the $50,000 mark, other devices were created to capture the giants. Sometimes it was gambling credit . . . chips . . . the freedom to lose without having to pay back the "marker." Occasionally it was simply greenbacks somebody had hoarded for the star from that morning's "skimming." But you will not get anybody to discuss this any more than you will get them to talk about a couple of unsolved murders.

Anyway, the stars began to come, though the one star whose personality was perfectly tuned to that of Las Vegas—Frank Sinatra—did not become a power in the town until the late 1950s, when he became the *biggest*. He first starred at the Flamingo, when it was owned by Gus Greenbaum, who, along with Mrs. Greenbaum, was mysteriously murdered.

The area came to have many Sinatra connections. For example, Ava Gardner once was hidden away up near Lake Tahoe waiting out a divorce from Sinatra. One afternoon my wife and I were driving around the beautiful lake region looking for her hideaway and found it not far from the home of the late Ty Cobb. The front gate had been left ajar, so we walked up the drive and knocked on the door.

Ava greeted us cordially and invited us in to meet her bullfighter chum, a strapping, virile looking Spaniard with bulging biceps and a gleaming white-toothed smile.

She decided we should all have a drink, and she said to her matador, "Get me a piece of ice." She glanced sharply at him and advised him, "That is not the same as a piece of ass." To us, Ava explained, "His English isn't so good."

Sinatra rapidly became the biggest, especially when Jack Entratter pulled him, Sammy Davis, Jr., and Dean Martin into the Sands family.

Entratter conceived the idea of getting Sinatra, Dean Martin, Sammy Davis, and Joey Bishop on the stage at the same time, and he decided to call it "the Summit Meeting," likening it to the summit meeting of the world leaders held in Paris.

The Sands' Summit Meeting on January 20, 1960, was a landmark. Sinatra, Dino, Sammy, and Joey—and Peter Lawford, whose brother-in-law JFK would soon become president—took over the stage and seemed to get more enjoyment from their ad-lib program than even the customers, who were ecstatic.

With those stars at the Sands every night for a couple of weeks, there was really no other place for a gambler to go. Between shows there might even be even a better show in the casino.

"Look! Dino's dealing blackjack!"

"Hey, Sinatra just won ten big ones!"

"Isn't that Nat King Cole . . . ? Did you see Pat Lawford over there with her brother . . . ? Sammy Davis just went into the restaurant . . ."

Everybody was happy and harmonious, and it seemed that it would last forever. Sinatra owned "a couple of points," two percent ownership of the hotel. If the hotel earned $2,000,000 in a year, he was entitled to $40,000. While this was a lot of money, Sinatra had been known to drop, or win, $40,000 in one night. Eventually Sinatra had 6.5 points. Entratter had 12.5 points. They were close friends, and between them they had 19.5 points; together they were the biggest stockholders in the Sands.

"The Summit Meeting at the Sands" took place while Sinatra, Martin, and Davis were filming a picture in Las Vegas called *Oceans 11*. Sophie Tucker was 70 years old that year and Paul Anka was 18, and they were sharing billing at the Las Vegas Sahara. *Spartacus* was the big buildup picture. Senator John F. Kennedy looked good for the Democratic nomination for president, but if he didn't win on an early ballot, look out for Adlai Stevenson and Pat Brown, the experts said.

Juliet Prowse, the leggy dancing beauty, was around the "Summit" with Sinatra. Mingling with them were Lucille Ball, Cyd Charisse, Dinah Shore, and Ingemar Johansson.

Jack Entratter sent his Summit stars a telegram that said, "You come to my summit meeting and I'll come to yours." It was signed "Khrushchev."

Comedy through insults was becoming popular. Sinatra found time to catch Don Rickles's act at the Sahara lounge and presented a gift to him. After opening it, Rickles said, "I'll say this for you, Frank—you're cheap."

Marlene Dietrich was singing "And One More for the Road." An admirer told her, "You know, you sing that better than Sinatra." "I think so too," Miss Dietrich said.

The glamorous Senator Kennedy arrived at the Sands for the Summit meeting and was introduced by Sinatra. Wildly uproarious cheering came from the crowd at the show, whereupon Dean Martin stepped up to the mike and in a soft, apologetic voice asked Frank: "What did you say his name was?"

The president-to-be had his arm around his brother-in-law Peter Lawford. Sammy Davis got in some fast lines about his people. Sammy then collapsed from lack of oxygen and lack of sleep, and he went to bed for 72 hours. Eisenhower was still president, and Bob Hope told the National Press Club an old one, that Ike told his pilot, "Take me anywhere—we've got troubles everywhere." Little did they know that troubles were developing everywhere in the country.

The show was colossal for Las Vegas. It focused attention on the city. There was a payola investigation going on in the East, and several disc jockeys were worried about getting convicted of accepting bribes. Rowan and Martin were a couple of pretty good comedians at the Copacabana in New York, but nobody ever suspected that anything like "Laugh-In" was in the offing. Their jokes weren't the freshest in the world. A typical routine would go something like this:

ROWAN, introducing the bandleader at the Copa: He'll do anything for you.
MARTIN: Yeah? Where are the broads?
ROWAN: No, I mean anything musical.
MARTIN: Where are the musical broads?

Those were the Sands's golden years, with the crowds pouring in to see, hear, and stare at that mad crew. Nobody could envisage any changes.

There was a lot of foolery that was amusing at the time because it was topical. On Dean's forty-fourth birthday, Peter Lawford came on stage in a waiter's coat, carrying a tray to serve a drink to Sinatra.

"Can you imagine what he'd have me doing if Jack had lost?" Peter asked the audience.

When John F. Kennedy became president, it was Sinatra and Peter Lawford who ran the pre-inaugural party, and the Summit crowd from Las Vegas moved into the Hotel Statler in Washington. Negroes had an important place there—Sammy Davis, Nat "King" Cole, and Harry Belafonte were upstairs in the setup arranged for Sinatra and Lawford. On the night of the gala, the man who would be sworn in as president in a few hours stood up in his box and complimented the performers.

"We have seen excellence tonight," he said.

"I want to run an ad in *Variety* with that quote across the top of the page," Sinatra said.

The new president might have been very friendly with Las Vegas —but he had a brother. Attorney General Robert Kennedy was interested in exposing racket influences in Las Vegas gambling. Thus, when the president made a visit to Palm Springs, he did not stay at Sinatra's house as had been expected. Instead, he was a guest of Bing Crosby. Sinatra and Peter Lawford had a misunderstanding, seemingly related to JFK's visit to Palm Springs. The friendship of Vegas and the new administration seemed to be over.

But something else was about to boil over on the back of the stove. On July 22, 1967, I reported in a news story that Howard Hughes was trying to buy the Sands Hotel for a sum ranging from $20,000,000 to $30,000,000 and this price would include the Sands's exclusive contracts with its big name stars.

Hughes, of course, had already bought the Desert Inn, where he lived in the penthouse. He had reportedly become annoyed about something at the Desert Inn, and said, "I'll just buy the place." The world's most celebrated recluse, Hughes was the subject of some of the tallest tales ever told. It was said that because he didn't want anybody to see him, he had himself smuggled into the hotel in the middle of the night in a refrigerator. According to another story, when he went to Boston to a clinic, he had himself carried not in a refrigerator but in a trunk.

Nobody ever saw Hughes—that is what created the mystery. Men who had worked for him for years and had been close to him would confess—reluctantly—that they hadn't actually seen the body of Howard Hughes in seven or eight years. They hated to admit this non-contact with the hero, and some of them would hint mysteriously that they had seen him but couldn't talk about it. Nor would they say *when* the contact had been made or what he looked like. All this added to the speculation about Hughes's health and undoubtedly triggered the suggestion that he was dead.

"I see him . . . I see him . . ." an old club companion of Hughes in the earlier days swore to me one night. "I don't have to tell you anything about it, and I'm not going to."

In these ways, the mystery was heightened.

It was speculated that Hughes hated gambling and that he planned to close down the tables and slot machines. That was more absurd than most of the other stories because one thing Hughes does not hate is money, and gambling brings in *lots* of money.

"I saw him walking around one night getting some air," a man told me at the Desert Inn. "It was about two o'clock, and he was wearing a long beard as a disguise. I know it was Hughes because he was wearing his famous tennis sneakers."

The man pointed to a seldom-used elevator. "He came downstairs in that elevator right there."

"I saw him on the street about a year ago," another supposedly reliable source informed me. "He was with four—no, three—other fellows. I *know* Hughes. I'm old enough to know what he looks like. How many other people around this town would know Hughes if they saw him? That's why nobody sees him. They don't recognize him."

It was all very eerie, as though show business were being influenced by a ghost. Still, there were those employees who were directed every day by memos and phone calls from the penthouse, from key people who claimed to be speaking for Hughes but who admitted they had never seen him.

Bizarre actions were attributed to "the spook." Here was a man empowered with the juggling of a $3 billion fortune, yet, according to one tale, he was troubled about a vulgar word spoken in one of the shows by a girl he had never met.

Memos and phone calls came down from the penthouse commanding that the objectionable expression be deleted from the act.

"This baffles the hell out of me," a stage manager said. "How the hell did Howard Hughes or his informants or his ghost or his secretary know that expression was in the show?"

Of course, nobody thought that Howard Hughes was skulking about the rehearsals disguised as a stagehand listening in on the dialogue. Yet some very serious people were puzzled about the manner in which he got the information. Nobody had been asked to submit a script. Nobody known to be representing him had sat in on the rehearsals.

"Could the room be wired?" they wondered.

"Could he have a closed circuit television hookup in his room?"

Ludicrous as it seemed, it was no more so than many other Howard Hughes mysteries. It was believed that even Hughes' secretaries, who conveyed his orders by memo or phone from upstairs, did not actually see him but were handed directives by a male nurse who, with Hughes, was barricaded against the outside world.

Particularly distressing was the fact that the employees of Hughes Tool Company—even those in purportedly responsible positions—had to wait for weeks just to find out what the man upstairs wanted them to do about a given problem.

"Is he too sick to give an answer?" "Did he ever get my question?" "Is somebody trying to make up his mind for him?" These were the simple questions, always followed by the big one: "*Is there a Howard Hughes?*"

"Did you hear there's a barber he told to wait for him to give him a haircut?" was one of the stories. "That barber's still waiting. It's four years now, and Hughes Tool is still paying for his room."

The arrival of Hughes Tool Company officials to the Sands—Hughes himself was never seen there—inaugurated a new, less personal way of doing business. The Sands and other hotels that Hughes acquired were computerized. Gamblers' junkets, which hauled well known players to Las Vegas free and gave them complimentary rooms, were discontinued or greatly reduced. A more careful watch was kept on the credit of the stars who gambled when they weren't performing.

Most of the stars over the years did some gambling, and they usually lost just as all the other players did. It was frequently reported that Joe E. Lewis blew his whole salary at El Rancho Vegas in one night. That statement could have been made about nearly every star at one time or another. It got to be a popular legend that "So-and-So can never leave Vegas for the rest of his life. He owes so much he'll have to stay in Vegas until he dies working off his debts." The story went on that the casino operators to whom So-and-So had lost so heavily were rough gentlemen who had virtually imprisoned So-and-So. I heard this story countless times, but I never found who So-and-So was.

Joe E. Lewis's name usually figured into the stories about compulsive gambling and big losses. His employer for several years was Beldon Katleman, proprietor of El Rancho Vegas, who watched over Joe E. almost like a mother, trying to get him to restrict his gambling. Joe E. was one of the action guys who brought big gamblers into any club where he performed. When El Rancho was mysteriously destroyed by fire, Joe E. went over to the Sands with the other action guys.

The story of Frank Sinatra's defection from the Sands and his transfer to the new Caesar's Palace is tangled and confusing.

A call reached me in New York that Sinatra had been unable to make a scheduled appearance at the Sands for a couple of nights because of laryngitis.

Then came another call that Sinatra had actually been in conference in Palm Springs with proprietors of Caesar's Palace, talking to them about selling them his Lake Tahoe Cal-Neva Hotel and making a new arrangement whereby he would leave the Sands to star at Caesar's Palace.

Then it became known that Sinatra had made an effort to sell the Cal-Neva to Hughes and that Hughes didn't want it. (The name of Hughes is always used in these reports although it was never determined that Hughes figured in any of these negotiations.)

At the peak of all this tension, when Sinatra was not making an appearance at the Sands supposedly because of laryngitis, he began gambling at the Sands. He soon hit a losing streak, and he was forced to demand additional credit. His request was refused, and a bitter argument followed, with Sinatra announcing loudly that he would never appear at the Sands again.

After hearing about this on Sunday, September 10, 1967, I phoned Sinatra's home in Los Angeles. His wife Mia Farrow answered the phone. I told her what I'd heard. It was mid-afternoon, and Sinatra was sleeping.

"When he wakes up, I'll have him call you," Mia promised.

I remember her reply because it wasn't evasive or tentative. She didn't say "I'll see if he can call you" or "I'll ask him to call you." Mia said: "I'll have him call you." She spoke like a woman with some authority around the house!

About two hours later Frank Sinatra did call me.

He must have awakened with quite a hangover, according to the reports I'd already received—and what another hangover was going to follow! It was generous of him to take the time to phone me on an afternoon in which (as it was to turn out) he had so many other matters requiring his attention. I will describe this Sunday afternoon and Sunday night (and the following Monday morning) of Frank Sinatra's life more extensively later in this book. But we might recall now that Sinatra had been monumentally insulted, at least in his own mind, by the casino bosses of the Sands, for whom he had done so much by bringing in customers who had gambled away fortunes to the hotel. To his way of thinking, they could never repay him for what he'd done for them. Likewise, there are old-time hotel operators in Las Vegas—who don't even care for Sinatra—who say that the Hotel Sands executives were out of their minds.

Frank in that return call spoke succinctly and wittily.

"What happened?" I asked him. "I heard they cut off your credit."

He replied they had done just that. We had heard he was into them for a tremendous figure—something like $200,000. Frank didn't say. He just confirmed that they had stopped his credit.

"They can't do that to you," I told him.

"They did it to me, and I did it to them," he answered.

"What did you do to them?"

Frank replied that he was walking out on his contract with them; he would never work for the Sands again. Frank did not say to me some of the things later attributed to him by others—that he had changed the place from a sand pile to a successful hotel and he was going to turn it back into a sand pile again.

His threat to part from the Sands was one of the most earth-shaking events in Las Vegas in several years. Immediately there were forecasts that he wouldn't do it, that somehow Jack Entratter would pacify him and bring him back.

However, on that Sunday afternoon, after he had talked to me, Sinatra returned to Las Vegas. He went back to Caesar's Palace, with whom he was still discussing the sale of his Cal-Neva Lodge. Then he visited the Sands, and in the early morning hours of Monday he got into a fight with Carl Cohen, the Sands casino manager. Frank lost some teeth.

Sinatra was renewing his demands for more credit and blasting those who refused him. A table was upset, a chair was thrown, and Cohen, usually a mild-mannered man, threw a punch that caught Sinatra in the mouth.

"Singer Tony Bennett left his heart in San Francisco, and Frank Sinatra left his teeth—at least two of them—in Las Vegas," Don Digilio wrote the next day in the *Las Vegas Review-Journal.*

That Monday morning fracas settled one thing: Sinatra was finished at the Sands, and the rift would not be patched up. Caesar's Palace met Frank's terms for Cal-Neva, and as part of the deal, Sinatra would star for Caesar's Palace. All this was arranged in one weekend.

To the rest of Las Vegas it meant that the Sands no longer had a lock on the biggest drawing card—Sinatra. And what about Dean Martin and Sammy Davis? Would he take them both with him to Caesar's Palace? Would they defect too? Nearly everybody believed they would, although here and there an expert declared that Dean Martin is an independent spirit who goes his own way,

The Hotel Riviera seemed to have an edge in trying to get Dino because the head man there, Eddie Torres, was a close friend. Still, Caesar's Palace had a lot of money to spend. And there was a new hotel going up—the International—built by a wonderman of Armenian descent, Kirk Kerkorian. The new hotel would undoubtedly undertake to secure a sensational opening attraction, just as all the other new hotels that preceded it had done.

The late movie actress, Anita Louise gave about twenty parties a year in the period just before she died. She threw one in Los Angeles, where I learned two significant facts about Las Vegas and its immediate future.

Sid Korshack, the prominent attorney and one of the powers with the Riviera Hotel, pulled me aside during the party and said "I have a couple of things for you. One is that Dean Martin is going over to the Riviera with ten points. They've offered him the presidency, but he doesn't know whether he wants that. The other is that the International has offered Barbra Streisand $1,000,000 to open the place for them.

"I know about that because we have Barbra under contract through a deal we made before she got so big. She wants us to let her postpone her commitment to us so that she can accept the International deal."

"Are you going to do it?"

"I'd hate to stop anybody from making a million dollars," he said.

The Streisand deal with the International will be talked about for a long time. After all, Barbra had tied with Katharine Hepburn for the Oscar for *Funny Girl*, and she was also starring in *Hello, Dolly, On a Clear Day,* and *The Owl and the Pussycat.* No star had been favored with bigger or better publicity. As a live attraction, the promoters could not have found anybody bigger.

So Bill Miller, who by then was helping the International with its bookings, signed up Barbra Streisand. The money, he said, was to be spread over a period of five years.

It broke down to $100,000 a week *plus*—plus how much, we don't know. Probably at least $10,000. As Marlene Dietrich a few years before had wanted more than Tallulah Bankhead was getting, Streisand wanted more than anyone else was getting.

The girl from Brooklyn who wouldn't fix her nose was getting more than double what Liberace got when he opened the Riviera fifteen years before. Barbra opened another new era of salaries that would lead to screams of alarm from some of the hotels unable to play in that league.

Bill Miller says, "I thought the Streisand deal was perfect for her and good for the hotel. We made an agreement not to discuss the figures. She was permitted to buy stock in the hotel at the market price, which was very cheap then. We charged $15 a person to see her. You put 4,000 people in that room with two shows a night, and you've got $60,000 a day without whiskey. So how much are we losing?"

Barbra bought 20,000 shares of stock in the International at $5 a share, and it went to $60 a share, giving her a paper profit of $1,100,000. (It subsequently dropped sharply.)

Undoubtedly her opening on July 2, 1969, was the most expensive and most glamorous up to that time. The new $60,000,000, 1519-room 30-story operation wasn't finished, and the air conditioning wasn't functioning properly in some areas. But all the big names of the time were there—including Andy Williams and his wife Claudine, from whom he later separated; Richard Zanuck and Linda Harrison, whom he later married; Jule Styne and Sammy Cahn, celebrating the fact that they'd become song-writing partners again; Tom Jones, the Smothers Brothers, labor leader Harold Gibbons, who found it wasn't safe to leave your table in that crowd (he left his, and it was gone when he returned), and Phil Harris and Alice Faye.

The celebrities' celebrity, Cary Grant, introduced Kirk Kerkorian at a cocktail party before the opening and again at the opening of the big room. Even with 2,000 seats there wasn't enough room.

Barbra had considered shock treatment for the opening night guests. Inasmuch as the hotel wasn't finished, she considered startling those who knew her reputation for high fashion by trotting out in dungarees and saying, "Well, the hotel isn't ready yet either." Then she would rush off stage and change into her flowing raspberry chiffon gown while the thirty-five musicians played the overture for four or five minutes. The shock value might be good, but was it worth the stage wait? Barbra sensed that the crowd would be restless after the long cocktail reception and the seating problem. Her husband, Elliott Gould, from whom Barbra was separated, discussed it with her and her manager, and she abandoned the idea.

Everybody leaped to his feet to accord Barbra a standing ovation at the end of her act. About twenty men carried floral pieces to her on stage. I was reminded of a mini Rose Bowl parade. Some of the critics were a little grouchy about the weather, the air conditioning, their table locations, or other problems. Barbra wasn't entirely pleased with her act, and she made some changes. It took her three or four days to establish the rhythm and pace she wanted.

When Elvis opened a month later on July 31, the hotel was functioning perfectly, and the crowd was gigantic. It appeared that Elvis the Pelvis was going to be as electrifying an attraction as Barbra had been. And he got off to a better start than Barbra, both professionally and, I suspect, financially. I'm sure that Colonel Parker, Elvis's manager, carved out an equivalent or better deal than even

Barbra got because he's been around those curves more years than has Barbra's manager, Marty Erlichman.

Colonel Parker waited until Barbra had closed her month's engagement. Then he smote Las Vegas with 200 radio spot announcements about Elvis at the International.

"This town has never seen a promoter like me," Colonel Tom declared. He had always regarded his boy as the greatest crowd pleaser in the world, and he may not have been far wrong.

"Don't forget, Elvis Presley went into the Forum in Los Angeles and took in $325,000 in one day," Bill Miller says.

His appearance was something of a gamble for Elvis. Barbra hadn't played a personal appearance in three years. He hadn't played one in nine years. In those nine years there had been the Beatles and the Beatlemaniacs, who had been anti-Elvis because they feared he would outlast the Beatles.

Now here he was, a saloon singer again, still emphasizing the pelvic movements, riding the guitar as if it were a bareback horse, doing those wild gyrations with the microphone. He was giving us his new record at the time, "The Ghetto," but he did not forget such old favorites as "All Right" and "Jailhouse Rock." During his act he hurled a challenge at Tom Jones, who certainly hadn't monopolized the female fans and never would as long as Elvis could move that pelvis.

Elvis brought a big newspaper crowd to Vegas as well as celebrities that included Burt Bacharach and Angie Dickinson, Wayne Newton, Totie Fields, and Steve Lawrence and Eydie Gormé.

There were other openings in Vegas that night—by Dinah Shore, Jerry Vale, Jane Powell, and Myron Cohen—which some of the reporters hoped to catch at a midnight show after Elvis's nine P.M. opening.

Then Colonel Parker tricked us. At the last minute he announced that Elvis would hold a 12:30 conference.

There had been rumors that Elvis might be making an announcement about his marital situation. Most of us newsmen were afraid to miss the press conference. We went and waited for a dramatic announcement. There wasn't any. All Elvis said was that he was glad to be there. Colonel Parker had effectively kept us from seeing the other competing stars and giving them publicity.

And that's the way it goes in Vegas. Everyone has to outdo the other, on the stage and at the gambling tables.

It's difficult for people of ordinary means to picture the way the "gambling barons" threw money around only twenty years ago. Jakie Freedman of the Sands staked $1,000,000 in the largest crap game on record at Joe W. Brown's Horseshoe Club in 1955 and finally broke even although he had been several hundred thousand behind during the game that lasted until ten A.M.

"Colonel Jakie" was betting $500 on every throw and backing each wager with $500 in odds. The experts on such matters said that when Freedman cashed in his stack of $100 and $500 chips and went home, he had outdone even the great games of Nick the Greek.

I have always been impressed by anybody who can treat a $100 bill lightly. One night in Las Vegas one of the owners threw my wife a $100 bill and said, "Go have fun, honey." She trotted off, won at a roulette table, and gave him back his $100 bill—which astonished him, since no woman had ever returned his money before.

This man must have been a participant in the "skimming"—the process of removing a few thousand in the counting room before turning in the "final figures." When the house was winning $100,000 a night, this thievery wasn't difficult as long as the skimmers were not too numerous or too greedy.

Tales of such opportunities lured "important people" to town. "Dandy Phil" Kastel, the supposed financial wizard for Frank Costello, was around the Strip, and so was Meyer (the Bug) Lansky. The police claimed that they told them to move on.

In the midst of all the gambling, there are unexpected paradoxes. For example, though you'll find the place swarming with Nathan Detroit types right out of Damon Runyon's *Guys and Dolls*, there are many earnest churchgoers who solemnly attend the "gamblers' Mass" held at 4:30 A.M. Sunday for croupiers, cocktail waitresses, cooks, bartenders and show people, at the Guardian Angel Shrine. There's another at five P.M. Sunday at the same church which has stained glass windows donated by Danny Thomas and Jerry Lewis. Frequently the collection basket is passed by a croupier or a dealer—who knows more about money?

"We accept chips," the priest says, "also personal checks. We are not proud."

And $5 and even larger chips are dropped into the basket. One of the regular plate passers is Tommy McDonald, long-time operator of the Singapore restaurant in Chicago, who became one of the bosses at the Las Vegas Stardust; and, as we wait for Mass to start, he bends over the pew, bragging to me about the number of churches in Las Vegas—close to 200, as Tommy tells it. (Tommy also estimates the population of Vegas to be 500,000, but other sources insist he is including much that isn't strictly Las Vegas.)

Just as churchgoing is common, so prostitution still is illegal, despite the fact that it is already legal in fifteen of the eighteen Nevada counties. Joe Conforte operates a brothel at Mustang Ranch, outside the county, and states that he does not actually manage his place—

"My wife Sally oversees things. A brothel needs a woman's touch. Things come up that only a woman can handle."

Conforte has made considerable efforts to legalize the oldest profession, but without success. Typical of the opposition is Eugene Murphy, the director of marketing at the International Hotel. A staunch Catholic who goes from Mass to his desk, Murphy frowned at the prostitution suggestion when I put it to him.

"We don't need any official stamp put on us saying 'This is Sin City,'" he contended.

Pointing out that conventioneers are a big part of the business, he added, "If we had legalized prostitution here, a lot of wives wouldn't let their husbands come to conventions." Money and morality complement each other in Las Vegas, or are made to do so.

The enormity of the business Murphy does not want to jeopardize is attested to by the fact that each major hotel must "win" $100,000 a night to keep going. If the "casino drop" isn't $700,000 a week, the hotel is in trouble. With more than a dozen major hotels and ten lesser gambling spots, the nightly win by the Las Vegas casinos is approximately $1,250,000. The average visitor probably leaves about $50 a night in the casinos.

With so much at stake, Las Vegas residents are realists, with no illusions about anything. They know sex is here to stay and that there are plenty of prostitutes floating around the casinos, looking for customers in the cocktail lounges, at the tables, and at the machines. One of the sex shops in the downtown area is frequently tended by a woman who greets customers cheerfully and tells them they can ask her anything because she's married.

Over in the dildo and artificial aids to sex section a man looks into a showcase and asks, "What's that thing with the little rubber bulb?"

"That's a special dildo for the man who can't maintain an erection," the woman answers in a voice loud enough to carry over the entire establishment. There is no whispering, no secrecy. "He puts his penis in here," she points out, "and then he blows it up by squeezing this bulb. It's the same as blowing up an inner tube in a tire."

Just as blithely, the woman discusses the sizes of the dildos, informing her assorted listeners that they start at six inches and go on. "Drop in any time," she says as her slightly embarrassed customers depart.

The people who have resided in Las Vegas for several years are just as realistic about its history. One of its best known murder cases —the double killing of Gus Greenbaum and his wife Bess in December, 1958—was never solved.

Greenbaum, sixty-four, was a popular fellow who'd helped to keep the Riviera open after it had gotten off to a faltering start. After lending the operators $500,000, he assumed control, and the hotel was a success when he and his wife were at their ranch house home in Phoenix, Arizona, that December night.

Greenbaum, unquestionably a gambling kingpin—he'd been in the Las Vegas Club, El Cortez, and the Flamingo before taking over the skyscraper Riviera—had maintained a Phoenix residence for twenty-five years.

The night of the murder Mrs. Greenbaum drove her maid, Mrs. Pearl Ray, home after the latter had finished her work. Then she drove back to the ranch house as she frequently did when they were in Phoenix.

As Mrs. Greenbaum left her car, she was waylaid near the back door by the killers, who are believed to have smashed her head with a wine decanter. Using her keys to enter the house, they fractured Gus Greenbaum's skull twice with the decanter. Then they slashed the throats of both victims with a large carving knife.

Coming to work the next day, Mrs. Ray found Mrs. Greenbaum

dead on a couch. Music was coming from a television set in Green-baum's room, and he lay sprawled in a pool of blood.

A private policeman had checked the exterior of the house on his rounds that night either just before or just after Mrs. Greenbaum returned home.

"Revenge killing—grisly gangland style murder," the police in Phoenix theorized. The Las Vegas police didn't get unduly upset about it. The murders *had* occurred in Phoenix, after all.

"Why did they kill Mrs. Greenbaum?" . . . "She must have known the murderers" . . . "But why was *he* killed?" . . . "He must have refused to cooperate with somebody." Those are the sorts of answers you get in Las Vegas today. Nobody cares very much.

In downtown Vegas, a huge figure of a cowpoke overhangs the street, making thumb-jerking motions to lure passersby into one of the casinos at a busy intersection.

You can't miss seeing him. In fact, for a time you couldn't possibly miss him because he would constantly say in a loud metallic voice: "Howdy, Pardner!"

Johnny Carson and some of the other show folk who live in Vegas part of the time allegedly took a shot at him with a bow and arrow—their own version of the game of cowboys and Indians.

But that wasn't his big problem. Some of the competitors and neighbors objected to the speaking and—as the locals say—"they cut out his squawk box."

Anyway, he is silent now, and, in the opinion of those who spend even a short time there, he is the only thing in Las Vegas that is.

2

There's Dough in Television: Milton Berle, Jackie Gleason, and Bob Hope

IN the beginning of laughter via television and particularly of the big money that was its reward, there was Milton Berle. He was later toppled from his throne by Jackie Gleason. Other comedians reigned for a while, but as the years passed by we realized that television was akin to a horse race and that the older, wiser horse on the track was resting during the earlier spurts of his fellow-entertainers, only to win in the stretch. The winner is Bob Hope.

I will not speak now of who is the funnier but of who stays on the air, and romps off with the money—which is the name of the television game.

Television, as it works today, is one of the twin pillars of show business. The other is the personal appearances initiated in Las Vegas and carried into the concert halls and arenas, in which a star can at least aim for the $304,000 the Beatles earned at Shea Stadium in August 1965, for one night's effort.

"Don't today's earnings make this the Golden Age of show business?" I asked Jack Benny, who has made quite a profit from laughter himself.

He hesitated. "I'm not so sure," he said. He thought back to 1938, when he was getting $800,000 or $900,000 a year and was one of the three top earners in America, according to income tax figures, which are no longer made public.

"Back when you could keep it . . ." he added with a rueful smile. Back then besides radio and movies and night clubs, there were the theaters on Broadway—the Paramount, the Capitol, the Roxy, and the Strand—which paid stars of Benny's caliber $50,000 a week for personal appearances, and—a sneer for the Internal Revenue Service—"you could keep it."

Television was little more than a toy in those years. I saw my first television program at the New York World's Fair in 1939–1940. It was a room-to-room hookup.

Who would have believed that because of that little tube we would become the most spoiled and lavishly over-entertained people in the world?

Who among even the dreamers could have predicted a citizen being awakened in his hotel room by television or radio, then being Muzaked down the elevator to the lobby, to a limousine with a television set, which runs two or three movies as he rides to the airport, where he can loll back with a drink and dinner in a flying theater which, in the jumbo jets, is showing movies on four screens?

Certainly Bob Hope couldn't have perceived it, nor could Milton Berle. As for Jackie Gleason, he was just fooling around. The big thing for some time had been Bing Crosby's radio program and the singing Boswell Sisters. And then the popular attraction was the Andrews Sisters—Maxine, Patti, and La Verne. They recorded "Nice Work If You Can Get It" with "Bei Mir Bist Du Schoen" on the flip side, and the flip side fooled them by selling a million right away.

The Andrews Sisters went to the Paramount Theater for a personal appearance, and when I visited them in their dressing room, they complained about a movie they'd made, saying, "Those producers just give you a pinch on the fanny and forget you." This was considered daring dialogue in those days. Even Jimmy Fidler, in one of his "open letters" on the radio, said that was no way for young ladies to talk.

"Pot of Gold" was on the air. Families congregated around their radios to listen to "Myrt and Marge," "Fibber McGee and Molly," and Cliff Edwards as Ukelele Ike playing "June Night," "Sleepy Time Gal," or "Toot, Toot, Tootsie, Good-bye." Who needed television, whatever it was?

Tom Dewey was going to be president—Alf Landon was going to be president the term before, but a funny thing happened to him on the way to the White House. Nobody gave a damn about the greatest thing that had come along, and the ignorance and lack of imagination of show people was appalling. Everybody was drifting along with the status quo, almost slumbering. Bob Hope frolicked into the Paramount Theater, doing five shows a day with Jane Russell, Jerry Colonna and the rest of the company, including Vera Vague. The mustached Colonna only had to say "Greetings, Gate!" and acknowledge a reference to Yehudi ("Who's Yehudi?"), and the audience was off in a fit of laughter. Jane Russell sang in Bob's show, and appropriate jokes were made about her celebrated bosom. She and Carole Landis (or Lana Turner) were known as the "Big Four"—and as for Jane's singing, it was said: "You can't take your eyes off her voice."

Jack Benny—with Rochester, Phil Harris, and Mary—was so big on radio that William Paley, head of CBS, lured him away from NBC by buying Jack's company, Amusement Enterprises, in one of the first such maneuvers, for $1,400,000. Jack had been earning a salary equivalent to that of George Washington Hill, the eccentric head of Lucky Strike cigarettes and American Tobacco in the years before. Paley commented later that bringing Benny over to CBS was a successful deal because "it made the network."

That arrangement was part of a battle between CBS and NBC that would continue indefinitely, eventually involving Hope, Berle, and Gleason.

Paley also moved Amos and Andy, Red Skelton, Burns and Allen, and Bing Crosby into the CBS camp, and NBC suddenly found that it no longer had nine out of the ten top shows. In fact, NBC was trailing CBS.

With such success with radio, it is not surprising that there was some hostility toward television at its inception. It is hard to understand now, but somebody brought out match packs imprinted "Help Stamp Out TV."

Some leading actors lacked economic foresight; a few were just waiting for the money to get good. The pay was so niggardly, the lights were so hot, and the audiences were so small in the beginning that self-respecting actresses such as Tallulah Bankhead vowed they'd never touch television.

Women were scared of television because the cameras gave them a squashed-in look. In 1946, Helen Parrish, then called "The First Lady of Television," told me that the camera distorted the appearance of her bones.

"I have to load my neck down with beads so the bones won't show," she said.

Everybody was pretty relaxed at first. Her sponsor was Tenderleaf Tea, but in one show Helen goofed and said "I've always used Lipton Tea." Nobody seemed to mind because apparently nobody was watching anyway.

I went to look at the "Hourglass Show," and on July 27, 1946, I reported that the eight to nine P.M. Thursday slot might some day be one of the best hours on television. I wrote: "But right now, in the pioneer stage, they start at eight but seldom run the full hour. No stage manager is rushing to get them off the air because nobody else is going to get on it anyway. It's a lot of fun being a television pioneer; a lot of fun—and very hot."

During those hot nights we did curious things when we got on those shows. We just walked around, as at a cocktail party—they did serve cool drinks because of the heat—we waved at the camera, and we had fun. There was no direction and no discipline.

"Do anything you like because nobody's seeing you. There actually aren't any receivers in town," they told you.

We didn't have a set yet. "You're going to get a free set for being on the program," somebody promised, but it never came, so we bought a set with a seven-inch screen for $350 on 7th Avenue. Jerry Lester was on, and I remember that my son, who was about four years old at the time, was enchanted when he saw Jerry Lester hold his foot up to the camera, and show the sole of his shoe. That was early television comedy.

Television sales were slow, and many people in New York watched it only in their neighborhood bars. Television needed somebody to induce the public to buy sets. The time was ripe for Milton Berle.

Milton Berle was the brashest young man in America. He wasn't great on radio because on radio you couldn't see him tickling the girls' midriffs, galloping around in long underwear, or blackening his teeth so that he looked grotesque. But he was already a millionaire from his theater and night club shows. "The thief of bad gags" claimed that he had become a top comedian by learning ten jokes a day.

"Ten jokes is a lot of jokes to steal every day," he said.

A very changeable fellow, sometimes he would deny he stole gags. Then he would say: "I was listening to Jack Benny on the radio last night, and was he funny! I laughed so hard I dropped my paper and pencil."

During a testimonial dinner at which Milton received the Interfaith in Action award for furthering religious understanding, somebody declared that he hoped Berle would live to be 102.

"I hope so too," cracked the guest of honor. "Then I would be as old as my material."

Milton was overenergized. Somebody called him "Public Energy Number 1." He'd been on some of those experimental television shows years before. He had a need to be seen and to be laughed at. After his own night club or theater shows he'd shoot off to other night clubs to get on the microphone in a guest spot.

He possessed tons of material. He'd had his nose fixed, and he developed a routine about that. "I've got a pretty good nose as noses run. I went to a plastic surgeon—one of those guys who run a clip joint for noses—and now I'm going to Hollywood to make some nosereels. Anyway, I have a lot of fun on my own hook."

Berle completely dominated the scene when he did his night club show at the old Carnival or the Latin Quarter. A waiter would walk through the room with the legs of a table upraised over people's heads. "Who shot the moose?" Berle would ask. Introducing singer Marion Colby, he'd say, "This girl is demure and very well reared. Looks good in front, too. Ladies and gentlemen, you've all seen such pictures as *The Killers, The Razor's Edge,* and *Best Years of Our Lives.* Well, this girl has seen those same pictures."

Milton's mother Sandra was almost always in his entourage. When there was an especially loud laugh from the crowd, Milton would say, "Thank you, Mother."

He liked to get the night club audience to participate in his act: "How old are you, dear? Oh, this girl is very shy. Shy about ten years. Darling, you're beautiful tonight. You look like you just stepped out of *Vogue*—and fell flat on your face."

Berle's salary went to $15,000 a week when he headlined at the Latin Quarter. I wrote in my column then that "Berle is getting the chance that might (or might not) make him the world's most famous funnyman. He soon starts regularly on *both* television and radio, becoming the first big comedian to attempt this in major fashion."

It was called a simulcast. I added that he would be the permanent emcee (or as he called it, Mental Case) of the Texaco Star Theater, "the best television presented thus far."

This was it—the beginning of the television gold rush. Berle was to get $110,000 a week for forty weeks. This $4,400,000 for a year's work (he would have twelve weeks off) was undoubtedly a record for the new medium.

Berle had all the sight gags, all the broad comedy, the singing, the dancing, the nonsense, and the energy that were needed. The NBC Texaco Star Theater was a brilliant success from the start, and the sixth floor of 30 Rockefeller Plaza became the place to be. Surrounded by his writers, stooges, and flunkies, Berle took command and became the first television king. He brought to the television screen many night club performers who had never before been seen by most of the American public. And some of his guests still weren't seen very much because Berle pushed, shoved, and edged them out of camera range so that he could monopolize the shot.

"Uncle Miltie"—somebody thought up that nickname for the kids—was soon the target of some jibes about screenstealing.

"The man who said 'Nothing is impossible' never tried to get between Milton Berle and a TV camera," one critic wrote.

As talk spread about the Berle show, the taverns increased their business on Tuesday nights.

Not only New Yorkers but people along the whole Eastern seaboard who had access to TV sets would cease their usual functions on Tuesday at eight when Berle came on. Night club business was off, movie audiences were down, and many shopkeepers closed up early so that they could rush home to sit with the family and watch Uncle Miltie.

More and more people developed sufficient curiosity to consider buying TV sets; the industry admitted that Berle's popularity sold more sets than did all the television salesmen combined.

"That's right," commented comedian Joe E. Lewis at the Copacabana. "Berle was responsible for the sale of more sets than any man living. I know I sold mine, and my brother sold his."

It's hard to believe that it was nearly a quarter of a century ago that Berle's popularity was at its peak. In May, 1949, when "Mr. Television" was given a testimonial dinner and was featured on the cover of both *Time* and *Newsweek* the same week, television was still very young. It had shot up like an overgrown boy.

"In Manhattan, diners at Lindy's gulp their after-dinner coffee and call for their checks as they did in the days of the Roosevelt fireside chats," *Time* reported.

Sid Stone, doing his memorable commercial for Texaco, became a celebrity just by being on the Berle show. His pitchman routine opening with "Tell you what I'm gonna do" was the first of the entertaining commercials.

Berle was "The Child Wonder," *Time* said, and according to *Newsweek* he was "Television's Top." His show was receiving a Hooper rating of 80 or better, which meant that four out of five sets were turned in to his show. Actually, the rating was probably closer to 100.

Regardless of all his praise and fame, Berle was an unhappy genius. CBS had tried numerous stars against him, including Frank Sinatra, and he had mowed them all down. Yet he was fidgety. One night before the big dinner, he told me, "I may not be back with Texaco next fall. There have been some little misunderstandings."

He was riding so high on the crest of popularity that even his rehearsals attracted a crowd. He was the king, and nobody dreamed that he could be toppled. Always a little breathless and perspiring, he wore a towel around his neck and was constantly blowing sharp blasts on a whistle for quiet. Directing his own rehearsals, he was De Mille, Curtiz, Lubitsch. He was painstakingly thorough about the music, the dancing, and the other performers' delivery—more concerned about their performances, in the rehearsals, than about his own. One heard stories that Berle sometimes forgot the punch lines of his own jokes. But he was so glib that he could make a mistake and recover easily by stating frankly that he'd fluffed.

One afternoon at a rehearsal I attended he had an attack of temperament. Blowing the whistle loudly, he shouted, "Clear everyone out of the studio who's not in the cast!"

The visitors left sheepishly. One of them was Milton's brother Frank. Others were important friends, top agents, and comedian Henny Youngman. Berle went on with the rehearsal, with the towel still around his neck and the whistle at his lips.

He was calling the orchestra leader to account. "What was *that* note?" he asked. "It doesn't sound so good!"

"By the way, Milton," I once asked him, "why do you use that whistle in rehearsals?"

"So I don't have to yell. It saves my voice, you numbskull!" he yelled.

In the summer of 1949 while I was in Columbus, Ohio, I found everybody curious about the Milton Berle show, though people there hadn't seen it yet (they would be viewing it as soon as the coaxial cable was laid).

"What's Berle like?" somebody asked me. "Is it true that he listens to all the other comedians and steals all their jokes?"

"No, just the ones he likes," I said, using a Berle-like answer to that type of question.

It reminded me that there had once been radio stars whose attraction was as compelling as Berle's. When I was a young reporter for International News Service in Columbus in the thirties, I did a story about the deathhouse at Ohio State Penitentiary. One night, as I waited near the warden's office to go inside and cover the grisly assignment, word moved along the grapevine that there was a delay. Maybe there had been a reprieve! Maybe the condemned man wasn't going to be executed tonight after all. The word crackled through the prison and caused general restlessness among the inmates.

We reporters grew nervous and restless too. What had happened? We waited. At last, several minutes late, warden Preston Thomas stamped downstairs from his living quarters.

"I don't miss 'Amos 'n' Andy' for anything," he chuckled, leading the way to the deathhouse.

Berle knew that CBS was laying for him—they knew that NBC had him so locked in that they couldn't buy him. CBS was looking for somebody to dethrone him, but Berle was cocky enough to think they would never succeed, for Milton Berlinger, the son of a paint salesman and a department store detective, was the undisputed king. He was also a ham in love with show business. He'd heard of overexposure but didn't believe in it. He was asked by his friend Irving Mansfield, the husband of Jacqueline Susann, to appear on the panel of a show he was producing called "This Is Show Business." The other panelists included George S. Kaufman, Clifton Fadiman, and Abe Burrows.

"You know about my NBC contract," Berle said. "I'm allowed to make ten guest appearances a year, and my price is $15,000 an appearance. Can you pay that?"

"No."

"Can you pay me $8,000?"

"No."

"Can you pay me $5,000?"

"No."

"Can you pay me $1,000, $500 . . . ?"

"No, no . . ."

"Can you let me have two tickets for my mother?"

"Yes."

"Okay! It's a deal."

Berle could not be stopped. He and I had developed a silly feud at about that time. Berle was barred from the Stork Club for some clowning there one night, and a couple of days later I printed that he was considering filing suit against owner Sherman Billingsley for $1,000,000.

The *New York Post*'s first edition had scarcely come out when he phoned me in a roaring rage to deny the item. I knew that the small and rather insignificant item was true, but I couldn't reveal my source. It was from within his own intimate entourage, and to have told him would have been betrayal.

Such feuds are stupid and uncomfortable. Here was a man I liked immensely, but because I'd printed something that, while true, he didn't like, I had to look past him without speaking when I encountered him in restaurants and night clubs, while he, on meeting me, had to stare over my head.

I didn't want any of it, yet I too felt a need to retain my self-respect. We bumped into each other one night on Broadway outside the screening of a Phil Silvers movie.

"Milton," I said, hoping I could get him to listen to the logic of my side of the argument, "will you listen for a second?"

He wouldn't. He roared and spluttered and embarrassed me and some friends who had attended the screening, and our feud continued, hotter and nastier than ever.

A few weeks later, I was given a birthday party by some of the Broadway press agents. There was a dais of speakers, mostly comedians, who had a gay old time ribbing me. The volunteer master of ceremonies was Milton Berle, who had prepared himself extensively with clever material for his introductions and for the roasting speech he made about me. Our feud was over. We were friends again, and I was elated. Milton Berle had exhibited a generous trait I didn't know he possessed.

Milton, like many other stars, needed an entourage to bolster his ego, to snap at sometimes, to applaud him frequently, to tell him over and over that tonight's show was the greatest hunk of entertainment in the history of the world. Waiting for him, preceding him, following him, and flattering him were five or six writers and stooges who, in the language of show business, "rubbed him down." The writers were constantly feeding him jokes.

But he never denied it. "I keep my wits about me," he said.

Often dramatic, he would stagger in from a show and groan, "Oh, I'm so tired, so sick, I'm going to fall . . . fall . . . right down."

"You can't, Milton!" his manager, Irving Gray, protested one night.

"Don't tell *me* if I can fall down or not," bellowed Berle.

CBS tried year after year to beat Berle. Finally, along came Jackie Gleason.

When Jackie Gleason was a minor night club comedian playing mostly outside of New York rather than in it, he used to send me some attempts at humorous fiction, written in epistolary style, addressed to "My Dear Friend, Hamilton."

I believe he used the name Hamilton because he had a close friend, a bookmaker named Frankie Hamilton, to whom he was in hock.

These letters were meticulously typed, probably intended as a slick version of the *Pal Joey* letters, and they were frequently signed: "The Great Gleason."

In those days in the late forties, nobody ever dreamed Gleason would indeed become The Great Gleason, for his career, compared to Milton Berle's astonishing success, had been one of near-failure. The letters that he submitted to me for publication were generally too long to reproduce in my column. Besides he wasn't a big enough name to justify frequent publication. I saved the letters, however, and I think now that they reveal a considerable writing ability and a lively narrative style that might have made him a short story writer if he hadn't stumbled into television.

One of his letters to his dear friend Hamilton goes as follows:

I am working at the Northwood Inn which is 11½ miles out of town. That means a daily trek to get there and back (to Detroit) of 23 miles. There is a healthy tab to make this trip by hack. (Three and a half clams each way.)

May I caution you never to arrive in Detroit single-O. All of the opposite gender are occupied in mechanical labor, and unless you can discuss triple riveting or applied welding, you are cooked.

I have been forced to cast my charms toward the line of girls appearing with me at the Northwood Inn. In particular, one named Rose.

To call Rose pretty would be elevating Karloff to a Harry Conover protégée. Albeit, as she had more hair than the rest, I took a liking to her.

While sharing a Sterno with Rose opening night at the bar, I suggested, as she lives in the same hotel, she share my hack to and from our place of employment. She readily accepted my offer and enhanced it by informing me that the rest of the line stays at our mutual hotel and she would feel a bit favored and too conspicuous if I didn't proffer my invitation to them too.

So that is why I am accompanied by six broads in a conveyance that comfortably seats two. I find myself wishing more and more that I had never grown up.

In another letter to his friend Hamilton, he made the following confession:

> My child life was one mad whirl of mumbly-peg and cubebs. What nostalgic memories permeate my reminiscence. Being an obese youngster, I was never to know the delight of riding a dumbwaiter down to the cellar or of taking the cup in a Peabody contest.
>
> One domestic duty gave me pleasure. It was exterminating rats at Houcker's Stable. After catching a cornered rat, we would pour kerosene over it and light it with a match.
>
> The rat, with a bloodcurdling squeal, would rocket itself around the stable, bash its head against a wall, and fly down the street.
>
> Egghead Rhodes, one of our gang quite imaginative and always looking for a thrill, decided one day to substitute a dog for the rat. The experiment proved disastrous. After the dog was lit, it whirled around and bit the pinky off Egghead's left hand. To this day, Egghead hasn't got a pinky on his left hand.

Fat Jackie used to recount these and other yarns at his table at Toots Shor's and Lindy's, and we considered him the funniest table comedian in the country. But privately we thought his night club act was spotty and that it was too bad that this poor fat man was wasting his life, sitting up all night boozing and throwing away his money. We thought he was never going to get anywhere.

"Thank God I got the pencil," he would say with a plump grin when he wasn't working. He went on eating, drinking, and enjoying life at Toots—using his privilege of signing the tab. He engaged in drinking contests with Toots, who, he claimed, was not a real drinker but "a slow sipper." That was like calling Billy Graham an atheist.

An often told story concerns one of these afternoon contests between Jackie and Toots, when each started with one fresh bottle. On this particular occasion Jackie called time out to visit the men's room, collapsed, and literally fell flat on his face in the stream of traffic between the bar and the dining room.

As he lay there, passed out, waiters and captains rushed to hoist his carcass out of the way, but Toots staggered up, roaring: "Let the creep lie there! It'll be a lesson to the bum not to try to drink with real drinkers!"

When he ate at Shor's—and he always was allowed to sign for it—Gleason would insult Shor about his cookery. "You serve the only soup that has to be carved," he howled one time. Often he lugged in sacks of food from other restaurants, claiming Toots' booze was all right, but his food was inedible.

Once when Jackie went to a feast at Toots' in honor of the late Grantland Rice, he sneered when the "charcoal-broiled sliced beefsteak" was served.

"Look, fellas!" he said. "Meat loaf yet."

He called to jockey Eddie Arcaro, "Do you know you're eating today what you rode yesterday?"

Refusing to eat Toots' special dinner, he sent out for a cardboard carton of pizza and was consuming that when the dinner ended.

Jackie was an "inside celebrity" in those years—not a big favorite with the public but working fairly steadily and a particular favorite of the late, late Broadway set, who liked him for his warmth and friendliness, and perhaps for the fact that he wasn't getting anywhere.

One night about twenty of us rode to Philadelphia in a special railroad car (equipped with cold running whiskey) to see Jackie open a club called the Mocambo. The owner charged an unprecedented $25 a head.

It was something of a disaster because the club wasn't ready. However, when Gleason came on and did impersonations of "Humphrey Pushcart" and "Lauren Bagel," who were then newlyweds, the crowd began to feel better. Gleason got $3,500 a week.

A month later he headlined at Billy Rose's Diamond Horseshoe and was frank with the crowd about his material. "See what you can do if you've got a little guts?" he said. He was so overweight at that time that he was referred to as Milton Berle's "favorite three comedians."

The idea of trying to get Gleason into television had occurred to Hollywood, which was planning to cast him in a series, "The Life of Reilly." But a couple of comedy writers, Coleman Jacoby and Arnie Rosen, saw something else in him. They had gathered film clips from a few pictures he'd done in Hollywood, and they had watched and admired him in some Broadway shows, including *Follow the Girls*. They envisioned him as a great funnyman operating alone.

They invited me and many others to sit still long enough to look at the clips they had assembled. I went with reluctance, for to me Gleason was a dedicated failure.

"Yeah, yeah, they're okay," I said afterward. "But they're sort of copies of Chaplin and Abbott and Costello and Laurel and Hardy, aren't they?"

"But with his own style! And is that bad?" they demanded. Jackie had indeed studied all those masters, and with his own bouncy corpulence, he used slapstick humor in his own way.

Jackie and Rosen continued to badger people, and they finally got Jackie Gleason on television—on a now forgotten network, Dumont, originating from what was considered a jinxed theater, the Adelphi on West 54th Street between 7th and 6th Avenues. The theater, later known as the 54th Street and the George Abbott, was like a nursing home—it was where old shows went to die. (It has since been torn down to make room for an addition to the New York Hilton Hotel.)

Having a television show in that stage theater was a sort of a freakish thing, and the neighbors across the way at Al & Dick's steak house and up at Max Asnas' Stage Delicatessen on 7th Avenue didn't expect much.

Still, Dumont's "Big Parade of Bands" and later its "Big Parade of Comedy," starring Jackie Gleason, did stir some excitement and did get fair ratings. For the first time Jackie Gleason was being taken seriously in the comedy competition, and he was considered a challenger for the throne of Uncle Miltie.

It got to be a little personal. Frank Sinatra, CBS's competition against Berle, booked Gleason as a guest, and Gleason predicted, "I'll fracture him!"

"Do you ever run into Berle?" I once asked Gleason.

"No, but I'd like to run over him," he answered. "Maybe I will, too, with my new Cadillac"—he got his new Cadillac as part of his guest star fee for appearing on Sinatra's show.

"And away we go!" was Gleason's opening line on his show, and the expression became so familiar across the country that in 1951 Gleason asked me to print a letter "To Whom It May Concern" blasting Berle for allowing Fatso Marko of his cast to use Gleason's trademark on the Berle show.

Without mentioning Berle by name, Gleason said in his letter that after Berle's show used "Away we go," he, Gleason, was accused of stealing it from Berle and that he "should be ashamed of lifting it."

"This man has been honored—justly so—for his great talent," Gleason's letter said. "He carries a title bestowed upon him by the public, a title that says he is the head man in television. But this title, like any title born of public satisfaction, will be taken from him when the public believes another is more worthy. I consider it unethical for this man to tarnish the title that will one day belong to somebody else."

It was pretty plain that Gleason himself had in mind becoming Mr. Television. The whole country was watching as the fat boy progressed. More than anybody, the sponsors of Milton Berle were watching.

Christmas and New Year's Day, 1954, saw it happen. Mike Kirk, a dapper, experienced advertising executive who often wore a derby, had been observing Gleason's growing popularity on behalf of his client, the Buick Motor Company. There is not much sentiment in the business. Gleason was the hot new property. Kirk wanted Buick to dump Berle and grab Gleason.

The news, which I obtained from Mike Kirk, was calamitous for Berle. The deal would take Jackie to CBS, which had long been waiting for an opportunity to sink Berle. CBS might even put Gleason on the air Tuesday at eight—the time slot that had for so long "belonged to Berle," where big time television really began.

Suddenly the one-time poor soul, Jackie Gleason, was going to be rich. Jackie reveled in the figures that Buick and his executive producer Jack Philbin were kicking around with Mike Kirk.

"Ralph Cramden," the bus driver, signed a contract that would pay him $7,000,000 for two years of half-hour shows, and $4,000,- 000 more if the option were renewed for a third year.

By a narrow squeak, it was the largest contract ever signed for television. Lucille Ball and Desi Arnaz had signed a contract in February, 1953, with Philip Morris and CBS for $8,000,000, but theirs covered two and one-half years.

Every few days Gleason was able to report from his vacation spot in Bel Air, California, that the money was still coming in. He was guaranteed $100,000 a year for fifteen years for pledging CBS his exclusive services between 1957 and 1972. He would get the $100,- 000 a year whether he worked or not—just so he did not work for anybody else.

Another bundle, of $350,000, was offered Jackie Gleason Enterprises to produce a summer replacement band show. He was also negotiating to do ten one-hour specials for General Motors in addition to his "Honeymooners," which, it was decided, would not move to Tuesday nights on CBS but would continue on Saturday nights.

The animosity between Berle and Gleason had reached a point where Gleason's representatives discussed these figures with enormous satisfaction. Gleason had not yet passed Berle in the ratings, but he was gaining. Mike Kirk explained to me that Buick wanted Jackie because he promised to perform certain good-will chores—hobnobbing with the Buick dealers, attending their conventions, things that, according to Kirk, Berle was not always available to do.

If Berle was shattered by the turn in events he didn't show it. Abe Lastfogel, head of the William Morris agency, spoke for him.

"Berle has the top rating and won't have any trouble finding a sponsor," Lastfogel said. "They wanted him to do more work. He wanted to do less. Besides, auto companies like to switch around. In seven years, Berle's had only two sponsors—Texaco and Buick."

Berle's pay at NBC would continue regardless because he also had an exclusivity contract: he was paid whether he worked or not.

But the Berle reign was just about over. "Mr. Television" was giving way to "The Great Gleason." The public was satiated with all the other comedians. Just before Christmas the ARB rating showed Gleason first, Lucy second, Dragnet third, Groucho Marx fourth, and Berle fifth.

"Gleason could have had anything he wanted," Mike Kirk said. As it was, he wanted and got just about everything.

While other stars boasted of their great industriousness in putting together a program, Gleason bragged about how little he worked.

"Did our rehearsal in an hour and fifty minutes," he once told me. "It usually takes the other boys three or four days."

At the time, Gleason was hobbling around on a cane, having taken a fall during a previous show and broken his ankle. He left his cane hanging on the edge of the stage as he literally chased his cast through a quick rehearsal. But that was Jackie. Like Dean Martin, he couldn't be bothered with a lot of foolish memorizing, he thought spontaneity was better.

CBS realized the importance of its catch and gave Gleason complete license in his wish to be creative. He spent $250,000 of network money to rebuild the interior of the CBS Color Theater at 82nd Street and Broadway in New York, converting it into "Café Mardi Gras," to be developed later, he hoped, into a television series he would produce.

"What's it all about?" I asked "Bullets" Durgom, Jackie's manager at the time.

"Jackie thinks people like night clubs but don't see them because they don't have the money. He wants to give them a big free night club TV show every Saturday night from nine to ten. It would keep them home so that they could see 'Honeymooners' and 'Stage Show,' which he's also producing."

Even though the Café Mardi Gras had Sammy Davis, Jr., Hildegarde, Noonan and Marshall, Paul Whiteman and Ray Block, and June Taylor's fifty "Glamorous Glee Girls," it wasn't a success as a TV pilot, and it was never heard from again. CBS must have marked down that $250,000 in Gleason's black book somewhere, to be recaptured from him later.

The reign of King Jackie, who fancied himself the modern equivalent of Diamond Jim Brady, is remembered on Broadway as the epitome of spending and frivolity. Books have been written about this plump comedian's extravagances. He said he was merely trying to live graciously. One day he arrived at Toots Shor's for lunch but didn't order food—he ordered an orchestra.

"If you had any class, you crummy creep," said Toots, in response to Gleason's request for some music, "you'd bring your own orchestra."

"Why, you miserable . . ." Gleason's words drifted off. "Say, that's a bully suggestion!"

In an hour, members of an orchestra that Gleason called Max Kaminsky's Heartburn Philharmonic arrived from as far away as Westport to accompany Gleason and Shor in their drinking. A woman customer came up to the piano near the bar to plead for Jackie's autograph and was bawled out by Shor.

"For askin' for this slob's autograph, never come back in here again!" roared Toots.

"I really wanted Joe DiMaggio's autograph," the woman whimpered.

"Okay. That's *class!* For that you can come in one more time!"

The concert went on for three hours. Gleason declared that he would never travel around town without an orchestra again.

Meanwhile, Gleason was again wanted by Hollywood. They needed him for the role of Lana Turner's leading man. He was kidded about making so much money, but it didn't bother him.

"I notice it was a quiet day for you yesterday," Jay C. Flippen told him. "You didn't make a million dollars."

Everything was done in the baronial manner by Gleason. CBS built him a castle in the woods at Peekskill, New York, which he called "Round Rock." He and Honey Merrill, his girl friend and secretary, rode to and from it in a Rolls Royce. The report that there was a bar in every room of the place was a slight exaggeration.

(Incidentally, Gleason had generally good relations with the press. But he once sent a threatening message to one reporter: "I don't care what you write about me, but if you ever write one word about my happy marriage, my wife, my children, *or my girlfriend . . . !*")

Gleason chose to do a Broadway musical, *Take Me Along,* and he got into a running battle with David Merrick, the producer, who made too many disparaging remarks about Gleason's rotundity. To some people, Gleason appeared to be trying to emulate John Barrymore. Merrick said that all actors are children and that he considered himself not a producer but a nursery supervisor.

"How do you like working for Merrick?" somebody asked Gleason.

"Merrick's working for *me!*" he replied.

All life was a party for The Great Gleason. When *Take Me Along* was ready to start rehearsals, Gleason invited Walter Pidgeon, Eileen Herlie, Ruth Warrick, and others of the cast to hold their first rehearsal at Round Rock, where, of course, there was plenty to drink. When he went into Doctors Hospital for surgery on the most famous stomach in television, for the removal of a cyst, he also gave that occasion a festive air.

Perhaps to celebrate his success, Gleason let the country know that he was proud of his drinking prowess.

"I drink to get rid of warts," he told me in one interview. "Not mine. Other people's.

"When I've been drinkin' a while, all the warts and wrinkles on other people disappear. The whole world becomes beautiful. The faces are all vague and lovely. I never drink for any reason except to get loaded and to get rid of warts. *Hey, Sydelle!*" he bellowed to his secretary Sydelle Spear. "Some more wart medicine!"

Jackie named the All-American Drinking Team, putting himself on it, although he acknowledged that Don Ameche was a neater boozer. "He can drink from eleven A.M. till midnight and still be a gentleman with every hair in place."

"They say Dean Martin can't really drink a lot because he has a bad stomach," I observed.

"A bad stomach won't stop a real drinker. He'll go ahead and ruin his stomach," Gleason responded.

Jackie and his managers were constantly negotiating with CBS for more money and other advantages. He threatened the network with a lawsuit if it didn't move "The Honeymooners" into an eight o'clock Saturday night slot so that he could collide with Perry Como on NBC. Each spring Gleason was uncertain about whether he would be back the next fall.

During one of these periods of uncertainty Gleason, sitting in his dressing room at the CBS Theater at Broadway and 53rd Street, said he'd like to work outside New York—maybe in California, where he could play golf all year.

His longing for balmier weather, reported in my column, attracted the attention of Hank Meyer, public relations man for Miami Beach, who immediately invited Gleason to beam his program from Florida.

"We might do it, pal!" Gleason told me happily.

His partner, Jack Philbin, didn't think so. "We could never move a whole show to Florida. And they don't have the facilities for building new stage sets for us every week."

Overcoming every objection and finding ways to make Gleason feel even more kingly than before, Hank Meyer brought Jackie to the growing resort city in a deal that was profitable for almost everybody. Gleason became Miami Beach's best huckster, though, as a rule, he did not remain there the entire year but went off to make a movie or to go on tour. He filmed *The Hustler* and, in Paris, *Gigot*. He was very proud of his work as a pantomimist in the latter film, in which he portrayed a mute.

Over a bottle of champagne one day, Jackie told Bill McCaffrey, Art Carney's agent, that Charlie Chaplin was very good "in *his* medium" but that "he would have bombed out after thirteen weeks on television."

"Chaplin *brags* about making thirty pictures in his life," snorted Gleason. "We do that in a matter of weeks. He admits he was a flop in talkies."

"You do admit that Chaplin is the greatest pantomimist?" McCaffrey asked.

"No."

"Then who is?"

Gleason, partly serious, partly joking, and partly full of champagne, replied, "I am—and any time Chaplin wants to start competing . . ."

"Your *Gigot* was in the Chaplin tradition," McCaffrey said.

"No, it was in my tradition!" Gleason ended the argument.

Hank Meyer had a problem keeping the king happy, preventing him from getting so restless or bored that he'd want to leave Miami Beach, so out at the Miami Beach Country Club appeared "The House That Jackie Built," right on the golf course where Jackie could sit at his desk in a luxurious office and contemplate his ratings, which were usually ahead of his competitors.

Miami Beach made him "creative consultant" for the new Statler-Hilton-Savoy Hotel (later the Playboy), and the hotel's rooms were named for Jackie or his show. Jackie's fee for this was a secret. But his partnership later was to annoy owners of competing hotels, who protested that Jackie was allowed to use the Miami Beach Auditorium for his television show. They pointed out that the owners of the hotels had to contribute to the auditorium as taxpayers and that Jackie was in competition with them. Brushing such complaints off, the Gleason entourage went ahead with plans for something more magnificent than heretofore dreamed of—a country club with five golf courses.

"Two more than anybody else has," somebody noted.

Jackie's CBS contract for 1966–1967 paid him $205,000 a week, approximately $8,000,000 for thirty-nine weeks, and he also was producing his own summer replacements, for $720,000. The next year he didn't want to work as much. At the age of fifty-one, he was only going to do twenty programs and ten repeats.

"CBS has asked me not to tell how much I am getting because the other actors will get angry," he said.

In 1969 and 1970, CBS became intrigued with demographics—the science of populations and people. Starting with the Nielsen rating for a given show, which gave an estimate of the size of its audience, CBS proceeded to break down the audience according to age. CBS decided that even its successful shows were appealing to groups that were too old for comfort. The network needed younger audiences and probably younger stars. It must build for the future. The oldest age groups would be dying off.

Red Skelton's ratings were okay, but he was dropped.

Jackie Gleason was another problem. Hard times were coming to television with the banning of cigarette advertising. Gleason's managers were hinting that Jackie wanted more money. He didn't want to do as many "Honeymooners" shows as before; he preferred doing variety shows. (They required less work.)

It all amounted to just too much. For the first time, CBS abandoned its conciliatory and cooperative attitude toward Gleason. The network did not renew his contract, though it did rerun some of his "Honeymooners" segments on Sunday nights.

Gleason could not have been happy about his rejection. It was the end of an era, and he marked it by moving himself and his new bride Beverly McKittrick from the Miami Country Club to a new development of his own near Fort Lauderdale.

On the morning of December 28, 1967, our C-130 transport plane, with several millions of dollars worth of entertainers aboard, was just lifting off the runway at Cuchi, Vietnam when the Vietcong snipers shot at us.

Bob Hope, riding shotgun up in the cockpit, did not do anything heroic. Nor did Les Brown or Phil Crosby. Nor did any of us bravely seize Raquel Welch in our arms to protect her. Her husband Pat Curtis was sitting beside her, as he had been during the whole tour.

Besides, we didn't know we'd been fired on until the pilot, Lieutenant Colonel Bob Parker, told us.

"Yeah," he remarked leisurely, accustomed to such things, "we were just fired on down there." That was a minute or two after our stomachs had noticed that we had made a rather abrupt rise during takeoff.

Seeing the shooting, he had spun around and gone into a quick assault takeoff in order to gain distance and altitude. As he spoke we were up and away from the shooting, still feeling the effects of the sudden steep climb.

It made the war seem very real and close to us. A helicopter had been shot down nearby. Lieutenant Colonel Parker, counting about fifty bullet holes in our plane, said we had perhaps been hit not only at Cuchi but also at Chu Lai and Da Nang.

"It was small arms fire," the pilot said. "It could have come from rifles five hundred yards or more away."

"Is it dangerous?" we asked him.

"Not until it hits you," he answered ominously.

Bob Hope had been through this sort of experience several times before, and he likewise endured it on subsequent junkets. When we dropped down at Clark Air Force Base in the Philippines, on the way to Guam and home, Hope joked about it.

"Sniping never bothers me," Bob said. "After all, I used to play vaudeville at the Palace."

I did not join the Hope troupe to Vietnam for two weeks for the purpose of getting a look at the star who had become the most successful and durable of all comedians—but that proved to be the end result.

"Why don't I go along?" I asked myself one day in November. I put the question to Hope's public relations representatives.

"He thinks he can fit you in, all right. But you'd have to go as an actor," they said. "You'll have to do a sketch with him, playing a reporter interviewing a GI who will be the sloppiest bastard you ever saw!"

After it was all cleared with the Department of Defense, I had qualms. "Do I really need this?" I asked myself. "I'm no kid anymore. Suppose I get shot at?"

Besides, I had an uneasy feeling about leaving home—for Vietnam —just before Christmas. I'd be missing the family holiday fun, opening the packages and so forth. Where would I be Christmas Eve? Probably much too far away to phone home. But I ultimately decided to go ahead.

At the Los Angeles Airport Les Brown took me under his wing, and I never had another problem or a fear. I saw a lot of Bob Hope. He was always in there swinging the golf club—which the GIs seemed to like—looking out at those faces of 25,000 to 30,000 GIs, giving them the greatest show within his very considerable talents.

In a way it was like a big traveling TV show because we were taped by television at every one of the twenty shows (before an audience totaling 200,000) by a professional crew whose cameras were constantly in front of us—because above the cameras were the all important cue cards.

Hope had once told me that when television came in, he resolved he was going to be good at it. He was going to get the best possible writing staff because material was the prime requirement for success. And now in Vietnam I saw the truth of his statement. It was the jokes, always the jokes. "Here's a good line for you . . ." he would chuckle as we were waiting backstage. "Did you hear this one . . . ?"

But I hadn't known before just how careful he was in his joke selection. Lyndon B. Johnson was president then. Jokes about him went down well.

"Things have changed at the White House," Bob would tell the boys. "The little Birds have flown the coop. There's nobody left but Mama Bird and Cock-a-Doodle-Doo."

It always got a roar from the boys. I mentioned to Bob that I'd referred to it in a column I had sent home.

"I wish you hadn't," he said.

"Why not? It's one of your best."

"I don't know . . . it may not be very good for the president back home. . . ."

He meant he felt the president might not like it or that the public might interpret it as a slap at LBJ, which he did not intend. He kept using the joke in Vietnam—he had used it at home, too—but when the Bob Hope Christmas show from Vietnam went on, Hope had scissored out Cock-a-Doodle-Doo.

It was the Christmas of Christmases for me. Those Vietnam days were sunny, hot, and humid. We would land—all sixty-three of us—an hour or two before a show. Rushing off the plane, we'd find a makeshift stage and dressing room and usually plenty of good fried chicken and cold beer. The scenery was always the same. We looked out upon an audience of 15,000 to 30,000 GIs who had been waiting there for several hours to see the show. Acres and acres of boys in khaki out there under that sun waited patiently for this slender contact with home.

It was a monstrous misrepresentation to say that the boys did not want to see Bob Hope—at least in 1967. They wanted to see him so much that those who didn't succeed in getting leave to attend the shows complained that they'd been cheated.

I might state that the sketch I did with Hope was a huge laugh getter. He came out in fatigues, usually wielding a shovel or broom, and gave the weariest salute ever seen. He identified himself as Private Westmoreland. He complained to me that he had a mail problem—they'd been mixing up his mail with that of some officer named Westmoreland, who had better watch himself or he was going to get in trouble. Asked what he did with the shovel, Private Westmoreland replied that he dug holes. And what did he do with the holes?

"Fill them back up."

"That's the stupidest thing I ever heard of," was my line.

"You think that's stupid! You're payin' the taxes to do it."

Hope conducted these shows in a masterful manner. This was already his seventeenth trip. He knew, of course, that the GIs had come to see the girls as well as to see him. At one point he would say to the girls, "Come on, leave the stage now. I'm the star. I'm the one they came to see. Isn't that right fellas?"

"No! No!" the boys would roar. Then Hope would bring back the girls.

One day the beautiful dancer Elaine Dunn almost came out of her costume, and there was a backstage joke, "We almost saw another side of Elaine Dunn." But it never went further, and at no time do I remember Hope getting risqué.

It was all carefully planned to enable the boys to escape the world of war for a few hours, and there was no political conversation or harangue, though Hope did thank the boys and tell them that their efforts were appreciated at home.

And then even on those hot days and nights, the troupe would end the show with "White Christmas" and "Silent Night." It was an awesome spectacle as thousands of GIs bared their heads and joined Barbara McNair and Elaine Dunn in song. The wounded soldiers lay in hospital cots or sat in wheelchairs in the front rows. It was difficult for us to control our tears. We had to keep reminding ourselves that we were there to cheer the soldiers up. Joining in the singing, we tried to keep our lips from quivering.

A helicopter flailing above us one day during a show was a definite annoyance—until a voice over the speaker interrupted the show to say:

"All medics report immediately."

Standing on the back steps of the stage, I could see stretcher bearers rushing battle casualties from the helicopter to the hospital a few hundred yards away. Unhappily, many of those wounded men died as our show was in progress. But Hope attempted to alleviate the tragedy and horror of war, at least for a time. And in the hospitals, where he took all of us almost every day to visit the wounded, he had the knack of cheering up the wounded by joking with them about their misfortunes. He could hardly have sympathized with them, for this would have emphasized the gravity of their injuries. One day, in fact, I saw him go into a ward where every patient was trussed up, and many were amputees.

"All right, men!" he shouted. "Everybody on your feet!"

He greeted a GI who had an unbelievable number of stitches: "Man, that's the craziest zipper I ever saw."

One young fellow who was a serious case attracted Hope, who smiled and said, "Where were you, fella? On the Hollywood Freeway?"

Day after day he put on this performance, as well as doing one or two shows and flying to the next area. He never got temperamental, never got out of line. He bent all his efforts toward trying to make people laugh.

On Christmas 1967, we all went to General William Westmoreland's house in Saigon, and, in a little speech, "Westy," who has the juttingest jaw I have ever seen, declared that he would still be there the next year.

"We'll be back," Hope said. Though all of us felt surely that the war would be over by Christmas 1968, we cheered.

Westy wasn't back the next year, but Hope was. The good he has done, the laughs he has brought to those boys, cannot be appreciated by those who have not seen his military audiences close up. I did.

Hope has seldom been given credit for the ecumenical jokes he has been using since the middle 1950s so I felt it was ungrateful of some New York church groups to withhold awards from him in 1971 because of his pro-government stance on the Vietnam War. Hope's efforts on behalf of our GIs have always stemmed from the best intention. And he has always tried to do his share for various church groups despite his good-natured jokes at their expense.

Most of his religious jokes were directed at Catholicism. Since his wife Dolores is an extremely devout Roman Catholic, the jokes were taken as such. Mrs. Hope's piety and zeal are illustrated by a story that Hope may have concocted. Supposedly Mrs. Hope had an audience with the Pope, and the Pope was overheard protesting to her, "But, Mrs. Hope, I'm already a Catholic!"

In the beginning, the religious jokes were a trifle shocking. Mild as they were, they were unexpected. Up to that time one didn't refer to religious differences.

"I went to a Catholic affair the other night," Bob declared in a typical opening monologue. "I know it was Catholic because when I came out, my car had been raffled off."

Hope keeps a close watch on his joke files. When I asked Bill Faith, Hope's public relations man in Los Angeles, to get me some of the first religious gags, for the sake of history, he said he'd have to get Hope's approval of the material.

"He doesn't even let his writers go through those files without his permission," he said.

"Hollywood Catholics are different from any other Catholics in the world," Bob said in one of his early ecumenical gags back in 1953. "They're the only ones who give up matzoh balls for Lent."

When Bishop Fulton J. Sheen was on television in 1956, taking viewers away from Milton Berle—Berle, incidentally, met the bishop head on, calling his show "Howdy Deity" and saying, "I only wish I had *his* writers"—Hope said, "Who can fight Bishop Sheen's writers—Matthew, Mark, Luke, and John!"

Hope said he loved appearing with Bishop Sheen—"He's the only one who gets a copy of *Variety* in Latin."

"In Los Angeles," he said on another occasion, "religion is our biggest industry. In addition to the usual religions, we have over 700 cults. And that's just in one block.

"Jack Benny is Jewish. Danny Thomas is Catholic. Red Skelton is Presbyterian. And they all go to the same place to worship—CBS.

"Every religion has something great. The Jewish religion has the Old Testament . . . the Protestants have the New Testament . . . and the Catholics have bingo."

When John F. Kennedy was running for president in 1960, Hope said, "It might not be so bad to have a Catholic in the White House. It's gonna take a miracle to reduce the taxes."

Hope has been receiving awards, plaques, scrolls, cups, gold-handled golf clubs, and other trophies for twenty years, from organizations that assured their success by getting his help. In 1964, Bob said, "I'll never forget the night I got the Brotherhood Award from the National Conference of Christians and Jews. It was a beautiful dinner. It was the first time I ever had lox and hot cross buns."

He told some GIs, "I have good news for you Catholics. It's official now. You can eat Spam on Friday."

One story that Hope enjoys concerns a priest blessing racehorses at the track in order to help them win. Each horse blessed by the priest came through a winner. A bettor who had watched each blessed horse win for several races decided, on the last race, to bet everything on the horse the priest went to visit.

That horse ran last. The bettor caught up with the priest and asked what had gone wrong.

"That's the trouble with you Protestants," the priest said. "You don't know the difference between blessings and last rites."

Later, a group of priests, who had doubtless been encouraged by Hope to venture into a debate about marriage for priests, began telling jokes that dealt with the subject. "I'm for it," one priest said, "but not for the reason you think. But there are a couple of monsignors and bishops I'd like to see stuck with mothers-in-law."

Hope had one joke about a raffle. A monsignor told one of his priests to buy some tickets to get things started. The priest won some His and Hers towels.

"Keep them!" the monsignor ordered. "The way things are going, you may be able to use them!"

In January 1969, when Hope's daughter Linda was married to Jewish agent and producer Nathaniel Greenblatt Lande at a joint Catholic and Jewish ceremony in Hollywood, one of the guests was then Vice-President-elect Spiro Agnew. He was gracious enough to walk across the floor from his table at a wedding rehearsal party to sit for a while at the table where my wife and I sat with the bridegroom's parents.

The wedding party was held under a series of tents said to cover five acres. There were about 1,500 guests at the reception, all drinking imported champagne. Dorothy Lamour's husband Bill Howard said the queue of people waiting to get into the powder room was so long, he decided to go home instead—to go to the powder room, that is. He returned to the party later. Mrs. Hope said, "Would you like to stay to dinner?—to about 200 people. Everybody said yes.

For this celebration, too, Hope's writers had prepared jokes and parodies. The party was so enormous, with many people not discovering until afterward that their best friends were present, that Hope once seemed to get away from the mainstream of activity.

"Will Bob Hope, wherever he is, please report to the bride's table?" somebody called out several times.

In a handsome tailcoat perfectly tailored to the lean figure that he preserves so well, Hope went to the mike in the main tent (the bride's table) and, as there was a murmur through the crowd, he said, "Ssssh, people, the owner's on. Quiet, or I'll drop the tent on you." He paused, then added, "Rarely do I do a benefit in my own home."

Sparing no one, he introduced Agnew ("He's the kind of golfer I like—not a very good one"), Bing Crosby ("He's working on his second set of tax deductions"), and his daughter, the bride.

"I traveled five years of my life and saw her so rarely," he said, "that she thought I was a gas meter man who was getting fresh with her mother."

It was an ecumenical wedding and reception if there ever was one. Once during the party Hope mentioned that his son-in-law Nathaniel Greenblatt Lande had changed his name. Originally, his name had been Nathaniel Greenblatt, but he had elected to take his mother's family name Lande and to use that as his own last name.

"When they were talking about changing his name and didn't know what to call him," Bob said, "I suggested Brownblatt . . . But nobody seemed to like my suggestion."

To review Hope's jokes over the years is to visit Nostalgia Land. It was generally said (by a generation that didn't really remember Will Rogers) that Will Rogers was greater. Some of these people said that Will Rogers is outstanding because he maintained a point of view. These same people have criticized Bob Hope for having his own opinions. Will Rogers came up with two or three jokes a day.

Bob Hope has a dozen to fifty. He is more flippant about the passing scene than Rogers was. The Rogers adherents seem to think that Rogers wrote his jokes without help. The fact is that Rogers used to tour restaurants and clubs, such as the Lambs and Friars, every lunch time, and he would mention the day's big news story, headline, or current subject. From these conversations would be sparked a number of witticisms, some of them from Rogers, others from his friends. Out of this and his own imaginative thinking Rogers put together his daily routines built around the idea, "All I know is what I read in the papers."

Hope might possibly have been more effective with fewer jokes, but he had cast himself as a rapid-fire monologist, using up tons of material. And it was supposed to sound fresh, topical.

Every morning Hope likes to take a look at the world and pick out a target for that day. When the New York World's Fair was in difficulty, causing problems for Parks Commissioner Robert Moses, Hope said at a banquet, "Only the real Moses could have saved that one." Bob Moses was there—and the applause was tumultuous. Dolores Hope, incidentally, cautioned him not to use that gag. Politics is, of course, one of his favorite and most effective subjects for humor.

He based one of his stories on the fact that New York City mayors are notorious travelers. "I saw Mayor O'Dwyer in the Easter parade," Hope stated in 1950 on his TV show. "He was wearing a top hat, white tie, and suitcase."

During World War II, Hope, then in his early forties, thought Eleanor Roosevelt's continuous travels very funny. Once when Hope, who was entertaining troops even then, had taken glamorous Frances Langford with him to some of the Pacific Islands, he quipped in a radio program:

"Frances was the first white girl ever to land on those islands— in fact, Eleanor was mad as hell."

Then, after saying perhaps he shouldn't make so many jokes at the First Lady's expense, he said, "I asked the president to apologize for me—in his next letter."

Hope, first and foremost, was a radio man. But in 1950 he got to work on television with his "$40,000 Easter show." Bing Crosby was still reluctant to appear on TV. He still belonged to radio. But Hope was eager and ambitious—and still only in his forties. He had decided where the big money was and that he was going to go directly to it.

The public excitement about a show costing $40,000 was enormous. Hope rehearsed upstairs over the old Lindy's, in the Nola Studios. Douglas Fairbanks, Jr., was his guest on the show.

The corridor there was the hot spot in New York. I rushed up and found composer Richard Rodgers sitting there looking forlorn, waiting to ask Hope to help him with a benefit the following September.

Remember, that this was about a quarter of a century ago. For more than twenty years people have been using Bob Hope's name for benefits.

"How dare Bob Hope keep me waiting?" laughed Richard Rodgers, who seldom had been put in that position. "Doesn't he know I'm here to ask him for a favor?"

Hope's generosity with his time for benefits can be demonstrated by an incident in 1959. Arthur Murray and his wife Katherine then had a successful television show. Murray regularly employed a trick for getting big name guest stars. He would give them a handsome fee, which they would turn over to their favorite charity. Both he and the guest star would be making a contribution to charity.

I was chairman of Fight for Sight, and we needed funds. I encountered Arthur Murray in Sardi's, and he said that if he could book Bob Hope for a razz-Bob type show, he would give our fund $50,000.

When I phoned Bob, he answered with typical Bob Hope acquisitiveness, "Make it $100,000."

Arthur Murray gulped. That was twice what he felt he could pay. Yet Bob Hope's appearance on his show was a great temptation.

"If I could make enough tape of you that I could do *two* shows . . ." ventured Murray.

"Okay, you've got a deal," Hope said. It would be a first—the first time Murray would salute one star for two successive weeks. It would be a record figure. The two-part special was advertised extensively in the newspapers. It was taped at the old Ziegfeld Theater, and Fight for Sight got its money. Not all the razzing was directed at Hope. Bob directed some of it at Arthur Murray.

"Right after the show," Hope said, "they put him back on Mount Rushmore."

In 1959, for example, old Droop Snoot, alias Ski Nose Hope, was warned by doctors to slow up because of an eye ailment, and he entered the hospital for a rest. That didn't slow down the never-ending flow of gags. He received messages of sympathy.

"I haven't been so overcome since Governor Faubus [of Arkansas] made me an honorary slave," he said. "My press agent has been doing a wonderful job for me. He got me on the cover of *Confidential.*"

(The scandal magazine actually did have a piece about him, but it was *not* arranged, of course, by his press agent. There was no indication that it ever bothered Hope.)

Hope has had few crises in recent years when he had to take a stand on any issue. There was a crisis back in the radio days when Hope's radio sponsor, Lever Brothers, decided he must not transcribe his radio program. Charles Luckman, the architect and builder, then American head of the sponsor company, insisted that his radio show had to be done "live." Hope announced that he had fired his sponsor. Luckman later left the company. The system of transcribing programs and taping or filming television shows is now so common that one is amazed that anybody objected to it then.

Hope's ratings in 1969 and 1970 were extraordinary. He did nine NBC specials. Eight were rated among the top twenty shows. Six were among the top ten, and the Christmas Special was number one. He also appeared on the number two show, the Academy Awards special, as "a Friend of Oscar."

The battle of radio, represented by Bing Crosby, against television, represented by Bob, led me to write:

> Lucky all of us! Today we're rich with entertainment and getting richer. In the next four or five years, we're going to be spoiled by great entertainment just by turning a dial. Well, we're all willing to be spoiled. . . . The whole country will become critics and not like anything.

Hope always used jokes about money. He must always have had a fondness for it. In the beginning, these jokes were aimed at Bing Crosby's wealth: "He just fell off his wallet," and so on.

As the years went on, Hope evidently got richer than Bing and Bing made jokes about Hope's money.

They got involved in oil adventures. Bob said they were going to put a sign over their latest well: "Opened by mistake."

"Are you an oil tycoon?" a reporter asked Bob.

"Listen, I own enough oil to oil a roller skate!" he said.

One day Bing Crosby was telling me how Bob had overtaken him and passed him in money making.

He also told me that, while looking at some maps of an exclusive section of California where he had acquired some property, he discovered a tract belonging to "Leslie Towne Hope."

"Leslie Towne Hope! That's Bob!"

The next time Bing encountered Bob he asked him how he had managed to get in that exclusive, aristocratic neighborhood.

"Somebody owed me some money and gave me a deed to that piece of property," was Bob's laconic reply.

Not known to the general public is the fact that Bob Hope continues to work because he *needs* the money—no joke. Much of his wealth, estimated in recent magazine articles as amounting to between $200,000,000 and $500,000,000 is invested in non-productive property. In response to articles about his wealth, Bob has told the magazine editors, "I wish I had writers like yours." He needs the money to pay his taxes and enormous living expenses. The truth is that Bob Hope's fortune is tied up in jokes.

3
The TV Revolution

TELEVISION played a more significant role in causing the revolution in show business than did anything else. Programs such as "Laugh-In" upset the rules governing comedy and demonstrated that satirical and risqué jokes could be sneaked past the censors. Audiences gasped when they heard such expressions as "dumb Polack" and "jungle bunny" (meaning Negro) coming from "All in the Family" but they grew accustomed to it, and some minority groups thought it was good for people with prejudice to be singled out and exposed.

"All in the Family," which drove some critics into a red rage and others into shrieks of hysterical laughter, could never have been screened a few years ago. To have the bigot Archie Bunker (played by Carroll O'Connor) talk *that* way about Jews and blacks would have been and still sometimes is considered outrageous.

"There was this pushy dame, see—you know the kind—they're somethin', them people, always in a big hurry—tryin' to get into a sale or somethin' to save four cents! What a tribe!" Archie said, explaining that his cab had been rear-ended by a woman driver. He was going to get a lawyer, and he particularly wanted a Jewish lawyer.

"If they're good lawyers, for all I care they could be Chinks," he says.

But he wants a Rabinowitz. When his liberal son-in-law says he's being a bigot, he says to his wife, "You hear that, Edith? Here I agree with him that they [Jews] are smarter and shrewder, and he has the nerve to say that I don't like Hebes."

His daughter Gloria says, "Even Jesus was a Jew."

"Yeah, but only on his mother's side," replies Archie.

George Friedman, writing for the Jewish Telegraphic Agency, liked the show, and said, "It is always funny, often brilliant, and makes its anti-bias points as it entertains."

The show was meant to be controversial, and it succeeded. *Daily Variety*'s review said it was "nothing less than an insult to any un-bigoted televiewer," that it was "a one-joke show, and a sick joke at that."

The revolution is not over. We can look for more changes. With cassettes, pay TV, and cable TV, show business will be compelled to move into many more new directions, probably catching us una-ware, as change has always caught us unaware. Most of us couldn't see the revolution coming, although we should have.

Yet television elected John F. Kennedy president, crippled the movie industry, killed night clubs, brought the Vietnam war right into our own homes as we were having dinner, and revolutionized education, making our children far smarter than their parents.

Television star Gene Barry, when awarded the Golden Globe as best international actor, was informed that due to his three series—"Bat Masterson," "Burke's Law," and "The Name of the Game"—he might have audiences of 2 billion viewers in one week!

When black comedian Flip Wilson's program became the highest rated new show in 1971 (with his characters Geraldine, Freddie the Bachelor, and the Rev. Leroy of The Church of What's Happening Now), it was estimated that he was seen by 16,770,000 people a week.

It would take a hit movie many years to be seen by 16 million people, to accomplish what one talented comic did in one night.

Still, at the beginning we underestimated TV's potential.

There were a couple of fiascos in the beginning that demonstrated the great potential of television. One was the "Great Mario Lanza Hoax."

Lanza, "the overstuffed tenor" who truly believed he was a rein-carnation of Enrico Caruso, who had said, "My voice is a gift of God, and I cannot take credit for it," was a sex symbol in the 1950s when the hoax was attempted. He was a prodigious eater and drinker, sometimes called "The Great Mouth" because he boasted about his talent as he roared around New York, Rome, or Holly-wood, eating half a dozen steaks and downing twenty or thirty bot-tles of beer, at one sitting.

"I am a movie star, and I should live like one," he said. "Nobody wants movie stars to be like the guy next door."

Temperamental and uncontrollable, he would report late for a call at the studio and explain that he'd been up all night listening to records.

"Whose?" he'd echo. "*Mine!*" He would gaze fondly into a mirror and say, "Mario, you sing like a son of a bitch."

He'd been slipping vocally and had been forced to cancel a $50,000-a-week engagement at the Las Vegas Frontier because his voice seemed to be going. He claimed to be suffering from laryn-gitis.

"Caruso also often had laryngitis!" he said. "I have Caruso's throat. If he can have a sore throat, so can I."

Yet for women he still had the sex appeal that made them want to tear his clothes off, and he was to make a comeback. He had thinned down to 215 pounds. His health was excellent, and his strong voice was back. He was going to show the world on Septem-ber 30, 1954, on the Chrysler "Shower of Stars" color show from Hol-lywood, that he was back in the groove, as good as if not better than Caruso.

Several newspaper people were junketed from all over the coun-try to watch Lanza earn his record $40,000.

All would have gone well if columnist James Bacon's wife hadn't gone to the beauty parlor. There she heard some gossip from a hair-dresser. Lanza wasn't going to be able to sing the songs he was scheduled to sing. The network had rushed in some three-year-old records. He was going to try to get by with a fake show.

So Bacon and others of the press were carefully watching for the fraud. After the show they accused the network and Lanza of mis-leading us. They denied it. Mario laughed and scoffed at the suggestion that he had had to use old records. He said it was all a big lie invented by the reporters.

The press kept hammering at the Lanza entourage. The network defense began to crack. Finally, they said yes, the songs had been prerecorded, but only two nights before. Prerecording of songs a few days ahead was already common.

But this was different. Here was a man who was supposedly making a comeback. Whether he had sung the songs three days ago or three years ago was of monumental importance.

The press gathered more evidence. Network President J. L. Volkenburg at last broke down and issued a statement saying that Lanza's doctor had warned that, due to extreme dieting, "it would be impossible for him to sing."

"CBS television felt that, both for the show and for the viewing public who were expecting to see him, it was better to present him in the way we did rather than to forego his appearance entirely and substitute another star for him."

When Lanza died on October 7, 1959, in a clinic in Rome at the age of thirty-eight, doctors said that he had suffered a heart attack but that he had also been a victim of dieting. He'd been undergoing the "sleep treatment"—using pills that caused him to sleep continuously for twenty-four hours. The obituary writers all mentioned the earlier hoax that did not work.

The exposed hoax of Mario Lanza was one of the first warnings to television that it could not fool the people; it should likewise have been a warning to the public to become aware of the immense influence and appeal of television.

Despite the revolution in television, Lucille Ball went on being top comedienne year after year. Coming to Broadway from Jamestown, N.Y., at age fifteen to study drama, she made up a new life story for herself—deciding she'd been born in Montana. She got a job as a chorus girl in a road company of Ziegfeld's "Rio Rita."

A short time later, one of Ziegfeld's assistants gave her some advice: "Go back to Montana and just be a happy cowgirl."

Meanwhile, Lucille had been eating at drugstore counters, watching carefully for people who bought two doughnuts but ate only one. She was, in other words, a saucerwatcher.

On Broadway she met an agent lining up "poster girls" for the Eddie Cantor *Roman Scandals*, to be made in Hollywood. She went there for six weeks' work—and has remained there for almost forty years.

There she eventually met that sexy Latin lover and bandleader Desi Arnaz (they appeared together in *Too Many Girls*), and the sparks began to fly. They married, battled, developed a vaudeville act, battled, went into radio, battled, went into television, where they put together "I Love Lucy," battled some more, and finally divorced. Lucille actually filed for divorce back in 1944 but never applied for the final papers.

In my memory I can still see a comparatively unknown Desi Arnaz leading a rumba band at the Copacabana in New York in the early forties. Jack Eigen had a radio show from the Copa lounge. He liked to interview celebrities. He couldn't always get celebrities, and when he couldn't he would interview Desi Arnaz. Those appearances with Jack Eigen were undoubtedly the most important events in Desi Arnaz's life at that period.

And they undoubtedly helped him get into the frame of mind he needed to become a popular television star—and a millionaire.

In the battling years, Lucille maintained that Desi was irascible and hot-tempered. She may have been right, but Lucille also had a low boiling point. Reporters remember their quarrels. The late columnist Florabel Muir arrived at the Beverly Hills Hotel once for an interview and found Desi sleeping in a chair in the lobby.

"Why don't you go home to sleep?" she asked Desi.

"I did," he said, "but Lucy locked me out."

Latin Lover Desi had lots of girls chasing him in those days. Lucille was always finding out about it.

"You should be more discreet," a buddy lectured him. "Stay away from girls that are known and recognized."

Desi heeded the advice. But the very next girl, an unknown, rushed to a magazine editor and sold him her story of Desi.

"I can't win," poor Desi said.

The firing of singer Julius La Rosa by Arthur Godfrey on the air in October, 1953, "for lack of humility" was another tip-off to America that television audiences were beginning to take a deep personal interest in their favorite programs and were going to have something to say about how they were conducted.

Julius La Rosa was only twenty-three when Godfrey, "the old redhead," so lovable, homey, and paternalistic, suddenly announced one forenoon that Julius had just sung his "swan song."

In a few minutes La Rosa was the second most talked-about man in America, Godfrey being the first. Today La Rosa, at age forty, is a successful radio disc jockey who does occasional night club appearances. He is a happy family man who can look back with satisfaction on the way the American public rallied behind him.

Shortly after Godfrey's announcement and the quick marshaling of sympathy for La Rosa, the news editors of major newspapers tore open the front page for new headlines when Godfrey's camp said that La Rosa seemed to have "gone haywire" over Dorothy McGuire, a girl singer on the show. Dorothy McGuire was married but separated from Sergeant John H. Brown, twenty-five, who was serving with the Army in Korea.

In all my years in reporting, I've never seen the press and public grow so agitated over what was really an insignificant incident.

Everything stemmed from the fact that Arthur Godfrey had become the most listened to and looked at television star in the country. On Monday night he had a half hour "Talent Scouts" show, an adaptation of the famous Major Bowes radio show. On Wednesday night he did an hour show, "Arthur Godfrey and His Friends." He also had a daily morning show of an hour and a half. Godfrey was on the air nine hours a week, and one and a half hours of it was in prime time, live. Probably nobody else has ever been on the air more in prime time; it is possible no one ever will be. His annual CBS advertising billings were $35,000,000—also probably a record.

The adverse reaction to his abrupt firing of the sailor boy he had discovered while he was doing a show in Pensacola, Florida, was so prevalent that Godfrey called a press conference to try to explain his reasons. Godfrey faced the press with a glass of milk in front of him. He had arrived on crutches, having recently undergone hip surgery.

Unsmiling, he told the reporters that La Rosa had "lost his humility—that wonderful quality I found in him."

How had he lost it? He had signed a managerial contract with

General Artists Corporation, which promised him at least $100,000 a year. Julius was getting out from under Godfrey's wing, and Godfrey, his discoverer, resented it.

Already there was a rumor that he objected to Julius's romancing Dottie McGuire, but Godfrey dismissed this.

"Julius is nuts about this kid the way a high school boy is nuts about the girl next door," Godfrey said. "As far as I know, they have not even had a date together. The boy went haywire, that's all."

Godfrey was wrong about the romance angle. Dottie, one of the three McGuire Sisters, whom Godfrey also had discovered, had already sent her husband in Korea a "Dear John" letter, and she was indeed dating Julius.

"When Dottie and I started to date, there was no hiding," Julius told me when we recently discussed the first big behind-the-scenes live television drama that actually had a soap opera quality to it.

"We went out to Meadowbrook to hear Frank Sinatra. There was no secret to it. I wanted to marry Dottie and there was nothing wrong with it because she was already separated from her husband."

Godfrey had decided several days before his announcement that he had to fire La Rosa, but he was uncertain about the method. He consulted Dr. Frank Stanton, the very serious, objective head of CBS, about the problem.

"We decided," Dr. Stanton later told Bob Williams of the *New York Post,* "that instead of having a press conference, the best way would be just to let everyone know it over the air. Maybe that was a mistake."

It was. Godfrey eventually had to hold a press conference anyway, and each statement he uttered stirred up the La Rosa fans further.

Poor Julius was no longer "shy, bashful, timid, a scared-to-death kid," Godfrey said. He was "obstreperous." He wouldn't let Godfrey's lawyer fill out his income tax forms. He was spending half of his $8,600 a year on fan mail and pictures.

"It makes me choke up to remember how Julie used to be and how he's changed," Godfrey remarked. "If he sang one bad song, he used to turn away from the mike with tears streaming down his face. At first he was cute and awkward, and then the awkwardness became studied. I found out he was rehearsing his awkward movements . . ."

The public and the headline writers cast Godfrey as the mean old boss interfering with the romance of two kid singers. Godfrey saw himself as the hero who was keeping a little girl true to her soldier husband off in Korea.

Angry mail piled up at CBS. Home viewers thought poor little Dottie looked strained, that she had tears in her eyes when she sang on the tube. Ed Sullivan signed La Rosa for his Sunday night program. He was offered big money in Chicago. Godfrey decided he'd better quit talking. "Humility" had suddenly become a dirty word to him. Godfrey later admitted that CBS had told him to "shut up."

Religious Differences May Block Dottie-Julius Nuptials was a headline. Julius was a Catholic. Dottie (whose mother was a Protestant minister in Miamisburg, Ohio) was about to be a divorcée.

CBS was worried about the damage to the Godfrey image. The managers arranged for him to appear with Ed Murrow on the successful and popular "Person to Person" program. Murrow toured Godfrey's Blue Ridge Mountain, Virginia, estate. By this time, Godfrey had become forgiving and meek.

He really loved Julius La Rosa.

"Which of your discoveries gives you the greatest pride?" Murrow asked him.

"Well, at the moment, I'd say Julius La Rosa."

"But you fired him, didn't you?"

"Yes, if you can call releasing him from his contract so that he can make ten times as much money firing him—yeah!"

"Were you wrong in firing him?"

"Sure . . . Well, I couldn't fire him that way again. I know now that it was wrong to do it that way, but at the time I thought it was the right way."

Julie and Dottie were seen having a quick lunch together before Julie went off to sing in Chicago . . . they were probably discussing their many problems . . . Dottie looked very sad (probably about Julie going away) . . . Julie got together with Godfrey for a picture to show there were no hard feelings . . . Dottie's husband in Korea was reached and said he wouldn't stand in the way of Dottie's happiness . . . See tomorrow's paper for the next exciting chapter.

The Julie and Dottie love serial intrigued even serious columnists such as Max Lerner. "Twilight of the Idol" was the headline of a think piece in which Lerner said Godfrey had revealed "a capacity for revenge on anyone who challenged his rule over his little empire. That is why there is meaning in the collapse of the Godfrey myth and the twilight that has enveloped this particular idol."

Jack Gould in the *New York Times* wrote that Godfrey erred "in forgetting his own humility while complaining that others had."

"After all, he was doing what he thought best for his own career, yet at the same time he was objecting to Mr. La Rosa's following his example. As events turned out, Mr. Godfrey may have made his first star by firing him."

The love story, moving as it was, did not result in a walk down the aisle for Julie and Dottie. Godfrey still tried to reunite Dottie and her soldier lad.

La Rosa was getting restless as he waited for Dottie to make up her mind. In January 1955, about fourteen months after La Rosa was fired, Godfrey, in the role of Cupid, flew Dottie and her husband to Florida in his private plane for what he considered a "second honeymoon."

Godfrey was bouncy and buoyant that Monday morning when he returned from Florida.

"I knew all along that this thing would work out," he told me. "I invited Dottie to bring Brown down to Florida. Why Brown is the nicest guy you ever met, and everybody knows how nice she is."

Dottie didn't have Godfrey's enthusiasm.

"We're just talking things over," she said.

The soap opera was on once again. La Rosa was reached in Chicago, where he was appearing in a theater.

"I am positively not giving up," he said (through a spokesman).

The "second honeymoon" didn't work out. About three months later, Godfrey made news again by firing nine performers, including singer Marion Marlowe and singer Haleloke.

Again there was a furor. Godfrey couldn't understand why.

"This time I fired people just as it's done in business organizations—and they still don't like it!"

Looking back to that time when he was "just a dumb kid from Brooklyn," La Rosa says Godfrey was good to him, gave him his first chance in show business, and was within his rights in firing him, although he feels that Godfrey did give him an undeserved stigma by saying he was obstreperous and lacked humility.

"He used to have us go to these ballet lessons," La Rosa smiled, remembering. "I didn't like them. I guess they were supposed to be good for you to help you to learn how to move. I asked to be excused from one session because I had to go to a family thing. He excused me.

"The following morning he dropped me. I got a notice that said 'Since you weren't at the dancing class, we don't need you on the radio and television show.' He had excused me, so I asked for an audience with him to discuss it. This was denied. I thought that was very pompous. Maybe he wasn't feeling well. I then committed the unpardonable sin of getting an agent. In a way I challenged him."

La Rosa added, "But if it hadn't been for him, I'd never have been in the business."

The Dottie-Julie romance tapered off after the failure of Godfrey's engineered second honeymoon.

"It broke up because of all the delay," Julie told me. "I resented Dorothy's acquiescence to all of Godfrey's demands. I figured, who the hell is he? She wasn't being fair to me. Yeah, it broke up over that. I would say that was the reason. I couldn't tell you the last time we dated."

La Rosa said he understood Dottie had become "Harriet Housewife"—"which I say with envy and admiration."

Dottie is now the wife of Lowell Williamson, an Ohioan who deals successfully in oil and real estate in Canada, and they have two sons. La Rosa married Perry Como's secretary, Rory (for Rosemary) Meyer, and they have a son and daughter.

A few people still recognize Julius La Rosa. On the street in midtown New York, occasionally one of them comes up to him all these years later and asks him about the Godfrey case.

A doctor wanted him to sing at a party, and he asked the doctor if he would perform an operation if he agreed to sing. The doctor replied, "Godfrey was right about you."

Julius laughed. "That story," he said, shaking his head, "was front page news for two weeks in this town."

The scene shifts from "Arthur Godfrey and His Friends" at CBS in New York in 1953 to "Laugh-In" at NBC in "beautiful downtown Burbank" in 1968. Producer George Schlatter, Dan Rowan, and Dick Martin brought about a revolution in comedy by following a policy that they insisted was not dirty or vulgar—just naughty.

They picked up the expression, "Sock it to me," which unquestionably refers to sex in its original meaning, and put it in the vocabulary of dignified Richard M. Nixon. "You bet your sweet bippy," also from their show, was heard in the nation's schoolrooms, for the kids loved "Laugh-In"—and probably understood it.

It was all done so swiftly; it was wild, insane, unbelievably impertinent, and, yes, naughty. In one sequence from the show a girl steps out of a shower, answers the phone, hands the phone into the shower, and says, "It's for you."

There were seemingly hundreds of film clips of outrageous sight gags, of girls in bikinis being body-painted, of pithy one-liners and impudent two-liners.

MAN: How can I believe you, Elizabeth? That child doesn't even look like me.

WOMAN: You're looking at the wrong end, stupid.

Or a whole news flash:

News of the Future: The Catholic Church will legalize the pill, it was announced today by Pope Leory, Jr. His father was not available for comment but his mother, the former Sister Mary Catherine, reached at Gluck's Hillside in the Catskills, said, "We like to think of the Pill as St. Joseph's Aspirin for Children."

In Arthur Godfrey's better days, in the 1950s, there could not have been any mention of the Pill if, indeed, there had been a Pill. But now, thanks to the revolution, Rowan and Martin were making jokes about it. On one program, actor Dave Madden said: "My fiancée just found out she's been taking aspirins instead of the Pill. She doesn't have a headache, but I do."

Viewers were asking, "How do they get away with it? Where are the censors?"

Rowan, Martin, and Schlatter sliced out the excessively off-color stuff themselves and put it aside in "the joke bank." Maybe the subject wouldn't be considered dirty in a few months. The revolution was liberalizing comedy just that swiftly.

Jump again, from 1968 to 1971, to a discussion about masturbation. Johnny Carson's having a non-comedic talk with the author of *Everything You Always Wanted to Know About Sex, But Were Afraid to Ask,* Dr. David Reuben.

There are no *Portnoy's Complaint* jokes here. Johnny's merely learning that the old idea that masturbation is harmful is considered false by Dr. Reuben.

Johnny pauses to comment upon their comment.

"A couple of years ago, if we even mentioned this work on TV, some NBC vice-presidents would be diving out windows," he says.

The topper came, however, in May, 1971, when that controversial bigotry show, "All in the Family," was given three Emmys by the National Academy of Television Arts and Sciences. It was voted the outstanding new series of the year. It was called a breakthrough and a landmark assault on bigotry (by some of the critics). *Saturday Review* said, "Television may never be the same again after the impact of this innovation." That's the same show we opened the chapter with: innovation—revolution—catches on fast today.

Sander Vanocur said at the 1971 Emmy Award ceremony: "I look back on the years 1963 and 1964 as the turning point—the beginning of a stream of news stories that were to transform the TV set into a nightmare machine.

"The shots that rang out in Dallas on November 22, 1963, changed the Soaring Sixties into tragedy. Television had its first assassination and murder, but not its last."

All that was in 1971, yet only two years earlier, in 1969, little Tommy Smothers was raising a brave voice and refusing to be censored. He and Jackie Mason went to war against CBS for deleting some of Mason's satiric remarks about the government policies on Vietnam—and some references to President Nixon that were mild compared to what's since been said.

"One of President Nixon's strong points is not saying anything," Mason maintained.

"The public felt that if a man doesn't say anything and doesn't know anything he won't make any mistakes because he won't know what he's doing. That's how he won the election."

CBS wanted that out, and also objected to Mason's few sentences on sex.

"I don't care for sex," Mason said. "I much prefer a musical concert. But lately I've begun to notice that if I don't get to a concert for a year and a half, I don't miss it. Let's be honest, did you ever hear of a guy getting up at five o'clock in the morning to go to a concert?"

The present programming leaders at CBS probably would have kept the Smothers Brothers on the air. If they like "All in the Family" and Don Rickles, they could hardly have objected to the kidding of Nixon about his alleged inertia and his purported ineffectiveness when he got off his inertia and tried to do something.

Interestingly, in 1969 black singing star Leslie Uggams failed sadly when she took over the Smothers time. She followed a controversial show and was non-controversial. Yet "Leslie Smothers," "Uggams Smothers," and the Smothers Sister—such tags didn't help —didn't have the zing and the ginger and the bite to follow the Smothers. Leslie was cancelled. Her show was pallid, conventional; it wasn't blue; it was conformist—and it was a flop.

Glen Campbell, who followed Leslie into the nine o'clock Sunday night spot with a non-controversial show, was a hit.

"So how yuh gonna figure?" as they say on Broadway.

You can't safely predict anything during show business today— least of all about television. The Ed Sullivan Theater at 53rd Street and Broadway is closed; for the first time. Lawrence Welk, who couldn't be stopped, has been stopped. "Sesame Street," just as respectable as Sullivan and Welk, is a hit. So is Carson talking about masturbation. *La Dolce Vita*, once a "blue movie," runs on TV unedited.

I will say one thing, for all the uncomplimentary observations that have been made about television's muffing its opportunities, it has nevertheless kept its nose clean and avoided being involved in any major scandal since the quiz show investigations.

Television never got the "casting couch" reputation that the movie producers and directors so justly earned for their industry.

One New York based TV show had such an incident. A girl arriving for an audition was asked—so the story is told—to take her clothes off. Had this been in the Broadway theater or at a movie studio, the girl would probably have had her clothes off before the gentleman made the request. But this was in the middle 1960s, and the girl was auditioning for a TV role. The girl complained to her mother who knew somebody important connected with the TV show. The gentleman left soon thereafter.

Television has not really developed any scandal-stained villains, as the movies did with Fatty Arbuckle and others. It hasn't produced any real-life murderers.

4

Where Have All the Night Clubs Gone?

ONCE in New York City, there was a night club . . .

Once, in fact, there were three or four—or 300 or 400—night clubs, which together offered a fascinating slice of American life. Young people today hardly know what a night club is—unless they've seen one pictured on television or in an old movie—yet there was a time when even some of the most scholarly citizens were influenced by the escapades and the vagaries of Elsa Maxwell and Lucius Beebe, who were the rulers of that world, along with Sherman Billingsley, an ignorant bootlegger from Oklahoma who had been acquitted of some trouble in his home state and had established himself as the arbiter of that phenomenon known as Café Society, Saloon Society, or the "Booze Who."

"What is a night club?" was a question asked in the 1940s and the standard answer was: "It's a place where the tables are reserved, but the customers aren't."

This allusion to the exhibitionistic traits of most of the habitués of the night-time world was justified. Inside the fabled Cub Room of Billingsley's Stork Club on 53rd Street sat one of the most extroverted and powerful of the pack—Walter Winchell, the gossip columnist of the age.

Writing notes in a bold lefthanded stroke, grabbing a telephone, stirring a drink, or eating a Winchellburger—(as the hamburger was called at the Stork Club in an attempt to boost Winchell's ego), he was the radio and journalistic oracle of the day, and you paid tribute to him when you passed table 50, which was akin to the throne.

Sitting with him within the area of the velvet rope, ruling upon the quality and eligibility of authors, editors, doctors, lawyers, actors, statesmen, and industrialists, was Billingsley.

It was said that certain tables were tapped or bugged and likewise the ladies' rooms and the men's rooms, so that Billingsley could eavesdrop on the conversations of the customers. Some of the information obtained in this way was purportedly handed over to Winchell for his column.

There sat Billingsley, a man without education or background or reputation for anything much except bootlegging, staring with cold eyes as he determined the Saloon Society status of many eminently successful people; and they sat still for this domination because they were lonely, because they wanted to be seen there, or because they wanted to have their names printed by Winchell.

One celebrity said, back in those pre-inflation days, that it cost him $50 to go to the Stork Club, but that it was worth it if he got a mention in Winchell's column.

When television arrived, "The Stork Club Show," with Billingsley as its foot-in-the-mouth host, was a Sunday night must because it was immensely funny, although the humor was unintentional.

The director was Yul Brynner, then a comparative unknown with few acting credits of importance and not even a bald head. The producer was Irving Mansfield, husband of Jacqueline Susann. The problems with the show were not their fault. There was nothing they could do. The trouble was their "star."

Fred Allen said Billingsley was the only man in television "who needs a teleprompter to say hello."

One night Billingsley had as his guest a man described as the King of Persia. Billingsley asked him, "How are things in Cairo?"

Each program contained an interview with a literary celebrity for the purpose of the inevitable book plug. But Billingsley was not inclined to scan the books of his literary guests, so conversation sometimes was difficult.

One male author was especially taken aback. "Well," Billingsley said, "I hear you writ a book."

Another night he was interviewing a famous English actress. "How old are you?" he asked her.

The actress mentioned an age that seemed right—to her at least —but Billingsley couldn't let it pass.

"I'd hate to be hanging since you were that old," he quipped.

Still, the glamorous names had a certain lure; they undoubtedly gave viewers some vicarious delight as they imagined themselves sitting with the host as he dispensed perfume, champagne, and the sponsors' cigarettes with a free hand.

One night Billingsley's guest was a Scandinavian singer named Carl Brisson, father of Fred Brisson, the producer-husband of Rosalind Russell. On camera Billingsley was shuffling some old photographs of people who had supposedly been in the Stork Club.

Billingsley exhibited a picture of his hated rival Toots Shor, who had a restaurant a block away. Shor had once been employed by Billingsley, but they argued, and Toots had opened his own place.

"Do you know him?" Billingsley asked Brisson.

Brisson nodded. "Good looking man," Brisson said.

"I wish I had all the money that guy owes." Billingsley smiled.

Brisson shrugged. He knew nothing about that. Billingsley muttered something else about Shor's debts. Unfortunately for Billingsley, Toots and his wife were watching the Stork Club show that night. Within a few minutes, Shor had reached his attorney Arnold Grant, and they were already planning the first law suit to test whether libel on television is similar to libel via the printed word.

During pre-trial examination, former Federal Judge Simon Rifkind, attorney for Shor, asked Joseph Busch, an associate director of Billingsley's show whether he knew that Billingsley had a criminal record and had served time in Leavenworth. Rifkind revealed that Billingsley had been sentenced to fifteen months in Leavenworth and had been fined $5,000 after being convicted with his brother in 1919 in a Michigan federal court for transporting liquor. He served three months and twenty days before he was released on a writ of habeas corpus.

Rifkind said he brought the point up to raise the question of whether "Sherman Billingsley is a person who should be allowed to ad-lib on a television network."

Shor sued for $1,100,000, naming Billingsley, the American Broadcasting-Paramount Theaters, the Stork Restaurant, and Mayfair Productions as defendants.

After almost four years of wrangling in the courts without going to trial, the rivals ended this one of their many battles on March 18, 1959, when Toots accepted $48,500 from Billingsley's insurance company and a letter of "sincere regrets" from ABC. Characteristically, Billingsley (and his lawyer, a man who had seen his own share of controversy, Roy Cohn) fulminated against the settlement, Billingsley snorting that he was going to sue the insurance company for yielding to Toots' suit.

Billingsley enjoyed "barring" people. Both Milton Berle and Jackie Gleason, after some feuding with Billingsley, were sent messages from the great host that they were no longer welcome, that "the rope" would be up to them.

For all his limitations, Billingsley did have the ability to lure celebrities to his establishment. He accomplished it by picking up their checks or by sending them champagne or gold cigarette holders. And they were a curious mixture of customers. Milton Berle was once heard yelling across the Cub Room to Lord Beaverbrook, "Oh Lord, come over here. I want you to say hello to the Ritz Brothers."

"The rope" was a moneymaker. In fact, at the peak of the Stork Club's popularity, Billingsley was quoted as saying, "The rope is good for $10,000 a week." Customers tipped well to get inside the Cub Room and to secure a choice table. The maitre d' would look frostily upon strangers and would claim that all the tables were "reserved" until a greenback was extended. It was the custom of the day for the headwaiter to share his tips with the operator of the club, Billingsley in this case.

Dapper little Joe Lopez, one of the Stork Club headwaiters, was on duty one night when Richard Reynolds, of the tobacco family, was departing after a convivial evening.

"Joe, what's the biggest tip you ever got?" queried Reynolds, reaching for his pocket.

"One hundred dollars, sir," replied Joe.

"The next time you are asked that, you can say $150," stated Reynolds, handing him that amount.

"Thank you, sir," said Lopez, bowing low as he pocketed the three $50 bills.

"By the way," asked Reynolds, stopping at the door, "who gave you that $100 tip?"

"You did, sir," smiled Joe.

Walter Winchell, the king of the columnists, was kind to me when I started covering the saloons. My wife said he was "an old sweetie," in the vernacular of the period. He had a six P.M. deadline for the old *New York Daily Mirror,* and at midnight or later, he often tossed me some items that were too late for him to get into print.

He was the world's champion one-way conversationalist. He would repeat most of his fifteen-minute Sunday night broadcast to you if you didn't squirm away. He committed many a "wrongo," but he was generous with plugs. People took advantage of him and his vast power in the show business world.

Once Charlie Danver published a small tale in the *Pittsburgh Post-Gazette* about the prankster who sent Winchell an item, which he printed.

The news item said, in effect: "Bandleader Jimmy Smith and model Janie Jones are middle-aisling it today." Danver discovered that the "news" had been taken from the "Pittsburgh Ten Years Ago" column.

"The embarrassing part," Danver wrote, "is that Mr. and Mrs. Smith don't know how to explain it to their eight-year-old son."

Winchell hung the dirty laundry of the world out on the line. Yet, as the late J. P. McEvoy, who was endeavoring to write a profile of Winchell, discovered to his surprise, Winchell was secretive about himself.

"Walter Winchell loves privacy," McEvoy wrote. "Not yours—his."

There was an unspoken but generally accepted policy among the columnists that they would not write about each other's peccadilloes. But not always. The late Dorothy Kilgallen once mentioned Winchell's being with a girl.

"Dorothy," he later said to Miss Kilgallen, "did you forget I am married?"

"No," she answered coolly. "Did you?"

The Stork Club—and all night clubs—was a comedy of human relations, with Billingsley barring people who were more desirable company than he was and Winchell sermonizing to people for conduct less godly than his own. During a battle over the future of the Stork Club television show, for example, producer Irving Mansfield was criticized by CBS for not attending rehearsals at the club.

"How can I attend them?" he demanded. "He's barred me."

Billingsley denied barring Mansfield and said, "Of course you're always welcome."

But when Mansfield returned to take over a rehearsal, he again discovered that he was barred.

Reveling in his power as the gossip king at the Stork, Winchell's judgment extended even to the life and death of people. One day he reported—and this was a long time ago when the disease was hardly mentioned—that So-and-So had cancer. So-and-So denied it.

The press agents were discussing it in Lindy's.

"So-and-So," opined one of the publicists, "had better have cancer or he's gonna get in a lotta trouble with Winchell!"

Another publicist shrugged it off. "WW doesn't use any of my stuff. I don't care what he says or writes."

"Whatsa matter, you?" shouted publicist Jack Tirman. "You an atheist or something?"

Mobsters were the behind-the-scenes owners of the smaller clubs, and when you consider that most of them had started out with speakeasies, their deportment was surprisingly good.

Henry Dunn, a one-time café performer with an act called Cross and Dunn, told me that he was doing his act one night in a speakeasy when a ringsider stepped onto the floor, said, "Excuse me," and pushed him aside.

"Sometimes a drunk would walk right across the stage to get to the men's room quicker," Dunn explained. "But this man was not taking a short cut to the men's room. He got me out of the way so that he could shoot a man across the room. He killed him."

The late comedian Jack Waldron used to talk about the Chicago clubs where, he said, "the boss would stab you good night."

There were indeed stabbings in Broadway clubs as late as the 1960s, although, in general, "that element" had been erased by the 1940s and 1950s, when Billingsley reigned.

By the 1940s the noisier clubs were just "rowdy." Over at the Club 18, at 18 West 52nd Street, the then unknown Jackie Gleason clowned with Jack White, Frankie Hyers, Pat Harrington, Fatso Marko, and some others. Their forte was insulting a female celebrity on the way to the powder room.

"Get a load of the hat on that broad!" was one of the salutes. "Hey, sister, what do you mean wearin' that? How the hell do you think we're gonna get laughs?"

As the subject of their jokes proceeded toward the powder room, one of the comics always said, "Mention my name and get a good seat."

Then a comic would come out with a toilet seat yelling "Garbo sat here."

Celebrities' birthdays were fêted strangely at the Club 18. A birthday cake would be magically produced, and the celebrity would be asked to cut it. As he reached to cut it, the whole cake would be torn from his grasp by some contraption to which it was attached.

"Get lost, you bum!" the guests would tell him in chorus.

Compared to this, the Stork Club and the El Morocco, its rival in the glamour world, were quite decorous. Billingsley continued to bar people, and I barred myself. Once he confused the identity of my assistant with that of another columnist's assistant. He said my assistant "was rolling up a house check by drinking." Actually, it was the other columnist's assistant. When told he'd made a mistake, Billingsley refused to apologize and said he "wanted the top man, anyway, and not any assistant." I decided never to go in there again, and despite many invitations from him and messages conveyed to me by intermediaries, I never did.

Increasingly Sherm was depressed and friendless. He battled the unions, which picketed his place. He got into an enormous row over refusing service to Josephine Baker, the Negro star. His right to carry firearms was challenged. Two of his captains started a rival club, the Harwyn, and attracted many customers who carried grudges against Billingsley.

Billingsley used to walk by the Harwyn himself to see who was going inside; later he would bar Harwyn customers from the Stork. His own club was beginning to fare badly. He quarreled with Winchell, whose power was declining.

The "balloon nights"—when you might grab a balloon and find a $100 bill in it, if you were a pretty girl who had caught Billingsley's eye—were long past. The bar was no longer crowded; sometimes you'd see only two or three drinkers there. The rope in the Cub Room was up even when there was nobody inside.

On October 4, 1965, as I strolled along East 53rd Street, I came to the Stork Club and saw a sign: STORK CLUB CLOSED. WILL RELOCATE.

The sign must have been placed there that morning, and it fell to me, of all people, to discover it. I wrote the obituary of the Stork Club for publication the next day.

A year to the day after he closed the club, Billingsley died of a heart attack at the age of sixty-eight. At the end he borrowed small sums of money from the same people he had once barred.

There was one man who seemed to wear a tuxedo every night.

John Perona, operator of El Morocco, had that look of urbanity and polish. Mr. Zebra Stripes, an Italian immigrant, also a former speakeasy owner, possessed all the social niceties that Billingsley lacked. He ran the most continuously exciting and financially successful club, and died leaving a fortune and a reputation of considerable dignity and self-respect.

Lean, handsome, youthful in movement and in speech, mannerly, hospitable but never servile, Perona was always the happy host.

His greatest pal was Errol Flynn. Flynn and Perona made quite a pair at the El Morocco Round Table—or at the George V in Paris in the summer. They traveled through France and Italy together and from there came happy stories, no scandals, about the escapades of a couple of older boys living out their lives. I was in El Morocco the night Perona and many others cried over Flynn's death.

"Elmer's," as El Morocco got to be called, did its share of barring too. One celebrity who was barred was Zsa Zsa Gabor. Perona had a colossal misunderstanding with Zsa Zsa during his friendship with her sister Eva. For years afterward, Perona, the suave, slick smiling proprietor, would not permit Zsa Zsa on the premises.

"You're just being stubborn, John," people told him.

"I know I am," he would say with a smile.

Howard Hughes used to go into El Morocco wearing tennis shoes and cheap suits in those days. John F. Kennedy visited there with many different girls. The Duke and Duchess of Windsor loved to sit in the Champagne Room and listen dreamily while the violinists played.

There was a night when press agent Chick Farmer phoned to inform me that the Duke and Duchess, freshly arrived from Europe after the scandal of their marriage, had just popped into Elmer's for their first visit, and why didn't I rush over and grab them for the first story about this monumental stop-off?

Captivated by his enthusiasm for such a piece of trivia, I rushed to the scene—this was at the old El Morocco, at 162 East 54th Street —to discover that I was minutes late.

The Duke and Duchess had just departed.

"The Duke's chair is still warm!" Chick exclaimed, disappointedly.

And that gave him an idea. Why didn't I sit in the seat that the royal derrière had just sat in and see how my flesh reacted to his seat? Would my commoner's backside notice any great difference when it perched in the seat just vacated by the so recent King of England?

"Then you will write yourself a beautiful column about it, mentioning El Morocco." Chick Farmer was already pushing me down into the seat that had been the Duke's.

I did just about as Chick told me, wrote the column, and received a raise on the basis of my imagination for doing something different in covering the night clubs. The credit should have gone to Chick.

There always seemed to be a story at El Morocco. Perona gave an annual New Year's afternoon milk punch party to which people brought their hangovers. On one of those occasions, Siri, a tall Scandinavian model, whispered to me that Prince Rainier, a playboy not then very well known in America, had spent the holidays visiting the home of the Jack Kellys in Philadelphia and that it looked as if there might be something going on there regarding the young Prince and the Kellys' daughter Grace.

"I heard about it through one of the embassies," Siri said.

I phoned the tip to the *Philadelphia Daily News* city desk, which tried to reach Jack Kelly but couldn't. We printed a brief about it anyway—the first news of the courtship of Rainier and Grace, although the big news was to come later.

As well as being exclusive, El Morocco was notoriously expensive. It had the world's costliest side dish—baked potato, $12—but that was with caviar, of course.

Not only the Kennedy boys flirted and danced at El Morocco. The Roosevelt boys were there before them—Elliott, John, and Franklin, Jr. Morton Downey was a young dandy who spent many evenings within its confines. And Douglas Fairbanks, Sr., recently separated from Mary Pickford, had been among its customers. Tallulah Bankhead was a young beauty—well, actually she was beginning to look a little wrinkled.

The club had been a long time at its East 54th Street location when John Perona decided to build a new El Morocco a short distance further east.

In the new club, at 307 East 54th Street, the Champagne Room was reached either by an elevator across the foyer from the check room or by an open stairway with carpeted steps. The beautiful ladies liked to ascend and descend those stairs while the gentlemen ogled. This route was variously called "the Stairway of the Stars" or "the Starway of the Stares." Perona, who in moments of happiness claimed he once had been a bus boy and now had been knighted by the Pope, was really proudest of the zebra-striped decor, which had been printed for him exclusively by DuPont.

Each club tried to outdo the other by providing special distinctions. At El Morocco the ultimate snobbism was provided by the "wrong side of the room"—the area *beyond* the dance floor that divided the room. It was nicknamed Siberia.

"I refuse to sit in Siberia," Peggy Hopkins Joyce had said, and many other people eventually made the same remark.

In this case, however, the distinction did not please the owner. He hadn't planned it, and he did not want half of his big room to be devalued. Henry Ford, Serge Obolensky, and some other notables obligingly sat on the "wrong side," and that took some of the chill off Siberia.

Nevertheless, Perona's maitre d's did "dress the room" and always were careful to display the most chic people at the most favorably located tables, usually at the right corner or first from the corner as you entered. And the maitre d's didn't have to be reminded not to seat Elliott Roosevelt's first wife and his third wife at adjoining tables.

The new club, which opened in 1961, did not produce any fights approaching the brawls they'd had at the old El Morocco in the forties and fifties. Perhaps the new place, with its red plush bar in the Champagne Room and the promenade down a Versailles-like hall of mirrors, was just too elegant for fighting.

One battle they talked about at the old club involved Morton Downey and Addison Randall, who at the time was married to Downey's ex-wife Barbara Bennett. Their argument went back to 1943. There had been bitterness among Downey, his ex-wife, and her new husband over the divorce. That night in El Morocco somebody threw a punch, and Randall was hit in the head and carried out. He had to be stitched up. To make it more of a family affair, Joan Bennett sat nearby with Walter Wanger, her husband at the time, but she didn't contribute anything. Not a word. The sisters weren't speaking.

The most famous fight of all involved Humphrey Bogart, two stuffed pandas, and a couple of girls who tried to steal the pandas. I shall cover that later in this book. Just let it be added that John Perona, his own best customer, was not present that night in 1949 when Bogart and Billy Seaman arrived with two stuffed pandas and ordered drinks for themselves and the pandas.

John Perona was Florida-tanned and looking a little tired when he opened the new club—with Otto Preminger, Henry Fonda, Billy Rose, Lucille Ball, Aristotle Onassis, the Duchess of Argyll, and other such fine folks trying out the new stairway. Sitting with him at the Round Table was his son Edwin Perona, El Morocco's crown prince. Edwin was not fond of the night club grind and would just as soon have been out of it, but it looked as if he was stuck with a gold mine—especially when John, who had been in the new club two nights before returning to Florida, discovered he had cancer of the spine.

Young Edwin took over entirely a few months later when John Perona died. But the grind proved to be just too much. He decided he wanted out and began looking for a buyer.

However, Edwin still had the club when, in August, 1962, Zsa Zsa Gabor was readmitted into El Morocco, seventeen years after she'd been barred. Seventeen years is a long time, but she *had* spat in John Perona's face—which everybody agreed was going a little too far.

Edwin Perona had been a boy when the Gabor feud began, but, of course, he knew about it. Then, one night, Bob Stralie, Zsa Zsa's boy friend, quarreled with her, left her, and went to El Morocco. Suddenly, while he was sitting at the Round Table with Edwin Perona, Stralie decided he wasn't mad at Zsa Zsa—that he loved her very much.

"You don't know how much she missed not being allowed to come to El Morocco all these years," Bob Stralie said. He grew sadder and sadder about it as it got later and later. "I'm completely broken up with her and I'll never see her again, but I do feel sorry for her not being allowed to come into El Morocco."

Edwin Perona broke down and said she could come in.

"It's been a long time," Edwin Perona said. "She did a lot of bad things in here but a lot of people did bad things in here."

And the escort who brought her back in was the man who had vowed he was never going to see her again—Bob Stralie. (Nine years later he was *still* seeing her.)

The new El Morocco saw a different clientele, presaging its end. It, therefore, came as no surprise, since we knew Edwin did not particularly like his job, when we learned he was *really* looking for a purchaser. The Duke of Windsor remained a regular patron, but he didn't do much dancing to the music from the shows. Lyndon B. Johnson, who had come in as Senator and Vice-President, and had always been greeted by "The Eyes of Texas Are Upon You," didn't get away from the White House to visit night clubs. Aly Khan was gone, Pofirio Rubirosa was gone. In the old days they had both danced away most of the night in Elmer's. Eddie Perona didn't see many people of his own age coming into El Morocco, and he preferred staying home nights on the big farm his father had left him in New Jersey.

Big 6-foot-4 John Mills, a back-slapping, hand-kissing Pole who ran Les Ambassadeurs in London, took over from Edwin and later said Edwin "was one of the smartest men in the world for selling to me."

John Mills, with his bluff, booming optimism, envisioned his El Morocco as a private membership club with a $100 fee to join. Sell enough of those memberships, old boy, and you'll have a bankroll to lean on. That's how he did it in London. You sat on the terrace of his club with a drink and watched the poor people go sweating by, and you were a happy snob.

Snobbish as America's upper classes were, they didn't embrace his private membership fee idea. Eventually big John concluded he had misgauged the spirit in the colonies. He looked around for a buyer, as Edwin Perona had done before him, and discovered a fine sort of fellow named Maurice Uchitel, who had once been called a textillionaire and "the shoulder pad king."

Uchitel quickly decided that the old El Morocco crowd of the Whitneys, Vanderbilts, and Astors had died or had become too old to go to night clubs, and he chose to transform the club into "young El Morocco."

Uchitel himself was a lean, boyish-looking, impeccably dressed middle-ager. He installed Peter Duchin's orchestra, experimented with discothèque music, and created a slightly psychedelic effect with twinkling lights on the ceiling. Uchitel spent his days with shopping center developments worth millions. But almost every night he was in the club greeting the customers, trying to make a success of something that seemed less and less likely to recover from a bad case of changing economic conditions.

Richard and Pat Nixon sat against the zebra stripes one night with Anita Louise and her husband Henry Berger—this was a little before Nixon had decided to run in 1968. Vice-President Hubert Humphrey entered with a political entourage of at least a dozen. Uchitel arranged for me to sit with both groups. Having such big names in the place nearly always increased business and gave the help a more cheerful outlook about what they had begun to fear was a dying business.

Uchitel spent a summer—and a lot of money—giving the place a new canopied Casbah look for its September 12, 1968, opening—its thirty-sixth.

"Socko El Morocco," the *Daily News* said.

One night Aristotle Onassis gave a party in the Champagne Room for Rudolf Nureyev, Dame Margot Fonteyn, and the ballet troupe. The check came to about $5,000.

"That's without the tip, of course," Uchitel told me.

Onassis sat with Cary Grant another night and invited me to join them. Eventually I asked Onassis whether he was going to marry again. At that time, we knew only of his romance with Maria Callas.

Smiling and enjoying the conversation, he lied through his teeth. He said he was not getting married again. "I've *been* married," he said, which I interpreted as meaning that he'd had it with that institution.

Having had it straight from the man himself that he wasn't going to get married, I discounted a rumor about two weeks later that he was going to marry Jackie Kennedy. I told my informant he was out of his mind and to stop spreading such ludicrous tales.

Times had really changed. The celebrity set had given way to a different pack of people.

Now the big names were the show business folk—Johnny Carson, Alan King, Sammy Davis, Jr., Joseph E. Levine, Peter O'Toole, Milton Berle. (Berle said one night, "This is a beautiful club. Who owns it this week?")

Maurice Uchitel saw the handwriting in the ledger. He pulled out of active operation and let his silent partner Joe Norban try his hand running the club. Billy Reed, long-time operator of the Little Club, was brought in as manager and chief greeter.

But too often there weren't many to greet.

The hatcheck girl kept a little counting device at her stand, and some nights it showed that there had been fewer customers than employees.

On May 3, 1970, Joe Norban gave me a birthday party at the club. At the party he handed me a note, which said that El Morocco would close May 24 for the summer "and will reopen as a private club in the fall of 1970."

My little birthday party was one of the last festive events there, with Berle, Joe E. Lewis, Dionne Warwick, Julie Budd, Gene Baylos, and Phil Foster contributing entertainment.

Business got even worse. Still, El Morocco tried to hold up its head. One night, with the club almost empty, there was one couple seated in Siberia. Even with most of the tables available, some captain had decided that the guests did not deserve to be seated in "the better side of the room."

On closing night May 23, 1970, which was lively because of some last-gasp publicity, people tried to tell the last operator, Joe Norban, that he should stay open. He knew that the activity was artificial.

"I go on record that I will not reopen it as a public club," he said. "There is no longer any night club business."

During the New York World's Fair of 1939 and 1940, Billy Rose, "the Bantam Barnum," or "the Basement Belasco," made a fortune at Flushing Meadows with the Aquacade, starring his wife Eleanor Holm, who later divorced him. And he made another fortune simultaneously with the Diamond Horseshoe night club in the basement of the Paramount Hotel on West 46th Street, where he titillated the male customers with beautiful long-legged chorus girls in brief, sexy costumes who kicked and sang and wiggled and waggled their fannies and pelvises.

"Billy Rose gets them both at the Fair and in town," people said.

A dozen clubs were trying to do the same. But during the "sexy sixties," the big splashy, flashy, razzle-dazzle floor show night clubs, featuring girls with large bosoms and very little dancing experience, began fading from Broadway. One reason was that New Yorkers were staying home nights to take advantage of the free entertainment on television.

The crushing blow was the death of the Latin Quarter.

For almost a quarter of a century New Yorkers had been walking up those red-carpeted steps at Broadway and 48th Street to see the glittering café stars—Willie and Eugene Howard, Ted Lewis, Harry Richman, Sophie Tucker, Mae West, Milton Berle, and Henny Youngman.

For years New Yorkers had sniffed loftily about "the Quarter," calling it a "tourist joint." Its appeal was supposedly directed to out-of-towners; the show was long, with acrobats, Apache dancers, jugglers, harmonica wizards—but you got a lot for your money, and the chorus girls did their best to show you their breasts although they usually had to wear pasties over their nipples (sometimes the pasties came unpasted, however, or the girls forgot to apply them).

Lou Walters, just about the best known café operator in the

country, was usually running the club either for E. M. Loew of Boston or for himself. Walters, a quiet, bespectacled little gentleman with a passion for gin rummy, was often joined at the Latin Quarter by his wife and two small daughters. Walters probably never suspected that some day one of his daughters would be better known to America than he—the little daughter being Barbara Walters, the television interviewer.

Those chorus girls, with or without pasties, were a big lure at the club, and their union, the American Guild of Variety Artists, didn't think they were sufficiently paid for their services.

Penny Singleton, the former "Blondie," a vice-president of the union, called for a chorus girl strike.

"It's not the raise she's asking that bothers me," E. M. Loew said. "I just can't get along with that woman."

Up in the dressing rooms the chorus girls weren't sure they wanted to strike. Chorus girls can be peculiar creatures. One girl told me that she so enjoyed romping around the stage exhibiting her body that she would have worked for nothing. But there were those who thought the $122 a week they got for thirteen shows was not enough and agreed with the demand for $150 a week.

E. M. Loew was getting increasingly irritated. He owned profitable drive-in theaters, so he didn't really need the Latin Quarter. He was also having a lease problem.

The union sniffed at his offer of $130 a week—shortsightedly for the chorus girl era was ending even though the Latin Quarter "cuties"—as they were so often called to their disgust—didn't know it.

Already, over at 10 East 60th Street, the Copacabana boss, wise and wily Jules Podell, had cut out his famous "Copa girl" line in January. Although he never admitted it, Podell probably foresaw a labor problem with his chorus girls and avoided it by dropping the line entirely.

"I want to try something new," Podell declared.

Actually, nobody felt very sad about the passing of the Copa girls. They had been beautiful and presumably necessary in their day. June Allyson, Olga San Juan, Julie Wilson, and Barbara Feldon had been among them. But by 1969, all girls could be beautiful, thanks to the new world of cosmetics, and some of the girls at the ringside tables were lovelier than the chorus girls. Besides, their dancing wasn't very good compared to what you viewed on television.

"If you can walk, you can be a dancer at the Copa," was the word around town.

"I find them just a stage wait," somebody said. "Who needs them anymore? We come to see Sammy Davis, not the girls."

So they packed up their tiny garments and departed, and the Copacabana went right on. The Latin Quarter girls continued to strike into the cold nights of February.

On February 20, 1969, we printed the obituary of the Latin Quarter. E. M. Loew and Lou Walters hung up a "Closed" sign on the front door.

"The Latin Quarter will reopen eventually at another location," E. M. Loew promised. It hasn't done so yet, and nobody's holding his breath. Lou Walters retired in Florida. And with the closing of the Latin Quarter, the night club era came, for all practical purposes, to an end.

The one traditional club that has stayed in business for thirty years, the Copacabana was ruled by the gruff, hard-driving Jules Podell. Sitting at a back table, he watched the floor show, scowling if it was bad, keeping the entertainers wondering whether he liked them and would bring them back. By shrewdly hiring performers when they were on the way up and getting them under contract for the future, he made sure the biggest café stars would bring in crowds for his floor show for a long time to go—from Joe E. Lewis, Perry Como, and Carmen Miranda to Frank Sinatra, Martin and Lewis, Johnny Ray, Tom Jones, and Don Rickles.

As a boss, Podell was dictatorial. Once, catching a waiter stealing food and putting it aside for a sneak snack later, Podell made an example of him. Setting up a table in the center of the kitchen, Podell commanded the waiter to sit down and then served him his best dinner, including wine. Then, with a frightening roar, Podell fired him, chasing him off the premises.

The only living kind of night club left is of the discothèque variety, an invention of the 1960s stemming from the arrival of the Twist.

"The Twist was invented by a woman trying to dry her backside with a towel while killing an ant with her foot," someone said.

A dance called the Twist leaped at America at the beginning of the sexy sixties and helped to prolong the life of night clubs for a few years. Looking back, I find the Twist the most incredible of all the fads. It was not made by snobs. The Taj Mahal of the Twist was a narrow, undistinguished little tavern on West 45th Street, the Peppermint Lounge, which, before its time of fame, catered predominantly to young men who wore no ties or jackets—unless they were leather jackets—and girls of dubious social status who mixed their chewing gum with beer.

Yet so great was the Twist rage that Bob Hope spoke of it at a banquet at the Waldorf attended by President John F. Kennedy. "There were so many VIP limousines out in front tonight, I thought this was the Peppermint Lounge," Hope quipped.

Martin Burden, the gourmet restaurant editor of the *New York Post,* sighed recently and said, "To think that my main claim to fame once was that I could sneak somebody into the back door of the Peppermint Lounge."

It really went back to the fifties. Attending the Cannes Film Festival, I heard people talking about going to a club called the Whiskey-A-Go-Go, where they danced to recorded music. The place was called a discothèque. It seemed pretty silly to dance to records, but the music was amplified and swingy.

Chubby Checker, a black singer, was alleged to have undone America at Palisades Park, New Jersey, on a sweaty afternoon in July 1960. Wearing a checkered jacket, he had executed the Twist and sung about it on Clay Cole's TV show.

Chubby's claim to be the inventor of the Twist was instantly disputed by Hank Ballard of Atlanta, who said he had recorded it a year before. And Joey Dee, the saxophonist leader of the house band at the Peppermint Lounge, likewise contended that he'd been doing it a year before Chubby. Nevertheless, much of the credit, or discredit, seemed to belong to Chubby and Philadelphia, which has produced so many singers. His record "The Twist" had simple lyrics and a jumpy, catchy rhythm.

In the beginning at the Peppermint Lounge, the Twist was done to the live music of Joey Dee (Joseph Di Nicola of Passaic, New Jersey) and a wild group called the Starliters.

Upon entering the Peppermint Lounge, after tipping a fellow who let you in through the back door, you saw a comparatively small dance floor and a few tables—and waitresses who, in the midst of taking your order, stopped to do the Twist.

The management encouraged the waitresses' enthusiasm. Some of the waitresses, in fact, were part-time go-go dancers who leaped on stage and twisted, solo, to the Starliters' music.

The dancing was unlike anything that had preceded it. The claim that it resembled a woman trying to dry her derrière with a towel was a reasonable description. In the Twist, nobody held anybody up close, and each partner seemed barely aware of the other's existence. Each partner would look at the other occasionally to make sure he wasn't dancing with somebody else, although if he should do so, it wouldn't be a serious violation of any rules, since there were no rules.

It was claimed that inasmuch as nobody held anybody close, the Twist wasn't sexual. But some of the contemporary dancers were. The Swim was tried out one night. It consisted of two people of the opposite sex getting down on the floor, one on top of the other. Then they made swimming motions. It didn't last.

"Twist parties" and "Twist evenings" became very big socially in 1961. They twisted at the Stork, the Harwyn, the Barberry Room, and the Four Seasons. Everybody made fun of it, but they got up and danced it.

"It's the shimmy dropped to the pelvic area," Arthur Murray said.

"It's like you're wearing itchy underwear and have to scratch yourself without using your hands," a go-go girl remarked.

The old King of Swing Benny Goodman watched in disbelief. "In my day," he said, "not only did boys and girls dance together, but you could tell which was which."

A lot of people hurt their backs when the Twist was at its peak of popularity. That jerky rhythm did it. Dr. Ben Gilbert, "the Broadway house doctor," who had offices near the Peppermint Lounge, set up a clinic there to handle the sprains of the Twisters. In Buffalo an orthopedic surgeon said he had treated several youngsters for dislocated kneecaps, and in Albany an auto salesman died of a heart attack after twisting at a company party.

Some puritanical citizens were shocked by the pelvic thrusts of the dancers, who sometimes seemed to attain intimacy even while remaining apart.

"They do get married later, don't they?" one woman was said to have asked.

An out-of-towner remarked as he watched the contortions, "If that doesn't bring rain, nothing will."

Of course those observations were also made about the shimmy and other "wicked" dances in the past.

The Twist twisted right along. Although Dwight D. Eisenhower criticized it, Adlai Stevenson not only approved it but did it. The country was electrified around Christmas 1961 to read that the First Lady had twisted in a Florida night club.

Bulletin! Correction! The Associated Press sent out a retraction declaring that it was not Jackie Kennedy who twisted. It was "a case of mistaken identity." Pierre Salinger, the White House presidential press secretary, asked for the correction.

The Lyndon B. Johnson administration was evidently pro-Twist. Perle Mesta gave a Washington party at which Carol Channing lured President Johnson's Secretary of the Treasury out onto the floor to do the Twist.

Carol was wearing white trousers and white boots with a black tuxedo jacket. They made a striking couple as they appeared on the nation's front pages the next day.

Shepheard's, the first big discothèque in New York, patterned after the famous Shepheard's Hotel in Cairo, opened on December 29, 1963, in the Drake Hotel. I remember how delightful it was to hear dance music played for our pleasure—great songs that we knew, backed by famous voices that we knew, on recordings selected by somebody who knew our tastes.

One of the women guests who didn't understand what a discothèque was turned to me and said, "Isn't that Sinatra's voice? I didn't know he was working here."

Shepheard's was plush, lush, social, softly lit, romantic, and continental—the exact opposite of the Peppermint Lounge, which was really a glorified beer joint. The only similarity between the two was the Twist and its variants that continued to fascinate dancers.

The word "disquaire" was invented to describe a young man considered a genius for selecting the record his audience would like to dance to, at, for example, 10:45 P.M.

And then came Arthur and the dance disease frivolously referred to as "Arthuritis."

Richard Burton had given up Sybil Burton and married Elizabeth Taylor. Sybil had the world's sympathy. Living in New York and looking for a new life, Sybil elected to join Roddy MacDowall and about eighty others who contributed $1,000 each to open a club called Arthur, located on the site of the old El Morocco at 162 East 54th Street.

On opening night, Wednesday, May 5, 1965, the night club reviewers had too much to do. The Latin Quarter was headlining Edie Adams. Eartha Kitt was opening at the Plaza Persian Room, wearing sexy derrière-hugging bell-bottom pants. We had to see them both and somehow managed to find time to visit Arthur.

Edie Adams was doing an "interpretation" of the First Lady—Lady Bird Johnson—with her thick Texas accent. Lady Bird was a good target for Edie.

"Ah made my husband what he is today—reeeich," Edie had Lady Bird saying. "Ah've been spending quite a lot of time in Washington since Mr. Johnson and Ah became Prezzahdent."

Rudolf Nureyev was the big fascination for femininity at the crowded Arthur opening. Rock Hudson and Ross Hunter couldn't find seats and left unhappy. Sophie Tucker and David O. Selznick were in the pack that could hardly get in and, once in, could hardly get out.

"I'm going to ask Nureyev to dance with me," Monique Van Vooren, the singer-actress known as the Belgian Bulge, said to me as she stood surveying the crowd.

Monique introduced herself to him ("We've met before," she told him), asked him to dance, and they did the Frug. They became such close friends that Nureyev was her house guest in New York five years later.

Arthur was instantaneously successful, and in 1966, the widowed Jackie Kennedy had succumbed to it and its crazy dances. Escorted frequently to Sardi's and then to Arthur by Mike Nichols, she danced the Watusi, the Frug, and the other offshoots of the Twist. The club people discovered that a former First Lady could be shoved and jostled like anybody else.

"I like to come here to scream," Danny Kaye said. "I scream and nobody can hear me," he told Sybil.

It was true that a scream made very little impression over the blare of the music. Those whose ears couldn't take it would go to a bar in the back—the Champagne Room of the old El Morocco, where the violinists once played Viennese waltzes for the Duke and Duchess of Windsor.

Although Richard Burton and Liz Taylor undoubtedly never set foot in Arthur, just about everybody else had some curiosity about it and its ear-splitting racket. Sybil Burton, like her former husband from a Welsh coal town, became a celebrities' celebrity, a magnet that pulled in the names during the late hours.

"I love everything about the stage except going on it," Sybil said once.

Studying acting in London, she met Burton while doing a small role in a movie for Emlyn Williams, who had adopted Burton as a protégé. Prematurely gray, she turned white-haired by the time she was twenty. She and Burton got married five months after they met, and she retired from acting very quickly.

But now Sybil was queen of the late set, reigning at a low table alongside the dance floor a few feet from the band platform.

She would be waving to the John Bentley Ryans, Gloria Vanderbilt, Huntington Hartford, Anthony Newley.

Yet, unlike her former husband and his new wife, who had been all over the newspapers with their romantic news, Sybil Burton hadn't been making any. Then she began to notice one of the young men on the bandstand near which she sat each night, Jordan Christopher, twenty-three, a meek-appearing, long-haired, quiet member of The Wild Ones, a musical group.

Jordan played the electric guitar, shook his tambourine, and sang, and it appeared that he and Sybil would have nothing in common. Sybil, a dozen years his senior, was from the London and Hollywood theatrical and literary world, with the added background of living in villas in Italy while her husband Burton made movies. Jordan Christopher was of Macedonian descent, the son of an Akron saloon keeper. His real name was Zankoff, and he had been married previously at the age of nineteen. He composed some of the rock music that The Wild Ones played, and he claimed that back in Akron he was the only boy who spoke Macedonian. He had even written a song, "The Ballad of a Macedonian Boy."

They had a whirlwind courtship. About six weeks after Arthur opened, they had a June wedding in Sybil's apartment in Central

Park West. People said it wouldn't last. But it did, and it continues to do so.

Jordan Christopher immediately joined the low table in the corner across from the bandstand where Sybil reigned, sharing in the secrets and private jokes of Princess Lee Radziwill, Leonard Bernstein, Truman Capote, Senator Jacob Javits and his wife Marian, Roddy MacDowall, and the rest of the elite.

Arthur had tone, class, and it had *names*. Teddy Kennedy was an occasional visitor. One night he and his brother-in-law Steve Smith participated in some family fun. They could hardly play touch football in those cramped quarters, but they played pitch-and-catch with sister Jean Kennedy Smith's handbag.

Of course it had snobbishness too, and the guardians at the door admitted no riff-raff. Outside on the sidewalk every night there would be a clamoring pack pleading to be allowed in. Fights broke out, taxicabs crashed into limousines, police cars arrived with sirens screaming. It was exciting and glamorous, and the owners of Arthur decided to try to spread Arthuritis across the country. It chose to infect California first and set about opening a couple of branches.

As always, there had to be a small shooting out on the sidewalk, a rumor that mobsters were trying to muscle in. Huntington Hartford and his wife Diane had a battle inside centering around a phone booth. Somebody got pushed down on the floor, Diane leaped into the phone booth and called police (who were outside on the sidewalk).

"Hartfords Trip the Fight Fantastic at Arthur," said a *New York Post* headline.

Nearly all the new clubs enjoy a brief popularity, then expire. Few have the staying power of the "old-fashioned" Copa, largely because fashions in music and entertainment change so fast nowadays. New kinds of clubs constantly spring up to replace the old— even if the old is only a few months or years old. That, primarily, is why the real night club era is dead.

Arthur persisted for four years. Its members and owners just sort of lost interest. Jordan Christopher decided to go into the movies, and Sybil no longer sat at the low table every night. The investors, including Rex Harrison, Lauren Bacall, Mike Nichols, and Leonard Bernstein, had more than doubled their money. So when night club owner Oliver Coquelin and some friends offered to buy the spot for $150,000, the Arthur group accepted.

Judy Garland joined the Arthur habitués during the last months and had fallen in love with the night manager, Mickey Deans. Then when Judy went to London for some engagements, Mickey Deans joined her and they were married.

Finally, the Arthur management announced that it would close the Saturday night of June 21, 1969. The newspapers predicted a big funeral type of party. Actually it came to end quietly. Sybil Christopher did not attend. She was in California with her young husband, making a movie.

I was not there to cover the last gasp. I had gone to the Bahamas to cover the Warner Brothers film festival. At Sunday breakfast, Danny Lewis of the *Bergen* (New Jersey) *Record* said, "You heard about Judy? Mickey Deans found her dead in London."

Judy Garland had succumbed Saturday night; Arthur had died Saturday night. The Sunday and Monday papers didn't carry a line about the passing of Arthur. They forgot Arthur and printed columns about Judy, which was proper. Judy was news for several days. Arthur was over. So was most of the night club era.

5

The Gentle Art of Ribbing

THERE are pessimists today who state that laughter has disappeared from the land. They do not hear any vaudeville jokes from the Palace Theater—or any night club jokes from the Latin Quarter because it is now a porno movie house—and they believe that fun has fled. The truth is that laughter has merely changed addresses. It has moved to television.

Twenty years ago you might have heard Bob Hope say from some theater stage, "I made a killing today in the market—I shot my broker."

You could have heard Henny Youngman say, "I had a very big day in the market—I sold two chickens."

Today you can hear the same comedians tell the same jokes on TV, and they are paid considerably more. Laughter is a much bigger business now than ever before.

There was a kind of nonsense and foolishness in the early days that I don't see now. When I came into this madland in the late fall of 1942, I was quite unprepared for the extroverts and exhibitionists I met.

On the radio Fred Allen was whining his complaints against the NBC vice-presidents.

"An NBC vice-president is a gentleman who doesn't know what his duties are and by the time he finds out, he is no longer there," Fred said. He also declared that every vice-president was given a molehill when he came to work at nine A.M. and was required to make a mountain out of it by five P.M.

Rushing out on my very first night on the Saloon Beat in a dinner jacket (to the amusement of my colleagues, who almost never went formal), I discovered that a "thing to do" on my new job was to attend the Leon & Eddie's Celebrity Nights on Sundays.

Short, big-bellied Leon Enken, the businessman in the combination that owned the night club at 33 West 52nd Street, where Toots Shor's later was built, had the quaint habit of spitting at people as he greeted them. Doubtless this was a dental weakness. Nevertheless, as I stood there at the door and reflected that this was one of the most important clubs in the nation, and he spat on me, smiling all the while, it *was* disconcerting—to say the least.

Tall, friendly, big-nosed Eddie Davis was on the stage welcoming the crowd who had come out to salute the week's celebrity, who might be almost anybody they could entice into the place. I say that with authority because subsequently I was the "celebrity" on a couple of Sunday nights when things were rough for them.

One momentous Sunday night the celebrity was eleven-times married Tommy Manville, who at that time was only up to wife number seven or eight—who could keep count? He and his bride were celebrating one month of wedded bliss. Tommy had a hired bodyguard, a personal photographer, and two pistols with him and his bride.

Tommy Manville had a passion for publicity unequaled in the world. He liked girls, but he married them only to get his name in the papers. He somewhat resembled an actor of whom it was said, "He is a very modest man, and he has three press agents to prove it."

When Manville got married, there was always a sizable story in the newspapers, and it remained news for two or three days. Eventually the big news dwindled to a mention in the columns. But when the columnists no longer mentioned Marrying Manville, the honeymoon was over.

One of his brides actually told me that Manville greeted her one breakfast time with a scrapbook.

"Look," he pointed. "Not one clipping in a week. We're through."

Everybody seemed to be a little crazier then—or maybe it was just that I was. I was present and very observant one night when an eminent first-nighter Jules Brulatour, who was tremendously wealthy, slipped off his chair and fell on his buttocks while watching a show at the old La Conga café.

They were having their usual thrilling dancing-and-singing opening, and Brulatour was sitting there with his platinum blonde wife Hope Hampton, when Brulatour suddenly hit the floor.

Brulatour was a portly, gray-haired gentleman with a stiff dignified manner. The floor's unwarranted attack on him took him by complete surprise, and he just sat on the floor for some moments, not believing a floor could be so unkind. I wrote in my column the next day that he had sort of sagged and went on the floor and had made sounds like a baby's—"Buh, buh, buh."

His wife provided very little help to him in his crisis. She became hysterical with laughter and declared it was the funniest spectacle she had seen in years. A couple of waiters and a captain helped Mr. Brulatour up, but he felt the need to brush himself off and retired to the men's room. I accompanied him.

"What happened?" I boldly asked him.

"I fell on my prat," he said.

I reported the event as fully as I could in my column, and Miss Hampton sent me some champagne in appreciation of my coverage of this rather historic fanny-fall.

Just a few doors away at another 52nd Street club, the 51 Club, I took a ride in a dumbwaiter one night with a stripper named Ginger Britton.

It hadn't been my plan to get in a dumbwaiter with her. Miss Britton had been quarreling with Harry Finkelstein, the proprietor, and I wished to report it.

"I cahn't do bumps and I cahn't do grinds and I cahn't roll my pants down in the back," she pouted. "If I cahn't do eyether of those things, my act is ruined."

Miss Britton was standing there in just her G-string, bare-busted, when a dumbwaiter ground to a halt and a man who'd been sitting inside it hopped out and walked away.

"What the hell was that?" I asked.

"He rode down in the dumbwaiter that comes down from backstage," the club's press agent, Lee Meyers, said. "They all do that.

That way they don't have to walk through the crowd in front of the club to get down here to the basement."

"I don't believe it," I said.

Miss Britton had tossed on a thin dress cut so low at the bosom that I could see all the way to her waist. Hearing me express surprise about the dumbwaiter, she spoke up in the adorable English accent that she'd picked up God knows where, "Cahn't you see how it's done? Come on, honey, you and me'll get in it and take a ride."

"There's hardly room for two," I muttered.

"Oh, come on, honey!" Bouncy Miss Britton climbed in, doubled up, and took my hands to pull me in.

The dumbwaiter was barely big enough to accommodate the two of us, at very close quarters. I squeezed in with Miss Britton, and if we'd have been any more intimate, we'd have been intimate. We were really close—alone at last in a dumbwaiter. I had to put my arms around Miss Britton to make more room for us. Lee Meyers now was pulling on the rope to haul us upward to the backstage area, but we were too heavy for him. The dumbwaiter wouldn't budge.

"Pull, you fool!" I yelled at him.

But we were too much for him.

Miss Britton unwound herself from me, and I disentangled myself from her and her charms, and we both got out. To show me how it worked, Lee Meyers hauled me up solo. But somehow, riding in a dumbwaiter alone is not as much fun.

A character named "Feets" Edson contributed to the nighttime gaiety. He was nicknamed "Feets" because he was talented at kicking people in night club fights. Sometimes he managed clubs; sometimes he ran the hat check concession. In the 1940s some of the big spenders (such as "Nucky" Johnson from Atlantic City) paid checks of $1,000 or more. Johnson once was buying for everybody and bought fifty-seven quarts of champagne at $25 a quart.

"Feets" told me his tricks of check-padding. One prominent man went to sleep in a club. Feets woke him and gave him a check. He went back to sleep. Feets woke him and gave him another check, which he paid. Feets claimed the gentleman paid the check nine times—and all he had was a cup of coffee.

"Another guy went to sleep at his table," Feets said, "so I got some empty champagne bottles and put them around at different tables. He woke up and I gave him a check for $800. He said 'What did I have?' I told him, 'You can see, can't you? You told all those people to have champagne on you.' So he paid it."

Grown men used up their energy and their intelligence in those couple of decades to "rib" people—to embarrass them by insulting them until they exploded into a rage.

Clark Gable was once the victim of professional ribber Vince Barnett, who inherited his talent in that field from his father Luke Barnett.

Vince Barnett, who was the master of several accents, also was able to carry off the pretense that he didn't understand English. His technique was bluntness. Seemingly a meek little man, he would be sent, for example, into the executive offices of a television company by a friend of an executive who wanted to play a joke on him. There he would pose as the irate owner of a used set that had broken down.

The executive would try to be nice to the angry customer, who would gradually drive him crazy.

"Vy," he would scream, going into his German accent, "you sold me a lousy zet and I spend $200 feex it. Now I vant my $200 and the price of the zet, $300, and cab fare and damages. I eefen took it apart myself and poot back togedder and can't feex it."

"All right," the executive said patiently, "we'll take care of you."

"Oh, ho—you're going to take care of me! Going to slug me. Going to beat me opp!" Shaking a finger under the executive's nose, he yelled, "You Nazi!" The executive, a Jewish gentleman, took off his glasses in exasperation.

"Oh, ho, you tage de glasses off! Vant to fight a poor old man. Now I call opp the district attorney on you, you storm trooper!"

Barnett didn't consider the rib a success unless he got the victim to take a swing at him. He had learned how to duck.

Vince Barnett usually posed as a distinguished foreign visitor. He was "Dr. Vojak, the German producer," at a Hollywood party given by Joan Crawford, and Clark Gable was the target. Barnett had found that Americans would usually put up with a lot of abuse from a foreigner because they felt there was a linguistic misunderstanding—but eventually they would blow up.

Gable had been in a little group that was talking. He walked away. Barnett saw his opening.

"Oh, de Great Gable valk avay ven I am talking," he sneered. "I am not acawstom to such discourteous pigs."

"I beg your pardon," said Gable politely.

"I don't accept no apawlogy. De Great Gable believes his publicity. How rude can a man be?"

"My good man . . ." said Gable.

"I am not your good man! De Great Gable thinks he can do anything because he really believes he is de Great Gable vot he reads in de phony newspapers vot he pays to get publicity."

"Listen," snapped Gable, now at the breaking point, "say 'the Great Gable' one more time, and I'll slap you!"

"So ho, the Great Gable is also a pugilist?" sneered Barnett, getting ready for the punch.

At that Gable blew his fuse and swung. Barnett ducked, and Gable hit Douglas Fairbanks, Jr., Joan Crawford's husband, who had been standing in the group enjoying Gable's discomfort.

Occasionally the father and son worked together. Their victim was once the celebrated divorce lawyer Jerry Geisler. It had been arranged that Luke Barnett would sit next to Geisler at a dinner where he was guest of honor and would trick him into an argument about law.

Speaking with brogue, he said, "Oh, I know the lah, I know the lah, I know the lah!"

"I know a little law myself," Geisler said, trying to confine it to a quiet discussion.

"A little is right," Barnett retorted. "You must be still studying."

"I am an honorary member of the bar association," Geisler declared testily.

"Oh—a politician?" snorted Barnett.

Geisler was boiling and ready to hit the elder Barnett, but when he didn't, Vince Barnett emerged from nearby and smashed his father—at least it sounded as if he did—and the father crashed loudly to the floor.

Picking himself up, he pretended that it was Geisler who hit him and began yelling, "You murderer, you!"

Geisler's friends at the main table, who had arranged for the ribbing, leaped up to lay hands upon "the murderer"—but decided to introduce him instead to the two professional ribbers.

Looking back on it, one feels that we must have had a lot of time

on our hands to go to so much effort for a joke. When General Nathan Twining was the new head of the U.S. Air Force in 1953, he was
the brunt of a joke at a garden party given in Washington by Elaine
Shepard Hartman.

Wearing epaulets and boots, Vince Barnett was there as "General
Emanon of Cambodia"—at that time, of course, Cambodia was a
country most Americans hadn't even heard of.

General Twining attempted to be patient and courteous to the
visiting general, but it was difficult because "General Emanon" was
rude, insulting, impertinent, and impossible.

The Air Force was smarting under some economy cuts at the
time, and the general from Cambodia harped on this delicate point.

"Why did you come to the United States?" General Twining
asked General Emanon.

"To buy some airplanes so we can be equal in air power with
you," the Cambodian general replied in an assortment of dialects.
"We're almost equal to you now! We have two planes and one bat-
tleship."

General Twining winced. Friends of Twining who had arranged
the prank changed the subject and introduced the ancient debate
of naval power versus air power.

"The Air Force never does the main job except in phony movies,"
General Emanon said. He got quite vociferous on this issue, and General Twining had trouble holding himself back. Then when General
Twining attempted to walk away, General Emanon called him
back. "Don't you agree with me that air power is just for supporting
the navy, General?"

General Emanon also infuriated General Twining by refusing to
shake hands, saying, "In my country, we don't have such a silly
custom."

When Twining learned that General Emanon was a ribber and
that Emanon spelled backwards is no name, he said, "To think that
I saw that fellow at another party a few months ago and didn't recognize him tonight."

6

Friendly Mobsters
I Have Known

SOME Broadway legends are told so convincingly that you want to believe them though your brain tells you to question them. One such story involves a New Jersey local.

There lived a racket boss who knew too much and had to be removed. Late one night, two hoodlums with guns, a piece of electric cord, and a bottle of brandy made their way into Longie Zwillman's twenty-room house in West Orange, New Jersey, and one of them said, "We got to take you, Abe. You're gonna hang yourself with this cord. And if you don't, we're gonna kill your old lady upstairs."

"You boys don't mean this," Abe said.

He was a big man, fifty-four years old with all his hair, which he combed straight back, and horn-rimmed glasses. He was said to be the king of the New Jersey underworld, but he had studied and acquired some polish, and his greatest treasure was his wife, his "old lady," a socialite, the former Mary de Groot Mendels Steinbach, who had gone to finishing school and had been a Junior Leaguer.

There had been talk of his romancing Jean Harlow once, but that was long ago, and now it was February 27, 1959, and the evil mind that had hatched this idea knew Longie Zwillman pretty well. The plotter knew that his wife was his link to respectability and that she meant more to him now than she ever had before.

"Come on, Abe," one of the hoods said. "Let's get it the fuck over!"

"What great brain dreamed this up?" Abe asked them.

"I don't know, I just work here," one of them answered. "We brought you this bottle of brandy to make it easier, Abe."

"You boys know I don't drink," Abe said.

"We seen you go pretty good at parties. Get started with the brandy, Abe; we ain't got all night."

"Why am I supposed to kill myself instead of you boys just knocking me off?" Abe asked.

"I guess you getting knocked off wouldn't look so good. Who the hell knows?"

Abe had feared he would be erased some day. It was one of the rules of the mobster game. But doing it this way was a rougher deal than he'd expected. Here he was in the midst of wealth, in a beautiful house that looked like an ivy-covered college dormitory. Around him were the well-manicured lawns and hedges, the high-powered cars, and somewhere, he supposed, were a couple of guys working for him whose duties included guarding his body. The fact that these two hoodlums had gotten into his house meant they were known to his bodyguards. Oh, well, the bodyguards were probably in on it, anyway. The orders had gone down, and nobody was going to do anything to stop it. Vicious murder would look like suicide.

"Could we make a deal?" Abe queried.

The two boys remained cold, expressionless, and unmoved. Tomorrow they would be at the track. Tomorrow he would be in the funeral parlor.

Longie thought of all the devices he'd hoarded over the years to escape being murdered—hidden guns, trapdoors, burglar alarms. They called him the "gentleman hoodlum," with his good manners and his own private tutor and his stockbrokers and his big donations to charity and his handball at the YMCA. But now the past had backfired on him.

"What am I supposed to have done?"

"Who the fuck knows?" They kept using that word.

Abner Zwillman began to consider that suicide might not be

so bad after all. The Senate Rackets Committee was hounding him about the Apalachin underworld meeting of 1957 and trying to tie him to the murder in the hotel barbershop of Albert Anastasia, the top assassin for the Mafia. They were on top of him again over the jury fixing in that hung jury on his income tax rap. They were probing his stocks and bonds, trying to see whether he wasn't the money behind the mob gambling operations. They were always saying he was the Capone of New Jersey, but he was just trying to be a gentleman of respectability, wishing they'd forget it. Hell, he'd only been in jail once, and that was for six months in 1928, for beating up a cheating numbers writer who deserved it.

"Take another good slug, Abe." They were holding out the bottle to him.

Abe was beginning to feel sleepy. His wife had given him a sleeping pill earlier for a headache. They'd had dinner out . . .

And so Longie Zwillman "committed suicide" due to "financial difficulties."

The gentleman hoodlum was found strapped to a wooden door brace. His neck was in the electric cord noose, and his feet were just a couple of inches above the floor. There were burns on his hands indicating that the visitors had found him resistant and employed matches or burning cigarettes to persuade him.

The curious thing is that Longie had become so powerful that he had become a little dictator; he was getting to be a nuisance to somebody in the mob, and he had to be dumped.

The above is the unofficial story of the suicide of Longie Zwillman, sworn to me by people who claim they know the real facts. It is labeled as quite preposterous and overly romantic by others, who say that Longie was simply "in a lot of trouble, got drunk one night, and did the Dutch act."

The mobsters I knew were always so charming and gracious that it would have been difficult for me to write anything bad about them even if I had ever wanted to be so careless.

From Lucky Luciano to Frank Costello, they were pleasant, smiling, never revealing any of the rough side that led them, so we heard, to kill people without compunction. They might be found having an ice cream specialty at Rumpelmayer's, where mothers took their young children for the same reason. Frank Costello's hobby was gardening. Meyer Lansky was a voracious reader.

Longie Zwillman sat across a restaurant dining room from me once, and I got a look at his back. That was about the extent of our acquaintance. He seemed to be less sociable than Frank Costello, who used to go regularly to the Waldorf-Astoria barbershop for a shave, a manicure, and numerous conferences.

Longie had been a friend of Toots Shor, who once testified for him in a tax hearing and also attended his funeral. One must remember that the rum-runners and beer barons of the twenties and early thirties were often prestigious people of a sort, and a man in the restaurant business got to know them all. Toots believes Longie would have gone down fighting in a battle with the two assassins or hangmen who came calling.

Longie didn't pop into Toots' casually. He knew his frequent presence there would do Toots no good. Longie had been a racket suspect carefully watched by the government for thirty years. Crime might have paid for him, but he likewise paid for crime, in the continual inquisition. In 1935, when he was only thirty, Longie was questioned for ten hours about the murder of Dutch Schultz. And his identification pursued him into middle age.

The routine was always about the same. The government would suspect him of being involved in some racket—slot machines, labor contracts, juke boxes. They would investigate him for months, questioning him, getting a strong denial, being unable to prove its case, then starting the cycle all over again with a new charge and investigation.

If it was frustrating for the government, it was a cause of constant irritation to Longie. "They are never off my back," he complained.

The official story of his hanging—the one issued by local authorities and generally printed by the newspapers—was that Longie was depressed and had been suffering chest pains. He had conferred with a heart specialist the day before his death.

Longie Zwillman was a fascinating figure. In 1956, a federal court jury in Newark deliberated twenty-nine hours before reporting that it could not agree on whether he had evaded payment of $38,911 in income taxes for 1947 and 1948.

Something of his suavity comes through in his response to the hung jury situation.

"I had hoped for a complete vindication," he said. He seemed saddened by the decision.

But eight months after his death, two of his associates, including his chauffeur, pleaded guilty to bribing a juror in that trial. They had pleaded not guilty when Longie was still alive, but after he died, they threw in the towel and gave up defending the man who had "hoped for complete vindication."

The mobsters moved into show business naturally enough from prohibition days, when they ran the beer, bootlegged the whiskey, and operated the speakeasies. The speakeasies became legitimate night clubs, and the mob guys became night club operators or, in some cases, posh restaurateurs. They had money from bootlegging, and some of them invested in more than one establishment. Then Las Vegas opened up, and there was their best shot of all.

The mobsters did not contaminate New York night life, as far as I could see. They didn't cut the whiskey more or make the floor shows worse than in the places operated by non-mobsters. And if they did attract some disreputable customers—and they did— some of them were most interesting, such as "Little Augie" Pisano. He left the Copacabana lounge bar one night with a pretty girl—the wife of comedian Alan Drake—and both of them were murdered in his car in such a mysterious manner that it has not been solved to this day.

Certainly Frank Costello made life more interesting around New York and he liked to eat out. Even in the last months of 1970 and early 1971, "F. C." was seen around his favorite New York restaurants as usual, looking a little stoop-shouldered from age but agile and peppery and alive—quite an accomplishment for a mobster almost eighty years old.

F. C. always denied—under oath, before the Kefauver Committee —the rumors that he owned a piece of the Stork Club or had a small investment in the Copacabana. Yet we always felt his presence and thought of him as the godfather of much of night life. He was "captain of the ship," one mobster said, the successor to Lucky Luciano. The late Mayor La Guardia, in his hatred of the racketeers, used to have his street workers constantly tearing up streets in front of some of the night clubs to harass them and to try to hurt their business.

Costello displayed a certain jauntiness as he sat there in a restaurant in animated conversation with a couple of other men in their septuagenarian years. He wore lively colored shirts and brown or gray suits. He did not attract attention because he preferred not to be noticed. He spoke huskily and apologized for his laryngitis, though the story was that he had cancer. Because of his aversion to publicity, frequently only the proprietor of a restaurant, the headwaiter, captain, and waiter knew that F. C. was in the place.

"Costello's over there," Toots Shor told me at lunch one day. Nobody else had mentioned his presence.

I went over to say hello. He was not at a showcase table—probably he did not want to be. We talked about making an appointment, and after a few minutes, he and his two old cronies left.

"Did you see Frank Costello?" I asked a couple of my friends who had been seated a couple of tables away.

"Was he here? Oh, I wish I could have seen him," said one, a hardened journalist who wouldn't have said that about the president of the United States.

There was an appealing quality about this man whom "Vito Genovese wanted to get rid of"—without success. Costello did not like to embarrass his restaurateur friends by going to their places when his name was emblazoned in the newspapers in connection with some new trouble, but he did observe his constitutional right as a free citizen to eat where he chose.

"How would you like to have all the money that fellow spent on lawyers?" Toots Shor proposed to me.

And how would I like to have the happy feeling he had when he recalled how former boxer Vincente (The Chin) Gigante had fired that slug at him on the night of May 2, 1957? F. C. had gone to dinner with a friend at L'Aiglon restaurant on East 55th Street across from the Hotel St. Regis. Costello evidently did not know the depth of Vito Genovese's disrespect for him that night, or he would have been better guarded.

Vito wanted to remove Costello completely from the scene so that he, Vito, would be supreme in the Mob's hierarchy. As F. C. emerged from a cab and stepped into the lobby of the Majestic Apartments on Central Park West, the lumbering Gigante, who was waiting there, called out, "This is a message for you, Frank," and fired that lone bullet at him, running off to crow that he'd scored a hole-in-one.

It made for a bloody evening for Costello. But Roosevelt Hospital declared that he was not seriously injured. Gigante later gave himself up when he "heard" that they were looking for him. Costello, however, refused to testify against Gigante, claiming that he hadn't seen the man who had shot him. Thus began a period when the legend arose that Costello was immune to murder. He was unkillable, extraordinary.

One time Costello called me to complain of an error in reporting his activities.

A television star who had formerly been a Cadillac salesman told me that Costello had once bought three Cadillacs for friends, paying for them with big bills that he carried into the Cadillac showroom in paper sacks.

It was history when I printed it, and it shouldn't have mattered, except that it might have induced some income tax agent to reopen a tax investigation that had been considered closed.

"This is Frank Costello," the voice said hoarsely, over the phone. His voice was cordial but firm. He didn't want any retraction, but somebody had told me a lie about him. He had never bought three Cadillacs, and he had never paid for cars with bills he carried around in brown envelopes. To me there was nothing serious about the anecdote, but to him, under the endlessly watchful eye of the Internal Revenue Service, there was.

One striking fact about all hoodlum personalities is that while they may be low in the public regard, they have powerful friends. My first interview with Costello, in 1947, was arranged by a newspaperman on a rival New York paper. He is now an important Hollywood name. He simply asked me one night, "How would you like to interview Frank Costello?"

I didn't think he could arrange it. Besides, I found myself wondering why he didn't interview Costello for his own paper. Costello was just gaining public recognition. He was eager to give the world the idea that he was retired from the slot machine business and was endeavoring to be a country gentleman among his flowers at his estate in Sands Point, Long Island.

"Who wouldn't like to interview him?" I replied.

A couple of afternoons later the reporter and I met in the cocktail room of a Park Avenue hotel.

"F. C. owns this hotel," explained the fellow who had arranged the interview. "It's one of his daily stops."

It's amusing now to reflect that then we knew almost nothing of the Mafia, of the Cosa Nostra. In fact, we hardly knew the word Mafia, and we certainly did not use it aloud. Costello was the leader of the Luciano Family (in acting capacity) in those years, enriching himself with the profits of slot machines, bookmaking, gambling casinos, and King's Ransom Scotch. I remember receiving a case of that Scotch from him for Christmas one year.

"What are the ethics involved here?" I asked one of my superiors, the late Ed Flynn, then city editor of the *New York Post*. "I received a case of whiskey from Frank Costello. What do I do with it?"

"Drink it," he commanded me.

"That's what I thought too," I said. As I pointed out to myself later, that was about all I could do because if I had sent it back, Frank Costello would certainly have been angry at me; and a columnist can't afford to have Frank Costello feeling animosity toward him.

Costello had a fear of paper-and-pencil reporters during these early days. Accordingly, I didn't display my notebook on our first interview. I kept ducking in and out of phone booths and the men's room to write down snatches of his answers to my questions.

He was in his fifties then, and he was smoking an English Oval cigarette and fingering a Charvet tie, which had some pretty Chinese girls' faces on it. The fellow who had arranged our interview was with us, but I thought Costello, out of bravado perhaps, got off to a rather bad start.

"I got no confidence in newspapers," he said, a compliment to neither of us. "Why should I overtax my larynx talkin' to 'em?

"I'm retired," he added. "I'm out of slot machines since a year ago. Listen, do I look like an imbecile? If I made the money in slot machines they say I made, I should be in the can for evading taxes. So why ain't I in the can? Because I didn't do nothin'."

Like other mobsters I've encountered, including Luciano the First—Lucky Luciano—Costello was anxious to proclaim his innocence and kept coming back to that.

"Listen, I love to live too much to do all that," he said. "When are we gonna get some warm weather?"—it had been a rainy, windy April—"I'm dyin' for that sun to come out so I can prune my trees and see my strawberries grow. I love flowers."

He ordered us another Scotch and water, and I went back to the phone to make some more notes.

"What the hell, nobody gives me a break!" he said. "I'm livin' thirty years in a radius of two miles. I can't be such a bad guy. They'd have run me out. I was in this town before Mayor La Guardia—before Dewey—before *you!* Has that crackpot La Guardia been able to run me out?"

Actually La Guardia had run Costello's slot machines all the way down to New Orleans. Costello was the legal winner. He got an injunction to prevent La Guardia from interfering with his slots, but La Guardia's forces busted them up anyway. And Costello gave in and dispatched the machines to Louisiana.

The newspapers had said that Costello was protected at all times by bodyguards but he denied that any of the ominous-looking strangers sitting around the cocktail lounge were his guards. It was said also that he always carried large sums of money with him for bribing purposes.

"How much cash have you got on you today?" I asked.

"Are you gonna district attorney me?" he laughed. He counted it: $450. He detected my disappointment.

"I had a little more before I left home today," he said. "While I was circulatin', I got three or four pretty good bites."

Costello—and Lucky Luciano before him—had a cardinal rule of success in gangsterdom, which one of them expressed very inelegantly: "Never cop no plea, and never scratch no paper."

"You don't want nothin' in the books against you," Costello explained. According to him, the forces of law and order, which he considered his natural enemy, had a trick of charging you with a crime far worse than the crime they actually caught you committing. You'd be outraged. You would face the possibility that they might convict you. Then when they'd offered to "reduce the charge," you would feel relieved, and if they offered to reduce it still more, you'd be inclined to plead guilty and go to jail. And from then on it would always be in the records. You did time for gun possession or whatever it was. You would be an ex-con.

"Never cop no plea." It was a good rule. "Never scratch no paper" —never sign confessions.

Costello was extremely businesslike, and it was hard to believe that he was the Mafia boss. He would scrape back his chair when you came to his table, leap up, and inquire, "How is your missus?" His talk would always be concerned with his legitimate business operations. As we were to find out later, he was also involved in stopping the Mafia from getting into the narcotics business. He was against it because he considered it too hazardous.

"Give yourselves a break and get out of it," he counseled them. "You want to get killed?"

Costello preferred wheeling and dealing in business and in political finagling. In fact he could not help but enjoy becoming a page one celebrity in the Kefauver investigation.

I met him just before his first appearance there.

I decided to try to see him away from the investigation. I phoned the private number he'd given me and left a message asking him to call me. I felt sure that he would. He did call me back—but I was out.

"This is Frank Costello calling," he said to my secretary, who asked where he could be reached. "I don't know, I circulate a lot," he added. But he would be at his attorney's office in an hour if I wanted to meet him there.

Already it was known that he followed a ritual of a morning shave at the Waldorf barbershop and an afternoon visit to the steam baths—a luxury, incidentally, that many mobsters allowed themselves. Jack Benny once said of the Waldorf shop, "It's so classy that you have to shave before you go in to get a shave."

On the day I met him he'd missed his third Waldorf shave because of his problems with the Kefauver investigation. He'd shaved himself at home. He'd acquired considerable assurance since the last time I'd talked to him, and he seemed quite unruffled about all the furor they were making about his supposed slot machine kingdom.

"It's just an annoyance," he said with a shrug.

He was quietly dressed in a double-breasted brown chalk-stripe suit and polka-dot tie. He sat at a small table in the office of his attorney George Wolf, and he answered my questions in a business-like manner. I would have preferred seeing him over cocktails because this meeting seemed a little awkward and stilted. I sensed that he had been coached on his answers even to my innocent questions.

Looking up across the desk at me, the inquisitor, F. C. said, "I welcome the chance to clear the atmosphere of a lot of nonsense that's been told about me."

"Did you make any statement to the committee about that?"

"Yes."

"What was it?"

"I'm not privileged to disclose it. You'll have to ask the committee for it."

Evidently Costello had added a new rule to the "Don't cop no plea and don't scratch no paper" dictum, namely: "Don't make no speeches." The man who was alleged to be a threat to all that was clean and decent was about as menacing in person as a librarian.

"You've heard the rumor that you're taking a pair of pajamas and a couple of bottles of whiskey with you when you go before the committee?" I asked.

"What's that for?" Costello bristled.

"A suggestion that you might spend a night in jail."

"That's a joke," George Wolf spoke up quickly.

"Jail!" snapped Costello. "That's crazy. I'm a witness, not a defendant."

Costello knew his rights and his position. He told me that he hoped the investigation would be over soon so that he could play golf again.

"Golf's my racket," he said. He wasn't trying to make a joke, I'm sure. That was my chance to be witty and say, "Kefauver doesn't think so," but I let the moment slip by.

The Valachi statement, detailing the shooting of Costello by Vito Genovese's crowd, had been well circulated by the time I next sat down with F. C.—and now over lunch at the Waldorf Peacock Alley he said, "To me, the Mafia is all a myth."

"A myth?" I asked. "Everybody says you were the leader."

"Sure, I know everybody says so. But it's my feeling it's a myth."

That was March 5, 1971. I'd told Costello that I was writing a book and that I wanted to clear up some points. He was seventy-five, but he was still bouncy and chipper except for his bad throat.

"This has been my worst winter!" he said. "Had laryngitis three times. My doctor says, 'Don't smoke, don't drink, don't talk!'" He laughed as he ordered a Scotch, lit a cigarette, and continued talking. "Doctor's orders!" he said.

He was in a denying mood, but he was humorous at the same time.

"I haven't sold Bibles," he said. "I was a bootlegger, I had slot machines, but I never cheated anybody. I never stole anything. In fifty years of investigating me, they never found anything except for that one time I underestimated my net worth by $20,000."

Discussing briefly the other kind of cheating—marital—he said, "A man who don't cheat I wouldn't want on a grand jury. Who the hell wants anybody like that? He ain't human."

He denied investing in the Stork Club or the Copacabana.

"I haven't been in the Copa in three or four years. I'm blasé. Shows don't mean a thing any more. I've seen so many. As for the Stork Club, Sherman Billingsley had union trouble. I said to one union leader, 'He's all right,' and he pulled off his pickets. Billingsley was so grateful that whenever I was in there, he overdone it with the perfume, and never no check."

Every place he entered, he said, there were rumors he owned it. He and J. Edgar Hoover, another frequenter of the Waldorf, had a running joke about that. Costello called Hoover "John." Leaving the barbershop one day, he saw Hoover and said, "Good morning, John."

Hoover said, jokingly, "Frank, I just found out you don't own this hotel."

Hoover invited Costello to have coffee. "I got to be careful about my associates," Costello said. "They'll accuse me of consortin' with questionable characters."

That was Costello's sore point. "Suppose we're sittin' here at lunch and two guys who might have a bad reputation come in here. They want to buy a drink. Who the hell am I to tell them that they got a bad reputation and we can't drink with them? They buy me, and I buy them. That don't mean to say I'm consortin'."

Costello's wife was taking a train trip to New Orleans, he recalled, and he had ordered tickets for her. Immediately a couple of FBI men found out and were around asking where Costello was going.

He complained to Hoover about that. However, Costello and Clyde Tolson, Hoover's aide, also joked about who had a good horse in that afternoon's racing.

"John, how many men you got under you?" Costello once asked Hoover.

"He says 6,500," Costello remembered. "Today it would be 16,000. I says, 'John, I don't want to sell you short. I always said you got the best force, better than Scotland Yard. But with 6,500 men under you you're asking *me* for information!'"

As he ordered us a second drink and lit another cigarette, Costello mentioned that he was smoking a filter cigarette because his wife had taken the non-filters away from him.

"Cancer . . . I don't think I ever had it." He shrugged.

"Polyps I had. Julie Podell and Joe E. Lewis had the same thing. They had theirs cut out. I didn't want anybody fooling around my throat. My doctor X-rayed my throat and gave me too much and hurt my larynx."

"But what did your doctor say you had?"

"I don't go by doctors half the time." Another shrug.

The most sensitive point of our talk was trying to get him to discuss the attempt made on his life. "You had a very narrow escape," I observed.

"Right in the brain! Just a quarter of an inch away." With his left hand he indicated the right side of his head.

"Do you have any philosophy about that? Do you think you might have been spared for some special reason?"

"Maybe. The thing was, I didn't deserve it." He meant that he didn't deserve to be killed, and therefore he wasn't. Perhaps fate or God intervened.

"Are you religious?" I asked.

"Sometimes. Without it we'd all be cannibals."

The Mafia "myth," he said, was a reference to "syndicates."

"Everybody's got organizations—syndicates. Four or five guys get together on a real estate deal—that's a syndicate. Your syndicate earns the right to some respect from the other syndicates. Four or five guys get together to build a highrise, that's another syndicate.

"I know everybody. They respect me, they come to me for advice, so they say I'm the head of it. I tell them to do it the proper way, the legal way. If it's illegal, I tell them what you gain in peanuts you lose in bananas. They come to me for advice, so that makes me the head of the Mafia!"

He shook his head. "I can't prove that there's any Mafia."

Costello professed to be puritanical about sex and prostitution. He claimed to be outraged by the book *The Godfather* not merely because it concerned a Mafia leader likened somewhat to himself but because it contained some shocking dialogue.

"A lot of guys sent me this book," Costello said. "Now I got a thousand books in my apartment, fifteen hundred books at my house. I never saw a four-letter word in a book before. Well, I read that line where the guy says to his wife, 'Where were you till three o'clock in the morning?' and she says, 'I was out fucking.' Well, I threw the book away. I couldn't read it. I got sick. This book here," he declared with indignation, "is a dirty book."

Without any mention of the Mafia's alleged connection with prostitution and the charges that Lucky Luciano had dealt in that criminal activity, Costello said, "I always hated a pimp since I was a kid."

He paused, looked away a moment, then asked with a sudden laugh, "Do you remember Johnny Wilson, the middleweight champion?" (He was champion from 1920 to 1923.) "We were crazy kids together. I lived at 222 108th Street. He lived at 219 108th Street. He was lefthanded and could hit like a mule.

"We were both about seventeen. On a Saturday afternoon all the prostitutes would be on the street, so Johnny and I would be out walking. I took my whip I got at Coney Island. We'd walk along, and I'd give one of the girls a shot in the ass. She'd yell and her pimp would come running out. I'd give Johnny the nod, and he'd bring up that left. Pow! Every Saturday afternoon and every Saturday night!

"How old would Johnny be? Well, I'm seventy-five. Johnny's the same age. When I had the slot machines in the late twenties, I gave him half a dozen machines."

Costello made another discovery recently, he told me, about the deterioration of morals. Always punctual, one day he found himself a half hour early for an appointment.

"I wondered how can I kill a half hour, and I'm thinkin' of going into Alexander's store to walk around. I never been in the store. I turn on Lexington Avenue. I think it's 59th Street, and I see a theater there in a brownstone house.

"I think how can there be a theater in a brownstone house? The admission is $3. I went inside, and I want to tell you—never in my life did I see anything like that!

"They're doing things in that picture I never even talk about or think about. This guy does things with two girls, and then there's two guys with two guys, and all I'm thinkin' is I don't want anybody to see me.

"I'm squirmin' around, and I put on my glasses, pull up my coat collar, and walk out of there like a real Dillinger. It was the worst thing I ever saw in my life."

Frank Costello, the supposed overlord of crime (although nothing was ever proved about him), shook his head as he remembered the experience, and said: "I coulda got picked up for going to a dirty show! That's all I need!"

Sometimes, it seemed as if life had become a gangster movie, only more so. In covering the night clubs, I found myself enmeshed in the underworld without quite realizing what was taking place.

They were real hoods, broken-nosed and scar-faced, from Murder, Inc., from "the Cleveland mob," from the Detroit "Purple Gang." They carried guns and fat rolls of money, and they were always extremely gracious.

One of the mob places was the old Greenwich Village Inn in Sheridan Square. It paid high salaries to top names in the entertainment world, but the place did very little business. It was operated strictly as a front "to keep some of the boys working in a legitimate business."

Lucky Luciano, Joe Adonis ("Mr. A"), and Meyer Lansky, later called "the chairman of the board," were circulating freely in those days. They might be seen in New York, Miami Beach, and Havana. We never knew the extent of their influence. Bugsy Siegel, later murdered for neglecting to pay back money he'd been lent to open a Las Vegas hotel, was around with his girl friend, Virginia Hill. They didn't seem to be frightened about publicity. The first time I ever met Siegel and Virginia Hill, they were in the Los Angeles hotel suite of *New York Mirror* columnist Lee Mortimer. The group was having some late drinks.

Virginia Hill Hauser, "the Queen of the Mafia," got into the New York night club scene in 1940. She began to make news because she had grown wealthy from dispensing her affections to Bugsy Siegel, Joe Adonis, and Chicago bookmaker Joe Epstein.

The southern girl who as a teenager had gotten her start as a waitress at the Chicago World's Fair became a one-third owner of the Hurricane night club. But then her financial mentor Joe Epstein ordered her to get out, and she obeyed.

Her partners—"there were a bunch of them," she told the Kefauver Committee Investigating Organized Crime—couldn't get a license, but she could.

Why was it that she could obtain a license? The Kefauver Committee went into that, questioning the pretty waitress who had made good.

As her answer seemed to indicate, she had learned to make men happy.

The Committee probed further. Where and how did she get her money? She seemed to have $40,000 or $50,000 lying around at any given moment.

"When I was with Ben [Siegel], he bought me everything. He gave me some money, and he bought me a house in Florida. And then I used to bet horses."

And she gave parties?

"It was the fellows I was going with who paid for the things. The fellows I went with—if you want to have a good time, have a party."

Chairman Estes Kefauver asked what kind of horse race tips she received and who passed them along to her.

"I used to know some people who gave me tips when they got them. Sometimes I would bet $100, $200, $500. It would depend on the horse."

"You seem to have taken very good care of your own finances," observed Rudolph Halley, the chief investigator.

"I take care of myself."

Still, she insisted that she knew nothing of the operations of the men who gave her money, that she had never been in business with them, that she had never carried money for them, that she knew nothing about any narcotics traffic. Men just gave her money, she said, and she took it.

Before going to Las Vegas to operate the new Flamingo Hotel for the mob, Bugsy Siegel impressed Broadway with his reputation for being a cold-blooded professional killer. Possessing great charm and warmth, he could also be as hard as granite.

Striding boldly into the Sherry-Netherland Hotel in New York one night and interrupting a meeting of some tough Italian mobsters trying to cut themselves a slice of his revenue, he began slashing them in the face, using the side of his open hand like a whip.

"I told you bastards to keep your hands out of my business. Now get out—all of you. The next time there won't be a warning." Although all the hoods were armed, none of them made a move to draw a gun. They knew Bugsy to be fearless and a little crazy, and his utter contempt for them made them docile and afraid. One by one, they left the hotel.

Exuding great sexual heat for the Broadway show girls, Bugsy Siegel went swinging around the speakeasies—the 5 O'clock Club, the Napoleon Club, Zelli's, the Park Avenue, and the Stork Club. Owney Madden and "Big Frenchy" controlled them. If the doormen carried guns they got $100 a week; if not, they got $50 a week. There was very little shooting, although the conditions would seem to have harbored violence.

Killer Abe Reles of Murder, Incorporated, was also around at the same time the hoodlums commandeered the slot machines, the juke boxes, many of the singers and record companies, and the night clubs and shows.

"How do you feel about killing all these people you don't know?" prosecutor Burton Turkus once asked Abe Reles.

"How do you feel sending all those people to the electric chair you don't know?" Reles retorted.

"The first night I couldn't sleep, but as time went on, I didn't mind it," Turkus said.

"Same here," snapped Reles.

Hoodlum "Waxey" Gordon, sweetheart of Gypsy Rose Lee, then a young stripper with an exquisite body, offered money to Florence Ziegfeld for a Follies show if he'd use Gypsy in the cast. Ziggy, pressed for cash, agreed.

The mobsters, accustomed to getting what they wanted and motivated by the vicarious lust most men experience in the presence of a beautiful, long-legged, voluptuous woman, often made it clear what they wanted from the Broadway showgirls who did dancing or singing routines in night clubs and stage shows they frequented. By means of threats and money they often got the girls they wanted. Many of them secretly backed night clubs and Broadway shows, which gave them a lever with the girls.

It was difficult to trace these "investors," but it was reported that mobsters had helped to finance "Lew Leslie's Blackbirds," "Earl Carroll's Vanities," the Cotton Club in Harlem (where Negroes were not yet accepted as customers), and the Club Ha Ha.

One of the most illustrious racketeers, renowned for his toughness, became an angel (backer) for night clubs. But he put his investment in the name of his mistress.

Visiting Hot Springs, Miami, and the other resorts, he kept his girl in hiding because he didn't want anybody to go tattling to his wife back in New York.

"You're really scared of your wife, aren't you?" somebody asked the hardened mobster.

"Scared of her!" he exclaimed. "Hell, she'd *murder* me!"

The hoods operated with considerable boldness and aplomb, and many of the authorities didn't know who they were. Forrest Duke, columnist for the *Las Vegas Review-Journal*, was at a Las Vegas assemblage once when the sheriff came to him and asked, "Would you know Meyer Lansky if you saw him?"

"I don't think so," Duke said.

"There's a fellow here we think is Meyer Lansky, and if it is, we want to run him out of town," the sheriff said. Lansky and his friends denied that he went to Las Vegas, but in 1971 he and some cohorts were indicted in connection with Las Vegas skimming.

The mob's technique for controlling a performer and getting most of his earnings from the "pieces" of them they acquired was developed in the 1940s and 1950s. A young performer would grant them twenty percent or as high as fifty percent of his income in return for a needed loan or possibly an advance just to get started in the business.

Vic Damone was one of the most noted victims of "the boys"

and their "generosity." He often cautioned younger singers against staying in the business, citing his own bad experience.

"I will never have more than twenty percent of myself for the rest of my life," he said.

The boys could do wonders, however. One virtually unknown singer suddenly drew astonishing crowds at every club where he appeared. All the tables were occupied by hoodlum types who were hysterical in their enthusiasm for him.

The orders had gone out to "Get the hell down there and see Jimmy."

Later comics could joke about such incidents. Phil Silvers got up one night in 1971 in a hotel supper club where an Italian singer was starring. Turning to one table filled with picturesque characters, Phil said, "It's nice to see the Sons of Italy here. Listen, I came from Brooklyn, the home of Murder, Inc., and we used to call you guys fags!"

One of the bad boys, a mobster nicknamed "Pretty" Amberg, had a fondness for puncturing people's faces with a fork. Milton Berle, then a young comic, didn't know Amberg was sensitive to remarks about himself. Glancing at Amberg's table one night at the old Vanity Fair, Berle said, "Oh, it's Novelty Night—you're with your wife . . . No booze on the table . . . Tourists!"

Amberg summoned Berle to his table after the show.

"Yuh know who I am?" he demanded. Berle didn't. "Next time I come in here—if I ever do—and I probably won't—yuh mention me and I'll kill yuh!"

Amberg grabbed Berle's throat and began pulling on his tie. Berle was choking helpless. Then Amberg reached for a fork, ready to tear Berle's face with it.

Suddenly another hand appeared and grabbed Amberg's wrist. The hand belonged to another well-known mobster. Berle was saved from the fork.

Amberg was later found dead in cement. His penis had been cut off and jammed in his mouth. This was the mobster's way of saying that the victim had talked too much.

Performers cross racketeers at their peril. For example, Peter Marshall, the television host, and Tommy Noonan were doing a comedy act one night at the old La Martinique in 1951, and they made the mistake of kidding some racketeers seated at a ringside table. As Marshall and Noonan left the floor at the end of their act, the ringsiders followed them toward their dressing rooms. They beat Marshall with a pistol butt, then threw a plate at him. He ducked, and the plate crashed to the floor. The proprietors, Dario and Jimmy Vernon, came running and broke the fight up. Frank Costello must have been well informed about the operation of La Martinique—though he denied owning any part of it—because Marshall remembers that he was there within ten minutes after the fight. Marshall also angrily recalls that the mobster who picked on him kept sneering at him and calling him "a Hollywood fag."

7

What Killed the Big Bands?

WHY are they no more, those sweet, sentimental, danceable, romantic big bands of yesterday—the Tommy Dorseys, Jimmy Dorseys, and Glenn Millers we used to know? The answer is simple.

The singers—the crooners—left the bands to go out on their own and make their fortunes. Then came the rock groups, and recording companies developed more of them.

"They were easier to promote and less expensive to record," says Willard Alexander, the agent and entrepreneur who booked the biggest name bands for many years.

"They blossomed into big money because it cost so much less to record three or four voices."

There were many other reasons. Glenn Miller, of course, didn't come back from World War II. So many musicians were called into service that about fifteen of the thirty top bands broke up and the record companies didn't build replacements.

Many big ballrooms closed. Young people lost enthusiasm for dancing to big bands. Why? They wanted something louder and wilder, something with a wail. They were part of an electrified, electronic generation. They became accustomed to amplified teachers' voices in school. They dug electric guitars, and the guitarists were the new poets, the new playwrights. It was a generation that wanted to kick and leap and go a little berserk on the dance floor instead of dancing cheek to cheek.

One suspects too that the new approach to sex may have contributed, especially when combined with drugs.

There was a time when young couples went dancing and afterward—in the back seat of a car or elsewhere—indulged in necking, petting, or went "all the way," depending on the depth of their passion. Dancing and a little booze formed a kind of middle ground. But with the frankness and casualness of the new sex, there is no middle ground. If a couple feels like copulating, they go to it immediately almost without any preliminaries. Who needed dancing or liquor to stimulate them?

So came the rock phase, acid rock, and rock jazz. There was the "distortion period," when many of the youthful enthusiasts were enjoying music under the influence of drugs because that had become their way of life.

But even these young people are growing older too, perhaps developing an awareness that it might not be safe to use drugs indiscriminately. At any rate, they are discussing the problem, and many of them are becoming apprehensive about hard drugs such as heroin. In the colleges, professors and administrators who have sometimes been timid about disputing their students seem to be hardening their positions. The result appears to be a reduction in the influence of "distortion music." Young people may well be turning back to songs of traditional melodies and lyrics—and softer singers.

Whatever happens, the big bands aren't likely to return. But the big bandsmen keep working. Count Basie is working forty-eight weeks a year and could do fifty-two. Buddy Rich is enormously popular once again, with a new age group that goes to hear him do a "contemporary jazz concert" at Barney Google's in New York. Duke Ellington, Benny Goodman, Woody Herman, Lionel Hampton, and others are employed as much as they want to be—and in Ellington's case, that means continuously. After a two A.M. "Battle of Music" with Woody Herman in Las Vegas, I saw Herman at the airport at eight, leaving for an engagement in Houston.

Still, I miss the aura of nostalgia, the glamour, the romance, of the big bands. They were an unforgettable part of our past. Even before the era of the big bands, I remember as an adolescent being awakened one morning by a victrola playing "Sleep," which must have come from Fred Waring and his glee club. I drove home from dances singing "June Night" and "Baby Face" and "Jada."

My fiancée and I got engaged to the brassy thump of the big novelty number "The Music Goes Round and Round" at the old Onyx Club on 52nd Street, New York, on New Year's eve 1936. The artists who wrote and sang it were not big bandsmen then; Mike Riley and Ed Farley had just six pieces, but they made a big sound—and a romantic sound.

Those dancing years were happy years. We went out to Meadowbrook or the Rustic Cabin in New Jersey, to Valley Dale in Columbus, to the Aragon or Trianon ballrooms in Chicago, or to the Palladium in Los Angeles, and the dance music of the great name orchestras made us feel and act romantic.

The big bands constituted an important strand of our social life in the late 1930s and 1940s. Those were the years of Glen Gray and the Casa Loma orchestra, Wayne King, Red Nichols and his Five Pennies, Red Norvo, Bob Crosby and the Bobcats, Eddy Duchin, Larry Clinton, Tony Pastor, Hal Kemp, Ray Noble, Artie Shaw, Jack Teagarden, Ted Weems, Ray McKinley, Teddy Powell, Charlie Barnet, Chick Webb, Russ Morgan, Art Kastle and his Castles in the Air, Frankie Carle, Fletcher Henderson, Shep Fields, Harry James, Charlie Spivak, Bunny Berigan and Paul Whiteman, the unforgettable "Pops."

Tommy Dorsey's theme song, as he tilted the old slide trombone for the folks, was "I'm Gettin' Sentimental Over You," and when he went into that one at Meadowbrook or the Hotel Pennsylvania, even people who hated to dance got up and danced.

Glenn Miller's theme was "Moonlight Serenade," and working with him at the vocals in those uncomplicated years before the war were Marion Hutton, Ray Eberle, and, later, the Modernaires.

"T. D.," as they called Tommy Dorsey, loved to clown. He gave a good show with Buddy Rich and Ziggy Elman as his featured musicians. On summer nights, lovers would go to the Astor Roof and hear Larry Clinton and Bea Wain. The gal vocalists were usually pretty, sexy, and gorgeously gowned. Dinah Shore was singing with Paul Whiteman; Harry James had Helen Forrest; Jimmy Dorsey had

Helen O'Connell and Bob Eberle; and Spike Jones had Helen Grayco. Tommy Dorsey over the years had Jo Stafford, Connie Haines, Edith Wright, Jack Leonard, Dick Haymes, and Frank Sinatra. They always had male vocalists so that they would appeal to both sexes.

There was no television yet, and the customers went to see the bandleaders and vocalists in the flesh and to dance to the music they'd heard on radio, on the NBC Red or Blue Network or on CBS. The fact that an orchestra leader had "two or three hours airtime" *made* him a big star without any other argument.

The bandleaders were celebrities, though it was whispered that several leaders couldn't tell one note from another.

"They're just put up there to wave the stick and sing a little and look handsome. They're really mob-supported. The boys put them in." That's how the stories went.

Guy Lombardo was such a fixture at the Roosevelt Grill with his Royal Canadians that Lawrence Welk didn't make much impression when he went in as a short-time replacement.

A woman came up to Welk one night and said, "What part of Canada are you from?"

Welk, a Dakotan with a Swedish sound, gurgled something that didn't come out clearly.

"Well, you are from Canada, aren't you?" she said. "You *are* Guy Lombardo, aren't you?"

The bands had an untold effect. So many of the songs and bands had special meanings for the public. There is much truth to the many "They're playing our song" jokes. And merely mentioned now, the names call up those memories: Alvino Rey and the King Sisters, Rosemary and Betty, the Clooney Sisters, who were with Tony Pastor, Jimmie Lunceford, Sammy Kaye, Earl Hines, Lionel Hampton, Les Brown, Horace Heidt, and Claude Thornhill and Johnny Long, whom they called "the old lefthander" because a pig had chewed on his right hand and forced him to play the violin southpaw. "A Shanty in Old Shanty Town" from Long's gang drove the prom kids wild.

Cab Calloway did "Minnie the Moocher" at a Johnny Carson tribute dinner in 1971. That was his big number in the late thirties.

In 1971 Dorothy Collins appeared at the Winter Garden Theater in *Follies,* a musical that Producer Hal Prince hoped would run for a couple of years. It took an old-timer to remember that Dorothy was once the singing discovery of bandleader Raymond Scott and, after his divorce, she became his wife. They did "Your Hit Parade" together, he as the conductor, she as the featured vocalist. Frank Sinatra was once grateful to appear on that radio program.

Remember Betty Hutton with Vincent Lopez? Ozzie Nelson and Harriet Hilliard at the New Yorker? Gene Krupa (who chewed gum fiercely and mouthed an expression about "fried potatoes" over and over as he beat the drums) forming his own orchestra? Marion Hutton—Betty's quieter sister—joining up with Glenn Miller? Those are the kinds of names that meant much to all of us in those comparatively innocent years.

Back then—it seems a million years ago—James Caesar Petrillo was the powerful boss of the American Federation of Musicians. He became notorious for calling musicians' strikes. He kept a collection of unfriendly cartoons about his strikes. One afternoon during an elevator operator's strike, I found him drinking beer at Toots Shor's. He told me he was tired because he'd just walked down eighteen flights of stairs from his office.

"Goddamn unions," he said, grinning, "will ruin the country."

Everybody's favorite gal singers were Ella Fitzgerald and Billie Holiday. In 1956, when Billie's book *Lady Sings the Blues,* co-authored by William Dufty, was published, it was discovered to have this remarkable opening paragraph:

"Mom and Pop were just a couple of kids when they got married. He was eighteen, she sixteen, and I was three."

Bespectacled Glenn Miller was loved by almost everybody who cared for dance music. He had a chubby, bald little road manager, George ("Bullets") Durgom, who later became manager of Jackie Gleason and is now vice-president of a major talent agency.

Bullets—so nicknamed because a little brother once called him that—was probably the first manager to race around the country romancing the disc jockeys, persuading them to plug the bands' records ahead of their arrival in town.

"There were four hundred disc jockeys then," Durgom said recently. "Today there must be forty thousand."

With the coming of the war, Glenn Miller's band traveled throughout the country and Europe playing for the troops. Durgom himself went into the service. One night Miller was in uniform at the Astor Roof when he saw Durgom, also in uniform. Miller said he was taking his band to Europe and needed a "band boy," or road manager.

"Want to go along?" Miller asked Durgom. "I can get you transferred."

Durgom wasn't craving that much action. "No, I'd better stay here," he said.

It was probably a wise decision. Glenn Miller's disappearance over the English Channel is one of the unsolved mysteries of the war.

Miller was happily married to a childhood sweetheart (with an orange ranch at Monrovia, California, named "Tuxedo Junction" after his famous song). Though there was little chance that he would have been drafted, he had enlisted in the army where he led a GHQ band that was virtually General Eisenhower's personal band.

Not long before he enlisted he'd nosed out Tommy Dorsey as "the best sweet band" in the *Downbeat* poll. His recordings of "In the Mood," "Chattanooga Choochoo," "String of Pearls," and "Little Brown Jug" were big sellers, and he reached his plateau during that bitter winter of 1944 and 1945.

Dramatic stories are told of Miller's last flight. The band, which had been living in the Little America section of London, had been driven from there by the buzz bombs to Bedford, England. After finishing a broadcast schedule, the band was going to Paris to make personal appearances before the troops.

Before they all left, Captain Glenn Miller, who had become Major Miller, threw a party for the band. He would go to Paris to make hotel arrangements and to prepare for the band's arrival. They would arrive the next day.

The weather was miserable. Miller's trip was to be made in an ancient plane known as the Norseman, a one-motor creation with far too little power to battle a storm, usually employed in VIP hops of very short distance. The Channel crossing itself was only twenty-two miles.

Glenn Miller was a very nervous plane passenger. The morning after the party, he walked around in the strong wind and icy weather, knowing that nothing was flying over the Channel. He wasn't very confident, he said to the officer designated to pilot him. "Maybe we ought to call this off."

The band members who had gone to see him off say that the flight officer began ribbing him humorously about being afraid of flying: "Do you want to live forever? Why don't you let somebody else enjoy your money?"

Johnny Desmond, Glenn Miller's vocalist with the band, heard from Captain Don Haynes, the band manager, that the kidding became more serious as Miller grew concerned about the bad weather and inadequate equipment.

"We only have one motor," Miller pointed out.

"Well, Lindbergh only had one," the pilot laughed.

"You don't have a parachute?" Miller asked.

"What do you want a parachute for? To jump into that icy water? It'll freeze you. But if you're scared . . ."

Glenn Miller finally got into the Norseman, and they took off for Orly . . .

The next day, when the band went to the airport to take off for Orly, they were told that everything was grounded. Twenty-four hours later the weather was still bad, again forcing cancellation of all flights. The third day the weather broke, and the musicians flew to Orly without difficulty. They went from the plane onto the airstrip and waited for Glenn Miller to greet them and fill them in on the band's future plans, including where they'd be living. They had made arrangements beforehand with Glenn that he would be on hand to meet them at Orly.

Glenn Miller failed to show up.

At first they thought it was just a normal delay. Captain Haynes, after a period of waiting, went to the control tower.

"I'm inquiring about Major Glenn Miller, head of the American Air Force band," Haynes told the controller. "The rest of the band just flew in from London. The major was supposed to meet us. He came in here about three days ago."

There was a chilling answer. "He never came in here. Nothing has been able to get in here for three days until you fellows arrived."

"The dreadful part of the story," says Johnny Desmond, "is that Glenn was probably lost thirty-six hours before anybody knew he was missing."

They didn't want to believe it. The army, the navy, and the air force began a thorough search as soon as they realized he was missing. Glenn Miller's probable death in the English Channel was withheld from the news media for several days while the military personnel continued their search in a frantic but waning hope that Glenn, his pilot, and the Norseman would be found.

One frightening theory was that the plane had been destroyed by English weapons. Seeing a plane out over the Channel when most air traffic had been cancelled by the weather, the English might have decided it was a German plane and shot it down. It is more likely, however, that the craft was simply blown into the sea.

For a long time Helen Miller, Glenn's widow, remained unconvinced that he was dead. "Nobody has seen him dead," she kept saying. "He'll come walking in here one of these days."

Finally in 1947 she conceded that he would never come back.

During the ten or twelve years after the war, "The Sentimental Gentleman of Swing," Tommy Dorsey, was constantly retiring, emerging from retirement, retiring again, or battling with his brother Jimmy Dorsey. Then, a dozen years after Glenn Miller's disappearance, Tommy died in a bizarre way at the age of fifty-one.

Tommy and his third wife Janie New were in the midst of a divorce action. They had been living in opposite wings of a $250,000 mansion in Greenwich, Connecticut, on advice of lawyers who had likewise ordered Tommy to keep his door locked—so that nobody could say their "separation" had been interrupted.

Despite these precautions, however, on the evening before Janie was scheduled to go into court next day to press her suit, charging Tommy with cruel and inhumane treatment, Tommy and Janie had dinner together—prepared with the help of Janie's mother—and drank a couple of glasses of red wine.

Tommy's agent, Vincent Carbone, was trying to reach Tommy. After dinner with Janie, Tommy apparently had locked his bedroom door just as the lawyer had ordered, and he settled down to watch television.

The next morning, Tommy's agent Vincent Carbone, who had been trying unsuccessfully to reach Tommy on his private phone, drove out to Greenwich, located Janie Dorsey, and went to Tommy's wing of the house. When repeated pounding on Tommy's door failed to evoke any response, Carbone got a ladder, put it against the wall of the house, climbed to a second floor, and entered the room through a window. Tommy was dead on the bed.

He had choked to death on food lodged in his windpipe and died probably between two and four A.M. Medical authorities said he must have gotten sick and had strangled after vomiting.

At first there were rumors of suicide. Police were confused by the release of a note that turned out to be a fake:

Dear Jane: Thank you for the dinner. It was wonderful and be sure to thank your Mom. I'm leaving early in the morning. Kiss Susie for me before she leaves for school. T.

Then another note—said to be genuine—was found, saying that he was glad he could start leading his own life again, "but thanks for the wonderful dinner . . ."

The authorities ultimately decided that there had been no suicide or foul play, that Tommy had indeed choked to death.

Tommy's funeral at the Campbell Funeral Home on November 29, 1956, opened with "I'm Getting Sentimental Over You" played slowly on the organ. A brass trombone lay atop the silvered copper casket. At the head of the casket was a spray of red roses with a ribbon reading, "Dearest Tommy, with all my love, Janie."

She sobbed and cried out during the service. Jackie Gleason, Paul Whiteman, Dick Haymes, and Nat (King) Cole were in tears or near tears as George Marlo, the eulogist, said, "At this moment, I feel Tommy is in the number one chair of the brass section in Gabriel's celestial orchestra."

Tommy's story is long and interesting, filled with fascinating anecdotes. Perhaps the most famous concerns Tommy, who was normally peace-loving (except when dealing with brother Jimmy), his beautiful actress wife of the time, Pat Dane, and their friend Allen Smiley. The three got themselves indicted in Hollywood in 1944 after heaving screen actor Jon Hall out of their apartment with a broken and deeply cut nose—so deeply cut that it was almost severed. Hall told the judge that he was stabbed and needed thirty-two stitches.

It turned out that a pleasant little party had turned into a free-for-all, and the exact reasons were hard to explain. Hall said that he'd put his arm casually around Miss Dane and that Dorsey demanded: "What are you doing to my wife?"

Hall also thought matters might have been made worse when Dorsey had asked him, "What kind of cigarettes do you smoke?" and he had answered, "Old Gold."

"I don't like them," Tommy had retorted.

But such quarrels appear to be slight quibbles, hardly the stuff to result in thirty-two stitch wounds. Moreover, after eight days of conflicting testimony, nobody seemed even to have answered the basic question: Who knifed Jon Hall? Tommy and Pat claimed they didn't, and Hall, the husband of radio singing star Frances Langford, who was on a USO tour with Bob Hope at the time, was very vague.

Eventually, the equally confused prosecutor asked that the case be dropped.

Smiley's lawyer, Jerry Giesler, said, "In all my experience I never saw such a crazy case."

Tommy was colorful, and his passing took a lot of gaiety out of the big band business. Tommy was fond of water pranks. He kept a siphon bottle handy on the bandstand to squirt water down the ballad singer's neck as she was singing a romantic number or to aim at Ziggy Elman while he was doing his solo. Sometimes he planted water-filled sponges in the seats of his musicians. Once he turned a garden hose on the band in Shea's Theater in Buffalo.

"You get pretty bored if you do nothing but let a thousand kids gape at you from two P.M. to one A.M. every day," he said.

For a time he had a thirty-two-room home at Bernardsville, New Jersey, and a hundred spare bathing suits for guests he'd occasionally invite out after finishing at the Astor Roof. They usually stayed until the next afternoon.

He enjoyed betting his guests that he could throw an egg over the top of his house without breaking it. He later explained that the first throw breaks only the yolk when it hits the ground. He couldn't do it a second time because then the shell breaks. He wouldn't explain all this to the friends with whom he wagered. He'd merely bet them he could do it, and win. Then he'd bet they couldn't and win again.

Jimmy was unable to go along with some of Tommy's crazy capers, and they had some arguments and even fist fights while they were partners.

"Mom" Dorsey, who outlived them both, used to say, "My Jimmy and my Tommy are good boys, but they will have their little scraps. The devilish part of it is that it's always about music."

One of their battles, back in 1934 when they were at Glen Island Casino, was hugely profitable. They were still billed as "the Dorsey Brothers." Tommy was leading "I'll Never Say Never Again Again."

Jimmy, the quiet one, put down his sax and growled that Tommy was beating too fast a tempo. Angered at this mutiny, Tommy stamped off the stand and didn't come back. Bing Crosby among others tried unsuccessfully to reconcile the brothers.

"I can't stand Tommy because he's always got a bunch of jerks around him. Another thing, when he's talking—and he always is—he leads off with a lot of corn," Jimmy complained.

Setting up rival musical groups, they soon had the largest slice of popular dance band business. Jimmy was called the King of the Juke Boxes, selling 5 million Decca Records, with Tommy selling 3 million Victor Records. Tommy was at the Astor Roof; Jimmy was at the Pennsylvania. Tommy's band had the attendance record at the Palladium in Hollywood until Jimmy's band came along and broke it.

"Nobody is happier to hear it than I am," Tommy said. Everybody tried not to laugh. The next trip out, Tommy's band beat Jimmy's record.

In 1947 Tommy thought swing music and the band business were dead and announced that he would retire to live on his ninety-six-foot yacht *The Sentimentalist*. But in 1948 he and the old slush pump were back on stage at the Capitol Theater on Broadway. Subsequently, I asked him what had happened.

"I didn't know what to do with myself," he said. "I got itchy to play. Pretty soon I was sitting in with every damn band that would let me, even in some little trap that had only three pieces. That convinced me that I would be a musician for the rest of my life."

Business, however, wasn't as good as it had been. Tommy formed a new group, cut his price from $3,500 to $2,000 a night, and insisted that ballrooms charge no more than $1.80 admission.

"We're off on another tour of one-nighters and expect to do well," he said. They did.

The Battling Dorseys got back together in the middle 1950s. Jackie Gleason put them on television as a summer replacement for his program. On "Stage Show," as it was called, they gave Elvis Presley his first important exposure.

The night after Tommy's death, I went over to the Statler (the old Pennsylvania), where Jimmy was making the funeral plans along with Jackie Gleason.

Jimmy took me into a bedroom apart from the others. "Brother and I had a lot of differences, but there hadn't been any serious beefs for the last three years," he told me. "Just Friday night we were all out till five A.M. and wound up at Reuben's.

"What am I going to do now that Brother's gone?" Jimmy asked me. "It's pretty late in life to start all over again."

Earlier that evening Jimmy, terribly broken up, went for a walk with Cork O'Keefe, the music publisher and agent, to try to calm his nerves. "I can't take it anymore," Jimmy said, and he backed into a doorway and cried for fifteen or twenty minutes.

Shamefacedly, Jimmy said to O'Keefe, "I bawled like a baby. That's kid stuff, isn't it?"

Jimmy usually called Tommy "Mac." Jimmy looked wet-eyed at O'Keefe and said, "As much as Mac and I fought, I loved him, and I don't think I'll be around for another year."

"You're crazy!" O'Keefe exclaimed.

Jimmy lost interest in life. He was paralyzed on one side, he suffered a serious fall, and then it was discovered that he had cancer. He was living alone, unhappily, in a Miami Beach hotel. A friend visiting him there said, "Jimmy, you've got to go home."

"Home!" he scoffed. "Where's home? Another hotel room?"

He did return to New York, however. But shortly afterward he was taken in an ambulance to Doctors Hospital. He did not come out alive. He died June 12, 1957. He had forecast that he wouldn't live a year after Tommy's death, and he was right. He lived only seven months.

The Dorseys were linked by a fierce family loyalty despite their frequent battling. Jimmy once slugged a customer who said his music stank. "It wasn't that so much," Jimmy said, "but I hit him when he said Brother couldn't play the trombone."

"Mom" Dorsey was the well from which that loyalty flowed. When Frank Sinatra began causing a furor while singing with Tommy's band, somebody asked her what she thought of him.

"He sings pretty fair," she replied. "But anybody who couldn't be a star singing to my Tommy's trombone ought to be shot."

One hot night in 1970, I dropped in at the Rainbow Grill next to the Rainbow Room in the RCA Building to have a little talk with Duke Ellington, who had been playing there for a week. I was surprised to find the Grill filled because business was hurting all over New York City, the stock market was in a sorry state, and people were saying in low voices, "You know, we've got a real depression on."

But at the Grill they had trouble finding me a seat. I sat with Jerry Brody, the boss of the restaurant chain running the Grill, his wife, and another couple.

"The Duke's jamming them in here," I commented.

"Oh, the Duke draws," Jerry Brody said.

To my further surprise, the minute the Duke Ellington band started a new set, the dinner guests leaped up with enthusiasm and danced, filling the dance floor. Just a couple of weeks before, Benny Goodman had mentioned that there was hardly any place left in New York City for dancing. Ellington stayed on for over an hour for the dinner show, clearly enjoying the fact that he was pleasing the crowd.

"The Duke always does more than he's supposed to do," Brody observed.

Ellington, in fact, wasn't supposed to play for dancing for the dinner show. He was scheduled to play for only an hour or less, but he was on considerably longer.

Duke was pleasing himself too. He told me later—Goodman said the same thing, incidentally—that the big satisfaction a musician gets is to hear and please himself.

With a wide grin, Duke announced at one point, "The first chorus of the next number will be played by our own piano player." That was Duke Ellington. When he was concluding the show, he led the orchestra in "I Love You Madly" and sang the lyrics in several languages, including Russian. As he walked off the floor several people approached to shake hands, and whether they were men or women, he laughingly kissed them on both cheeks.

The Duke strolled back into a small side room and sat down. I sat across from him as he discoursed on his newest ambition—which, at the age of seventy-one, was to write some successful lyrics.

"I never had a hit with any of my lyrics," he admitted to me. "I never pressed myself as a lyric writer because I always had a lot of great lyric writers with me."

Recently he had been happy about writing the lyrics for "Love Came." Oddly enough, it had been exhausting exercise, though writing the melodies has never been tiring for him.

"When I got through with the lyrics I was so tired I couldn't write the music," the Duke informed me. "I called Billy Strayhorn and I said, 'You write the music, man; I got my kicks from the lyrics.'"

Duke remembered an example of how easy writing has been for him. "In 1923 or 1924," he said, "Joe Trent and I wrote a show in one night. That comes from being illiterate and not knowing you can't write a show in one night.

"Nobody had told us it couldn't be done. It was *Chocolate Kiddies,* and it played the Winter Garden in Berlin for two years. Everybody in it became a star. Adelaide Hall was in it and Josephine Baker was in the chorus."

To write, the Duke said, "All you have to have is physical isolation —and whatever is in you bubbles out of you." But that's not as easy to get now as when he rode the trains. Now he travels on planes and doesn't want to miss the dinner or the movies, and by the time he's handled those, he's completed most trips without writing anything.

He constantly employs about a dozen bandsmen. "The big bands," he says, "are damned expensive. But music to me isn't a business, it's a compulsion. So if I write something tonight, I want to hear it tomorrow morning. That means keeping the band together and working all the time."

Giving credit to luck more than ability, Duke claims, "There are a lot of guys who know much more about music than I do, but I had the good luck to be heard."

Starting out in his late teens and twenties in New York, he was ready to audition with his band for a date at the old Cotton Club in Harlem at noon. But the kid Ellington had to hustle five more musicians. When he finally assembled his collection, it was three P.M.

"The guy doing the hiring heard us, and he said, 'Hire them!' He hadn't heard the other bands that were waiting. He only heard us.

He was late getting there, too! And the Cotton Club was our launching pad."

Duke has encountered race problems, but he has always met them head on. In the days when Negroes couldn't get rooms in better hotels, Duke arranged for his band to travel in two chartered Pullman cars, and a baggage car.

"We would park it on a siding, just like the president of the United States traveled," Duke said. "It earned us respect."

Not generally known about the Duke is the fact that while he was a prize lover at one time, in his septuagenarian years he is the happy grandfather of three. He is usually surrounded by women. They like him for his gracious courtliness. Duke's second wife Evie doesn't often appear with him at the celebrity functions he attends because she's not in the best of health. People wonder about the woman seventeen years younger who usually accompanies him. That's his divorcée sister Ruth Ellington, whom he has placed in charge of his far-reaching music business, assuring her and her children of a substantial income for years after he's gone.

Duke's son Mercer Ellington manages the orchestra and also plays trombone, trumpet, and French horn.

Mercer's daughter Mercedes is one of the apples of grandfather Duke's eye. Landing a dancing job with Jackie Gleason's show, she was one of the first black dancers on television and subsequently went into *No, No, Nanette.* Generally, it has been her policy not to reveal to prospective employers that she's Duke's granddaughter. A grandson has worked as bandboy for Duke's orchestra.

"The King of Swing" they called Benny Goodman, and he was the inventor of "The Ray."

He was a very young bandleader when swing began—in his middle twenties—but he was a stern, perfectionist boss, with a practice of glaring disapprovingly over the top of his glasses at his men when they weren't playing their best. He couldn't tolerate sloppiness or carelessness. He was mad about music, and he expected the musicians in his unit to share his enthusiasm and dedication.

So he would glare at the culprit, who naturally felt ashamed. It became such a familiar routine that the boys in the band referred to his accusing stare among themselves as "The Ray."

"If you're interested in music," he always contended, "you can't slop around. I expect good things from you. If I don't think I'm getting the best, I sometimes show you with a frown."

"Do I still do it?" he said in answer to my question during a recent interview in his apartment during preparations for a concert tour of the Italian Riviera, where Benny Goodman and Swing were still appreciated. "I wonder." He smiled a little. "Could be . . ."

He had a plush, well-groomed look about him—expensive clothes, a king-size apartment, fine leather shoes, which he put up on a hassock as he lit a cigarette and chuckled about that Italian tour. He was really a remarkable gentleman, a boss type, but a truly dedicated artist. He went shouldering through the apartment, calling to his secretary, "Muriel . . . where all are we playing in Italy? Venice, Livorno, Lugano, Montecatini. Places we can't even pronounce."

"Are they one-nighters?"

"We call 'em concerts. I guess everything's a one-nighter. We play in beautiful concert halls, and it's an event. The halls are so beautiful, just built for music, and you're geared up when you walk in. The musicians are a band I've used over there before, some English fellows I think are pretty damned good. I feel comfortable working in Europe. The whole thing is a big rat race unless you enjoy it and I enjoy it in Europe."

He was still playing his kind of music.

"This music in the discothèques drives me nuts," he confesses. "Oh, I run right out. My band makes a good bit of noise, but we make a different kind of noise."

The least appreciated facet of Benny Goodman is his determination, which enabled him at the age of forty to change his entire style and to adopt a new technique for playing the clarinet. It was a painful switch-over.

Consider that in 1937, when he was twenty-eight, he had them swinging in the aisles at the old Paramount Theater and was making jazz history. His famous "Carnegie Hall Concert" recording, cut in 1938, is still selling.

Then in 1949, he began taking lessons from classical clarinetist Reginald Kell, who used both lips while Goodman had always held the mouthpiece between his front teeth and lower lip. For Goodman, this was like learning to play all over again. He also had to have his finger calluses removed by a doctor and to develop new calluses with his new finger technique. He had to make use of and cultivate a set of facial muscles he hadn't previously used. In effect, he was forced to start his career all over again.

B. G. achieved it, of course, and he shifted from jazz to playing the classics, appearing with both the London and New York Philharmonics as soloist, while Aaron Copeland and other composers wrote concertos for him. The word "virtuoso" seems to fit him, but undoubtedly his favorite numbers include "Honeysuckle Rose," "Stomping at the Savoy," and "The One O'Clock Jump."

Goodman helped to break the color line in the big band business in the 1930s. He was assisted by his brother-in-law, wealthy John Hammond, a jazz worshipper, who could afford to take chances— and did.

"We never thought about a man's race when we were starting out," Benny remembers. "We heard colored music—we loved it— that was all."

First, Goodman recruited Teddy Wilson, the great Negro pianist, for the Benny Goodman Trio (which included Gene Krupa), and then he brought in another black, Lionel Hampton, and made it the Benny Goodman Quartet.

"One Negro is all right, but two Negroes, no," some of the out-of-town bookers told him.

"Take them or you don't get me," Goodman replied. He and Hammond made it work. By the 1940s nobody seemed to notice that blacks and whites were playing together.

But Goodman, a pioneer in integration, was mystified as years went on, when overzealous and uninformed newcomers in the civil rights movement phoned to ask whether he was going to use black musicians in his orchestra.

"I always have," he would say. "I always have. Why not now?"

B. G. believes that his first Carnegie Hall concert, on January 16, 1938, was the first time integrated musicians ever appeared on the concert stage in New York. He wasn't yet thirty years old when he walked out on stage in tails, counted the beat, and lifted his clarinet to start the blasting. It was a night of challenge and great expectancy. Just sitting in their seats in that plush hall listening to jazz, or swing, seemed a little crazy to some people in the audience. But they were willing to listen.

On stage blowing away was trumpeter Harry James, about whom there has arisen a famous anecdote.

Purportedly he was so impressed by himself and his fellow musicians at being in such an aristocratic, artistic atmosphere that he said, "I feel like a whore in church."

The applause that struck the musicians was as surprising to them as their music was liberating when it reached out to the audience. It was quite an organization that B. G. had assembled—Ziggie Elman, Teddy Wilson, Bobby Hackett, Lionel Hampton, Cootie Williams, Gene Krupa, George Koenig, Chris Griffin, Vernon Brown, Babe Russin, Hymie Shertzer, and Art Rollini. Martha Tilton was the vocalist.

Thirty years later, on January 17, 1968, Benny Goodman held a reunion of that band in his penthouse. Several of the musicians had become famous leaders on their own during those three decades. Harry James's remark was still amusing but no longer true. No jazz musician playing in Carnegie Hall could honestly feel like a whore in church any more. B. G. had made them very respectable—even sought after.

Benny was rich now, but maybe he wasn't having as much fun as in the earlier days when he was playing for dances at the old Pennsylvania Hotel. He had more contact with people in those days. One night after work he was sound asleep in his room when a loud knocking and screaming awakened him.

"I want the money you owe me!" somebody was roaring.

The owner of the voice claimed to be a waiter from the Copacabana, and he said Benny had just been there and run out on his check.

"I haven't been to the Copacabana!" Benny yelled back, pulling his pants on and trying to outscream the waiter. Others on the floor had been awakened and were siding with the waiter.

"Aw, for God's sake, I wasn't there, but how much was it?" Benny shouted through the door.

"Fifty-eight bucks."

"Of all the swindles!" Goodman howled. "I'll give you the money, but tomorrow I'll be over to the Copa to take care of you."

Benny flung the door open angrily and discovered that the yelling waiter wasn't at his door but at the door of the adjoining room. As it turned out, the guilty check-dodger in the next room hadn't arrived home yet.

8

The Hollywood Scandals

WHO was the number one scandal lady of the golden age of show business? Ingrid Bergman . . . Elizabeth Taylor . . . Mia Farrow? They were great beauties with tremendous potential as seductresses, but (and I don't mean to insult them) if they were the worst—or best, depending on your viewpoint—then scandal was in a bad way. Yet their affairs were and are the stuff of movie magazines and even, I'm sorry to say, of columns.

Liz Taylor, it is true, snatched two husbands away from their wives: Eddie Fisher from Debbie Reynolds, and Richard Burton from Sybil Burton. But since she traded in Eddie Fisher for Richard Burton, does Eddie really count? Isn't that like a fisherman throwing one fish back in because it isn't big enough?

The Burtons' scandal—Burton himself always refers to it as *la scandale*—was disappointingly brief and rather dull and dreary afterward, with no breathtaking side features. Burton just announced one night to Eddie Fisher, at the Fishers' villa outside Rome, "I'm in love with your wife—*Get out!*" and Eddie Fisher scrammed, leaving Richard and Elizabeth to their lovemaking in what he had thought, until then, was his house. One cannot be surprised that Eddie Fisher was a shaken man ever after, always doing strange things, which led to his professional decline and ultimate bankruptcy. The real explanation may be that Eddie Fisher never got over his love for Elizabeth Taylor and her rejection of him after she tumbled for the great Shakespearean actor Richard Burton.

Although the Liz Taylor, Ingrid Bergman, and Mia Farrow cases fit loosely into the "hushed-up Hollywood scandal" slots, none happened in Hollywood, and none was really hushed up. Liz Taylor, married five times, stole Eddie Fisher away from darling Debbie Reynolds at Grossinger's in the Catskills "Borscht Belt" in upper New York, and she burgled Richard Burton from Sybil in her starring role as his Cleopatra in Italy, feeding him rich pasta and powerful vino every night while she worked her personal magic on him. None of it was hushed up because Liz has never been secretive, and what Elizabeth wanted Elizabeth usually got.

When I first began to circulate in this world of glamour and glitter, Liz was not yet cast as a scarlet woman. She was just becoming a genuine star at the age of twelve in *National Velvet*. Still, when, in 1950, Liz married Nicky Hilton, the hotel chain heir, somebody with great foresight said, "He'll make a fine first husband."

The gossip began at once. It was not about Liz, however. Nicky, the eldest son of Conrad Hilton, was drinking and gambling on the honeymoon, not paying attention to his honeymoon duties. Liz was brooding. Soon there was a report that the bride and bridegroom had split up.

I received a telephone call from Los Angeles from Arthur Forrestal, a veteran publicist for Conrad Hilton, Sr., who asked me for a favor. He wanted me to publish a story to the effect that the rumors about Liz and Nicky severing their relationship were not true.

"To prove it to you," he said, "I would like you to have dinner with the two of them tomorrow night at the Waldorf. They will tell it to you themselves."

They were to arrive in New York from California, he said. I agreed. It sounded like a good story.

The next day he phoned me again. Our dinner date was cancelled. They were not coming to New York together after all. The split was on.

Liz Taylor once said, "I guess the world thinks of me as such a scarlet woman, I'm almost purple."

I've always found her a down-to-earth—even a down-to-earthi-ness—girl, suffering from the "handicap" of her beauty and sexual-ity. She'd been engaged to football star Glenn Davis and William D. Pawley, Jr., and at seventeen had caught the perceptive eye of Howard Hughes, then forty-four. When Liz got together with Mike Todd, there was no need to suppress anything because both were free. Liz was divorced from Michael Wilding. She was merely changing Mikes.

As for Todd, he was a high-riding, big-spending widower, sort of a contemporary pirate with personality. Gambling, borrowing, bluffing, conning people, charming them into loaning him more money, he had finally hit it rich with *Around the World in 80 Days* and was trying to make himself a living legend by reminding peo-ple that he who was once a bum was now a millionaire.

About twenty-four, to Todd's forty-eight, Liz was captivated by his flippancy and possibly by his flexible code of ethics. He pre-tended not to be overly enchanted by her, and some witty fellow, noting the age difference between this gorgeous gal and this grand-father, commented naively:

"What can Mike Todd *possibly* see in her?"

During their extraordinarily blissful marriage, with Mike hurling gifts at her all over the world, Mike and Liz had an idyllic friend-ship with Eddie Fisher and his wife Debbie Reynolds. Young Eddie literally worshipped Mike Todd and copied some of his traits and mannerisms—including smoking expensive cigars.

Then in March, 1958, Todd's ice-covered chartered plane crashed, killing him, author Arthur Cohn, and the pilot, and Liz was a bereft widow before the whole world.

The first girl friend to reach her side was Debbie Reynolds. The two couples had been a happy foursome in the Mediterranean on Todd's yacht.

Four or five months later, rumors reached the big ears of the gos-sip columnists about Liz Taylor and Eddie Fisher.

Let me interject that I have never been ecstatic about the part of my profession that requires me to report on marital breakups. It has always been merely "a job" to me. If I were a political reporter (which I have been) and discovered a swindle, or if I were a sports writer (which I have been) and came upon a major swapping of star athletes, I would have reported them and would have hoped to be first.

Anyway, columnists, despite what some readers may think to the contrary, have ethics. We never contribute to the breakup of a marriage—we only report those that have already broken up.

Still, simply because many stars were especially accessible to me, I probably got more inquiries than most reporters from editors who would call and say, "Hey, Earl, do you think there's something going on between Liz Taylor and Eddie Fisher?"

This is not what I had hoped to do with my life when I was a Sunday school teacher back in Ohio, but I was the fellow who might get the story first for my paper and syndicate, so I would sigh and start making phone calls. I made it my rule to obtain and report both sides of the story, if possible, hoping from sheer selfishness that the *next* time they got a divorce, as they probably would, they would remember my fairness and maybe call *me*.

So there it was in my column on Friday, August 29, 1958, under the heading "The Low-Down on the Higher-Ups," about Mrs. Todd, who had been widowed the previous March:

> Elizabeth Taylor and Eddie Fisher were dancing it up at the Harwyn this morning, Eddie having been Mike Todd's close friend and now sort of an escort service for Liz. They saw *Two for the Seesaw* the night before.

That was all. There was no reference to Debbie Reynolds, who was back home in California.

A Labor Day weekend was coming up. Liz and Eddie were going to the Catskills together, to Grossinger's, for the holiday. It all seemed in good taste—Jennie Grossinger, the proprietress, was a good friend of Debbie's. And, after all, Eddie had worshipped Mike Todd, and Liz and Debbie were such close friends. What could be wrong?

George Bennett, then the Grossinger's press agent, invited me to join them. "With Liz Taylor there, you never know what might happen," he said. I accepted, and I took along my wife, my mother-in-law, and my son. It was all very cozy and familial.

I was most cautious in reporting their activities during that holiday weekend because, if there were any romancing, I wasn't clever enough to nail it down. It was clear that Eddie was the dutiful cour-

tier to Liz during every step she took that weekend. They got into a
station wagon and rode through the rain to an auditorium, where
Eddie received an award. Liz caused a near panic in the dining
room. Hundreds wanted to gaze upon her beauty. Eddie helped
to shield her from the mob. Nobody had ever generated such excitement in the mountains.

"Where's Debbie?" Eddie was asked over and over.

"Oh," he would smile, "she stayed home with the children in
California."

"Labor Day alone with the kids in California while her husband's
here with Liz Taylor—how cozy!" somebody said.

But Labor Day was over, and Eddie was flying home to California,
and Liz was winging to Europe, and that would be the end of it.
Another crisis avoided.

However, just as a protective measure, we followed through on
how Eddie was received when he returned to the arms of Debbie
and the kids in California.

By phone we learned something startling. Debbie went to the
plane to meet Eddie, only he wasn't on the plane. In addition,
Eddie hadn't notified Debbie he wasn't coming. It seemed he'd told
somebody else to tell her, and the somebody else forgot—or was
afraid to.

In fact, Eddie was still in New York with Liz, who had cancelled
her trip to Europe. They were going to dinner and seeing shows,
and Eddie was working on his television show.

If the story about the weekend and the husband missing on the
plane had never been reported, perhaps the Eddie Fishers' crisis
would never have come to a head. But as soon as we got the facts
in type, Eddie returned somewhat sheepishly to California. Meeting
reporters, he wrung his hands and declared that he and Debbie
had talked things over and "hoped to work it out."

A year before, when Liz Taylor's Mike was still alive and buying
her baubles, Eddie and Debbie had talked about divorce. Then
Debbie learned she was going to have her second baby.

"We called off divorce plans even though we'd gone so far as to
prepare an announcement," Eddie confessed.

Hollywood columnist Sid Skolsky and I got together on a couple
of special articles headlined, "The Fight at the Fishers," explaining
to any who might be interested just what had disrupted the

domesticity of Debbie and Eddie—and the true role of the widow Todd.

One thing seemed to clear Liz's fair name—or at least to rip a part of the scarlet letter off her well-filled blouse—that part about the Fishers having planned a divorce long before.

Liz wasn't a home-wrecker after all. She and Eddie were just helping each other in a time of mutual loneliness.

"Elizabeth Taylor doesn't figure in this at all except that she happened to be alone when he was alone," one of Eddie's advocates explained to me. And he was alone a lot.

"Debbie is less an extrovert, less flamboyant, more stay-at-home, than Eddie," asserted Skolsky, my accomplice-in-gossip.

"Debbie startled some of her friends among the stars by making some of her own clothes. At times she can be severe. One Hollywood celebrity called her 'an angel with spurs.'

"When she was warned that she should work frequently in pictures and continue to be a glamour girl lest she lose her husband, she boasted: 'I will never lose him!'"

And that was actually the end of the marriage. There exists no record of Liz's ever calling on Debbie as Debbie had called on her when Mike was killed. Of course, the moralists of the press, who had excoriated Ingrid Bergman, enjoyed the disaster. Both Elsa Maxwell and Dorothy Kilgallen preached in print about the wicked Liz. Liz in turn had some graphic four-letter word answers for them.

But that was just the beginning of their troubles. Eddie's popularity skidded after his marriage to Liz (which Debbie had coldly consented to). Hollywood gave both of them the freeze and didn't invite them to parties. Liz, "the other woman" in the mind of the public, was blasted in mail to the studio by people who said they'd never go to see her pictures again. The Theater Owners of America contended that they could not possibly give their annual award to Liz for Cat on a Hot Tin Roof—"it would be out of the question at this time." They gave it to Deborah Kerr instead.

Liz, who was lonely and worried about what would happen to Eddie and herself, was getting the same icy treatment that the American public had given Ingrid Bergman.

Eddie and Liz took off for London, where Liz had always been a favorite. Just a year after their romance was revealed, Eddie did a

BBC telecast there. Privately, Eddie told me he hoped for good reviews in London—they might help him to re-establish himself on television in America.

"I need some good press notices," he confessed.

Compared to the mature-looking Liz, he looked almost like a little boy, with his hair longish, Italian style, having been cut by Liz, who was always running her hands through it.

The impression of his being a schoolboy stayed with us. Some comedian said: "Eddie Fisher marrying Liz Taylor is like trying to flag down the Broadway Limited with a paper match."

Eddie's London reviews were excellent, the couple returned to New York and went straightaway to Grossinger's, where somebody had thoughtfully removed from the walls an old photograph of Eddie and Debbie in their happy days there.

Liz's loyalty to her bridegroom when he was fighting a comeback battle was impressive. She was ill, with a temperature and a hacking cough, but she resisted going to the hospital because she wanted to be at the Waldorf Empire Room when he opened there just before Thanksgiving 1959.

She promoted in the grand Michael Todd manner. She let the word leak out that she'd attend both the dinner and supper shows, knowing that her presence would attract hundreds to the hotel lobby and make it a carnival night. Then she invited seventy VIPs as her own guests and picked up a check for about $1,500.

Her excuse was that it was an anniversary for them; they had been married six months.

Afterward Liz gave another party for the VIPs at Leone's restaurant starting at two A.M. and really warming up at about three.

From there, Liz went into the hospital. Doctors said she had contracted double pneumonia as a result of her stubborn refusal to come in before Eddie's opening. A few days later, Eddie and I rode up to the hospital to visit her.

"She hates hospitals," Eddie revealed. "She's been in about fifteen of them. She resents anesthetics. They can't seem to knock her out. When Elizabeth had Liza [Michael Todd's daughter], she had a Cesarean against the advice of about twelve doctors. Then she's got a bad back and a bad throat."

Unquestionably, Eddie had been given a new shot of confidence by his bride. He was especially elated that Liz had secured a part for him in her next movie, *Butterfield 8.*

"I'm gonna play a piano player named Eddie," he said. "I never acted before. Elizabeth plays a lady of the evening."

The great turnabout in their fortunes occurred in February and March, 1961, when Liz almost died on the operating table in London during a tracheotomy. The seriousness of her illness was known to show people. In the Poodle Room at the Hotel Fontainebleu in Miami Beach, Joe E. Lewis raised his glass to friends and said, "Instead of saying 'Cheers' or 'It is now post time,' let's say a little prayer for Liz Taylor."

So critical was the surgery that Liz was said to have been dead —and to have been brought back to life. These dramatic reports, true or not, suddenly made the one-time scarlet woman a heroine, a figure of sympathy.

"They saved her life," Eddie stated. "Elizabeth is overwhelmed by the letters and cables from people saying they went to churches and synagogues to pray for her recovery."

As Eddie was preparing to bring Liz back to America, he talked to me in the famous Oliver Messel suite at the Dorchester. Liz's two miniature Yorkshire terriers were romping around the suite.

"She won't need any nurse going home; I'll be her nurse," Eddie said.

Elizabeth required a wheel chair and turtleneck type collars, as well as new necklaces—"diamond and ruby bandaids"—to cover her scars. Liz, of course, walked off with the Oscar for *Butterfield 8* a few weeks later (and said some years later that she didn't deserve it).

The public was in love with Liz again. But it only took a year for her to become the "other woman" again. While Liz was in Rome filming *Cleopatra,* she was rushed off to a hospital again, this time reportedly after taking an overdose of sleeping pills.

The gossip about Liz and her co-star Richard Burton was just starting. The studio people from Twentieth Century-Fox, sitting over their drinks in the Snakepit, the downstairs bar at the Hotel Excelsior in Rome, said Liz had taken the pills because Burton couldn't marry her. He was already married to Sybil, a rather possessive woman, who was back in London.

Writing about this later, a former secretary of Burton claimed that Liz had reached a point of desperation. She had told Burton, "I can't live without you," and Burton, drinking and desperate himself over his own situation, had said, "Then die . . . die . . . die." Incidentally, most of his acquaintances find this picture of Burton hard to accept.

"I won't dignify those stories by answering them," Eddie Fisher said when questioned at the time. He insisted that it was all malicious gossip. He was still clinging to the hope that Liz and Burton would break off.

Ten days after the hospital incident, Liz turned thirty. Eddie invited my wife and me to a birthday party for her at Rome's luxurious Hostarian dell'Orso restaurant. The party was supposed to silence the rumors about Burton.

But it didn't, and one reason was that Burton wasn't there. Producer Walter Wanger and director Joseph Mankiewicz attended. Liz danced twice with Roddy MacDowall. She and Eddie did not dance together.

Liz and Eddie left at midnight—very early for Rome—and the rest of us went back to the Snakepit and speculated about whether they had really patched it up. The consensus was that they hadn't.

Burton had never intrigued me as an interview subject, but now that he was rumored to be Liz's choice for a soul mate, the situation called for a meeting. I succeeded in getting a lunch date with him out at Cinecita, where he drank some red wine and said that all the talk about his being a film matinée idol was "bloody nonsense."

"I haven't made enough films, and I'm too old—I'm thirty-six," he said. "And I look about 5'2". I'm 5'10½". But I'm so wide or my head's too big or something, and so I come out on film with an odd shape."

Burton has friendly eyes and a solid, wiry look. There wasn't any doubt that girls—and some men—had crushes on him. It wasn't gentlemanly to ask him about the stories about Liz, but I did notice that he looked up with great interest when somebody came to the table and remarked that she might be doing a scene that afternoon.

"Is Liz going to work?" He glanced up in pleased surprise. "You don't know what fame is till you walk down the street with Liz," he said. "Liz, Eddie, and I went to Bricktop's one night. It was empty, but the word spread to the Via Veneto, and when we tried to leave, we couldn't get through. They were trying to pinch her, and they got very insulting. She was torn to bits."

For a month columnists and glamour reporters ran wild. Would it blow over or would Eddie and Liz get a divorce? If they got a divorce, then certainly it would mean that Sybil was going to give Richard a divorce so that Liz and Burton could marry.

Trivial as all this may seem years later, at the time it was of monumental importance to journalists. The man who knew the inside story was a celebrated lawyer and author, my friend Louis Nizer, attorney for the Fishers.

Back in New York I learned that Nizer had been summoned to Rome by his clients. That made a headline. He must surely be going to Rome to arrange for a separation, a settlement, or a divorce, we speculated.

But we wanted to nail down the story, clinch it, end the guessing. Nizer informed me that he would be having dinner that night at the Algonquin with Ben Bodne, the owner, and Harry Hershfield, the great storyteller and after-dinner speaker who wrote a humor column once a week for the *New York Daily Mirror*.

"Drop in, I might have something for you," Nizer invited.

I got there a little after seven P.M. I'd hardly sat down with them when Nizer got a phone call. The operator said Rome was calling. This could be it! What a story I might have tomorrow!

After taking the call, Nizer returned to the table, reached into his pocket, pulled out a typed slip of paper, and handed it to me: "Elizabeth Taylor and Eddie Fisher have authorized me to state that their marriage is terminated and they will obtain a divorce."

"It's all yours," Nizer said with a kindly smile.

All mine! It was almost 7:30. My paper, the *New York Post*, had gone to bed at least three hours earlier. I had the biggest story in the world, and nobody to give it to, no paper to print it in.

I was about to say to Nizer, "You couldn't hold this off until tomorrow?" when he said, "You've got a couple of hours. I've called a press conference for nine P.M. to give this out generally."

A two-hour break he'd given me—but where, oh where, could I print it? Rushing to a phone booth, I called my Los Angeles outlet. Due to the time difference, it could still get the big scoop into print. I phoned a few other out-of-town papers, but it was the New York exposure I desperately wanted. Well, if I couldn't get it into the *New*

York Post, maybe I could at least give the scoop to the Associated Press.

Phoning the Associated Press, still aquiver with my big exclusive, I got a deskman who wasn't as impressed as I was. In fact, he seemed to doubt that I really *had* the story and decided to wait until the press conference so that he could really be sure.

Thanking Nizer for giving me the exclusive but not revealing my secret heartbreak, I returned to my office to grieve. How unfair fate had been to me! An hour or so later, I went out onto Broadway and stopped to pick up the *News* and *Mirror*.

What was that headline? *"Eddie, Liz Divorcing."* In the *New York Daily Mirror*.

Where and how had the *Mirror* gotten it? "By Harry Hershfield."

I had been scooped by my good friend, the after-dinner speaker in his seventies. While I was wondering what to do with my story, Harry had simply and quietly phoned it into his paper.

In the years since, Mr. and Mrs. Burton have been courteous hosts and delightfully personable. The Burtons nowadays are not passionate discothèque-goers. But Skip Ward, who had been in *The Night of the Iguana* with Burton, was insistent that the Burtons accompany him and the girl whose house guest he was—Stella Stevens —to Bumbles.

"We must, luv," said Burton.

"Why?" demanded Liz.

"We must, luv," he repeated.

She didn't want to go. But they were soon there, and suddenly it was Burton who wished he hadn't come. One of the managers was being overly gracious. Burton complained to Liz, "This man is fawning over me!"

"Considering everything,"—Liz said—meaning the place and the company they were in—"you're lucky to have *anybody* fawn over you."

And with that, she hit him in the face with her purse and ran to her limousine. She hurried away to spend the night with Beverly Hills socialite Mrs. Edie Goetz. Burton made a rather unsteady attempt to overtake her on the outside of Bumbles, but he did not catch her. It took him an hour or so to figure out where she'd gone. And when he finally found her, Liz unleashed some of her more vivid vocabulary in his direction and declared that was the last time Burton would be her tour conductor.

"Yes, luv," he agreed docilely.

Next day Burton sat pensively in the Beverly Hills Polo Lounge sipping a drink.

Liz approached his table and clobbered him in the mouth.

"Care for a drink?" He didn't seem surprised or in the least ruffled. Liz sat and had a drink.

"Oh," a friend of theirs told me, "they do that all the time."

Before Liz and Eddie and Liz and Burton, there was, of course, the love of Ingrid Bergman and Roberto Rossellini.

These glamour romances have a way of sizzling and sputtering for a time at low key, then suddenly exploding with horrifying reverberations. Ingrid's affair with the flamboyant but erratic Italian director was known to the movie world for many weeks, but it was not mentioned in print because Ingrid was married to Dr. Peter Lindstrom. It could not be concealed for long, however, because in the summer of 1949, while Ingrid and Roberto were making a movie in Stromboli, Ingrid was reported to be pregnant. There is nothing like a pregnancy to expose a clandestine romance.

Ingrid, the merry type, enjoyed companionship. Dr. Lindstrom was quiet and studious. Having been impressed by one of Roberto's films, Ingrid had written him a letter saying, "If you ever need a little girl with a Swedish accent for a picture, let me know . . ."

Reading this letter from one of the most beautiful women in the world, Roberto didn't write or telegraph—he rushed in person from Rome to Hollywood. Thus it all began.

Now it was August, and Ingrid and Rossellini were returning from Stromboli to Rome. With them they brought the big questions: Was Ingrid getting a divorce? Was she going to marry Rossellini? Was she pregnant?

The publicist-intermediary who knew the answers was Ingrid's press agent, Joe Steele of Hollywood. I discovered to my great disappointment while I was in Rome working on the story that he intended to give the news break to International News Service out of his loyalty to columnist Louella Parsons, who was associated with INS.

I had been led to believe that Ingrid had not yet made up her mind about what she was going to do. Very late at night I had gone to the Stampa, the press wire office, to file my story to New York saying that Ingrid was still trying to reach a decision.

My eyes wandered to the telegraph printers. Suddenly I noticed an International News Service story quite the reverse of what I'd been told—Ingrid had decided to divorce her husband and retire.

Quickly locating Joe Steele, I accused him of the worst of treacheries and told him that I would make the rest of his life miserable if he didn't demonstrate his good faith by arranging an exclusive interview between me and Miss Bergman.

In almost cloak-and-dagger fashion, I was taken the next night to her hideout apartment at an address I didn't know and wasn't able to learn because Steele rushed me in and out.

Miss Bergman was understandably nervous as she walked into the living room and faced the first reporter she'd seen since the storm had broken over her affair with Roberto. She was going to marry Rossellini, she said, and far from retiring, she and he would make many movies together, and perhaps they "could rule the film world, artistically speaking."

She could envision herself in Italian films; she would be "an international star."

Roberto had done much for her self-confidence, she stated. Convinced that she didn't have attractive legs, she had always kept them covered. But in the Stromboli film, Roberto had insisted that she show her legs, wearing her skirts knotted so that they would show all the way to her thighs as she climbed a rock.

"If my legs are ugly, it's all right because it's artistic," she said, laughingly quoting Roberto.

"Why is there so much criticism of me in America because of this?" she asked me. She mentioned that Lana Turner, Paulette Goddard, Joan Crawford, and other stars had changed husbands without being blasted.

"It's out of character for you. Everybody thinks of you as being a steady, husband-loving wife."

"But why?" she demanded. "Then if I had been a bad wife, it would have been all right? Am I being punished for having been a good wife?"

Defending Rossellini, declaring that he hadn't broken up her marriage, that it had been coming for some years, Miss Bergman then solemnly stated to me that she was *not* pregnant.

"The *New York Times* printed that I am pregnant," she said—I'm sure she had some other paper in mind—"and I told Joe Steele, 'If anybody prints that I am pregnant, *sue!*'"

(Miss Bergman subsequently laughed about this and told me a month later, when Steele had returned to Hollywood, that one day she sent him a cable: "*Don't sue anybody.*" She *was* pregnant by then.)

Our secret interview ended with Miss Bergman showing me the scars she'd gotten on her legs when climbing the jagged rocks on the volcanic island where the picture was filmed.

Eventually the censure of Miss Bergman for leaving her husband to go with Rossellini became more tumultuous than had ever been anticipated, and the moralists of the glamour press assailed her. Her picture was later boycotted by some groups. I'm afraid I half-heartedly joined some of the puritans, writing that she had misjudged public opinion.

All this criticism hurt her, and when I was in Italy a year later, she refused to see me at first. But then she invited me to Fiuggi, the mountain resort town where she was living for the summer, and she showed me baby Robertino who, she boasted, was already four inches longer than the average baby his age.

"I bawled you out, good, didn't I?" she said, referring to her earlier refusal to see me. "I felt very proud and strong afterward. When all this happened, there was such a wall of hate in America, and so many people raised holy hands to heaven, that I became very bitter and hard."

It was easy to see how she could have fallen in love with the colorful, reckless Rossellini, who had five cars but was frequently broke, often rushing from one bank to another to borrow money to shoot his next scene. He was always late for appointments. The Italians said, "When he's half an hour late, he's ahead of time."

He once was *eight days* late for a meeting with one of his film units. But he had a certain flair that appealed to people. Once as we sat at a sidewalk café, a slight breeze blew out the flame of his cigarette lighter. He then held the lighted lighter down inside his shirt against his hairy chest as he relit the cigarette. Italy then had a law permitting a citizen to put a photographer in jail for taking a picture without permission. When the Rossellinis were involved in such an incident, Roberto would put the offending photographer in his red Ferrari and roar off to jail with Ingrid and little Robertino at his side.

"Then Roberto gets to like the photographer and is sorry he has to take him to jail to protect the baby and me against them," Ingrid said. "Sometimes we stay with the photographer. We have spent many happy evenings in jail."

Emotionally, Ingrid paid dearly for her happiness with the charming Rossellini. In 1952, while she was in a hospital in Rome awaiting the birth of her twins, she was stunned to read a news story from Los Angeles quoting her daughter Pia as saying that she didn't love her mother. This came during a court battle, and Rossellini charged that Pia's mind had been poisoned against her mother. It took a few years for this difficulty to be straightened out happily for mother and daughter.

Ingrid stayed away from America for over seven years. In January, 1957, she left Paris, where she was doing *Tea and Sympathy* on the stage, and she flew to New York to accept the Motion Picture Critics' Best Actress award for *Anastasia*.

By 1957 the fickle American public had either forgiven her or decided that her conduct was none of its business. Steve Allen filmed an interview with her from Sardi's and said he hadn't had one protesting phone call, although about thirty people registered their objections by mail.

Crowds were so great on West 44th Street that auto traffic had to be turned back. Kirk Douglas, Mel Ferrer, Audrey Hepburn, John Huston, Edward G. Robinson, Henry Fonda, and Burgess Meredith kissed her. Holding a big bouquet of violet orchids and yellow tulips, Ingrid said happily that she might return to America that year with Rossellini, the man responsible for her long exile.

That, to repeat, was January, 1957. In November of that same year something else in the way of scandal was let loose. Ingrid and Roberto had abruptly reached the end of the road in their relationship. Roberto was trying to get their marriage annulled. He had a young Hindu sweetheart, Sonali Das Gupta, and Ingrid was being girlishly coy about her romance with Swedish producer Lars Schmidt.

"When are you going to get married?" I asked her in London.

"I wish I knew," she replied.

"Your answer implies that you are going to get married."

"*You* can say that! Anyway, I'm very happy about everything."

The following summer I found Ingrid glowing with pleasure as she was filming *The Inn of the Sixth Happiness* outside London, though it wasn't easy for her to glow because she was dressed as a peasant girl from China, with real dirt on her face. Her marriage to the mild-mannered, bespectacled Lars Schmidt was approaching. Ingrid was forty-three years old and confident that this next marriage would last forever.

Her career was going well. When the picture was finished, the London newspapers headlined that Queen Elizabeth II wept when she saw it. Critics called her "the Divine Ingrid" and said she was "greater than Garbo."

The *scandale*, as Roberto had called it, was now almost a decade in the past. Ingrid had suffered a thousand heartbreaks, indignities, and humiliations. Now, sitting on the doorstep of her trailer dressing room, she laughed at the twists and turns of her life, and she grew lightly philosophical.

"You're basically a happy person, aren't you?" I said.

Smiling, she answered, "I'm adaptable. You know, you can't expect to have happiness all the time. And you shouldn't because you'd be a monster. You wouldn't grow up to be a human being."

I didn't quite understand that. Laughing some more, she elaborated.

"I'm grateful for the good things but also for the unhappy things. Because if you don't have some suffering, you don't understand it in others. You can't be patient and tolerant with them. But more than that, if you only have happiness, you don't understand what happiness is. You have to have sadness to appreciate how sweet happiness can be."

It's possible that the Hollywood scandals may be much less scandalous than back in the Fatty Arbuckle days, when studio public relations chiefs were constantly covering up indiscretions of its male stars. "Sex orgies" then were just called parties.

Visiting male stars were often taken to a "Black Knight" sex ritual in a private club in New York. Naked girls paid tribute to a naked Black Knight in a casket, sometimes copulating in the casket.

A famous leading man, married, and with a good image, was found naked there in a police raid, and his studio, one of the biggest, went on a spending spree to keep his name out of the papers.

"It cost the studio $50,000," was the underground report at the time. The leading man's fair name still has never been tarnished, and he walks among his friends and his family with his head held high.

Confidential magazine came along in the 1950s, published by a flip, sharp, racy Broadwayite named Bob Harrison, who was to rehash almost every Hollywood scandal ever heard. It is amazing now to review it and see how much he got away with, how successful he was financially, and how little he was penalized.

Before *Confidential* he had been printing girlie or cheesecake magazines with titles such as *Titter, Wink, Hush-Hush, Uncensored, Low-Down, Eyeful,* and *Flirt.* He always had several curvy girls—models, I presumed—sitting around his editorial offices.

The Kefauver investigation of crime demonstrated to him that the nation was hungry for gossip because the whole country seemed to be willing to stop work and watch witnesses tattle on their friends or acquaintances in the televised hearings.

Determined to capitalize on this yearning for gossip, Harrison launched *Confidential* and was eventually selling 3,700,000 copies on the newsstands—outselling even *Reader's Digest* and *TV Guide* with his screaming headline articles such as:

"The Untold Story of Marlene Dietrich."

"Billy Daniels and His Blonde Baby Sitter."

"What Robert Taylor Doesn't Know about that Redhead."

And there was one headline that said: "NAMED—The Fall Guys In The Jelke Trial"—which was concerned with the famous call girl trial and listed some of the "Johns" the newspapers hadn't identified.

Harrison was proud of his product. He frequently asked me, "What do you think of my magazine?"

"I think it's a disgrace," I would tell him.

"You think it stinks now," he would say, "but wait till you see the next issue."

Operating on the theory that there was some truth to nearly every piece of gossip and his belief that nobody would do much about his printing the gossip, Harrison employed some working New York newspapermen and newspaperwomen to take outlines and meager facts from "researchers" and whip them into lightly written scandal stories without any personal knowledge of their veracity.

Some "researchers" were call girls. One male celebrity who had decided to have affairs only with prostitutes (because his wife usually caught him when he was cheating with a starlet) discovered his whole adventure told in *Confidential*. His prostitute had run and sold her tale to Harrison.

For a couple of years Harrison reported the activities of the famous of Hollywood, and then they began suing.

Robert Mitchum had grown increasingly touchy over the years about a story that he'd gone to a party naked and covered himself with catsup.

"This is a masquerade party, isn't it?" he supposedly said. "Well, I'm a hamburger, well done."

Errol Flynn also sued for $1,000,000, objecting to a story that he had taken several prostitutes as guests on his yachting honeymoon with Patricia Wymore.

In 1955, when the hatred of Harrison was at its height, Errol Flynn happened to encounter him in El Morocco. Flynn was drinking, but he was convivial and not inclined to pugnacity. I was sitting with Flynn when he called across to Harrison's table, "How about settling for $100,000 right now? I have a check with me, good on any bank. *You know I've got you!*"

Harrison leaped up and planted a kiss on Flynn's forehead. "I love you!" he said.

Brushing him away, Flynn said, "Isn't that assault? Can't I sue for some more?"

With Harrison was his lawyer, Dan Ross, and he did persuade Flynn to discuss the article. Flynn said it referred to their honeymoon "in Hollywood," when actually they were married in Monte Carlo. "The whole article's bungled, and you'll pay," declared Flynn.

As the drinking increased, Flynn grew lighthearted about it and began bargaining with Harrison about a settlement.

"How about $200,000?" teased Flynn. That got another refusal. "How about $100,000? How about $50,000?" Harrison and his lawyer laughed off those offers, too.

"Well," said Flynn, in a cheery mood, "in that case, how about a two-year subscription?"

The country thought it was going to get an earful of juicy scandal when Harrison was prosecuted for allegedly publishing obscenity by the state of California. Only two stars appeared—actress Maureen O'Hara and singer Dorothy Dandridge—both to deny the stories *Confidential* had published about them.

The strange case had a strange ending. There was a hung jury, and the state and the defense reached a compromise. The obscenity charges against Harrison and eleven others were dismissed, and the state's earlier charges against five corporations and eleven individuals were narrowed down to a charge against two magazines, *Confidential* and *Whisper*. They were fined $5,000 each, a mere trifle.

What did the trial prove? Primarily that Harrison was indeed able to get away with his brand of journalism. Did the state let him down easy in their reluctance to open its files to more scandal cases? Was there an understanding that Harrison would behave himself and never do it again? He announced he would revise the magazine's format, and he later stated that he had sold out to a "syndicate," which he said was a "very successful power group founded for that purpose."

Harrison was never extradited. He circulates around the New York restaurant scene today, deprived of the fame he once had, publishing magazines that have never attained even a small part of the success of his greatest and most lucrative venture.

"I don't know about its being a financial success, in the long run," Harrison told me earlier this year. "The trial cost us four hundred thousand dollars. We had three sets of lawyers. Oh, the lawyers! We flew witnesses from Europe. We cabled, we telephoned, we hired more lawyers."

Harrison settled a lawsuit brought against the magazine by Liberace. The magazine paid him $40,000.

It was all most educational for Bob Harrison. Lee Mortimer was then a gossip columnist for the *New York Daily Mirror*. Mortimer pretended to be Harrison's enemy and to be contemptuous of his publication. He also objected to Harrison's using the title *Confidential* because he'd written a book called *New York Confidential*.

"We were really very good friends," Harrison said recently. "Mortimer wanted to keep the controversy going. We would meet at a phone booth in a little hotel on East 52nd Street and exchange information so that he could keep writing about *Confidential*. It was a big help to me.

"I took in millions. I paid an income tax one year of a million. But the lawyers! Oh, the lawyers!" Bob Harrison held his head in despair.

9

Drinking, Diddling,
and Divorcing

BEFORE the old Hollywood passed away, around 1970,
the so-called cinema capital of the world was famous for indulging
in the three Ds—drinking, diddling, and divorcing.

Then when the conglomerateers arrived with their cold com-
puterization and turned studios into ghost towns, Hollywood continued to drink, diddle, and divorce.

But the gaiety had gone. Once you could laugh about the romantic
propensities of Howard Hughes or share a bawdy joke with W. C.
Fields, Al Jolson, Fanny Brice, or Eddie Cantor. Everybody was
rich. I once asked Jack L. Warner, "Is it possible to lose money on
a picture?"

"I don't think so," he replied after about half a second of thought.

But when the bankers and the accountants from the conglomer-
ates came marching in, fun fled the town. You could hardly expect
"the smiling cobra," James T. Aubrey of MGM, or Charles Bluh-
dorn of Gulf & Western or their Wall Street associates to be howling with laughter over enormous losses.

"More films are being shot in Spain alone than in Hollywood," Hank Grant wrote in the *Hollywood Reporter* in March 1971. "The only place that's busy here is the unemployment office."

Anita Louise had forecast to me a couple of years before that one studio would literally become a cemetery. Except for a zoning law prohibiting such construction, she spoke the grisly truth.

It had all been predicted. On October 8, 1969, *Variety* asked: "Can Hollywood Studios Make It?"

Thomas M. Pryor wrote: "It would no longer occasion surprise if all the majors were to sell off their studios."

In Paris, Gene Moskowitz interviewed Darryl F. Zanuck, producing a page one banner: "Film Biz In Need of Change . . . Pushes a Streamlining" in short, layoffs, slashes, retrenchment!

How sadly different from those earlier, more prosperous days when all Hollywood seemed to worry about were the three Ds. Once, so the legend went, columnist Louella Parsons looked at her husband Dr. Harry Martin lying on the floor, quite "under the weather" at a late party, and called nervously to some friends: "Oh, do help me wake him up. Doctor has to operate at seven."

I remember other incidents from that era. W. C. Fields was reported to be dying in a rest home. Gene Fowler, the eminent author and prankster, and Dave Chasen, the restaurateur, were going to visit him, and they invited me to join them. Full of merriment and booze, Fowler took Fields a cake, and he stopped at a hardware store to buy a file to insert in the cake—to escape the rest home, of course. Fields was able to drink a martini with us, and he enjoyed the cake-and-file joke. Fields had been quarreling with everybody during his illness, and one of his verbal sparring partners was the owner of a building in which he had lived before his illness.

"Bill," Gene Fowler said, "I have some news for you. Your landlord is very sick."

Fields' lips turned up in an effort at a smile. "Aw," he clucked like a small boy, "you're just saying that to make me feel good."

This was during the period when the funeral of Harry Cohn, one of the most hated men in Hollywood, drew such an overflow at the chapel that one cynic said, "You give the public what it wants . . ."

Al Jolson left Hollywood and came to New York on the Super Chief and 20th Century (or Broadway) Limited to do a radio show, and he was met by song writers offering to cut him in for half of the royalties if he would sing their songs and put his name on the sheet music. They would give him co-author credit.

"Hey, Al!" they'd say, thrusting a lead sheet at him. "Here's a song you just wrote."

Jolson was one of the pioneers of candor on the air. After entertaining troops in England, he was asked by an interviewer, "How did you like that warm English beer?"

"As far as I'm concerned," replied Al, "they can pour it back in the horse."

The aforementioned Gene Fowler was a heroic drinker who sometimes started early in the day. Once he arrived at Pat O'Brien's house while Pat wasn't yet awake. Pat's daughter apprised him that Fowler was there.

"Is he drunk?" asked Pat sagely.

"I don't know," the daughter said. "But he's wearing a New York Giants uniform and has a bat on his shoulder."

Bing Crosby and Phil Harris were still good drinkers in those days. Leaving Hollywood for a tour of the South, they arrived in Tennessee, where a reporter asked the purpose of their trip.

"We came to lay a wreath on the grave of Jack Daniels," said Phil Harris, who apologized for Crosby's not drinking as much as usual. "He heard from his liver," explained Phil. "It said, 'I quit.'"

Nobody suspected in those happy days that this glamourland of dazzling blondes, muscular males, and flexible expense accounts would some day be split up into fiefs of Gulf & Western, Commonwealth United Corporation, and Kinney National Service (which started modestly as Kinney parking lots). Their thinking was centered on more entertaining, if less earth-shattering, events. For example, no one knows how many people swore they witnessed a diddling scene at either the Brown Derby or Mocambo one night between a beautiful brunette actress and a handsome continental director—under the table. The story is that they forgot themselves in their passion and that quite a number of people saw them engaging in oral lovemaking. The number of people who swore they saw it exceeded the capacity of the restaurant, and in later years it was almost impossible to meet somebody who hadn't been there looking on that night.

I was *not* there, and I never had the courage to ask the glamorous brunette, whom I know fairly well, whether the story is true, though I was tempted to do so many times. Perhaps I shall just send her this chapter with a few question marks on the margin.

Samuel Goldwyn was then the world's greatest malapropist and was getting off lines such as "If Franklin D. Roosevelt was alive, he'd turn over in his grave." A verbal contract, he claimed, "is not worth the paper it's written on." "All the lies they tell about me are true."

When Goldwyn brought out *The Best Years of Our Lives,* he charged $2.40 for the Saturday and Sunday performances, a steep price in 1946.

"I don't want to make a nickel on this picture," he solemnly stated at the time. "All I want is for everybody in the country to see it."

Acquaintances of Goldwyn debated whether Goldwyn really perpetrated the twisted witticisms attributed to him. They suggested that they were carefully thought out by master publicists Irving Hoffman and Howard Dietz, who undoubtedly circulated, if they didn't invent, the great "include me out" line.

A visiting columnist like me could get invited to lunch by Goldwyn at his studio and listen carefully for him to utter a gem such as "Anybody who goes to a psychiatrist ought to have his head examined." I lunched with him more than once, anxiously waiting for him to say Mussolini instead of Rossellini or to declare that "The dictionary is nothing but a lot of words." He certainly said of Fredric March, "I'm overpaying him, but he's worth it," and, speaking of the high salary paid to a certain third baseman, he scoffed, "I wouldn't pay that much to a *first* baseman."

I did catch a few. He was weak on titles. The Poor Richard Club of Philadelphia came out "The Poor Richman Club," and Sammy Davis' "Mr. Wonderful" became "Mr. Wonderman." He also had respect for the picture *Withering Heights.* He told me, however, that when the press quoted him, they didn't quote the twinkle in his eye, meaning, I guess, that he was kidding.

Goldwynisms, however they came about, had a relevance that intrigued Manchester Boddy, then the editor of the *Los Angles Daily*

News. He requested me to ask Goldwyn if he would be interested in wiring a daily gag box, as Will Rogers had done.

"Tell him no, thanks, I wouldn't," Goldwyn said. "Do you think I want people to think I'm stupid?"

Ray Bolger gave me an answer to the question of whether Goldwynisms were authentic.

Bolger learned that Goldwyn was planning a picture with a great dancing role. He managed to wangle a golf date with Goldwyn, hoping Goldwyn would suddenly be hit with the thought that Bolger should get the part. They played pleasantly enough, but Goldwyn concentrated on golf, never mentioning the picture. Bolger became increasingly anxious. At last, over a drink in the clubhouse, Goldwyn unbent.

"Ray," he said, almost confidentially, "don't mention it, but I'm looking for a great dancer to do a wonderful role in a new picture."

"Is that so, Sam?" Bolger knew then that the message had reached Sam, and he couldn't wait for the offer to come.

"What would you think," Goldwyn asked, "of Gene Kelly?"

One of the great diddlers of that day, of course, was Howard Hughes, who was on his way to becoming a billionaire. He bought RKO Studio for $8,825,000, flirted with buying MGM, made such hit pictures as *Two Arabian Knights, Hell's Angels, Scarface,* and *Front Page*—and greatly assisted the economy of Hollywood by placing numerous beautiful young starlets under contract.

Although these girls constituted a potential harem for Hughes, some of the starlets lamented that it wasn't true: that they seldom, if ever, heard from him. He just forgot them.

Once in the 1960s, while staying at the Beverly Hills Hotel, the bell captain allowed me to look over the list of guests on a chart.

Almost the entire third floor was occupied by a "Mr. Glenn."

"What Glenn is that—John Glenn, the astronaut?" I asked.

"That's Howard Hughes," they told me.

Hughes, or "Mr. Glenn," occupied four and a half bungalows in addition to the rooms on the third floor, paying a monthly rent of $30,000. Deathly afraid of being kidnapped, he kept a staff of security officers at the hotel, and they could be seen idling around one hotel suite day and night, usually watching television while awaiting orders. In his fear for his life, Hughes wouldn't allow the proud staff of the Beverly Hills Hotel to serve him. He had his *own* staff.

He was most persistent when in pursuit. He knew how to flatter women, and he had the means to do it. When Ava Gardner's mother was ill in the Carolinas, he offered his private plane to fly Ava there and to take medical help—and he was in the cockpit himself.

Hughes gave ladies his personal attention, and one wondered how he found time to do it all. Ingrid Bergman was his target for a while, though she apparently spurned his advances. He had offered to fly me to San Diego to see my sister in July, 1946, at the very time he crashed and narrowly escaped death in his army photographic plane. As I related earlier, I was enormously flattered by his kindness toward me until I learned that he thought I was going to be interviewing Ingrid Bergman aloft and that this would present opportunities for him to get better acquainted with her.

Once Miss Bergman was in a plane that was parked in Kansas City Airport, trying to sleep. Hughes was annoyed that another TWA plane's motor was roaring nearby.

"Turn that off!" he commanded. "Miss Bergman's asleep in there!"

Hughes had two hobbies—planes and girls—and he was ten times busier with his hobbies than any other hobbyist, as the girls told me. He gave away many rings and fur coats, but he also knew how to get rid of girls.

One night while in Hollywood he wanted to break a date with a girl. He decided to try to convince her that he'd gone to New York and couldn't get back. Calling a friendly phone operator in a New York hotel, he persuaded her to connect him with the girl in Hollywood and let him talk to her through the switchboard as though he was in New York.

"I'm tied up here and can't get back due to the weather," he told the girl.

"I don't believe you're in New York," the stood-up girl said.

"Call me back here at this hotel collect," Hughes challenged her.

She did. Hughes, still in Los Angeles, took the call as if he was in New York. The girl apologized for doubting him.

"I hope," Hughes rebuked her, "that'll be the last time you'll mistrust me."

In the summer of 1947 Hughes was on the carpet before the

Senate War Investigating Committee, making several senators look foolish about their inquiries into the expense accounts rolled up by his publicist, Johnny Meyer, in connection with building a flying boat for the government. Proving himself his own master publicist, Hughes met various reporters at two or three A.M. and fed them exclusive stories, always in his favor, of course.

I was living in Los Angeles that summer. Once he arrived in an old car at his office in the Goldwyn Studios, and he came in, with tennis sneakers slapping the floor, to give me an exclusive angle. The next meeting was different.

"I'll see you in the back room at the Players Club at two-thirty," he said. "I'll have a girl with me. It's dark in there. Don't write anything about seeing me there or tell anybody. I don't want Louella Parsons running something about me being out with a girl during this investigation."

In the semi-darkness of the room, the girl sat at the table with us as he talked, but Hughes never introduced her. He had a passion for mystery even then.

The comedian of the investigation was publicist Johnny Meyer, who later entered the employ of Aristotle Onassis (he's a man who knows how to pick employers!). Hughes' fortune was estimated at a trifling $500,000,000 then. He had money to toss away, and Johnny helped him toss.

"Let's give a party," Johnny would say, and he became the world's fastest check-grabber and signer.

"You're Mr. Hughes's guest," he would often announce to one and all. Unbelievably self-confident, Meyer would brook no put-down attitude from his boss. He called him "Junior," asked him, "What are you, a genius or something?" and at times would tell him, "You're nuts." Johnny eventually left Hughes when one of his own oil wells came in. They remained respectful toward each other, however, and Hughes ultimately engaged another man with the same name for the job.

Questioned about some of his "entertainment" checks, which included drinks and meals for starlets, Hughes could honestly say, "I don't know anything about them. That's Johnny's department."

"Didn't you ever look at his expense accounts?" I asked him.

"Hell, no. I've got better things to do!"

Seeing Johnny Meyer around now with Onassis and his wife

Jacqueline, I marvel at the importance of "the great check-grabber" in those days. Not surprisingly, he was needed as a witness to explain some of those checks, and likewise not surprisingly, he was missing. He did the great disappearing act before Hughes did. Hughes assured me that night at the Players Club that he knew where Meyer was—he had dispatched him to South America to sell some planes.

They nailed Hughes down for a press conference, and while waiting for him to appear—he was an hour late—I learned from his public relations representative, Carl Byoir, who'd been his press spokesman for several years, that he'd never met Hughes.

Concerning the expense accounts, Hughes had a vast, sincere ignorance. He was frequently penniless and had to borrow cab fare. On his trips to New York, he became extremely fond of Robin (Curly) Harris, a press agent, who took him everywhere around town and always paid the checks.

"That's a wonderful man . . . never lets me pay for a thing," Hughes told Johnny Meyer.

"Junior didn't know that Curly was working for him and was turning in expense accounts to me for everything—probably padded!" Johnny Meyer said.

Johnny was the ultimate check-grabber. One night in El Morocco a man in his party went to the men's room. On the way out, he tried to tip the attendant.

"Oh, no, sir," bowed the attendant, "you're the guest of Mr. Meyer."

Parties of all sorts are staple fare in Hollywood, which can never have enough of them. There are many true stories of guests going into a bedroom to get a coat or hat left on a bed only to find the hat or coat on the floor and the bed occupied by two or even three guests.

Anita Louise was one of Hollywood's busiest party givers in the couple of years before her death. She entertained twenty or thirty times a year. At one of her parties I was foolish enough to say good night before the main event—which was unscheduled.

The remaining dozen guests were sitting around the bar. They included a famous actor, a famous producer, and their young wives.

We'll call them Actor Jones and Producer Smith.

Down on the floor Producer Smith had Actor Jones's wife in his arms and, in front of the remaining guests at the party, was fumblingly trying to copulate with her.

Actor Jones's wife was not resisting especially, but Producer Smith was too inebriated to carry out the act.

Actor Jones was a large, muscular, outdoor fellow, and he and his wife are quite tender with each other in public. Sitting at the bar, looking down at his wife and Producer Smith attempting to fornicate, he declared in a loud voice:

"I think it's about time somebody introduced me to Mrs. Smith!"

They didn't join in the act, however, and make it a foursome. The word of the "floor" show spread swiftly around Hollywood and soon became almost as famous as the alleged incident at the Brown Derby or Mocambo involving the beautiful actress and the continental director years before.

Actor Jones and his wife came to New York shortly thereafter and were as loving as usual.

"I saw you at Anita Louise's party," I reminded them.

"Oh, yes, were you there?" they said.

"Unfortunately I had to leave early," I said.

That probably conveyed to them that there had been one fewer witness than they thought. As for the famous producer, Mr. Smith, he did not attend any parties for a while. His young wife reportedly beat the hell out of him.

Now that the revolution in films has destroyed the studios, ending the reign of the tycoons and installing bold young independent producers with practically no money in positions of leadership, the King Henry VIII years of Louis B. Mayer, Harry Cohn, and Darryl F. Zanuck must sound very unreal. The wealth the movie moguls had to fling around gave them a power over the lives of their male and female stars that truly made them emperors in their Hollywood realms.

"Don't you understand," a Hollywood friend said to me, discussing Louis B. Mayer, "that these tycoons, when they get rich, collect the best paintings, the best horse flesh—and the best woman flesh?"

Female flesh, in reality, was cheap. Starlets threw themselves and their bodies at the czars. But call girls were also used. In some executive offices in the administration buildings the afternoons were set aside for sexual high jinks. A good lunch was often followed by a matinee with a young beauty in the executive's office. Visiting his office ostensibly to discuss a role in a picture, she would make oral love to him, the preferred method of intercourse because he probably didn't have a bed in the office. It got to be almost a daily routine with some executives far below the mogul or tycoon rank. If the girl showed promise, the executive might pass her on to one of his associates. Since so many were available, there was no need to be greedy.

The high potentates of filmdom were truly men of power and often of mystery with their own private dining rooms to which only the other powerful were invited, luxurious limousines, and many additional special privileges.

Harry Cohn seemed always to be arriving from Las Vegas with rolls of greenbacks in his inside jacket pocket. Where did he get the money? Was he somebody's silent partner? Did he know somebody who was skimming?

Hollywood was full of racy gossip about these men and women. Howard Hughes was a bachelor, entitled to as many girls as he wished, and was alleged by the story bearers to have from twenty to fifty beautiful creatures stashed away in apartments here and there, under contract to him as a movie producer—though it was never claimed that Hughes took advantage of these young things. With the busy schedule he had, he just forgot them, as the story went, but they continued to receive their pay checks, waiting and wondering when they would hear from him. A further tale about Hughes concerned the fact that he occasionally ran into a girl who insisted that he marry her. Hughes was reputed to have his own little marriage ceremony prepared for these sticklers. He supposedly would take them to a mountain top and perform the marriage service himself. Most of the stories about Hughes were similarly fanciful.

"D. F. Z."—Darryl F. Zanuck—was the tycoon most envied by his high-ranking colleagues because he was clever enough to spend millions of company money building up screen careers of girl friends who never really should have had careers.

All they ever really had was Zanuck, with the big cigar, dark glasses, white mustache, and black tie.

The last of these girls was a French model, Genevieve Gilles, forty-four years younger than the old gray twentieth century fox.

"You know Genevieve, don't you?" Zanuck would say through his cigar when he was escorting this girl, still in her very early twenties, to 21 or Trader Vic's in New York. (Zanuck was one Hollywood tycoon almost never seen anymore in Hollywood.)

Zanuck's passion for youth caused his separation from wife Virginia in the middle 1950s. Mrs. Zanuck remained in California, and Zanuck went on to live in hotels in New York and apartments in Paris. Mrs. Zanuck never bothered getting a divorce.

"Even if she weren't Mrs. Zanuck, she still wouldn't be able to get a good table in Romanoff's," people used to say when Prince Mike Romanoff's was the place to be.

Close friends said that Mrs. Zanuck continued to love her husband and hoped he would come home some day after he had had his fill of youth.

He may have hoped for the same. However, the family breakup assumed the proportions of a Greek tragedy in 1971, when Darryl F. Zanuck had to discharge his son Richard Zanuck as president of Twentieth Century-Fox in one of the film company's many reorganizations. Mrs. Zanuck sided with her son.

Zanuck was still seen with the model Genevieve. He was looking older, she looking no older but perhaps more chic. D. F. Z. still had not had enough youth.

Zanuck had first seen Genevieve in Paris, where he also courted her predecessors, Bella Darvi, Juliette Greco, and Irina Demick. Genevieve made a film short about fashion that filled Zanuck with hope for her chances of developing into an important screen personality. When she emerged as a star in a picture called *Hello—Goodbye*, one of the film critics referred to the movie as "a $5,000,000 screen test."

This sort of gossip cut deeply into the egos of Zanuck and Genevieve. In an interview with me, Genevieve herself brought up the reference to the "$5,000,000 screen test."

It was a sensitive subject because the company was in desperate financial straits, and Zanuck's personal position was in peril. For the head man to be risking that kind of money on a girl friend was certain to make the stockholders go berserk. When the publicists at the film company learned that Genevieve had talked to me about the "$5,000,000 screen test," introducing the subject herself, they asked me to soften her references to it. I agreed. We cut it down to a "$4,000,000" or even "$1,000,000 screen test."

Zanuck splurged more spectacularly, of course, with Bella Darvi, the Polish girl who helped to break up his marriage and succeeded in keeping him in her clutches for years while she gambled away a fortune. Anyone visiting the casinos at Cannes, Monte Carlo, or Deauville was likely to see her gambling madly, usually with Zanuck at her side.

Zanuck and his wife were together in Paris when they met Bella, and the three hit it off so well that they invited her to visit them in California in 1951. When Bella was living with them, they changed her name from Bella Wegier to Bella Darvi—the Darvi being a combination of *Dar* for Darryl and *vi* for Virginia.

Presumably unknown to Mrs. Zanuck, Darryl Zanuck was already in love with Bella, and although Bella Darvi had no acting experience, he decided, in his crazy passion for her, to make her a screen star. She became one of his biggest disasters.

The Egyptian, with Bella playing the role of a courtesan, was a big joke, but funnier yet was the fact that Zanuck thought she was good and became more devoted to her than ever.

The truth must have reached Mrs. Zanuck by this time because Bella Darvi was taken off the list of house guests, and she subsequently came to New York, where she lived in an expensive Park Avenue hotel. I interviewed her there after her expulsion from the Zanuck household by Mrs. Zanuck, but I found most of her comments too candid for publication. She had no reticence about discussing her role as the mistress of a famous man.

In all, Zanuck gave Bella three chances in pictures, and the cost must have amounted to many millions. Additionally, he contributed to her expenses in the years after. It was quite sad, after he had finally removed himself from her influence, to see her down-and-out at the casinos, trying to borrow money on jewelry so that she could continue to gamble.

The classic days of Hollywood were the "wolf pack" days, before men were called studs. Zanuck was not a wolf. He fell in love with girls and stayed in love with them. The others, I fear, were triflers. Dick Haymes was going through all the girls at all the studios, and

Richard Burton was reported to have said to one of his leading ladies, when she resisted, "Are you going to be an exception?"—the only one of his leading ladies who wouldn't?

Porfirio Rubirosa visited New York and Beverly Hills. Fearsome tales were told of the reasons for his success as a lover.

The allegedly insatiable Aly Khan conquered Rita Hayworth, Gene Tierney, and probably many others. It was his "thing," in the days before there was such an expression, to take a girl out on the lawn and into the shrubbery between courses at a dinner party. Beverly Hills residents admired Aly Khan for his singleness of purpose. He didn't drink much. He had better things to do.

When Aly and Rita were about to get married in the town of Vallouris on the French Riviera, a reporter for a Paris scandal paper had the bravery to write that Rita Hayworth, "getting married next week to Aly Khan," was expecting a baby. This was shocking journalism then.

The same reporter had the additional bravery to arrive at Vallouris to cover the wedding. Aly Khan heard he was there and confronted him.

"Are you the reporter who wrote that my fiancée is expecting a baby when we're not even married yet?"

"I am."

"Don't you realize what a terrible thing that is to do to my father, the Aga Khan, the head of millions of Moslems, and to me, who will some day be the head of millions of Moslems? Don't you know what a terrible thing you have done to me?"

"But," replied the journalist, "I never said you were the father."

(How I wish I had said that!)

Alfred Hitchcock once told me that "all love scenes started on the set are continued in the dressing room after the day's shooting is done."

In other words, the leading man and leading woman get themselves worked up before the camera and finish the scene afterward. "Without exception," added Alfred, who also said that it could happen at the lunch hour too. He would not say how he was so sure of this, nor would he mention names.

Many of the stories doubtless are part of a growing myth. A famous actress told me that she had been in her dressing room one day when her phone rang, and she discovered she was on a crossed wire.

"It was Cary Grant talking to Sophia Loren. He told her how desperately in love he was with her. He wanted to divorce Betsy Drake, marry Sophia, and take her around the world. She told him not to be foolish."

Later I asked Sophia Loren about this story. "Whoever told you that is not your friend," she said. "It never happened."

Some of the strangest stories about Hollywood are only peripherally concerned with sex. For example, Rita Hayworth herself at times quiet and brooding, at times a veritable conflagration, contributed to the town's lore. After her divorces from Aly Khan and Dick Haymes, she married James Hill, the writer-producer and partner in Hecht, Hill, and Lancaster Productions. For a time they lived cozily and quietly in Beverly Hills.

One night Bernie Kamber, the director of publicity for Hecht-Hill-Lancaster, was invited to the Hills' for dinner.

"Rita doesn't entertain much, but she'd like to have you over," Jim Hill said.

Kamber was flattered. He anticipated a gourmet dinner prepared under the eye of the great sex goddess.

Rita and Jim greeted Bernie enthusiastically, and Jim poured Bernie a drink. Rita wasn't having a drink, she was too busy darting into the kitchen to watch over the dinner preparations.

Coming back to chat with the guest, Rita suddenly made the observation to Bernie, "Do you know you look a lot like Ed Sullivan?"

Bernie had never before heard this comment about his looks. While he mumbled a "Well, thank you," Jim Hill said to Rita, "Oh, he looks nothing at all like Ed Sullivan!"

"I tell you he's a carbon copy of Ed Sullivan!" Rita said, raising her voice.

"And I tell you," said Jim, "he looks no more like Ed Sullivan than I look like Sophie Tucker!"

"And I tell you . . ." shouted Rita.

"You must be sneaking drinks out there in the kitchen!" declared Jim.

Suddenly both rushed to the kitchen, and in the battle that ensued, the dinner was soon splattered over the kitchen. Jim ran to a clothes closet to get his coat and that of his guest, and then he led

Kamber in a dash to his car in the driveway. In their haste to get away from the anger of the housewife who was seeing pink Ed Sullivans, Hill swung the car up against the side of the wall. But there was no damage, and they escaped uninjured.

Hill took Kamber to dinner at a restaurant.

A couple of days later, Hill meekly told Kamber, "You know, Rita feels awful about what happened the other night. She'd like to do something nice for you."

"Ask her," replied Kamber, "not to have me to dinner."

Similar stories can probably be told about all kinds of people. What makes the Hollywood stories more interesting is that they often deal with superstars, who range in modern times from Greta Garbo to Joan Crawford to Lana Turner to Marilyn Monroe to Barbra Streisand to Raquel Welch; and from John Gilbert to Clark Gable to Richard Burton to big John Wayne.

I love them all, but they're such a collection of characters, so inconsistent, unpredictable, and supersensitive that their actions always make good copy.

Long ago, when Frank Sinatra threw Ava Gardner and Lana Turner out of his house in Palm Springs while he was married to Ava, I reported the fact in headlines. Ava didn't object. But after I revealed that, during an interview with her, she had walked around barefoot and had said she was a sharecropper's daughter turned a millionaire, she sent word she wouldn't see me anymore.

Ava is quite a personality. When she first came to New York she was quite naive. I interviewed her during a dinner meeting and she ordered an old-fashioned.

Sipping from the glass, she said to the waiter, "That's the best old-fashioned I ever drank."

"Wait'll you see how good it is when I put some whiskey in it," said the waiter.

Carole Landis, whom we all loved, killed herself over Rex Harrison long before he was known as "Sexy Rexy." In World War II days, Carole was dancing with a British soldier who admired her bosom, which was projecting considerably from her low-necked blouse. They were then called V-necks. She was attending a party at a USO canteen where they were trying to raise money to send food abroad in "Bundles for Britain."

Looking pointedly at her breasts, her dancing partner said, "Is the V for victory?"

Miss Landis replied, "Yes, but the bundles are not for Britain!"

Marlon Brando once flared up at me for asking him about his playing an army officer with homosexual tendencies in *Reflections in a Golden Eye*. In another meeting, however, he was so charming and hospitable that I was overwhelmed. He'd just finished an extremely difficult scene and was clearly exhausted, but he trotted around his dressing quarters serving *me* tea.

I called Sammy Davis, Jr., "the world's greatest entertainer" before anybody did. Still, when I found out on a Thanksgiving that he was breaking with Mai Britt and asked him for a comment, he informed me that I couldn't print it because "the lawyers are going to release it Monday."

After I published the story the next day, he became angry and refused to see me the next time I caught his show. He switched back to his usual friendly good humor a few weeks later when we next met.

Barbra Streisand's famous nose got lots of attention from me. Producer Ray Stark told me, "I've employed the two most beautiful girls in the world: Elizabeth Taylor and Barbra Streisand."

"Who did you say were the two most beautiful girls in the world?" I asked.

"Elizabeth Taylor and Barbra Streisand," he answered.

"Either you're out of your mind, or you've lost your eyesight," was the tenor of the mail I received. Miss Streisand evidently liked my references to her beauty, but one day when I reported that she'd worn a wig at a party, she called me personally to declare that she never wears *anything* false.

"I am sure about the falsies," I replied, having just seen her bust overflowing her dress in *On a Clear Day*.

John Wayne was always a man of character. Sure he drank and swore, but so did everybody. I was the first to get news of his combating cancer, but he deprived me of the story in an honorable way. Learning that he'd had a lung operation and beaten the disease for the time being, anyway, I phoned him in Los Angeles and persuaded him to let me write the story.

In fact, I told him I had the story and was going to print it unless he strongly objected.

It was ten o'clock at night in New York. I put aside my notes on the talk with him and decided to write the story later. I went around my New York beat. A couple of hours later I phoned the city desk of the *New York Post* to tell them I had the John Wayne cancer story.

A desk man on the *Post* said, "We already got the story from the Associated Press."

How could that be, when he'd told it to me, after I had persuaded him to let me print it?

I found out that Wayne had phoned his friend columnist James Bacon in Las Vegas to tell him about it. He and Bacon were close; Bacon knew of the cancer, but he had agreed not to print the story. When I finally obtained Wayne's consent to use it, he naturally decided he should give Jim Bacon the go-ahead too. So I was beaten out of my scoop in a way that I really didn't mind.

Joan Crawford, as big a superstar as any, who still carries herself like a star, once told me that the great love of her life was Greg Bautzer, whom she never married. She had problems in her marriage to Douglas Fairbanks, Jr., because Doug Fairbanks, Sr., and Mary Pickford were then the king and queen of Hollywood and not certain whether they should welcome Joan into their royal circle.

"Uncle Douglas turned out to be adorable to me," Joan told me later. "It was Mary Pickford that I had my doubts about. What could they have expected? Doug and I were only eighteen at the time, a couple of kids. Mary and I became good friends later."

(Mary Pickford was very ill and confined to one upper room in Pickfair in 1971. She saw very few people and had only a few "good" hours a day.)

Joan Crawford was haunted all her life by a rumor that as a young actress she'd made some stag movies so lascivious that if they were ever shown, they would have driven her out of public life.

But the pictures were shown, and they didn't drive her out of public life. They weren't Joan Crawford.

Freely discussing them with me, Joan said, "Louis B. Mayer and Eddie Mannix [head of the MGM studio] looked at those pictures and said that if they were of Joan Crawford, they'd eat them.

They were just pictures of some other chubby girl. When I was sixteen, I weighed 145. I never saw the pictures. If Mayer and Mannix were satisfied that they weren't Joan Crawford, that was enough for everybody and the issue was dropped. But the rumor has lingered on all these years.

"Anyway," added Joan, "stag movies in those days would probably be so innocent now that they could be released as a feature!"

Peggy Lee was a superstar of song. Usually soft and loving, she once bawled out a Las Vegas audience for being noisy, and she refused to continue her show. Then she apologized.

When she appeared at the old Basin Street East in New York, she wore such an unflattering dress that I thought she was pregnant. I went back to her dressing room and asked if she was expecting which wasn't considered very gentlemanly since she was single at the time. It turned out that it was just that kind of a dress.

Raquel Welch with her famous luscious figure is a good actress off stage and offscreen. I know because I was taken in by her.

Sitting in her hotel in Rome with Pat Curtis, the press agent she later married, she kept from me the fact that she'd been married before and had had children.

That trick is often played on reporters, and there is nothing more embarrassing. You've just written a piece about this innocent young kid who's beginning to find out about life and how she's looking for a nice boy who's just as naive as she is—and you discover that she's been married. Oh, well, Jennifer Jones did it to New York reporters thirty years ago.

Of course, not everyone gets away with everything all the time. Take the case of a male celebrity whose name I shall not mention. He was purportedly a great lover. But when a particular star wanted to find out whether he was really great, she found him most disappointing in bed. She happened to write about her unhappy bedtime story in a letter to a friend, revealing intimate details of the "great lover's" unsatisfactory performance. The letter came to the eye of Irving Hoffman, the Broadway press agent, columnist, and prankster. He had copies of the letter sent to friends all over the world, destroying the great lover's reputation.

If that sounds familiar, it's because Jacqueline Susann learned of the story and made it a part of her novel *The Love Machine.*

10
The Making of a Sex Symbol

ACTRESSES have busy minds. They're always changing them. Actresses also have tricky little devices for getting your attention, and some of them are adorable. Some of the aforesaid wisdom I gathered all by myself while observing what was once one of Los Angeles' principal industries, creating sex symbols.

One of my first and most bitter experiences with the mind-changing of a build that was getting a buildup was an interview I did with Marie McDonald, "the blond bleachhead" who, because of her voluptuousness, was known as "The Body."

Marie was very proud of her bust. Marie was very proud of everything she had and, God knows, she had plenty of everything.

The buildup of The Body was just getting launched when the promotion men brought her to New York, lodged her at the Gotham Hotel, and ran the press boys and girls in like sheep to exclaim about her. She was about the first of the Hollywood actresses to get the sex symbol buildup; she had been a hatcheck girl at Leon & Eddie's not long before. Jayne Mansfield did it later. Both ladies had fierce energy and a willingness to go to extremes to get publicity.

Jayne Mansfield used to wake up early in the morning, call her press agent, and say, "What kind of pictures are we going to take of me today?"

A publicist named Bernie Kamber, who later became president of a film company, took me to the Gotham to interview Marie Mc-Donald. It was a day in June, but The Body was in bed with a cold.

The Body could have pleaded illness, but she chose to proceed with the interview. It was mid-afternoon, but she got out of bed and got dressed—in a gold lamé dinner dress. It was a peculiar choice for three P.M. but it bulged in all the right places, leaving no doubt as to how she got her nickname. It was caressingly tight around the bosom, the pelvis, and the buttocks and may have inspired the description, "She looked like a chiffonier with the top drawer pulled out." The Body sort of swam through the room with a breast stroke when she walked.

Marie was always on the defensive, ready for an argument. I mentioned something about the gold lamé dinner dress, and she leaped at me vocally.

"I guess," she said petulantly, "that I am supposed to go around in a sweater all the time."

"I never said that," I replied.

"No, but the photographers always act insulted when I show up in a suit!"

"But you've got nothing to hide," I said.

"You can say that again, bub!" Marie drew a deep breath and held it—and her bosom looked like a couple of balloons. It was a very convincing demonstration of her rightful claim to physical fame. "You can see that I don't need that artificial stuff to give me a figure because, brother, I'm loaded!"

"You sure are, sister," I said, "but out there in Hollywood, where there are so many girls who wear padding . . ."

"Isn't it revolting?" Marie shook her head sadly. "Why, at Paramount I was the only girl there who had her own figure."

At the mention of Paramount, Bernie Kamber and I paid strict attention to every word because several female stars on that lot were noted for their sexy figures.

"Don't tell me," I said, "that Dorothy Lamour wears falsies!"

"Dorothy Lamour's sarongs are specially built," The Body said with a tight little smile.

"Well, I'll never believe that Joan Fontaine wears 'em," I shot back.

The Body laughed at my naiveté.

"Haven't you heard that story?" She alleged that Miss Fontaine had come on the set with a beautifully rounded figure on a very hot day. After complaining about the heat, "She pulled out her bust pads and started fanning herself with them."

I hadn't heard the tale, but in my capacity as a writer on entertainment, specializing at the time in physical culture, I was glad to learn about it. I took it all down in my notebook, with The Body watching me write it and Mr. Kamber witnessing the remarks.

A few days later the interview appeared in the *Los Angeles Daily News,* and there was hell to pay! Everybody involved jumped on Marie for exposing the inside bust information about Hollywood.

Agent Vic Orsatti, Marie's husband, bawled her out by phone. Jimmie Fidler, then a powerful radio commentator who was sort of godfathering the picture business, attacked her on the air. Dorothy Lamour got mad at me.

Marie did just what a lot of other people would have done.

"Wilson's a goddamned liar," she said. "I never said any such thing. In fact, I never even saw him."

Fortunately, Bernie Kamber backed me up, assuring people that Marie had not only said everything I printed but also a lot more that I had decided not to use because "it might get her in trouble."

But Marie's resilience was astonishing. She went about Hollywood charging that I had damaged her reputation.

A few weeks later, my wife and I were in the old Dave's Blue Room in Hollywood with Edith Gwynn, then columnist for the *Hollywood Reporter.* She had defended me and excoriated Marie. We hadn't been there long before we spotted Marie at another table. She saw us at the same time.

Charging over to my table, Marie blasted me with an opening salvo of "Earl, how could you get me in trouble with all my friends like that?"

"Get *you* in trouble!" My wife and I rose to our feet and the tops of our voices at about the same second, with Edith Gwynn joining in. My wife was threatening to belt Marie with her bare fist and knock the head off The Body.

"And I always thought you were a lady!" Marie yelled at my

wife, while Edith Gwynn said, in almost a shriek, "I always knew you weren't."

The Body and I eventually patched up our quarrel and I did several interviews with her over the years, and frequently reported her night club appearances and the various phases of her love life. The Body taught me, in the course of her promotional buildup, one valuable lesson: when interviewing an ambitious actress, always try to have a witness.

In those days starlets signed the infamous seven-year contracts, which they later charged made slaves of them, although when they signed the contracts, they seemed heavenly. A studio started a girl at perhaps $150 a week; the next year her salary went to $200 a week, and the third year, to $250. For a girl who'd been a waitress, night club dancer, or chorus girl $50 to $75 a week seemed a fortune.

The girls were sent to acting school on the studio lot, and they spent hours in the photo gallery, posing for cheesecake pictures that were sent out to decorate the amusement pages of the world. They didn't do much acting; they weren't ready yet. They were occasionally given a walk-on though not necessarily assigned any words. Most found the job much less exciting than it had promised to be when they signed the contract. Moreover, they discovered that there were option clauses in the seven-year contract. The studio had to pick up their option every six months or year, and if it didn't, they weren't starlets anymore.

The studio also had "loan-out" privileges. If it didn't have a picture for a girl, it could loan her to another studio that did, and the other studio paid her studio a rental fee for the starlet. However, the girl didn't get the money—her studio did.

"Servitude," the starlets called it.

The composition of a fascinating biography of the starlet was part of the buildup. To say that she was simply a night club chorus girl was not exciting enough to get newspapers to print big stories and cheesecake pictures. Accordingly, the studio press agent would concoct some tale about her being a countess who had been spirited away from her family by gypsies—or God knows what.

It had been a press agent grinding out such a biography of Marie McDonald who had given her the name, The Body.

The starlet had to memorize this life story and was supposed to tell it as the truth whenever she embarked on a picture exploitation tour.

Frequently, a starlet became trapped in all the lies she was telling and admitted she was the daughter of a taxi driver in Brooklyn or a vegetable peddler in the Bronx.

The tolerant public didn't really care much what her background was, and sometimes it helped a girl to have a phony buildup exposed.

The Marie McDonald life story, which ended in October, 1965, when her body was found slumped over a dressing table in her home in Hidden Hills, California, was an extreme case of a starlet who did not make good.

Cora Marie Frye was her real name. She was born in Burgin, Kentucky, but her mother, a one-time Ziegfeld girl, eagerly pushed her into dancing and singing classes and beauty contests in New York. At fifteen she quit school and went to work as a John Robert Powers model. She was married at sixteen, divorced at seventeen, then performed in the chorus of George White's 1939 *Scandals* and was, for a brief interval, a vocalist with Tommy Dorsey's orchestra. The big opportunity arrived in 1941, when she received the precious starlet's contract with Universal pictures.

Marie dropped the name Frye and took her mother's stage name; she also changed from brunette to blonde. For some reason, she was referred to in the first publicity broadsides as "the Yuk Yuk Girl." But the publicists couldn't fail to notice her body, and thus she became The Body—a title that, she often said later, was probably unfortunate. Without the title, though, Marie probably wouldn't have received as much attention as she did because her acting talent remained undiscovered until her death.

However, she did have a knack of getting publicity and being inventive. When she was married to Harry Karl, the shoe manufacturer who later married Debbie Reynolds—Marie in fact was married twice to Harry Karl—she figured in a sensational "kidnapping." Disappearing from her home in Encino, California, in January, 1957, she came to light wandering in the desert near Indio a day later. She was 100 miles from home.

Marie charged that two men kidnapped her in her pajamas and housecoat and took her on a wild ride during which they stopped off at a delicatessen for a turkey sandwich.

The story didn't have the ring of veracity to detectives. Looking around her home, they found a novel called *The Fuzzy Pink Nightgown*. It concerned an actress who was kidnapped in her pajamas and housecoat by two men who stopped to buy turkey sandwiches.

They also found a ransom note in The Body's mailbox. It was made of words clipped from headlines in a newspaper. Looking further, they found the newspaper from which the words had been clipped—in her fireplace.

Marie admitted months later that she had made up the story because Harry Karl had been suing her for divorce, and she was angry at him. Despite all this, Marie eventually won a $1,000,000 divorce settlement.

And then, suddenly, Marie began to follow the drug route. Suffering from a stomach ulcer, she sought relief in pain-killers. She was treated in Las Vegas for an overdose of sleeping pills. While making an appearance in Sydney, Australia, she disappeared from a psychiatric clinic at dawn in a white hospital gown and blue nylon negligee. Two days later she turned up at her apartment, apparently unharmed but unwilling to talk about her adventure.

In June, 1962, while she was still a very beautiful forty-year-old, I went to see her at the Latin Quarter, where she was having a battle with comedians Pepper Davis and Tony Reese over who was to close the show.

Marie used a simple method to avoid opening the show. She arrived late so that the club had to put Davis and Reese on first—which, of course, meant that Marie would close it.

"And they're not supposed to sing 'Rockabye'—that's one of my songs," Marie kept saying. The comedians claimed they'd been singing it there for two weeks before she had joined the show.

As usual she was enjoying a fight. Marie told the audience about it and later followed the comics into their dressing room, railing at them. She cried every step of the way.

Marie was losing importance in 1962 and always appeared glad to see me, despite our earlier differences. I believed she knew I was sympathetic because I understood some of her weaknesses after writing about her for nearly twenty years.

"Being a woman, I'm entitled to cry, so I cry," she said. "My eyelashes wilt, and I have to be made up all over again."

A year later Marie was tripped up by California state narcotics officers for forging a prescription to obtain the drug percodan, which at the time was popular with narcotics users. A druggist in Sherman Oaks became suspicious of a prescription blank with the name of "Rita Morrison" on it and checked with the druggist whose name was also on it. The druggist said he had not given any Rita Morrison any prescription for percodan.

Wearing dark glasses and looking drawn and haggard, Marie went into court, pleaded guilty, and was fined $250 and placed on three years' probation.

And that's the way it was on October 21, 1965, when her sixth husband, producer Donald Taylor, found her unconscious at her dressing table, lifted her into bed, and called a doctor, who pronounced her dead.

"There were lots of pills around," one policeman said.

"Marie McDonald Dead—Suicide Hinted," proclaimed one headline.

The Los Angeles coroner stated that she died from "acute drug intoxication, either by suicide or accidentally."

Marie died three years after Marilyn Monroe succumbed to an apparent overdose of sleeping pills and liquor—"a probable suicide." The coroner undertook, as he did in the case of the Monroe tragedy, to get a correct answer to the questions about Marie's death from a team of consulting psychiatrists and psychologists.

There was one thing that shocked many of us when Marie was found dead. Most of us had half-forgotten she was still alive. Marilyn Monroe had so far surpassed her as a provocative sex symbol that we didn't think of Marie any longer.

The funeral at Forest Lawn had none of the flamboyance of Marie's busy life. Approximately fifty people attended. The mourners included her sixth husband, her fifth husband, and exactly one actor, according to Associated Press—Efrim Zimbalist, Jr., of "The FBI" television series. Beyond that, nobody in Hollywood got his name on the list in the funeral chapel register. A pity.

Junkets were part of the buildup technique—usually a press junket to the premiere of a film in some "exotic" place, ranging from Honolulu to Tulsa. (There once was a junket to Zanesville, Ohio.) For example, Terry Moore, one of the sex symbols getting a buildup, reaped publicity on a brilliant Hilton Hotel junket to Istan-

bul in June, 1955. Terry's charms had already excited Howard
Hughes and Glenn Davis, the West Point football star who was the
Joe Namath of the period. In addition, she was the guest of Nicky
Hilton, the ex-husband of Elizabeth Taylor.

The excitement around Terry Moore made some of the other stars
—Carol Channing, Diana Lynn, Mona Freeman, Irene Dunne, Ann
Miller, and Merle Oberon—seem a little quiet when we arrived at
what was once Constantinople.

The splendor of the trip was such that the two rival Hollywood
gossip columnists, Louella Parsons and Hedda Hopper, both joined
it. That made it sticky for the stars because an actor was supposed
to declare his loyalty. Louella allegedly had more papers than
Hedda on her syndicate list at the time. Therefore, some of the stars
declared their undying fealty to Louella even if that meant slighting
Hedda—which none of them wanted to do.

With such publicity opportunities, Terry Moore and her advisers
decided that they would go all out. She had already made the news
once, in Korea in 1953 when she did a striptease spoof for the American soldiers, who saw her end up in a mink bra and white ermine
panties. It couldn't have been very erotic with all that clothing covering her charms, but the army brass got nervous when the pictures
were printed. Terry Moore charged that the army had kicked her
out of Korea. She made the complaint in Las Vegas, where she
was wearing a transparent gown. Terry was obviously ahead of her
time in garnering publicity.

Anyway, when our Pan Am Stratocruiser—"The Flying Carpet," a
doubledecker with a bar downstairs—arrived in Istanbul the weekend of June 11, 1955, the Turkish photographers regarded it as a gift
because they'd never had such a wealth of glamour.

Terry Moore was most cooperative. She was always talking
about how strict a Mormon she was and how studious she was—
how she studied Shakespeare for four hours a day. At the same
time, she often left people with the impression that she and Howard
Hughes were going to be married.

Soon after our arrival, a Turkish paper, the *Milliyet* published a
highly indelicate picture of Terry (her legs were not carefully
crossed). She burst into tears when she saw it on the front page and
cried as though she'd been stabbed in the heart. "They trapped me!
They took it from a sneaky angle!" she cried.

We all studied it carefully. There was shapely and bosomy little Terry sitting on a little bench, her hands across her knees, barefoot. But the photographer had shot from such a low angle that he got a complete portrait of her pelvic and derrière area. One got the impression that Terry was wearing no panties, yet there was a little triangle of white there. To students of such matters—and there were several on the junket—it appeared that this little triangle of white was Terry's panties, or that it had been inserted there by a retouch artist to shield the uncovered area.

One could draw all sorts of conclusions, and that's exactly what Istanbul did. The main conclusion was that when the photo was taken, Terry was bare.

"Why, I had on panties—I was fully clothed when it was taken. The photographer asked me to rearrange my dress, and I did it all in good faith!" Terry wept. "Then they retouched it and made it look worse. This is a terrible blow! What will all my Mormon relatives think? And just when I've been working so hard on my Shakespeare."

A nice question of journalistic ethics arose. Louella Parsons, Hedda Hopper, several other newspaper people, and I were all guests of Hilton Hotels on the junket. If we printed a story about Terry's panties (or lack of them), it would not help the hotel. It was a trivial local story, really. Should we telegraph anything home on it? Why not forget the whole thing?

Suddenly all the power of the glamour press seemed to be concentrated in the lobby of this new hotel in Turkey, far from New York and Hollywood, trying to decide whether to expose the story of Terry Moore's bottom to the world. Finally the word came down from upstairs that Louella had volunteered *not* to file the story. Then Hedda agreed that she would *not* file the story. I was a lesser journalist, but I agreed that I would *not* file the story.

I can happily report that to a man we all broke our word and filed the story.

The Hilton Hotel couldn't get the paper to surrender the negatives; in fact, the photographer said, "I've got other pictures that are worse."

That set Terry off on another Niagara. "Mother will have a stroke! And my grandfather, who was a Mormon Bishop . . ."

I tried to be a peacemaker. I went to the *Milliyet* offices. The publisher, Ercument Karacan, offered to have his photographer take some more discreet photos of Terry. She refused to permit that.

"It was the cameraman's fault," she moaned. "I trusted him because he was a Moslem." Terry was reported to be taking sedatives and wasn't able to study Shakespeare even for one hour a day.

To try to right any wrong they'd done, the publisher, editor, and photographer came to the hotel, went up to Terry's bedroom, and presented her with a negative of the revealing picture.

"Oh, thank you so much!" gushed Terry, and she made a little ceremony of burning the offending negative.

Terry flew off home to resume her studies of Shakespeare.

And the publisher, editor, and photographer went back to their offices with smiles on their faces. They had held back the negatives they claimed were more revealing than the one they had printed!

All publicists and press agents agree that the best buildup job ever done was Jayne Mansfield's promotion of herself. She had a stronger career drive than any of the others. She also had an effective Hollywood press agent, Jim Byron. Jayne named her pet Great Dane for him, calling the dog Lord Byron.

Jayne surrendered all privacy and considerable dignity to the daily job of getting her name and picture in the papers. Her home, whether it was a house, apartment, or hotel suite, was always open to reporters, and photographers were constantly running in and out, stumbling over her dogs and cats or her little daughter Jayne Marie.

When she first came to New York in 1955, flaunting a forty-inch bust, with the leading role in *Will Success Spoil Rock Hunter?* Jayne stayed for a few nights in the expensive apartment of a man from the garment district who had climbed his way up to Park Avenue. His apartment had a shocking pink carpet. Jayne arrived with Lord Byron, a photographer, some luggage, and me.

Lord Byron was frisky and immediately began romping around the apartment. After a few turns, which almost upset me and also the Park Avenue admirer who had invited her in, Lord Byron saluted the shocking pink carpet in the way that dogs have always saluted carpets.

Jayne moaned, "What'll I do?" and then to the 120-pound beast, "Once more and I'll spank."

The photographer was there with the idea of getting a picture of Jayne in a towel. She undressed in the bedroom while we waited in the living room. Lord Byron went a little wild when she came out in the towel and charged playfully at her, knocking her over and cutting her leg.

"My, how he's grown up," Jayne said, getting up off the floor. Lord Byron charged at her again, knocking her down again, and Jayne shouted at us, "Why don't you men do something?"

She eventually fed him some hamburger and locked him in the bathroom. Then she sat there sniffling about the loss of her poodle, which she had dyed pink to match her Jaguar. The ASPCA had somehow got the idea that the poodle's death might have been caused by the dye job.

"I broke down and got hysterical when they asked me about that," she told me. "It hurt me so much that anybody would think that."

Jayne was kind-hearted, very much like the little girl whose voice she often used. Her passion for pink and for heart-shaped bathtubs and swimming pools was part of her childishness. She was relentless in her need to be a movie queen and would willingly go to the opening of a drug store or a supermarket to get photographed.

While Jayne was in the stage show, for which she was required to be at the theater well before eight P.M. she would often go to a movie premiere to get photographed with the arriving celebrities, and then rush to her stage show. The absurdity of a stage star going to a movie premiere on the night of a performance never got through to Jayne. After all, if her picture didn't run in New York, maybe it would run in Beirut or Bangkok. It was all part of her buildup, which had been going on for about three years.

Jim Byron planted small items about Jayne in the Hollywood trade paper columns in the very beginning of the buildup, and then —this was before the Broadway play—she went to Florida on a promotional trip for a picture called *Underwater*.

Jane Russell was the star of the film, but Jayne Mansfield in a tight red bathing suit, got all the publicity. Playwright George Axelrod saw a picture of her and cast her in *Will Success*, the base of operations she needed for her continuing exposure.

The show played in Philadelphia before coming to Broadway, and the advance talk about Jayne and her bosom made Jayne Mansfield a star even before the show opened in New York. She was a star purely as the result of publicity.

If Jayne Mansfield had stolen the Florida party right out from under Jane Russell, she was willing to do the same on Broadway. Jayne would attend *anything* if there were photographers there.

Even when she was under the influence of Broadway press agent George Bennett, who adored her and tried to dissuade her from being so eager about publicity, she did not change her mind.

"Public relations is more important than publicity," Bennett assured her.

But Jayne didn't agree with Bennett; she was convinced that the only way to be a star was to get your picture in the paper. In fact, she would often phone reporters herself to give them stories.

One Sunday night she called me about one of her admirers, whom I'd met at a party she attended. He was supposed to have been an Italian count. Jayne had found out the night she phoned me that he was actually a sexton at a church in Long Beach, Long Island. She had learned the facts because he'd just died, and the truth had come out in his obituary.

A girl with dignity would probably have preferred to keep the matter secret. But to Jayne it meant a story for the papers and more pictures of her.

In fact, Jayne wished to improve on the idea by going to the funeral parlor and kissing the forehead of the playboy sexton while photographers snapped her picture. She also wanted to place a rose on his corpse.

"It's ghoulish," George Bennett protested.

Nevertheless Jayne did get the story published about her playboy count being discovered—in death—to be a sexton. And she was proud of it.

Covering Broadway, I sometimes encountered Jayne four or five times a day and night, always on some publicity-seeking mission. She was a freeloader. She simply would not pay. She felt that the restaurants or clubs would get publicity from her being there. Always frank with the photographers, she warned them not to show the scar on her left breast. She was witty, intelligent, and good-humored if a little too squealy at times. She was always good company. There was nothing wrong with her except that she had the compulsion to build herself up as a movie queen.

"What is the secret of your success?" I asked her when she really hadn't achieved any, except for getting into the Broadway show. I was interviewing her for *Playboy,* for which she'd been a Playmate in February, 1955.

"That red skin-tight bathing suit I wore in Florida."

"What happened to it?"

"I washed it, and it shrunk."

"Are you still growing?"

"Growing where?"

"Where else?"

"I stopped growing when I was seventeen at forty inches. I started developing when I was ten. I was terribly sensitive about it, especially when I was thirteen. I wouldn't wear a bra because I thought that if I went without one, that would de-emphasize my bosom, which was what I wanted. It didn't de-emphasize it. Nothing could. I got over my sensitivity, though, and now it's my bread and butter, of course. It used to worry me that everybody stared at my bust. It doesn't worry me so much now, but I would prefer it if they stared more at my face."

Jayne's mother, the former Vera Jeffrey, a schoolteacher, said that Jayne was a child prodigy. If she wasn't, she did at least get married at sixteen while still in high school to Paul Mansfield, and, as she once put it, "We had a baby nine months and ten seconds later."

Jayne's figure was always outstanding, and she earned some money while still a young mother by posing for an art class at Southern Methodist University in Dallas.

"I posed nude once or twice, but mostly I wore a leotard with nothing under it. I didn't make as much when I wore the leotard, but I wasn't so embarrassed.

"I guess I was the only model who ever brought a baby to art class with her. Jayne Marie was just a few months old. We couldn't afford a baby-sitter. I'd stick a bottle in her mouth, and as long as she didn't make any noise, everything was all right. Every so often I'd have to change her diapers."

Her husband got drafted, and while he was away, Jayne was busy thinking about the future. More and more she came to believe that she and her size forty bosom had something to offer Hollywood. When her husband came home, she packed him and Jayne

Marie and her bikinis off to the West Coast and immediately began visiting the movie studios. Her first professional role was on the Lux Video Theater in October 1954, a small part in *The Angel Went AWOL.*

She had her bust in the door by this time and got cast as the lead in a movie, *Hangover,* with Laurence Tierney and John Carradine.

"I often wonder whatever happened to *that,*" Jayne said.

And then she bought the skin-tight red bathing suit. "Not much cleavage, but nobody seemed to mind," she reflected.

She and Paul Mansfield were in the throes of a divorce by the time she hit New York, and she was in love—for the time being, anyway—with Robby Robertson, an airline pilot, a tall, good-looking, adventurous guy with charcoal gray hair, who later married Linda Darnell.

"I'm a big girl, and I have to have a big guy. There aren't any others that are so perfectly made for me and I'm so perfectly made for." She didn't leave any doubt that she was talking about sex.

Jayne would often remember at these moments that she was also in love with Nick Ray, a Hollywood director. Coming into an inheritance of $6,000, she bought a Hollywood home—"to have a home for Jayne Marie," she said. Her husband declared in the divorce action that she wasn't a fit mother and that the *Playboy* pictures proved it.

"I have a very stainless character," Jayne retorted.

In her constant quest for a big, well-muscled man, she went to the Latin Quarter one night to see Mae West's show.

"I want two things here tonight," Jayne said, "a steak for my dog and an introduction to Mr. Universe."

Mr. Universe, Hungarian Mickey Hargitay, was appearing in Mae West's show. He had medals acclaiming him as being "the best built man in the world." Jayne was determined to find out if it was true.

Next thing we knew, Jayne was in love with Mickey Hargitay. They were cooing and purring at El Morocco early one Sunday morning, and Mickey, a giant who was blond and weighed 230 pounds, informed the press that his wife in Indianapolis was divorcing him. He insisted that it was not because of Jayne. Mickey and his wife had been a dance act—"then I got interested in body-building and became Mr. Universe," he added.

"I was present when he spoke to his wife's attorney on the phone," Jayne spoke up. "His wife must be a very sweet woman."

Somebody was crude enough to ask her about Nick Ray. "I've gone from Nicky to Mickey. I love Mickey because I love to be loved back—real strong."

Mickey, 6'2", with biceps like a watermelon and a chest that seemed almost bigger than Jayne's, was surprised but philosophical about the interest that "vomans" took in him.

"The vomans vait for you and grab you and kiss you," he said in his Hungarian accent. "Some nights I get so aggrawated at them. They say, 'Let me feel you muscles.' Dey give you phone numbers. I always velt it should be a man who do dose things. One vomans vant me to pose in her house for five days, and she give me $3,000, but I must pose in no clothes. She say she is a skoolpter."

On June 7, 1956, the headlines blazed: "Mae West's Strong Men in Battle." And Jayne Mansfield really seethed; the headlines didn't say that the battle had been over Jayne Mansfield.

What had happened was that Mae West and her muscle men, including Mickey Hargitay, had reached Washington, and Miss West had called a press conference in her dressing room to refute stories that she was miffed because Mickey had been paying too much attention to Jayne and neglecting her.

Into the argument walked one of Mae West's weight lifters, Chuck Krauser, a healthy lad of twenty-four who evidently caught Mickey by surprise and knocked him to the floor before he knew he was in a fight.

Speaking through cut lips, Mickey explained, "Krauser had a tremendous jallusy for me because Miss West show awfection for me. Miss West has been very opset since I am vith Jayne. All in a sudden, he hit me like a train three times. I get knocked out. I get a cut in the eye and lips, and I hurt my knee ven I fall down unexpectedly."

As he was taken off to the hospital to be mended, Miss West, then sixty-four, called out to the ambulance driver, "Get him back early. We got another show to do."

Mae swaggered about and enjoyed the attention.

"Hargitay was just an upholsterer for years, and then I glorified him and it went to his head," she stated. "He's the old Mr. Universe, last year's model. They've already named a new one. He said I fired him because of Mansfield, but that's not true. The show winds up this week, and I go into summer stock. He started making remarks about how I was jealous of him, and Krauser, who's sort of a boy friend of mine, just knocked him down and beat him up."

Miss West then gave her frank opinion about Jayne.

"As for this Mansfield, I think she's a dangerous publicity-seeker. Maybe if she went to school and learned how to act, she wouldn't have to do that."

Jayne, however, thought that she was doing exactly right.

"A year and a half ago," she told me one night, "I was selling candy at the Wilshire Wiltern Theater in West Los Angeles for about $35 a week between small acting jobs. Men would walk by and say, 'How about a date, honey?' Now I make about $1,250 a week with *Rock Hunter* and television shows and things. And I haven't changed very much physically. I think I looked better then than I do now. I'd just come from Texas, and I had a certain freshness."

Wasn't she doing the cheesecake pretty strong?

"I wouldn't like to see my daughter do cheesecake, but a certain amount is necessary."

After the Broadway show, they made *Rock Hunter* into a movie starring Jayne, with a part reserved for Mickey, and Jayne settled down in her first Beverly Hills house, where she seemed always to be running around in a towel. When we visited there, we would soon have a couple of chihuahuas in our laps and kittens underfoot, while two Great Danes would be howling from a long concrete pen.

And the following week they were getting a pinto pony.

In a breathless voice, Jayne was trotting and bouncing around the house, telling her plans.

"Mickey's going to build us a heart-shaped house with a heart-shaped pool in Bel Air, and we'll have all our dreams come true. We want our careers to boom, and together we will reach the tippy-top of the highest mountain. Mickey has everything every woman has ever dreamed of. It's amazing he has so much."

Mickey, who was living nearby and not yet married to Jayne, looked at her worshipfully. He looked thinner.

"Like Jayne," he said, "I try to keep my waist down and my chest up."

Jayne's passion for publicity never slackened. Hollywood hadn't objected to her getting her name in the papers—and her pictures—until the night of a big welcome party for Sophia Loren at Romanoff's. Sophia, too, has a celebrated bosom; and she was sitting at a table alongside Clifton Webb. Sophia sat erect and ladylike with a warm little smile, when a photographer came over hunting for something a little different.

From somewhere came Jayne. She was in the lowest-cut gown ever seen until then; she wore no bra, and everything was hanging out. Jayne stood just behind Sophia and Clifton Webb and bent over for the photographer. The resulting photograph was as if Jayne had laid her two breasts on a platter for the world to see. One could see between her breasts down to her navel. Jayne's eyes were on fire, as she smiled delightedly at the camera.

"Isn't that the goddamndest picture!" Hollywood was soon asking. It was a remarkable photo for those days; it would be noteworthy even for today.

"She went too far this time," Hollywood said.

To Jayne, though, it was the right move. She had come to the party in that gown hoping to steal the evening from Sophia Loren just as she had stolen a picture from Jane Russell in a red skin-tight swim suit.

"Do you think you went too far?" I asked her.

Jayne answered with another giggle. "I shouldn't have bent over; there was nothing under the dress but me. But I didn't know how I would look bent over."

Jayne was cast in *The Wayward Bus*, probably her best picture, but it seemed that her buildup had gone as far as it could possibly go. She was getting $25,000 a week at the Las Vegas Tropicana, where she and Mickey were already making a muscle man out of their baby son Mickey Jeffrey Palmer Hargitay, Jr. I photographed Mickey holding the baby standing up in the palm of his big hand.

"Ven he is seventeen, he vill be Mr. Universe," predicted Mickey.

"This is a job," Jayne said. "You have to get that eight hours, and you can't drink. Alcohol's no good for your looks."

But Las Vegas was tempting. There a person could never get to bed. She and Mickey liked to gamble. And Jayne thought the house should keep her in chips. The house could only go so far.

"Tell the house we're empty," I heard her say one night in the casino at the Tropicana after she and Mickey had tossed in their last chip.

She and Mickey waited for more chips. None came. But a message arrived from the house: "We're sorry."

A wiser person would have read the danger signals; Jayne didn't. In fact, she had become such a publicity grabber that she was even suspected of faking when she, her husband, and a companion (Jack Drury, her press agent at the time) were missing for sixteen hours after their small boat capsized off the Bahamas. Their boat had tipped while they were water skiing off Nassau. They were picked up by a search ship after they'd been marooned all night on a rock about forty feet wide. Jayne, dressed only in a bathing suit, found the February night sharp and chilly.

Reporters meeting them after their rescue were frankly skeptical, and Mickey Hargitay immediately said, "I know what you are going to say. I love this voman. Do you think I would be damn fool enough to take a chance with her life?"

But how did she happen to have her press agent with her on a water skiing trip?

Drury and Mickey told an alarming story of the boat's tipping over, of Jayne being knocked unconscious, of Mickey saying, "This is it, she's gone, she's gone."

Drury said that as Mickey groped for her and picked her up, unconscious, he saw sharks and screamed, "Sharks, sharks!"

The Nassau Yacht Club butted in to say that no sharks had been seen in those waters for many years.

It is sad to say, but Jayne Mansfield, who had once been a fresh breeze in the newspapers, was becoming a large bore. She had overdone her buildup. Although she'd always protested that she hadn't and wouldn't pose nude, she had quite obviously done so for *Playboy* in 1962 or thereabouts because an obscenity warrant was issued for the arrest of the magazine's publisher Hugh Hefner.

Jayne "writhes about seductively," the lawyers said, and Nassau County District Attorney William Cahn called the photo "hard-core pornography," adding, "I don't think this issue should even have been sold to adults."

Then in Cleveland a judge decided that a movie she'd made, *Promises, Promises,* was obscene. There were three scenes in which Jayne "displayed fully her elephantine charms, accompanied by writhings, squirmings, and gyrations," the judge said after the jury reached its decision.

Characteristically, Jayne called a press conference in Cleveland. She was barefoot.

"There are two scenes in which I appear nude for a brief moment," she said. "The only objections I've heard is that the scenes are not long enough."

American studios lost interest in Jayne, so she went to Italy, where her love for Mickey Hargitay cooled. She had tumbled for Enrique Bomba, the assistant director of a picture in which she starred. Many of her American friends also fell away from her. They didn't like to see her drop Mickey, who was doglike in his devotion to her. When I saw her later, in New York and Rome, she had drifted into the continental way of life, with sex and drinking the most important goals to be achieved each day.

Finally, and with a great rush, just about everything went wrong for Jayne. After a divorce from Mickey, she married producer Matt Cimber. Soon she was divorcing him and becoming very friendly again with Mickey Hargitay.

She left four of her five children in the charge of her daughter Jayne Marie and Mickey while she took off for South America on a personal appearance tour, and her youngest child Tony, who was nine months old, was bundled off by his father, Matt Cimber, to his mother.

The next blow fell in 1967 when Jayne's daughter Jayne Marie, then sixteen, got some publicity. She turned herself into the West Los Angeles police, saying she didn't want to go back to live with her mother because one of her mother's male friends beat her with a strap and hit her. Police took pictures of the welts on her body. Jayne's lawyer and new beau, Samuel S. Brody, protested on Jayne's behalf. Dr. Murray Banks, a psychologist, sided with Jayne, too, saying she had spanked her daughter "like any good parent" and that the punishment "wasn't as severe as it probably should have been."

While that was a real incident, so many things happened to Jayne that one could seldom distinguish the facts from mere publicity. For example, just before she was scheduled to open in a show at the Westbury Music Fair, her secretary phoned *Newsday* to suggest that Mickey Hargitay was flying in to help Jayne divorce Matt Cimber—and wouldn't that be worth a picture?

One year before, just as Jayne was due to open in another show, there'd been a sidewalk encounter between Hargitay and Cimber that appeared to have been arranged in order to create publicity for Jayne.

"It's beginning to look as if Jayne's penchant for publicity is the only contribution she's equipped to make to the stage," wrote Allan Wallach. "Jayne is a young woman who is abundantly endowed, but not notably with talent for acting, singing, or comedy."

When Jayne was decapitated in an auto accident just outside the New Orleans city limits on June 29, 1967, she was thirty-four and not anxious to reach thirty-five. She had been appearing in a supper club in Biloxi, Mississippi, quite removed from the lights of Broadway and the glamour of Hollywood, and she was rushing through the night to do a television interview in New Orleans.

Her death was the most theatrical and dramatic thing that ever happened to her, but it lacked the glamour she adored. It was about 2:25 A.M. She and her attorney boy friend, Samuel S. Brody, were in a Cadillac sedan with three of her children, being driven to New Orleans by Ronald B. Harrison.

Ahead of them was a truck hidden by the mosquito-fog it was spewing out and also by a curve. The Mansfield car slammed into the truck with such force that the roof was peeled off.

Jayne was sitting at the right in the front seat with Brody at her left between her and the chauffeur. Three of her children—Miklos, eight, Zoltan, six, and Maria, three—were asleep in the back seat with four chihuahuas.

Attorney Brody's head was crushed when the sedan's dashboard was crumpled and rammed back against him. Chauffeur Harrison's body was thrown across the highway, Route 90.

Jayne also was hurled out of the car, and her long hair became entangled in the wreckage—causing her head to be severed.

The children were injured, and two of the dogs were killed. A bracelet Jayne had said was worth $10,000 was found in the engine.

Thus exited Jayne Mansfield who never really became a movie queen, the superstar, she had longed to be. But she apparently did go out in a reasonably happy frame of mind. She had visited the Keesler Air Force Base near Biloxi the previous afternoon, and when the boys saw her famous bust, they whistled madly. Those press agents, those Boswells of the Bosom, who had ballyhooed her build so zealously, would have been happy to see that her breasts hadn't lost their appeal in that dozen years of headline hunting.

Jayne was to have been interviewed on television at noon that day on WDSU. She had done two shows at the Biloxi Gold Coast Club, and the club owner had sent her and the group to New Orleans via his car and driver. They had been scheduled to spend the night at the Hotel Roosevelt.

Mickey Hargitay, who remained her close friend after their divorce, had spoken to her a couple of days earlier from New York and planned to fly to New Orleans to visit her and the children. She had been happy about everything, he said.

"I never saw her depressed," he said. "She was always in the clouds no matter what happened."

Perhaps it would have been better for Jayne if she had been unhappy occasionally because some things should have made her unhappy.

Never acknowledging that any adverse occurrences were career setbacks, Jayne always thought of herself as going onward and upward. She was a girl of many sides, a sex symbol who had been married three times and had numerous affairs. At the same time, she was a dutiful mother, who could never have enough children and enough pets, and who took them with her even in the middle of the night.

Jayne never grew up—she only grew out. A psychiatrist gave the opinion that she had the body of an adult but the heart of a little girl and that her house was like a little girl's playhouse.

Jayne wanted to be Marilyn Monroe. When Marilyn died, Jayne tried to replace her as the great American sex figure, to beat out Carroll Baker and the other contestants, but America had already seen all of Jayne, literally and figuratively. She had nothing left to show, and the American film companies weren't interested in her. Jayne had shot her bolt with her never-ending battle to build herself up, and when the great opportunity came, it was too late for her.

She was drinking a quart or more of whiskey or vodka a day at the end, taking diet pills, and getting little sleep, and the toll of dissipation was beginning to show in her face. Frequently, when she felt convivial, she would hunt out some discothèque late at night and go dancing, throwing herself into the dance with the wildness of voodoo witch doctors.

One friend said that she had tried to kill herself at least twice toward the end, partly because she had come to realize that she was always going to be "a second class Marilyn Monroe," never her replacement. But this evidently was the only period that Jayne was ever depressed. She was almost always the optimist, usually believing that tomorrow would bring the stardom that she had long been seeking.

One could moralize and say that it was a wasted life, that Jayne might better have spent all that time trying to learn to act, hoping that publicity would come to her through excellence of performance. But Jayne could not allow herself to take the slow way.

Anyway, with a figure like hers, it was difficult for people to take her seriously.

At her funeral at Pen Argyl, Pennsylvania, Mickey Hargitay, the father of three of her children, was the dominant figure. Like most of her later life, it was a mob scene, with several thousand people waiting along the route to the cemetery. It was July 3, 1967, and there was almost a holiday atmosphere in the crowd. In fact, some people had brought picnic lunches.

The crowd was looking for celebrities. There were no celebrities except Hargitay, but among the 100 floral pieces was one from Bob Hope.

The casket was draped with 500 roses, with a large heart-shaped floral piece in the center. Hargitay kissed the casket before leaving the gravesite in Fairview Cemetery, where Jayne's mother, Mrs. Harry Peers of Dallas, had a family plot.

"Jayne had a soft heart, as soft as butter," Hargitay said. He had sent a spray of thirteen roses, one for each of the years he had been married to Jaynie, as he called her.

Despite their divorce, Hargitay felt that Jayne was legally married to him at the time of her death, and a New Orleans judge who released her body to him seemed to share his opinion.

Jayne's mother wept softly into a handkerchief that she said Jaynie had bought her in Paris when she was there with Mickey on a visit.

It probably would have pleased Jayne that she continued to get publicity after her death. She left no will, and there was a dispute over the division of the estate, which was estimated at about $400,000. Attorney Brody left two wills naming Jayne as his sole heir, but a court ruled that Brody's estranged wife should be named administrator of his estate. Hargitay was to get $180,000 from a double indemnity insurance policy, and Matt Cimber, Jayne's surviving husband, was to get one-sixth of the estate. The twenty-eight room house was sold in a court-ordered auction for $180,000. Jayne owed $70,000 in mortgages on it and $9,000 went for commissions for the sale.

Her five children were the biggest benefactors. She left them some $15,000 each.

The cleverest of all buildup jobs was the one done for Jane Russell and *The Outlaw*, by Russell Birdwell, the veteran Hollywood press agent who had little to work with except Miss Russell in a tight sweater.

"He had Howard Hughes's money behind him," another member of the profession says enviously.

Birdwell believed so strongly in the power of publicity that he endeavored to build himself up at the same time. He wrote articles and ads telling of his prowess as an image-builder. As he sold Miss Russell, he sold himself, and people were convinced he was the greatest.

The Marilyn Monroe buildup was achieved by the public relations staff at Twentieth Century-Fox, headed by Harry Brand and including Perry Lieber and Roy Craft. The latter, who was assigned to Marilyn personally and traveled with her, was so affected by his experiences with her that he eventually gave up the business to operate a small newspaper far from the madness of Hollywood.

The overall effect of Marilyn's buildup was possibly greater than Jane Russell's, and some would argue that it was the number one job. The disclosure that Marilyn had posed nude for a calendar picture—that she had only done the sinful thing because she needed the money—was a masterful piece of press agenting engineered partly by Marilyn herself.

At least Marilyn's bosom was seen out in the open. Though Russell Birdwell induced millions of men to slaver over Jane Russell's measurements, they were seen only in a sweater or in the imagination. She was never really exposed; she was an unfulfilled promise—and that's why I call hers buildup number one.

Is the day of the big buildup over? There are those who even refuse to be stars nowadays because they reject the star system. Actress Barbara Loden, the wife of Elia Kazan, wearied of working in movies under people who knew less about films than she did, decided to try to produce a script she'd written and revised over a period of nine years. Miss Loden, who established herself as a gifted actress in the stage show *After the Fall*, went to various filmmakers, including the underground crowd, and asked how they raised money.

"They wouldn't tell me," she says now.

"One man told me 'New York is built on a rock and Boston is built on money.' I couldn't figure out what he meant until somebody informed me that he had a rich Boston widow who was backing him."

On a trip to Johannesburg, South Africa, she and Kazan met a man of Lithuanian descent who was operating lion country safaris in Florida and California. He seemed to have gold mines and other businesses. They kept in touch. Meeting later on, the friend asked Barbara what she was doing.

"Trying to produce a picture I wrote," she said. And she explained further that films could be made, with small crews and without studios, much more cheaply than in the years of the film moguls.

"How much would it cost?" the friend inquired.

"About $100,000," Barbara Loden said.

"I'll give you the money," he offered.

"You're kidding," she replied, astounded.

But he wasn't. He put up the money and didn't interfere with the production—didn't even ask to be shown the script. He was literally a silent partner. Miss Loden finished *Wanda* and gathered excellent reviews. The Lithuanian was not only happy with the arrangement but asked to be associated with Miss Loden on other projects.

Though other actresses are eagerly waiting to be considered stars, Barbara Loden didn't want that at all and insisted that the billing read "With Barbara Loden" rather than "Starring Barbara Loden."

"The days of the big stars are past," she insists.

"Young people don't want stars as much as they want stories that are true and relevant."

I challenged her that Elliott Gould on his own and without any obvious buildup had become a star. Fans were rushing to see him in everything he's done.

"The word in the business is that they're not going to see his current show," she replied.

Barbara mentioned that we'd seen each other about every five years, when something new happened to her.

"I'll see you five years from now, when you're a star," I said.

"I hope not!" she said.

I cannot believe there will be no more buildups. For even when an actress is attacking the star system, she is building up either herself or a picture and thus using the buildup method she is assailing. As long as there are beautiful, well-endowed, talented actors and actresses, there will be buildups.

11

A Gallery of Rogues: Mike Todd, Joe E. Lewis, and David Merrick

MIKE TODD was unquestionably the most brilliantly successful con man I ever knew on Broadway. Although he died rich, he was for many years the town's most colorful nonpayer of bills, and when forced into bankruptcy in 1947, he had been spending big as usual and listed liabilities of $1,105,616.78 against assets of $275,360.70.

"I spend money as though I had it," he often said as he lit a dollar cigar and ordered champagne for everybody, with never a thought as to how he was going to pay for the cigar, much less the champagne.

In 1946, long before he courted Elizabeth Taylor, he was about to marry Joan Blondell. She had left Dick Powell for him. As was his custom, Mike was pretending to be in the money, though he was broke.

Nobody was more gifted at borrowing money. Mike had already

A Show Business Gallery

*the great and
not so great!*

Humphrey Bogart concentrates on a 1955 script.

Earl Wilson

The young Frank Sinatra and friends.

Dean Martin showing
off his new nose.
David Workman

Lou Costello, half of the Abbott and
Costello comedy team, and Dino—before
his nose job.

Dean Martin is
crowned "Mr.
Wonderful" by
Gail Renshaw,
iss World–U.S.A.
1969, with whom
he was linked
romantically.

Ingrid Bergman in Italy, 1950.

Don Ameche and Hildegard Knef, 1

Latin star Ricardo Montalban a
Gloria de Haven, 19

Ingrid Bergman and her third, Lars Schmidt, 1959.

Liz Taylor and husband, producer Mike Todd. The marriage was the third for both.

Eddie Fisher, Liz's fourth, and Liz during their stormy and ill-fated marriage.

A 1955 photo of a voluptuous Elizabeth Taylor.

Liz Taylor soon after her appearance in MGM's *Father of the Bride.*

The battling Burtons in one of their quieter moments.
Joseph Munster

Durling the filming of *The Comedians* (1967) Elizabeth
Taylor experiments with Cyril Swern's sound equipment.

Liz in *Reflections in a Golden Eye*, 1967. She personally edited the seminude bare-bottomed photos taken by the crew's still-photographer.

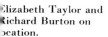

Elizabeth Taylor and Richard Burton on location.

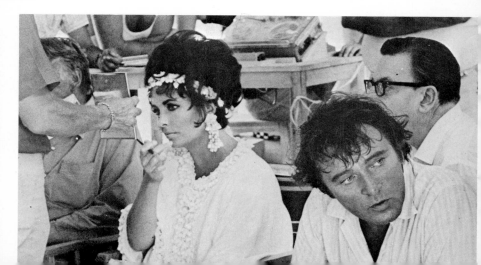

Richard Burton.
Robert Penn

Rex Harrison in his Academy Award winning role as
Julius Caesar with Burton as Marc Antony in the film
spectacular *Cleopatra*. 　　　　　　　*Robert Penn*

Tragedy-prone Dorothy
Dandridge, star of
Porgy and Bess.

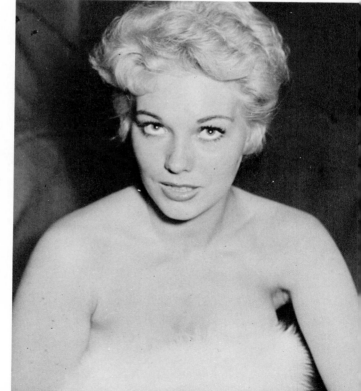

Like many actresses,
Kim Novak helped her
career by posing for
cheesecake photos.

Earl Wilson

Marilyn Monroe at the start of her remarkable career. Her looks and sex appeal took the American viewing public by storm.

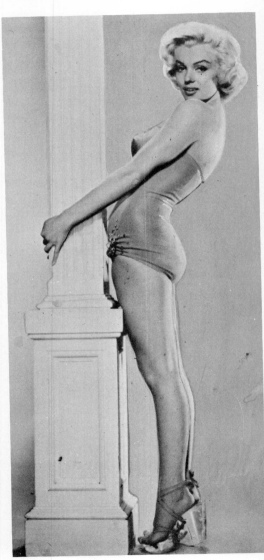

Marilyn Monroe and baseball great Joe DiMaggio, her second husband.

Earl Wilson

Marilyn during her marriage to playwright Arthur Miller. The seemingly ill-suited marriage provided unlimited material for gossip and speculation.

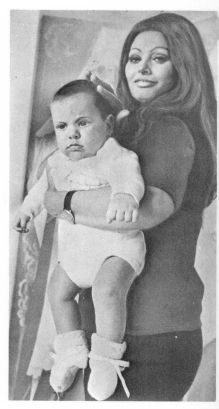

Sophia Loren and child by her Italian director-husband Carlo Ponti.

Grace Kelly with restaurateur
Toots Shor at a party
before her marriage to
Prince Rainier of Monaco.
Earl Wilson

**Jayne Mansfield totally
overshadowed Sophia Loren at
Sophia's first big Hollywood
party, in 1957.**
United Press International

Jayne Mansfield in a
familiar pose.

ne, muscleman husband Mickey
rgitay, and their baby.

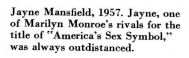

Jayne Mansfield, 1957. Jayne, one
of Marilyn Monroe's rivals for the
title of "America's Sex Symbol,"
was always outdistanced.

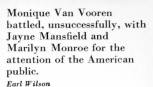

Monique Van Vooren
battled, unsuccessfully, with
Jayne Mansfield and
Marilyn Monroe for the
attention of the American
public.
Earl Wilson

Yvonne de Carlo (lower left).

Sue Ann Langdon (lower
right) shows her bare bottom
in the European version
of *The Rounders*.

Caroll Baker, sexy star of several not-so-successful films in the U.S.,
discovered that her talents were better appreciated in Europe.

Author Jacqueline Susann and her
poodle, the title character in her book
Every Night, Josephine.
Tim Boxer

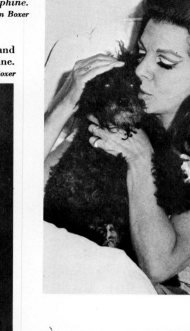

Lucille Ball, perennial television and
screen actress-comedienne.
Tim Boxer

Jane Russell.
Tim Boxer

Jason Robards, Jr.

At right, singer Tony Bennett.
Lower left, Lana Turner
(America's former "sweater girl")
still attracts a crowd of admiring
fans. Lower right, two great
ladies of the American theater:
Lauren Bacall and Ethel Merman.

Tim Boxer

Earl Wilson

Terry Hall and mother Ruby Keeler. Ruby starred in *No, No, Nanette* during its 1970-1971 revival.

Tim Boxer

Actress-turned-executive Joan Crawford (right) and Paulette Goddard.

Tim Boxer

Henry Fonda.

Tim Boxer

Television talk show host Johnny Carson escorts Diana Holland to dinner at the Waldorf Astoria.
Tim Boxer

Xavier Cugat enjoys dinner with his wife Chiaro at La Scala.
Tim Boxer

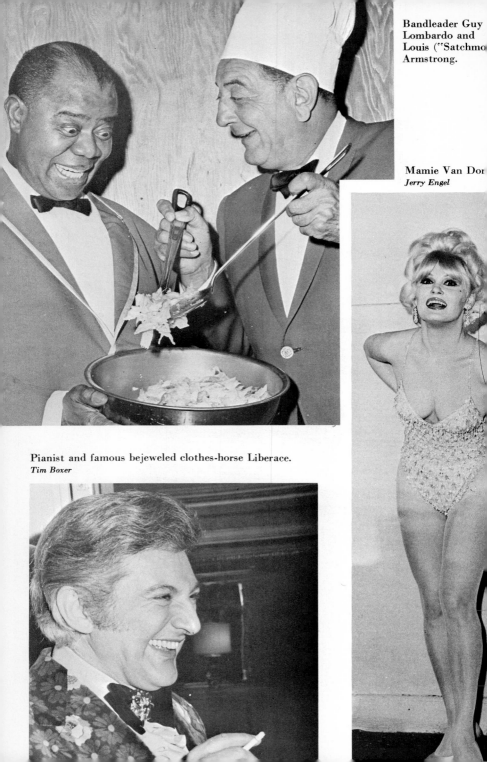

Bandleader Guy Lombardo and Louis ("Satchmo") Armstrong.

Mamie Van Dor
Jerry Engel

Pianist and famous bejeweled clothes-horse Liberace.
Tim Boxer

Ali Mac Graw.
Tim Boxer

Talk show host David Frost with Diahann Carroll.
Tim Boxer

Romantic twosome Julie Christie and Warren Beatty.
Tim Boxer

Dustin Hoffman.   *Alpha Blair*

Sharon Tate, actress and model,
before her gruesome murder.

Dustin Hoffman and Chief Dan George, co-stars of *Little Big Man.*
Alpha Blair

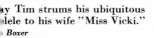
y Tim strums his ubiquitous
lele to his wife "Miss Vicki."
Boxer

Elliot Gould and Jennifer Bogert.

Jude Jade (left) and Sylvia Miles,
ninhibited and outspoken advocates
the new morality in entertainment.
Tim Boxer

Bob Hope, comedian and
tireless entertainer of
America's overseas troops.

Suave and ageless
Cary Grant.
Tim Boxer

Comedian-turned-director Jerry Lewis.
Tim Boxer

Peter Ustinov.
Tim Boxer

Faye Dunaway,
embodiment of the
"Now" look.
Alpha Blair

Johnny Cash, country and western singer.
Tim Boxer

George Harrison, former Beatle.
Tim Boxer

Dionne Warwick,
celebrated singer of Burt
Bacharach's hits.
Tim Boxer

Mick Jagger, notorious lead
singer of The Rolling Stones.
Tim Boxer

Roger Daltrey, of the rock group
The Who, "does his thing"
at the Metropolitan Opera House.
Tim Boxer

Gerome Ragni, co-author (with James
Rado) of the lucrative "American tribal
love-rock musical" *Hair*.
Tim Boxer

Tom Jones, Welsh-born
singer and the object
of female affection.
Tim Boxer

Michael Butler (left), the producer who astounded theatergoers with *Hair*, and
Peter Yarrow, folk singer and songwriter, formerly of Peter, Paul, and Mary.
Tim Boxer

Racquel Welch.

uel Welch in an eye-catching costume.
Tim Boxer

Husband and wife Paula
Prentiss and Dick Benjamin.
Tim Boxer

Jack Lemmon (left) and
Gerry Mulligan and his
wife, Sandy Dennis, celebrate
their completion of *The
Out of Towners* at
Le Directoire, 1969.
Tim Boxer

**Broadway was
astounded by the
frankness of
Oh, Calcutta!
Where does the
theater go from
here?**
Friedman-Abeles

Patricia Hawkins
and Alan Rachins
in a scene from
Oh, Calcutta!
Martha Swope

Oh, Calcutta!, the
first of many
American plays to
show "everything."
Friedman-Abeles

The Midnight Earl
in hippie disguise.
Tim Boxer

Earl takes time out from his rounds
to relax with two actresses from
The Love Machine.

confessed his sad plight to Lee Shubert, the theater owner, who was not known for giving money away.

Shubert phoned another wealthy New Yorker who was similarly taken with Todd's "lovability," for Todd had undeniable charm.

"Want to shoot $1,000 on your friend Mike?" Lee Shubert asked. "He's getting married to Joan Blondell, and he's flat. Shall we each put in a thousand?"

That night Shubert and his friend saw the newlyweds celebrating at a wedding supper. Todd regally sent them a magnum of champagne. He also invited them on the luxurious boat he'd chartered, complete with musicians.

"He was making like a millionaire, but he was really operating on the two grand we'd lent him," snorted Shubert later. Shubert, a millionaire many times over, would never have indulged in such irresponsible flamboyance, but he felt a bit envious of anybody who could carry it off as Mike could.

During his earlier life, when he was dodging creditors or conning them, Mike was gambling that some day he would hit that magic number in the great roulette table of life. He did so with *Around the World in 80 Days*, but it's doubtful if that could have made him any more generous with his own money than he'd been with other people's money in the earlier days.

"Tapped out" was his usual condition. But he had a knack of persuading an angry creditor to lend him still more money. Soon after he became a Broadway personality, I heard the story of Mike's going to a newsstand at the Algonquin Hotel, asking for the morning papers, and offering the clerk a $100 bill.

"I can't change that," the clerk said.

"Who asked you to change it? Keep it," Mike said.

Mike's honesty about having a streak of the con man in him was part of his charm. A one-time carnival barker, he continued to talk like one and would frequently pretend to be less knowledgeable than he was because he thought it made him more colorful. This trait unquestionably made many women want to mother the poor lad.

He was "young Mike Todd," thirty-five, a cocky, cigar-frazzling Broadway promoter, putting together a *Gay New Orleans* for the

New York World's Fair, when I first interviewed him in 1940. He made a typical Todd mistake.

"I'm going to reproduce Beale Street," he said.

"Beale Street," I suggested timidly, "is in Memphis."

"You see?" He shot out a pointed finger. "I'm exactly the guy to do New Orleans. I've never been there. I don't know what it's like. But I know what the public thinks it's like!"

A couple of years later, I wrote an article for the old *Liberty* magazine, "The New Ziegfeld," describing Todd's system of getting angels—how he convinced people who had money that they should give him some.

He woke me one morning in great anger, saying I had to kill the article. He had seen an advance copy. He had phoned the Chicago offices of *Liberty* and had demanded that distribution of the magazine be halted.

His objection was to my reporting that he had induced Gypsy Rose Lee, who was his girl friend at the time, to help finance *Star and Garter,* in which she was starring.

"A guy takes money from a dame—he's a pimp," Mike protested.

Another objection, which he didn't mention, was that his wife Bertha Freshmen didn't know about Gypsy's interest in the show, but she did know about their feelings toward each other; he knew the article would stir up things at the family hearthside.

Liberty couldn't and wouldn't hold up distribution.

Characteristically, Mike thereupon sent his employees to the Times Square newsstands to buy all copies of *Liberty* so that his wife would never see one.

Several years later, when he was moving his office from Broadway to Park Avenue, he looked into a closet and said, "What the hell is this?" Hundreds of old *Liberty* magazines were still there.

Mike's lofty attitude toward his creditors was unbelievable. When his own employees complained that they hadn't been paid for some weeks, he rebuked them. "What are you trying to do—make me lose confidence in myself?" he demanded.

He would then go to the race track and lose thousands.

He had briefly been a gag writer for Olsen & Johnson and could give a comedy twist to any difficult situation. During a crisis with a labor union demanding more money, Mike insisted he was not making a profit and couldn't grant a raise.

"But your publicity department claims you've got a hit show and are getting rich," a reporter pointed out. "What do you say to that?"

"Both departments are functioning perfectly," Mike grinned.

"You're a chiseler," Lee Shubert once told him.

"Now I've been called a chiseler by the champion chiseler," Mike retorted.

"I made you!" Shubert shouted.

"Another one!" Mike puffed his cigar. "I'm gonna form an *I Made Mike Todd Society.*"

When Mike became a Hollywood producer without actually making a Hollywood picture, he got more publicity than the producers who actually produced pictures. His early "producing" was all talk and plans. He always rode planes, claiming that he could only sleep in the air. A couple of times I saw him board midnight planes for Hollywood and loll back in the lounge. A stewardess whom he seemed to know from previous trips took off his shoes and socks and gave him a foot massage.

Completely lacking in responsibility where money was concerned, Todd once borrowed $600,000 from Chicago's Colonel Henry Crown to buy into Delmar race track. En route, he stopped at Joe Schenck's Beverly Hills home, where he was often a house guest. Finding several high-flying acquaintances in a table-stakes poker game, Todd leaped in and lost $60,000. Colonel Crown eventually got 28¢ on the dollar in the bankruptcy action that haunted Todd for nine years. Characteristically, Todd always pretended to be puzzled by the attitude that moneyed people had toward money. It never bothered or impressed him.

"I saw him win seventy thousand dollars in five races in Belmont Park," publisher Billy Wilkerson wrote in the *Hollywood Reporter* when Todd died. "At Delmar, I saw him win nine thousand dollars in the first two races and end up losing twenty-eight thousand—twenty thousand of which he did not have. There was no change in his appearance either time.

"The lovable rogue," as Lee Shubert called him, found *Around the World in 80 Days,* his only picture, a fitting outlet for his art of conning the great. He cajoled big names into making guest appearances, which he called "cameos." Aware that people considered him a charmer, he played himself to the hilt.

Noel Coward was conned into agreeing to bring Todd together

with Sir John Gielgud over lunch in London. Gielgud had no intention of taking a role in the film. Lunching with Todd was just a favor Gielgud was doing for Coward.

"Mike began playing Mike," said author-humorist S. J. Perelman, who wrote (and got an Oscar for) the picture. "He was waving his cigar, slapping his thigh, and spouting carnival talk.

"In less than an hour, Gielgud had his arm around Mike and was asking when he could get his lines. Todd had amazing magnetism."

Borrowing money right up to the end to finish the picture, Todd emerged as the genius he always said he was when it turned out to be a smashing success, with a theme song that haunted the airwaves. Now he was able to bawl out people who had called him "Borrow-a-Million Todd."

Where did he get the money? Tommy Manville's socialite sister Lorraine Dresselhuys loaned him $2,500,000. William S. Paley of CBS put in $1,000,000 for an eight percent interest.

"Walkin' around money," flipped Todd. "Wait until the real scratch starts rollin' in."

In October, 1957, Todd gave one of his biggest flops—"A LITTLE PRIVATE PARTY TONIGHT" it said on the marquee of Madison Square Garden—for the first anniversary of *Around the World*. It was for "18,000 friends." It was shown on CBS, and Mike got paid for that.

"Don't bring presents," the invitation from host and hostess Mike Todd and Liz Taylor said. "Have so many already, we'll share them with you."

Everything went wrong. Mike announced they were going to give away a Cessna plane, three Edsels, and three Fiats as door prizes. Most of the prizes didn't turn up. In addition, the waiters took advantage of the situation, and some of them *sold* champagne instead of giving it to the guests. The beer wagon ran out of beer. Tony Curtis, Red Buttons, and Lou Nova, the heavyweight boxer, had champagne, Nova explaining he'd tipped a waiter $5. Ginger Rogers, not knowing you were supposed to pay the waiter for your supper, stayed hungry and thirsty.

Of course, Mike wasn't to blame for this chaos. He was busy at the television with Senator Hubert Humphrey, a comparatively new friend. Mike kept saying, "I may make this bum President of the United States," but Humphrey enjoyed it.

In keeping with the Madison Square Garden atmosphere, they had a circus parade, and Sir Cedric Hardwicke had a close call when he almost fell off an elephant.

His distress was apparent as the parade moved around the Garden. He was gasping and slumping over when he got off the elephant backstage. I heard a woman who'd just run up call out to him, "Open your collar!" He did. He was red-faced and fighting for breath.

"My damned howdah slipped, and I thought I was going off," Sir Cedric said.

During the confusion, some of the "guests" tried to walk out with stoves, washing machines, and other prizes that were supposed to be donated in drawings. Many of them were stopped at the door. Todd and Liz, who elected to abandon the party before it was over, left word that the "prizes" would be dispensed later. For this Todd was blasted in the press. He was accused of extending his promotion gimmick a few days more. The guests who'd never succeeded in getting champagne unless they paid for it did not forgive Mike until he died—which was in March of the following year.

Mike claimed he owed his success to smoking expensive cigars. "Cigar smokers are successful because they always want to make more money so they can smoke better cigars," he said. He himself had cigars with bands reading, "Made Especially for Mike Todd."

Todd was one of the few fathers who urged a son to squander money. He told Mike, Jr., to live dangerously. Among his prized possessions was a private plane he operated so extravagantly that his son complained.

"My son is gettin' too old for us," he remarked with a wry grin. "He disapproves of my old lady"—that was Liz Taylor—"and me stopping off in New Orleans to have dinner on the way to New York from Palm Springs. I keep tellin' him that you can't take it with you."

After the death in 1971 of George Hamid, Sr., the Lebanon-born owner of the Atlantic City Steel Pier, I came upon a story of how Todd, when well-fixed, treated those who had once befriended him.

The story came from George Hamid, Jr., who told me that when Todd visited Atlantic City one of the many times he was broke, he persuaded Hamid, Sr., to stake him to a considerable sum.

Years later, young Hamid bought some theaters in Atlantic City. Todd, by this time a big success with *Around the World in 80 Days* about to be released, was consigning it to theaters around the country in association with United Artists.

"It was going to be a bonanza and I needed it desperately for June, July and August," Hamid, Jr., said.

But the terms were extremely difficult. First, the theater had to convert to 70-mm. film, and that cost about $25,000. The film company would take 70 percent of the receipts, giving the theater 30 percent.

"It was too steep for me," Hamid, Jr., said. "I begged for a break. United Artists told me the only person who could change it was Mike Todd.

"We went upstairs to Mike's office and I explained my difficulty. I couldn't afford the $25,000 to convert nor could I afford to pay 70 percent.

"Within 10 minutes, Mike ordered United Artists to write a contract in which the first $25,000 of the receipts would go to the theater for conversion—after that we would pay not 70 percent, but 60 percent for four weeks, 50 percent for four weeks, and 35 percent for the balance.

"The United Artists representative said, 'Mike, this is a serious departure from our policy.'

"Mike looked straight at him and in his brusque way said, 'This boy's dad helped me when I really needed it and I'm going to help him now.'"

"The Aristotle of the Bottle," comedian Joe E. Lewis, was given a nationwide drinkathon testimonial on Sunday, September 13, 1970, at the Las Vegas Riviera. To say that it was an "unforgettable night" would be erroneous. The truth is that some of the guests didn't remember the *next day* what had happened the previous night.

The hero of the evening lived up to his reputation for dramatic showmanship by collapsing at the microphone while trying to gurgle a thank-you speech. Many of his fellow imbibers got tears in their eyes, believing he had suffered a stroke on his night of honor.

He was so confused by booze that he forgot the lines of a parody of "My Way," which he had done many times. He began sinking at the knees. Dean Martin and a couple of other guests held him up and assisted him to a wheel chair and an elevator, which took him to his room.

A great gloom descended on the audience that had come from all over to pay homage. Had he suffered another stroke? Was this his exit? While they stood there as though in mourning for the greatest guzzler of them all, I rushed upstairs, arriving just behind the doctor.

Stretched out on the hotel bed was Joe E., inert as if he were in a coma.

I shared the fears of the others. He had been a great friend. Many times I had helped to steer him home.

The doctor stretched out a hand and took Joe's pulse. Instantly recovering, Joe E. opened his eyes, hiccoughed slightly, and smiled weakly.

"Hey, doc," he mumbled, "how about a drink?"

"I don't drink," the doctor replied.

"Not *you! Me!*" Joe E. said.

Joe E.'s self-prescribed treatment worked magically, and a couple of hours later he was in Dino's Den drinking as usual.

He'd given us a truly suspenseful few minutes. Here was a man who had suffered a stroke, diabetes, an ulcer, the loss of most of his liver, removal of polyps from his throat, and a slashing across the face when he was a young comedian. Yet nobody could deny that he was "in pretty good shape for the shape he was in," as they used to say. He adored that one song, the parody to "My Way," which he sang in his official capacity as "Abbott Emeritus" of the Friars. And if the sequence is incorrect here, it's because he never got it quite right, either.

This is about what Joe E. had wanted to say that night:

> My friends all tell me, "Joe,
> You drink too much, your life you're losing,"
> But they're all dead, and I'm still up here,
> Alive and boozing.
> I know I drank a lot,
> Threw up on every highway;
> I was a souse but not a louse,
> I did it my way . . .

I don't like rock and roll;
I do things the rock-and-rye way.
Let's be friendly,
Pick up a Schenley,
And do it my way.

For what is a man without a Scotch?
It's like Tom Jones without a crotch.
My doctor told me the other day;
Yeah, my doctor died just yesterday.
They're full of bunk,
Let's all get drunk—and do it my way.

And now the end is near
At last I face the final curtain
Farewell to my career
I'll leave my broads
To Richard Burton.

Tony Zoppi, the Riviera public relations man who had the idea for this tribute, had been promoting it for weeks. Joe E. was then "between sixty-nine and seventy-one"—and there was no accent on youth. "Swifty" Morgan, the octogenarian "gentleman jockey," was pushed into the dining room in a wheel chair. Joe E., paralyzed on the right side, leaned slightly on the arm of one of his friends when he went to the dais.

Dean Martin said to a startled woman in the audience, "Yeah, I need glasses, honey." The specter of age kept insinuating itself all evening.

Wonderful old Harry Richman stood up and threw out his chest robustly, evoking whistling and handclapping. But when he resorted to simply mouthing the words for his recording of "The Birth of the Blues," a few of those who could remember him in his thirties and early forties could hardly hold back tears.

The crowd gawked at Jack Benny, George Burns, George Jessel, Tony Martin—adults all. This was a night of "fun and laughter," and they remembered Joe E. Lewis' famous lines. "While in the hospital, I took a turn for the nurse" . . . "They say money can't buy love. If they'll give me $5, I'll do my own shopping" . . . "If I had my life to live over, I wouldn't have the strength" . . . "I follow the horses, and the horses I follow, follow the horses" . . . "They don't make girls like that anymore. At least I don't" . . . "My doctor warned me that if I didn't stop drinking, I'd die. But I told him I know more old drunks than old doctors" . . . "Remember the words of Tennyson: you're never drunk as long as you can lie on the floor without holding on."

Dean Martin and Frank Sinatra were scheduled to host the party, but only Dean could make it. According to Dean, Frank was not able to attend because of a recent fight at Caesar's Palace.

"Frank was an unwanted child," Dean said. "Now he's wanted in five states. But you have to give Frank credit—or he'll bust up your joint."

They gave Joe E. Lewis some $1,000 checks for his favorite charities: Santa Ana, Arlington Park, Aqueduct, Belmont, and Churchill Downs.

Joe E. was far ahead of his time with double entendre jokes, which he did inoffensively. His big hit songs in the middle 1940s were "Sam, You Made the Pants Too Long," which is about a tailor who literally did make trousers too long, and "The Groom Couldn't Get In," a double-meaning little lament about a wedding party where the hall was so crowded that the bridegroom couldn't get in.

Joe would intone in his memorable way:

> The Groom couldn't get in.
> The butcher got in, the baker got in,
> His uncle who used to play horses at Jamaica got in.
> But no room for the groom.
> The groom couldn't get in.
> The preacher got in,
> The teacher got in,
> Even Vincent Lopez and his goddamn piano got in.
> But the groom couldn't get in.
> No room for the groom.

Joe E. was also one of the early users of "fractured French," which in later years would be something like "franglaise." "La petite chose," for example, was translated "Your fly is open." In his sly way, Joe E. would sprinkle among the "Voom, voom, voom" musical arrangement and dance steps some social comment, which would hardly be recognized as such by his listeners.

One night a guest in the audience was Bob Harrison, the publisher of *Confidential*. When Joe E. mentioned his presence, there were boos.

"Please, ladies and gentlemen," pleaded Joe E. with a grin, "be fair. With a little bit of a break, this man might now have been making a living as a procurer or selling dope."

Disc jockey Jack Eigen had left the Copacabana lounge in New York to go to Chicago to practice his art.

"Jack Eigen has been forced out," Joe E. said one night, "by a vicious outburst of common decency and good taste."

Joe E. delivered such lines with such bowing and smiling that the people named were usually complimented. One night Vincent Lombardi, the great football coach, was having dinner in Toots Shor's, and Toots was expounding.

"Be fair, Vince, be fair to Tootsie," Joe E. implored him. "Toots may be loudmouth and a big slob, and he may reek of bad taste, but in spite of all that, he's very annoying."

One of Joe E.'s favorite tales of his later years concerned his calling me once in Miami Beach to invite me to the race track. I was in Miami Beach to emcee a police and firemen's charity benefit and was staying with my wife at a hotel not among the best known. But the doorman at the hotel was anxious to impress me with the big names they occasionally had there.

"Do you want to go to the track with me?" Joe E. had asked that afternoon.

"Got to work," I said. "But maybe my wife would like to go."

"It was really your wife I wanted to take," Joe E. said. And he picked her up, and off they went to the races while I stayed at my typewriter. Toward the end of the afternoon, I finished and called for a taxi to take my copy to Western Union.

When I returned, the front doorman was gloating.

"I told you we had a lot of celebrities," he said. "Joe E. Lewis just dropped his tomato off here."

Beloved Joe E. died at 4:13 P.M. Friday, June 4, 1971, at New York Roosevelt Hospital, aged 69. One of the last coherent remarks he uttered was, "How are the Mets doing?"

He had the drinkers' disease, acute liver trouble, plus a kidney condition and diabetes. In keeping with his way of life, he drank—

heavily—right up till the night before he collapsed and sank into a coma.

His long-time friend, Bobby Gordon, ex-dancer and gag writer, found him unconscious in his room and rushed him to the hospital by ambulance.

Riverside Chapel was too small for all the friends who wanted to get in. They stood in the street; they stood in the back of the chapel. Joe E. was Standing Room Only at his funeral. In a way it was sort of a funny funeral. We had all come early to be sure of seats. We waited 45 minutes to an hour. Suddenly the hush in the chapel was broken by soft laughing. The friends began quoting their favorite Joe E. Lewis anecdotes and quips. Soon they were chuckling about Joe E. in almost every row. As somebody said, Joe E. left us laughing.

It's possible that the most acerbic sense of humor on Broadway belongs to producer David Merrick.

When Jackie Gleason warned the stage manager in July, 1960, that he might be out of *Take Me Along* with a stomach ache, Merrick sent back a typical Merrick reply: "Tell Jackie that I sympathize with him deeply because when he has a stomach ache, that's like a giraffe having a sore throat."

Gleason's sensitivity about his weight was well known, and he fired back. "Merrick does have a sense of humor," Gleason retorted. "If he didn't have, he wouldn't look like that."

Actually, Merrick invited this duel of insults. While at the Beverly Hills Hotel, I ran into publicist Bill Doll, who asked me if I'd like to hear Merrick speak his mind about Gleason.

"For publication?" I asked. After all, Gleason was starring in Merrick's show. It wasn't customary for a producer to open up on his star.

"Sure, for publication," Doll said, and we met at the Polo Lounge, where Merrick opened fire. Gleason had been out of the show previously with laryngitis. Merrick raised the question of how Gleason came to be sick.

"I'm sure that Jackie wasn't feigning that illness," Merrick said. "He may have sat up all night in front of an open window wearing wet pajamas, but he had laryngitis."

Gleason claimed that Merrick hated actors.

"Hate them? Not at all. I merely think of them as children, and I consider that I am running a children's camp. I am not a producer but a playground supervisor," Merrick retorted.

It went on like that. Gleason said that Merrick was "not called 'The Abominable Showman' for nothing," and that "Merrick really believes I had a stomach ache because he gives one to everybody near him."

Merrick, formerly a lawyer, felt he had outwitted Gleason early in their dealings. He maintained that he'd heard Gleason was going to "get sick" if he didn't get his own way. Merrick took out a big insurance policy on Gleason's possible nonappearance.

"When he found out that I would make just as much money when he didn't appear, he was furious," Merrick gloated.

Merrick's sense of humor is so sly that it can't always be detected. Two years after the Gleason exchange he reported that there was a champagne shortage in Paris. "Jackie Gleason was there last summer," he explained.

Was he feuding with fellow producer Alex Cohen? "He doesn't have the qualifications to feud with me," Merrick responded loftily.

Merrick seems to enjoy his reputation for being difficult in his relations with actors. One night at a restaurant with Mickey Spillane, he said, "They call me the Mickey Spillane of Shubert Alley."

He had a small war with Anna Maria Alberghetti during the run of *Carnival* and a considerably larger one with Pearl Bailey when she left *Hello, Dolly!* on tour, claiming she was ill.

I happened to be in the middle of that last one.

After Pearl left the show in Dallas and Merrick had to close it in Milwaukee, Merrick wasn't speaking to Pearl. But they both showed up as judges of the Miss Universe Pageant at Miami Beach in July, 1970. They sat in the same judges' box just a few feet apart, went to the same judges' interviews with the contestants, walked through the same lobbies, and went to the same judges' meetings—without speaking to each other.

I was a judge, and Merrick wasn't talking to me either.

Our problem revolved around the Swedish beauty Etan Aronsen. Several months before, one of Merrick's close friends told me that Merrick had introduced Miss Aronsen as his wife at a party at Raffles, saying that they had just been married. Merrick enjoys secrecy and at that time was often able to keep his whereabouts secret from his publicists. Inquiry of the press agents revealed that Merrick had already been asked about the likelihood of getting married and had told them to say, "I'm too young to get married."

When I published the rumor of a marriage and the girl's name, his press agents gave me the gag as the only thing they knew about it, except that he had flown to London. Returning, he was constantly seen with Etan Aronsen, and he remained mysterious about their status. A few times he baffled people by saying, "Meet the future ex-Mrs. Merrick," which, they concluded, indicated that they were married, yet when they thought it over, he hadn't really said precisely that they were married.

Publicly, nobody could pin down the fact that he said they were married, although one night a photographer who had taken their picture was bold enough to ask the lady her name afterward. The photographer said she had replied, "Mrs. Merrick."

Accordingly, Merrick wasn't speaking to me at the time of the beauty pageant—or maybe he was—it's not always easy to tell. He's been known to fire off a telegram, "Never print my name again," and then to smile and make a small joke in Sardi's next day.

Just after I printed the rumor about his marriage I saw him in Sardi's, and he made a noncommittal comment about it. He said something to the effect, "I may have made a mistake. I hear it's hard to get parts for those foreign models."

Now he and Etan Aronsen were at the pageant, and we were all avoiding each other's eyes; it was very uncomfortable.

We judges were interviewing the contestants one noontime. One of the rules stipulated that each contestant had to be interviewed by each judge before going on to the next event.

Then one of the executives called out, "Has everybody talked to Miss Bailey?" and then, "Has everybody talked to Mr. Merrick?"

That was too much for Pearl Bailey, who sang out, "I haven't talked to him, and he ain't talked to me."

Merrick grinned and started talking to Pearl in an indirect way, through me. "Ask her about her health," he suggested.

"Haven't needed one pill since I got rid of Merrick," Pearl replied. "Got over my Merrick's disease and feel just fine."

Pearl had been saying she'd been invited to the White House by the Nixons a few months before and had taken Merrick with her. She made clear she wasn't taking him along on another trip she was making to the White House in a few days.

"She stole a chair the last time," Merrick needled her.

Pearl had to laugh at that one. She hadn't stolen a chair, but she'd gotten such a firm grip on one chair that they all realized she was going to take it home with her. Pearl and Merrick went back to stony silence later, but Pearl did tell me, "Nobody else likes him, but I do. I really have a feeling he likes me too. My daughter passed him on the street, and she was hurt because he didn't smile. I told her, 'Don't worry, honey, that man doesn't smile.'"

He may not smile, but he does chuckle softly. The first time I interviewed him he seemed to me to be so quiet and colorless that I had difficulty getting a story. He was just a lawyer who'd gone into producing. I tried to probe his background as a lawyer, but he didn't care to talk about it. When he was born on November 27, 1912, in St. Louis, they called him David Margulies. When he was thirty-seven in 1949, he produced his first Broadway show, *Clutterbuck,* employing various promotion gimmicks to move it. One device was to have pages in hotel lobbies hustle around singing out "Call for Mr. Clutterbuck." He also ran limerick contests—centered, of course, around Mr. Clutterbuck.

Still he was never personally flamboyant in the manner of Billy Rose or Mike Todd—who never had a fraction of the hits Merrick enjoyed. But flamboyant he could be *professionally,* as when he brought in a show called *Subways Are for Sleeping.* This musical was disliked to a man by the seven New York drama critics. The satanic mind of David Merrick had probably been toying with the idea of his next step in this stunt for some years. By searching the New York phone directories, he found individuals who bore the same names as the critics. He invited these gentlemen to attend the show and, of course, they loved it—not being drama critics—and they permitted their names, photographs, and their high praises of the production to be splashed across a full-page advertisement, which Merrick ran immediately.

The *New York Times* critic Howard Taubman, who had blasted the show, discovered in amazement that the other Howard Taubman adored it. "A triumph!" exclaimed the other Taubman. "Only once in thirty years!"

The other reviewers got similar tweaks in the whiskers by Merrick's quoting their name-alikes. It cost Merrick several thousand dollars, and it probably didn't fool the public a bit because the newspapers printed stories about the gag ad. It was just an expensive joke on the critics—"a delicious gag," Merrick called it.

The quotes were mostly quite outrageous. John Chapman in the *New York Daily News* had called the show, "noisy, energetic, and good-natured." Merrick's John Chapman called it, "The best musical of the century."

When the *New York Herald Tribune* discovered the fakery, it killed the ad.

Merrick engaged in running battles with the critics. He had one with Walter Kerr, claiming that Kerr's wife Jean influenced him. If she nudged Walter, he laughed and liked it, Merrick hinted.

Kerr admitted that this could be true. "She likes me, that crazy girl," Kerr replied. "Surely, somewhere, sometime, someone must have liked you well enough, Mr. Merrick, to give you a dig with an elbow. No? Ah, well."

12
One of the Barrymores

THE great Barrymores are all dust.

There is no royal family of the theater to replace Ethel, John, and Lionel. Except for their old movies now seen on television, most memories of the Barrymores will be Jack Barrymore's boozy performances in *My Dear Children*, when people came to see whether or not he was drunk.

That was in 1939. The play was "an embarrassing burlesque of his own life," one critic said; his co-star was his wife Elaine Barrie, and the director was a comparatively new participant in the theater, Otto Preminger. "The Great Profile" died in 1942 at age sixty. It was a sad final curtain for the handsome Hamlet of a generation before, whose good looks aroused women to the best or worst that was in them.

The great Barrymores were already at the end of their careers when I began covering Broadway. Though I knew all three slightly, it was John's daughter Diana whom I knew best, and I was not far away when she played the last scene of her life and lost out to love and liquor.

"I have the family sickness—drinking," Diana frequently told me.

"I am always fighting the battle of the bottle. This is the stuff that killed Daddy, and it will kill me."

She called the turn correctly. When she died at thirty-eight after a final party at her second-floor rear apartment at 33 East 61st Street, across from the Colony Restaurant where she'd made a final appeal for more whiskey, she was clearly a victim of drinking and sleeping pills, although it was called a heart attack.

Diana's death caused me to write a column on January 27, 1960, headlined: "The Killers: Pills and Liquor."

> The strange death of Diana Barrymore emphasizes the peril of the liquor-and-sleeping pills combination, which Miss Barrymore resorted to when depressed—as do many others on Broadway.
>
> Miss Barrymore, when in her cups, could be served water instead of vodka without detecting the difference. Then she'd forget how many pills she'd taken. "Did I just take a pill or didn't I?" she asked a friend a few nights ago. "Oh, well, I'll take another one," she said, adding that hers had to be strong enough to "knock out a horse, or a Barrymore."
>
> Quite a few headlined mystery deaths have been due to this combination. An investigation of how users get enough pills to hoard them for their gloomy nights might be in order.

Marilyn Monroe and columnist Dorothy Kilgallen, were of course among those who went the route that Diana took.

Diana was twenty-five—and unemployed—when I first met her back at Christmas time 1948, when she was a shapely, vivacious brunette with very little acting experience. She was already, as she said, "making personal appearances at the Unemployment Insurance queue."

They got $18.50 a week in those days. "That $70 a month is not to be sneezed at," she said. "They all do it, including the *big* people. The other day there was a very prominent dame in a mink coat in front of me and a very prominent drunk behind me." The specter of unemployment never troubled her for long, however, because the royal family of the theater had all gone through it.

"Father," she told me, "once had an apartment without a bed in Washington Square. He could afford either a bed or art materials but not both. He bought the art materials and slept on his books. My aunt Ethel, a famous beauty, had twelve flops before she got *Captain Jinks.*

"I had a millionaire who wanted to marry me, but he said his wife would not act. I said that his wife wasn't going to be me. I'm afraid that when I'm sixty, I'm going to be starving in a cheap hotel room on my unemployment insurance."

Diana told me all this sitting in her East Side apartment surrounded by Christmas presents and numerous pictures of her father, uncle, and aunt. It was all rather light and merry as she recounted how one of her friends, Count So-and-So, had "left" his gold and diamond cigarette case for a while "at the Provident Loan Company."

"The family disease" held Diana in its grip as the years went on. Then one day an opportunity arose for her to get her own television talk show.

It was to originate from the Grand Central Building, and I recall it clearly because she asked me to be her first guest. She would interview me. Arriving at the studio that night a little ahead of time because I had expected Diana to be a little nervous, I found the place almost deserted. Diana had not arrived; nor did she.

After waiting for a half hour, I left, feeling very much snubbed. Diana, of course, had been "under the weather." The next week Faye Emerson, the wife of Elliott Roosevelt, took over the program. She was not only a smash success, but in a few weeks she was one of the biggest things in television—especially around the bosom. Her cleavage was gag material for columnists and comedians for weeks.

Diana eventually arrived at a point in her life when she wanted desperately to do any kind of acting. She was candid, friendly, easy to get along with, and still young, and she told her troubles to the whole world. She had been drinking, she said, since she was fourteen. In her determination to act, she had taken refuge in another kind of acting. She had to put on an act—in the restaurants, night clubs, and theaters—pretending that she had cured herself of drinking when she knew that she had not and probably never would. In her own way, she was as afflicted as Marilyn Monroe was by her heritage. Marilyn was haunted always by the terror that she would go insane as some of her family had, and Diana lived with the fear that she had the Barrymore "family sickness" and that it was incurable.

In January, 1956, Diana voluntarily entered a psychiatric sanitarium in Westchester County to fight alcoholism. And she told me that she would gladly discuss it for publication.

"I'd be very delighted if you'd just write that Baby—that's me—decided she can't do it by herself because she thinks it's psychiatric, so she's going away," she said, then added, "I've signed in for six months." Her half-brother Leonard Thomas was footing the bill. "And there'll be plenty to foot, but it's all right because he just struck uranium."

She had been in street fights, she had been arrested, she had lost jobs.

"I've been in hospitals, and I've tried Alcoholics Anonymous twice. I was just recently in Doctors Hospital, but one week later, wham! Right back on the old bottle again."

Diana went back in memory to discussions she'd had with her father about drinking. "I wasn't very old then—just old enough to mix his drinks. At that time I drank like people. Now I drink like an idiot. One hundred proof bourbon if I can get it—rather expensive. When I'm alone, I drink, and when I've got friends in, I drink. People with my problem drink any old when."

Already she'd been married three times, but in 1956 she was single, although she'd fallen tragically in love with Tennessee Williams. Her friends lectured her constantly that this could never mean anything. Nevertheless she hoped it would with the same desperation that drove her to attempt to be an actress.

Evidently Diana wanted the public to keep *au courant* with her progress in the Battle of the Bottle. She phoned me in May, 1956, to tell me she had quit drinking, just on will power, and wasn't even touching wine while appearing in the play *The Ivory Branch* at the Provincetown Playhouse. She was earning $30 a week.

The treatment at the sanitarium had scared her.

"They gave me the same suite Daddy had," she said. "I decided I didn't want to be one of those drunks who came reeling into the place. One man very proudly told me he had been a patient there seventy-eight times. I'm on the dry, and I'm going to stay on the dry. I can look in the mirror now. My face is getting back its heart shape. I said to myself the other day, 'You're not so bad looking, my dear, when you're not drinking.'"

Eventually, however, she went off the wagon with a crash. Then, in 1958, she notified me that she was trying again, this time with Antibuse.

"I've been on it two months today. They say that if you drink while taking Antibuse, you won't die, but you'll wish you could. For two months now I've been swigging ginger ale and no-cal orange soda." She was in the Tennessee Williams play *A Streetcar Named Desire* in Fort Lee, New Jersey.

The next year was torture for her. She openly told people of her love for Tennessee Williams. "If I could only get that monkey off my back," Diana said, meaning Williams.

1960 came, and on New Year's night Diana phoned me that there had been a row in Harold's Show Spot on West 45th Street involving her escort and that she had been an innocent witness. A singer had been hit, and the singer had accused Diana's escort.

"It was my first drink in two years," she said. "I just had a little vodka in my orange juice."

Later the same night she called me back in considerable triumph to say that she hadn't had a real drink. "The bartender told me there wasn't any vodka in my orange juice. When you haven't been drinking for so long, it's hard to tell."

But she had been skirting around it, drinking light wine and vermouth, which she thought weren't threats to her sobriety.

On the night of Saturday, January 24, Diana was drinking again. Mrs. Essee Kupcinet, wife of my friend Irv Kupcinet, the popular Chicago columnist, had been with her and was trying to prevent her from drinking. Mrs. Kupcinet took a drink out of her hand and left her to return to her hotel.

Soon Diana ran out of liquor. She phoned the Colony Restaurant about one A.M. and pleaded with Gene Cavallero, Jr., the owner, to let her have a couple of bottles of whiskey.

"I can't help you," he apologized. "It's illegal to sell in bottles or to send anything out."

"I can come over for it," Diana said.

"Everything's locked up," Cavallero stalled.

She got no liquor there, but she may have succeeded elsewhere. She reached a couple of men friends, one of whom dropped in on her at 3:30 A.M. Monday.

"She was very upset," he said later. "She was moaning that all her pals had walked out on her. That wasn't unusual for her." He stayed till 5:30 A.M.

Another friend, an actor, said, "I walked out on her when she was drinking. God, I never should have. She phoned me, and I hung up on her."

A maid found Diana dead in bed.

She left no notes, nothing.

That was 1960. Diana, who wanted to be remembered, was recalled only with pity. Eleven years later, however, her name appeared in the New York papers in a bank advertisement. It was an "unclaimed deposit" ad, and it stated that Diana Barrymore still had a deposit there of $16.

13
Bogie and Bacall

ON the brisk, snowy night of January 29, 1945, nine days after Franklin D. Roosevelt had begun his fourth term as president, I crunched along 52nd Street, in New York City, to have a drink at the 21 Club with Humphrey Bogart. I hoped the drink would give me courage enough to ask Bogart, still a married man, whether he was going to marry a young model turned actress named Lauren Bacall.

It was a vastly exciting, dramatic, and historic winter, and the news I was hunting was trifling everywhere except in the world of show business.

"The best dressed men," the saying went in January, 1945, "are those in uniform." The Allies had Hitler, Mussolini, and Japan on the run, but V-E Day, Hiroshima, and V-J Day were still a few months in the future. Vice-President Harry Truman had no image, and the world was hardly aware that he had a daughter named Margaret. Most of the country didn't know much about Lauren Bacall, either, though it was to learn quickly when she sat on Harry Truman's piano. In New York City, the comedians were pecking away at Mayor Butch LaGuardia's inadequate snow removal, alleging that his method was just to push it back and forth in the street.

"The Little Flower," they said, "doesn't remove the snow. He wears it out."

Franklin D. Roosevelt, who would be going to Yalta in a matter of four or five days to meet with Churchill and Stalin, was something of a god to many people in the forties. To others he was the devil. To Bogie he was "The Man." On the night that I saw Bogart, the newsstands displayed an issue of the *Saturday Evening Post* featuring an article by Bogart—"I Stuck My Neck Out"—describing how he'd supported FDR for a fourth term. Later, he joyously quoted from one of three thousand letters he had received in response to the article: "No matter who wins the election, you are a son of a bitch." Bogie framed it.

Bogart was one of the darlings of the decade not as much for his acting as for his public mischievousness. He and his wife Mayo Methot, whom he called "Sluggy" because she was always slugging him, were known as the Battling Bogarts. When they went to Africa to entertain the troops for USO camp shows, their friend Peter Lorre prophesied, "You'll get kicked out of Africa."

"I've got news for you," Bogart reported after they returned. "We also got kicked out of Italy."

Anyway, having a drink with Bogart was quite a distinction even in 1945. He had been nominated for an Oscar for *Casablanca*, with Ingrid Bergman in 1943, and he was one of the ten top box office stars, yet, though we admired him even then, nobody among us suspected there'd ever be a Bogart cult.

He had come to New York by way of his friend Louis Bromfield's farm near Mansfield, Ohio, to promote his newest movie *To Have and Have Not* with Lauren Bacall as his leading lady.

Miss Bacall had already been widely promoted as "The Look." Not "The New Look" of several years later—just "The Look." Miss Bacall would point her face, nose, and chin downward and turn her eyes upward. It has a devastatingly sexy effect even now, but in 1945 it was stupendous.

Traveling with Bogie to New York was my good friend Jack Diamond, a movie publicist of extraordinary ability whose function it was to keep Bogie out of trouble or get him into it, as circumstances required. Diamond appeared to have a publicity "natural" on his hands—a romance between the two stars of the picture he was promoting. Unfortunately, an alert newspaperman knowing

Diamond's publicity touch was skeptical of any real attachment between Bogart and Bacall, who was not yet old enough to vote and about twenty-three years younger than Bogie. The story was so good it is possible that it was "encouraged" by Mr. Diamond. That was the way I felt—and he was my friend.

Still, Bogart was never known to engage in publicity frauds. He lived the year around in a world of make-believe, false faces, and toupées, but he remained a realist who could stare you down and say, "Now let's cut the crap and have a drink." So was there truth to the rumors?

On a previous trip to New York, Bogie had bought me a drink at 21, and we'd discussed Lana Turner's attractive backside, whereupon I remarked, "Lana's callipygian."

"She's what?" He put down his drink and glared.

"She's callipygian. That's an adjective from the Greek meaning to have beautiful buttocks," I said.

"You're making that up."

"It's in the dictionary," I said. I knew it was because I had looked it up a few days before.

"You're lying!" He called for a phone and asked the operator to get the *New York Times*. She must have been surprised when he told the operator, "This is Humphrey Bogart. I'm at 21 with Earl Wilson having an argument. Is there such a word as callipygian, and if there is, what does it mean?"

The operator connected him with the reference department, and Bogie repeated his inquiry. He sipped his drink while we waited. The reference department eventually gave him its report.

Bogie glowered. "I'll be a son of a bitch," he said. "There is such a word, and it means a dame that's got a beautiful ass."

One Saturday my wife and I had had a long lunch with the Battling Bogarts, who were appropriately battling that day. Sluggy was not the most tactful of wives. She called Bogie "Pa" and gave the impression that he was about ready for retirement.

"If Pa can keep his teeth and his hair for five years, we'll be all set," she said, evidently meaning that they could settle down and fight in peace.

Then Sluggy got sluggy, and the lunch broke up. They went to their hotel. When I phoned later to ask whether there had been any casualties, Bogie said, "Hello," and then there was the crashing sound of glass being splintered against the wall.

"My wife just missed me with an ashtray," he said coolly. "I don't know what's wrong with her aim lately. Maybe she's thrown her arm out."

By 1945, when the marriage was over and Bogart was again a bachelor, George Frazier, then entertainment editor at *Life,* sat down to write a profile of Bogart. With his wild sense of humor, Bogie pretended that *he* was going to write a profile of Frazier.

"Now, let's see," Bogart said one day, getting Frazier on the phone, "you attended Berlitz, where you played left tackle, and Dale Carnegie's, where you alienated Dale Carnegie, which is hard to do. You were sort of a dull creep, weren't you?"

Thereupon Bogie dispatched a wire to *Life:*

> George Frazier life story impossible. He has absolutely no color. Nothin happened to him except that he was born, and his wife sleeps in the top of his pajamas. Suggest cancelling entire story.

Looking back on those days, I feel it must have been the most amusing phase of New York show business history. The "Oomph Girl" Ann Sheridan was at the Stork Club Cub Room every night with her great love Steve Hannegan, and she explained that "Oomph is a noise a fat man makes when he bends over to tie his shoelaces in a phone booth."

Edgar Bergen had just given an engagement ring to a beautiful model named Frances Westerman, and I rushed over to El Morocco one afternoon to see it and write about it. They would one day become the parents of Candice Bergen. Red Skelton was in town on furlough from Camp Patrick Henry, Virginia, where he was a private. Carole Landis, who would ultimately kill herself over Rex Harrison, was a sexpot in a Broadway show called *A Lady Says Yes.* The Jack Benny and Fred Allen radio shows were big Sunday night attractions, and comedian Morey Amsterdam was causing trouble, claiming that the hit song "Rum and Coca-Cola" had been burgled from him.

Mike Todd was just emerging as a Diamond Jim Brady type of big spender. The night before, Todd had given a $10,000 party at Tavern-on-the-Green to celebrate the opening of his musical *Up in Central Park.* My wife and I were among the approximately six hundred guests who rode to the restaurant in horse-drawn victorias.

Mike Todd, who had not yet met and married Elizabeth Taylor, was then wedded to Bertha Freshman. Frequently during the party, Bertha could be seen kissing the *New York World-Telegram* critic Burton Rascoe. Chewing hard on a big cigar, that was to become his trademark, Todd protested, "No play's so bad that a producer's wife has to kiss a drama critic."

That was one of the few parties I've attended at which the bartender gave us a full bottle of champagne and told us to take it with us when we asked him for a glass. When we left at four A.M., the horse-drawn victorias were no longer available. But taxis were there to replace them. And a doorman stepped up and softly said as we left, "The cab ride home will be compliments of Mr. Todd."

They were carefree, exciting days in the world of show business, and I thought that to be in the thick of them was heaven.

Sitting at a corner table and wearing a white flower in his lapel, Bogart was leisurely propped against the wall when I joined him and Jack Diamond. A devotee of martinis at that time, Bogie had doubtless imbibed a couple, but he was still sober and in extraordinarily good humor.

Leaning over Bogart's table was Jack Kriendler, the tall, erect, mustached co-founder of "Jack and Charlie's 21." In those days it was the hangout of Robert Benchley, George Jean Nathan, Billy Rose, and Monte Woolley.

Although 21 did not allow autograph hounds or celebrity buffs on the premises, Bogie inevitably attracted people to his table.

A man from Mexico came over to inquire after the health of one of Bogie's sisters—only to learn that she had died years ago.

A sailor sat down uninvited and began reminiscing about events twenty years earlier. "You're an old bastard, aren't you?" Bogie said.

"No, about the same age as you," the sailor retorted.

Bogie liked that.

Then an army lieutenant arrived at the table to report that he had unfortunately stepped through Bogie's hat and wished to pay for necessary repairs or a replacement.

How Bogart's hat got in the path of the lieutenant's foot is a little misty now. But Bogart forgave him, and the lieutenant then undertook to pick an argument with him about a special tommy-gun Bogie had used in one of his movies. The lieutenant was skeptical of Bogie's cleverness with the weapon. At that time Bogie, John Wayne, and Errol Flynn were winning the war almost by themselves in the movies. As one critic had written, "Errol Flynn was never braver."

"Remember, you're an officer and a gentleman," Bogart remarked to the lieutenant. He was feeling so happy that he was discouraging arguments.

"The appointment as a gentleman is only temporary," the lieutenant snorted.

"You're proving that." Bogart gave the lieutenant his back, and he left the table.

With the table to ourselves, we were maneuvered by Jack Diamond into a discussion of the new movie. That led immediately into talk about the new actress.

Finding Bogie in such high spirits, I decided to pop the question at once—I didn't want the precious opportunity to escape.

"Do you intend to marry Lauren Bacall?" I asked him.

"You're goddamned right!" His hand and the glass in it hit the table. "As soon as I get my divorce, I'm going to marry Baby."

I had my notebook open. He saw me writing down his noteworthy scoop, but he offered no objection. In fact, he seemed elated to have said it to a columnist. And he began saying it all over the 21 Club in a remarkable example of a man wearing his heart on his sleeve.

"Did you ever see Baby?" Bogie suddenly asked me. (I was still writing furiously in my notebook.)

"I've done a telephone interview with her from here to Hollywood, and that's all," I said.

"We set that up for him," Jack Diamond informed Bogie.

"Well, let's drink one to Baby!" He paused. "I shoot off my mouth too much," he said. "But you know something? I'll let you in on a secret. I'm in love again—at my age!"

That the thrice married movie tough guy with the rough-cut face was in love again became increasingly evident to everybody within earshot that night. Digging into his suit, Bogart produced his wallet and extracted two snapshots.

"Look"—he was beaming upon the snapshots—"she's a real Joe!

"Doesn't wear shoes." That meant she was down to earth.

"Right off the streets of New York." He had come from New York himself, so that was complimentary too.

We were witnessing a moment of truth with a great guy. Those snapshots he was showing us were personal and important. They had shaken up a man reputedly unshakable. Bogart was irreverent, iconoclastic, disrespectful toward people on pedestals; he was civilized, urbane, intelligent; he couldn't tolerate the platitudinous, and I don't think he could do anything caddish or ungentlemanly —except during his moments of extreme overindulgence, and, of course, there were such moments. They were the only times that Bogart was ever boring.

Primed by still another drink, his enthusiasm for Miss Bacall increased, and his proclamations grew somewhat louder. But since he was generally liked by everybody at 21, he was forgiven by the other customers, who simply smiled.

"Are you still talking about her?" one customer finally inquired. "You're very boring."

Bogart just laughed. "I'm in love. Do you mind?" he grinned.

When we eventually decided to leave, Bogart called for his hat, having forgotten the Army lieutenant's warning about it. The 21 Club has always had one of the world's best hatcheck systems, but there must have been an overflow of hats that night. Bogart's hat had sure as hell been stepped in. It had no top.

Nevertheless, the granite-chinned movie star put on the hat and wore it out into the cold January night, with the top of his head bare. Humphrey Bogart was not a man that Stetson or Cavanaugh would be proud to call their own, but he was a happy man.

"You'll want to see Baby when she comes to town in a couple of days," he said. "You'll fall in love with her like everybody else has. She's a real Joe. Do you think you can stand meeting her? Do you think you can take it?"

Pocketing my notebook and my scoop, I went home and wrote my column about Bogie and Bacall. About six days later, I met Bacall, the "real Joe" who didn't wear shoes.

"Bogie was glad that you got the scoop since you're a young guy just starting," Jack Diamond had reported a couple of days later.

It was the day of the Big Buildup. Lauren Bacall had arrived on the 20th Century Limited, the deluxe New York Central train, as movie stars did in the forties. The arrival of a movie queen was sufficiently exciting to cause a mob scene at Grand Central, and each newspaper usually assigned a photographer and feature writer to cover the event. Miss Bacall went as soon as possible to the Gotham Hotel, where Bogart was already registered. Lauren Bacall wasn't yet twenty-one, and she hadn't yet been seen on the screen, but she was about to become a movie queen and the bride of a top movie star.

While she was in another part of the suite freshening up, Jack Diamond remarked, "That girl changing her dress in there doesn't know she's a star. She began to suspect it when they gave her a big reception in Chicago. But she'll find out in this town that it's really true. She's a star." He spoke the word "star" with reverence, for he was a creator of stars.

From the very first, Lauren Bacall had class—something beyond star quality. Because of her age she needed it. She knew that, because of her buildup, she was already resented by some people who had never seen her and that she had to convert those critics. Furthermore, the term "the new symbol of sex" had been tossed about, stirring some hostility among more conservative elements.

The Look was supposed to be sexy, and that's what we watched for as she swung out in handsome beige slacks, gold slippers, and a rather unimpressive sweater (she is small-chested). She walked into the room in a long, loose model's glide, wearing no stockings, accompanied by a brown dog she called Droopy. When she ate her chicken salad, Miss Bacall gave Droopy some crumbs from her plate.

After a time (goaded into it, I imagine, by Jack Diamond), Miss Bacall moved over and sat on the couch beside me and tucked her feet under her. (My paper, I must explain, had sent not one but two glamour specialists to scrutinize Miss Bacall. It hadn't meant to send two, but my wife had gone along with me.)

"How do you feel about becoming the new symbol of sex?" I asked Miss Bacall.

She flashed a nice smile. "I haven't thought of myself like that at all." She spoke in a light, joking manner, tossing back her hair, which one of the ladies of the press had described as the dark gold of corn syrup. "I don't know what all this is—but it's a lot of fun. It's just been the maddest thing you ever saw in your life. People draped on stairways gaping at me. And me sitting at the station to give the photographers leg art. Why, nobody even looked at me in Hollywood, so I can't believe this. I think I'm dreaming!"

She turned on another wide smile and tossed her head back again. She always had the bearing of a lady.

"You're pretty long-legged," I said.

"Yes, that's where I get my height. Somebody called me a long-leggedy beastie."

As Jack Diamond had predicted, Lauren Bacall was overwhelmed by her New York reception and bewildered about becoming a star.

"They just want to see me, to see how good or bad I am," she remarked to me. "Isn't that it? I'm on trial?"

If she was indeed on trial, she certainly triumphed at her first big meeting with the New York press, and she's been its favorite ever since. At first she captivated them with her own naturalness, and later she was regarded in an almost sacred light because she was Bogie's girl, his wife—and, finally, his widow.

"You used to be an usherette around here, didn't you?" I asked her.

"Yes, it was fun. I did it while I was going to drama classes. There I was, saying, 'Tickets, please,' in my most resonant voice . . ." She did an imitation of Tallulah Bankhead's voice.

While modeling, she posed for a picture that caught the eye of Mrs. Howard Hawks, wife of the director, and she was asked to send some information about herself. Instead of sending it, Miss Bacall delivered it in person. She was signed immediately for motion pictures.

Bacall's capture and occupation of New York City continued for about a week, during which time she and Bogie were frequently seen in night clubs and restaurants.

"You know the broad, don't you?" Bogart would say, waiving any formal introduction.

A new luncheon club, the Celestials, invited her to appear. Paul Douglas, the emcee, introduced her by saying, "Miss Bacall made a picture, she made history, she . . ."

"Made Bogart!" piped a voice in the back, a voice not heard by everybody.

Overhearing it, I sent her a penciled note about it. She tucked it in her purse and told me she would preserve it.

"Bacall will be returning to Hollywood shortly, and Warner Brothers should know that she charmed the hardboiled press with her good sense and lack of anything phony," I wrote on St. Valentine's Day, 1945. "Her big boosters are the newspaper photographers, who were afraid she'd be stuffy. They were planning to fold up on her. But she wasn't, and they didn't."

Two days later, Bogart left New York to return to Hollywood, leaving Bacall behind, and I was surprised to see that he was still on his good behavior.

With Bogart out of town, New York City quieted down. Indeed, it got very quiet starting just a few days later, at midnight February 26, 1945. The wartime midnight curfew went into effect, and Toots Shor made his famous crack, "Anybody who can't get drunk by midnight ain't tryin'."

Billy Rose's Diamond Horseshoe and John Perona's El Morocco and all the other spots began warning customers at 11:30 to "drink up—we're closing"—which brought cries of "Quick, two double Scotches!"

The waiters removed tablecloths and piled seat cushions on table tops to prove they meant it. So the customers ordered triple Scotches. A few speakeasies stayed open. But the clubs moved up their eight o'clock dinner shows to seven and their midnight shows to ten, and there was a general recognition of the curfew.

A posh club called the Monte Carlo got rid of its customers at midnight by having the orchestra play "The Star-Spangled Banner." While the patrons were standing, the waiters pulled their chairs away so they couldn't sit down again.

It took three months for my column about Bogie planning to marry Bacall to be formally confirmed. The announcement, April 28, 1945, carried by the news services, said simply that Bogart would marry Lauren Bacall "as soon as the present Mrs. Bogart obtains her divorce."

"Betty" Bacall took on, in her marriage, one of the most difficult assignments in the history of mankind—and fielded it magnificently.

This lanky blonde kid was not a drinker; she was not a slugger; she was under twenty-one; and she was marrying a Hollywood character whose name was a synonym for hell-raising and who had already flunked matrimony three times. Furthermore, she was hoping to devote a great deal of her time to her own career.

It didn't take Bogart long to free himself to marry Bacall. Mayo Methot hastened her divorce by going to Las Vegas. The death of Franklin D. Roosevelt on April 12, 1945, left Bogart shaken more than anything had in years. By May, he was almost ready to get married, if very nervous about the prospect.

While visiting the Warner lot in Hollywood, I found him pedaling around on a bicycle, and I caught up with him in a house where he and Barbara Stanwyck were filming *The Two Mrs. Carrolls*.

"I have a feeling something terrible is going to happen at the time we're getting married," Bogart said.

"What could happen?" scoffed Miss Stanwyck.

"Maybe the guy who is supposed to marry us won't show up. Or I'll louse it up by dropping the ring. Baby was going to wear gloves. I talked her out of that. That'll make it easier with the ring. She comes up to me every day and crouches and holds up four fingers, three fingers, whatever it is, and says 'Only four more days.' 'Only three more days.' She's wonderful!"

"You're the most nervous bridegroom I ever saw," his pal producer Mark Hellinger told him.

"I believe in the institution of marriage," Bogie replied.

"Obviously, Bogie, with number four coming up," Barbara Stanwyck said.

"What you need is a drink," Hellinger suggested.

"No, I'm on good behavior. I don't drink anymore," Bogie answered.

"I know, I know," nodded Hellinger. "That's Joe E. Lewis' line. You don't drink any more. Just the same amount as always."

Any bride or bridesmaid would have said that Bogart was the cutest thing in the land. *Modern Screen* carried an article by him listing his choice for the ten most beautiful stars. His first choice was Lauren Bacall.

The couple took the train to Louis Bromfield's farm near Mansfield, Ohio, for the wedding on Tuesday, May 22, 1945. The nervous bridegroom did not drop the ring. The war with Germany had ended a couple of weeks before with Germany's unconditional surrender. The married Bogarts returned to Hollywood, where all the brainiest people were debating about how the German people should be punished.

The gossipy lady journalists of Hollywood conjectured in the fan magazines about whether Betty would prove herself a Bogart tamer. Could she take it? Would she go into 21 with him as Mayo Methot had done, mumbling, "We aren't well today?" Would Betty be heard saying, "Poppy's going to eat something today, aren't you, Poppy?"

"All right, just as soon as I've had a double martini," Poppy would say, back in that other marriage. Would it be like that?

It wasn't at all. Although Bogie had a huge reputation as a saloon fighter and party pugilist, some of the fights were fakes. He and Broderick Crawford, who had participated in fake fight scenes in the movies, often restaged them at parties, pretending they were real. They loved to find a house with a balcony where they could scream and yell and swing wildly, take falls, leap up, swing again, take more falls, while the guests, thinking it was a genuine struggling match, rushed to separate them.

The only real complication arose, said Crawford, long-time drinking buddy, from Bogie's satanic sense of humor, which inspired him at times to start fights in bars and then make a quick exit, leaving everybody else to get bloodied while he was on his way home to have a pleasant drink.

"He would start a beef and leave me to do the fighting," Crawford said. "I would find him in the apartment with a big smile and a big drink. 'Well,' he'd say, 'how'd you make out?'"

Betty went along with his devilry, even participated in it. Bogie seemed to revel in getting barred by the Stork Club and El Morocco, and Betty was right there at his side the night he deflated Sherman Billingsley, the proprietor of the Stork, who was conducting a very poor television interview show from the Cub Room with the impression it was good.

The incident occurred when Betty and Bogie had been happily married for a few years. They were going around town, having some drinks and some fun, when Bogie got the idea of dropping into the holy of holies and insulting the arbiter of Café Society, as Billingsley was called in the columns.

Seeing Bogart and Bacall seemingly sober, Billingsley welcomed them into the snobs' room, ordered the captain to bring them a bottle of champagne, and then sat forward to tell them of the success of his club and his television show.

Bogart led him right into a trap. "How do you manage to do these interviews so well?" Bogie asked him.

"Well," "Sherm" answered, trying to be shy, "I just act natural. I just tell them to be natural too. If it's a man I tell him to be himself and not to feel strange."

"Why, you miserable ham!" Bogart interrupted him. "Don't you know you stink up the whole show?"

"Wh-what's that?" Billingsley's mouth fell open. Nobody had ever talked to him like that in his own club.

"Your show is lousy, you're lousy, and you personally stink!" snapped Bogart. "What actor do you get to say 'Hello' for you? It's too big a word for you to say all by yourself."

Billingsley trembled with rage and began yelling at Bogart, who yelled back. The Cub Room customers, unused to hearing anybody yelling at Billingsley, saw Sherm get to his feet and shout, "You can't come in here and insult me. Get out!"

"Bar me! Go ahead and bar me!" Bogart got up too, but he was laughing. "That's what you want to do—bar me from the Stork Club. Well, I consider it a tribute to my good taste to be barred from this hole."

"O.K.! You're barred!" roared Billingsley. "Don't *ever* come back."

"And even if you do invite me back, your show is still lousy, and you still stink!" Bogie and Bacall hurried out of the Stork Club howling with laughter.

One night a few months earlier, Bacall had let Bogie off his leash, and he had become embroiled in the famous incident with the pandas at El Morocco that got him more publicity than had his winning the 1951 Oscar for *The African Queen.*

It was really a trifle, but it got blown up. On September 27, 1949, my column read:

> *B'way Bulletins:* Humphrey Bogart was barred from El Morocco by John Perona because he and Billy Seaman brought in two large panda dolls and sat at a table with them as though they were girls. (Hey, John, you're barring people just for *that?*)

A couple of days later, another newspaper decided to make the incident that year's Bogart *cause célèbre.* Model Robin Roberts and banker's daughter Peggy Rabe claimed that they had been the victims of Bogart's wrath at El Morocco. He became irate, they stated, when they playfully attempted to take one of the stuffed panda dolls from his table.

"Bogart grabbed my wrist and shoved me down to the floor," Robin Roberts maintained.

Then, she said, Miss Rabe's escort, John Jelke, did the chivalrous thing and went after Bogie with a plate. A struggle followed—it was alleged—and Bogart was hit with a saucer. He and his male companion left hurriedly, presumably to describe the evening's fun to Lauren Bacall, who had stayed home.

Bogart retorted that the pushing, shoving, and saucer-flinging was all pure fiction. Nevertheless, Robin Roberts charged Bogie with assault. A process server handed him the papers at 8:30 A.M.

"Why did you have to come so early?" was Bogie's reaction.

The case was thrown out of court, but of course, Bogie had to explain it to Bacall. I found them at 21 on Monday noon and took them a newspaper headlining the Great Panda Robbery. Bogie was abashed; Betty Bacall was vastly interested—in a humorous way.

"It's about time you got some dignity, old boy," she told him. "You're pushing fifty! What were you doing with pandas anyway?"

Toy pandas were a weakness of Café Society never thoroughly explained to me. Previously it had been kewpie dolls. You bought one for your girl, and she put it on her pillow or someplace, and it cost you $10 or $15. It was absolutely useless and nonsensical, yet a lot of people indulged.

"Well," Bogie said, "I was with Billy Seaman [a canned goods millionaire and run-around] and we picked up these two panda dolls at Reuben's restaurant because we couldn't stand to look at each other."

"*That* makes sense," Lauren Bacall said.

"As a matter of fact," Bogie added, trying to improve the story, "I was buying them as a present for Stephen [their 8-month-old son]."

"Why two?"

"Well, we started in a modest way with one, but we decided that one was lonesome and should have a companion," Bogart replied rather lamely.

Entering El Morocco with the two pandas, they naturally asked for a table for four and placed the pandas on chairs just as if they were women companions. They happened to see Johnny Meyer, the playboy-publicist, at the celebrated Round Table, and they excused themselves from their companions and went to call on Johnny.

So there sat the two lady pandas brooding morosely because of their lack of male companionship.

"Suddenly," related Bogie, "there's a screaming and a squawking, and a girl hollering, 'I'll bet I can get one of your pandas.' She grabbed one. I said, 'I'll bet you can't,' and I grabbed it back from her."

"Did you knock the girl down?" Bacall quietly asked.

"Somebody may have *fallen* down," Bogie conceded. "I may have fallen down myself. Who isn't a bit unsteady at four o'clock in the morning? But if she went to the floor, that's her fault. I never hit a lady in my life."

"Never, Mr. Bogart?" Lauren Bacall said.

"Oh, maybe an old wife some time or other," Bogie shrugged. Bacall tossed back her head and pretended to be the outraged wife. My own opinion was that she found the whole episode boyishly Bogart. "I can't let you out of my sight!" she said.

El Morocco barred him permanently. "I've been barred from so many clubs, I'm going to have to open my own," he complained.

Betty got her revenge, anyway. When they went to Belmont race track, Baby was presented with a special Hawaiian orchid. When they returned to the hotel from the track, Betty, who was going shopping, asked Bogart, "Would you take this orchid back to the room for me?"

"Sweetie," replied Bogie, "wouldn't I look silly carrying an orchid into the hotel?"

"I guess you didn't look silly carrying a panda into El Morocco?" she shot back at him.

"Touché!" Bogie toted the orchid into the hotel.

Later, Bogie would often say to me, when we sat down for an interview, "Who can we louse up this time?" but I believe the Great Panda Robbery chastened him. Besides, he was the father of Stephen Humphrey Bogart, then two years old, and he was trying not to forget his responsibilities as a father. The happy parents took Stephen to 21 for lunch on one of their visits, and Bogie demonstrated how he had taught Stephen to hate the names of certain night club owners—especially those night club owners who had barred his father.

"Do you like John Perona?" Bogie asked the child, who said no.

"Do you like Sherman Billingsley?" Another no from Stephen.

But a couple of times Steve lost interest and said yes—to the great merriment of Bogie's audience.

"There's an ugly rumor you've reformed," I mentioned one time.

"What did I ever do but point out the right of a man to get a little drunk?" he demanded. "You know, for that I got fan mail?"

He laughed. "I get fan mail for all the wrong reasons." He managed to put on a phony frown. "Something happens to people who drink, I always say. They live longer."

He really believed they did, which put him in the same league with Toots Shor, who once made the assertion, "Whiskey never hurt anybody." Bogart assured me that he hadn't reformed but was only trying to coax the world to adopt a program of more decorous drinking.

"You can't have decorous drinking when women are present." He was downing a Scotch and water, and he noticed the effect of his words on Baby. "Women don't drink attractively. They should be allowed one cocktail as an appetizer and made to drink that at a table. They look a little crooked when they drink. They fix their hats till they get them tilted and cockeyed. Their faces fall into grotesque patterns."

"What kind of women have you been drinking with, old boy?" Bacall twitted him.

"You don't have fights in men's bars," Bogart went on. "The fights are in night clubs—when women come flirtin' around."

"I thought you were in El Morocco with a panda," she flung back.

By 1954, Bogart was unmistakably henpecked, and the Bogarts were one of those rare ideally married Hollywood couples. Bacall and Bogie had made two pictures together after *To Have and Have Not*—*Key Largo* and *The Big Sleep*—and then she had gone out on her own in *Young Man with a Horn* (with Kirk Douglas) and *Designing Woman*. Then came her delightful achievement with Marilyn Monroe, *How to Marry a Millionaire*.

"Baby's impossible since that picture," Bogie told me when he stopped in New York on his way to Italy to star in *The Barefoot Contessa* with Ava Gardner. "She's a very talented broad, but she's also very hammy. I'd be completely overlooked at home if it hadn't been for *Time* saying they'll put me on the cover. I've regained some prestige."

Why was *Time* putting him on the cover?

"I'm a very colorful fellow. I offered to bet them $500 they wouldn't go through with it, but they wouldn't bet. They wanted names of some close friends of mine they could get stuff from. I gave them the names of Bob Benchley, Mark Hellinger, and Charlie Butterworth."

"They're all dead," I pointed out.

"I told you I was colorful," he said.

Bogie was giving a lunch for eight at the St. Regis, and one guest was a girl I did not recognize. I leaned over and asked him who she was, and he said, "Oh, she's my mistress." He paused and grinned at me. "That's a conversation stopper for you, isn't it? She's kind of my secretary and hairdresser."

"Why do you need a hairdresser?"

He ran his hand back across his thinning hair.

"To put on my toupée. There's a scoop for you, Mr. Wilson!"

In January, 1955, the Wilsons were invited to drop in at the Bogarts' place in Beverly Hills. Bacall was at the studio. Bogie was helping mind the kids—Stephen and their little daughter Leslie. I remember Bogie yelling at them, "No television"; they ignored him and watched television. Stephen was lying on the floor inside a leopard skin watching Captain Video.

"Hey, Stephen . . . Hey, Stephen . . . Hey, *Steve!*" Bogie kept yelling at him. Steve ignored him.

When Bogie yelled, "Hey, *Sam!*", the little boy said, "What, Daddy?"

All of a sudden Bogie and Bacall were celebrating their tenth wedding anniversary. Thinking about it made one feel aged, for the world had changed morally and politically in that decade into a modern coliseum in which the gladiators were suave, polished, elegantly dressed liars, cheats, thieves, and pirates, who practiced payola and other forms of bribery while perjuring themselves before grand juries.

Dwight Eisenhower was President. Jayne Mansfield's breasts were getting as much publicity as Dagmar's. People were saying that a beautiful girl like Grace Kelly ought to get married, and Barbara Marciano took the subway home (with me beside her) after her heavyweight champion husband Rocky Marciano knocked out Archie Moore in the ninth round.

Barbara and some of her friends had gone to St. Patrick's Cathedral to light a candle before the fight—and that's about all the religion there seemed to be. There were alarming rumors that some of the big radio and television quiz shows were rigged—that seemingly respectable people were being fed the right answers. But nobody believed the whispers that a brilliant man from a famous scholarly family would cheat. We kept discrediting it—right up to the time he admitted his guilt.

There was money around. A Texan sitting in a hotel room on a hot day was urged to remove his coat.

"Can't," he said. "My shirt's not monogrammed."

Bogie brought Bacall to New York in October, 1955, took off his shoes and socks, put his bare feet up on a coffee table, and, with his hat on and a glass in his hand, received callers from the press in order to plug his latest picture *The Desperate Hours.*

But he did it under mild protest. A young press agent from Paramount kept trying to slide a word in about the movie while Bogie was discussing the Holmby Hills Rat Pack with me.

"They say this is your best picture yet," the press agent ventured.

"Oh, drop dead," Bogie retorted.

"No kiddin'. A lot of critics think you might get an Oscar."

"You guys been out buying a few votes," Bogie grumbled.

"When are you going to flatten somebody again?" I asked.

"I told you I've retired from fighting," he yawned.

Lauren Bacall came in then, sniffed as she observed her husband's bare feet on the coffee table, and moved around the room. Trying to taunt him into an explosive comment, I asked her if she had tamed him into this effeminate state where he would no longer hit anybody.

"It's age." She tossed her head characteristically. "He's just turning fifty-six. When he turns sixty-five, watch out!"

Ironically, he was 56 when he died, and though none of us knew it, that day when Bacall said, "It's age," he hadn't long to live. My talk with him that day was one of the last I had with him before his cancer was diagnosed.

I was a camera bug then, and I took a picture of him. It has been on my office wall ever since.

In the background of the snapshot there's a hotel room dresser, its top loaded with whiskey and soda bottles. With his glasses on, Bogie is reading a press release about his movie. In the foreground are Bogie's bare feet, his slippers on the floor, and, on the coffee table, a folded copy of the *New York Post* with the big headlines: "*Ike Better.*"

The headline referred to President Eisenhower's fight for life after his first heart attack. Bogart, looking ruggedly and scornfully healthy, was to die of cancer of the throat at his Hollywood home on January 14, 1957, about fourteen months from that day. The seemingly enfeebled President Eisenhower, however, would suffer three more heart attacks, surgery for gastrointestinal obstruction, and congestive heart failure, before he died at seventy-eight on March 15, 1969.

When I left his hotel room that day, the young press agent said, "By the way, was he as natural as that before he hit the top?"

"He's always been natural since I've known him, but he's always been at the top since I've known him," I said.

"Maybe that's why," the press agent said.

The news that Bogart had cancer of the esophagus cast sadness throughout the English-speaking world. He was one of the bravest of the brave. In March 1956, about five months after our talk, he was on the operating table for eight hours, undergoing surgery that one doctor called "the worst any human being can undergo."

His stomach was raised twelve inches. Two inches of his esophagus were removed, and one rib was discarded. The public was told that the operation had succeeded, but Bogart lost thirty-five pounds.

Then they gave him three-million-volt radiation treatment at the Los Angeles Tumor Institute. Still his condition did not improve.

"Why not discuss it?" Bogart queried. "It's a respectable disease. Nothing to be ashamed of like some other diseases I might have had." Sneering at the idea he might not lick his disease, he continued to sail his sixty-five-foot yacht *Santana*. The surgeons doubled their efforts to sustain him with nitrogen mustard treatment.

Lauren Bacall never left him. Bogie commended his wife for her attentiveness. "That's about the only way there is of separating the broads from the ladies," he said.

Christmas was sad at the Bogarts, and they canceled their usual holiday party.

On New Year's Day, Paul Douglas and restaurateur Dave Chasen visited Bogie at home. Bogie had no strength, but he showed plenty of spirit.

"You'd better give me a pill and another one of these"—he held out his Scotch and soda glass to Bacall from his wheel chair.

After ten minutes, Chasen suggested they leave (doctors had recommended only brief visits), whereupon Bogie exploded.

Following their guests to the driveway, Mrs. Bogart asked Chasen if he could get her husband a special type of lobster—"I can't get him to eat anything," she said.

Returning to New York after the Hollywood visit, Paul Douglas told me that Bogie's bravery, expressed in letters mailed to editors around the country protesting against their gloomy reports of his condition, was gallant but unjustified. Douglas had observed Bogart trying to pick up the phone.

"He didn't seem to have the strength," Douglas said.

On Friday night before the fateful Monday in January, 1957, Bogie complained—one of the few times—about "the pressure in my chest."

Saturday was a bad day; he had trouble breathing. Usually he kissed Lauren Bacall and said Good night, but on Sunday night he put his hand on her arm and, in his gravelly voice that had not been altered by cancer, said, "Goodbye, kid."

The funeral on January 17 was remarkable in many ways. John Huston, who had directed Bogart in *The African Queen*, which won Bogie his Oscar, delivered a simple eulogy at All Saints Episcopal Church—if anything that John Huston does can be described as simple. At precisely the same time, Bogart's body was being cremated at Forest Lawn Memorial Park. His ashes eventually were put to rest there on a hill overlooking Hollywood.

Three thousand people lined the streets outside the church. On the movie lots, a minute of silence was observed. In the place of a casket in the church, there was a glass-enclosed eighteen-inch scale model of the *Santana* he loved.

Lauren Bacall had asked Rev. Kermit Castellanos, the church rector, to preface the services with a reading of the Ten Commandments.

"He believed in them; he lived by them," the rector said. "I read them now as a foundation of his faith."

John Huston, with his rich, deep voice, declared in his eulogy, "No one who sat in his presence during the final weeks will ever forget his sheer display of animal courage. After the first visit—it took that to recover from the initial shock of his wasted appearance—one quickened to his grandeur, expanded under it and felt strangely elated, proud to be there, proud to be the friend of such a brave man."

Turning then to the thirty-two-year-old widow, Huston said, "As Bogart was brave, his wife was gallant. He gave no thought to death; she knew it was there, every hour of the day and night. And out of the power of her love, she was able to hide her grief and go on being her own familiar self for Bogie—a flawless performance."

Appropriately, a tiny gold whistle was placed in the urn for Bogie's ashes in Memorial Park. It was a memento of their first picture together, *To Have and Have Not*, and inscribed on the whistle were some words from the film: "If you need anything, just whistle."

Fourteen years have passed. As I sit in Lauren Bacall's apartment in the wondrously aged Dakota Apartment complex at 72nd Street and Central Park West in New York, it is 1971, and Miss Bacall, at forty-six, is lean, laughing, and seemingly happy. She has had the best work year of her life as the singing and dancing star of the hit Broadway musical *Applause*.

How did she do it—a singing and dancing debut at forty-five?

"Oh, she's a tremendous worker," Jason Robards, Jr., her husband for a while in the years after Bogie's death, told me.

"Jason didn't really see much of me when I was actually working on this, though," she said.

Hers is the remarkable story of an actress who had given up movies, which she felt hadn't treated her well, to become a brilliant success on the stage.

"I finally feel that I have an identity that is clearly my own, and I'm grateful for that. It's taken me a hell of a long time to get it," she tells me.

"Quite a while?"

"Well, if you call a lifetime a while . . ." She lifts her head in a proud way and looks past the flowers and plants at the window, out into Central Park.

It is three P.M. and she is playing with some lunch on a small plate in the living room. On the walls are many paintings and photographs, and I notice one of Bogart and Bacall. But I have been warned that she doesn't wish to talk about Bogart. I do not entirely believe this, however, because on previous occasions she has talked to me about him and has told me that she has kept the clipping of my column in which I announced that she and Bogie would be married.

"Do you remember the first time you met Bogie?" I manage to ask.

She sits up. "The first time I *met* him, Howard Hawks brought me down to the set to a film he was making, *Passage to Marseilles*. That was when Howard was trying to decide about *To Have and Have Not*.

"And *then*"—Miss Bacall has a way of underlining words in her conversation for emphasis—"not too long after that, I was walking into Howard's office, which was a bungalow at Warner Brothers, because I knew that Howard was showing Bogie my screen test to see how Bogie felt about working with me, a new young thing.

"As I was walking into Howard's bungalow, Bogie was coming out, having seen my screen test. I remember he looked at me and pointed and said, 'We'll have a lot of fun.' I don't think he realized quite what fun he was going to have."

She laughs deeply saying this. "It was to put me at ease, and it was terrific. I was a *baby*. I was *Nineteen*.

"I went down to the National Press Club in Washington. I wasn't married to Bogie then. Charlie Einfeld, the head of publicity at Warner Brothers, took me. Vice-President Truman was also a guest. Mr. Truman came over and started to play the piano. Somebody said—probably Einfeld—'Get on the piano.' So I sat on the piano. The next day the picture was all over the country, and I had nothing to do with planning it. I was a total novice about those things."

"Do you think anything Bogie said kept you going after his death?" I ask.

"Certainly he contributed to the kind of human being I am today. He had tremendous respect for the acting profession—for real actors, not for flukes. He always felt one should work at one's trade and not just sit back and wait for that wonderful part because if you do, chances are nothing will come along. Even if things are not as good as you'd like them to be, you can still learn. You're functioning. Perhaps you're using not all of yourself but some of yourself."

"You weren't happy in pictures?"

"I had a lot of bad luck, and I had to fight my way along. I got lousy reviews for *Confidential Agent*. I had no choice but to turn down things and go on suspension. I was lucky that I was married to a man who could support me well. I had never wanted to be a movie star anyway. As a kid I always dreamed of being in the theater. Actually I am grateful because if I had had it too easy in films, I would never have tried the theater."

Two years after Bogie's death, she was in Spain filming *Flame Over England*, when Leland Hayward asked her about doing a Broadway stage farce, *Goodbye, Charlie*, written by George Axelrod.

"I told myself, 'Well, you've got to find out, kiddo,'" she says.

She was then thirty-five. She'd never been in a play. Suddenly she was the star of one. She had to learn about projecting her voice. "In films, you don't have to worry about projecting—you have the microphone hanging over your head."

After that, she began referring to herself as a "survivor." She'd been good enough to survive, and staying alive was the aim of the game of life.

Somebody said in a fan letter, "You should not say 'survivor' but should say, as Faulkner said in his acceptance of the Nobel Prize, 'I have prevailed,' which is a more appropriate statement." Miss Bacall, however, continued to call herself a survivor.

Next, David Merrick offered her the lead in *Cactus Flower*, and she played it for two years on Broadway without missing a performance. Everybody loved her in it, although Miss Bacall wasn't too sure about Merrick, who, she said, never dropped around to see her or to thank her for not missing a show.

"When *Applause* came along, I was scared to death," the new, more confident star says. She looks back on those moments of horror. "But then I'm *always* scared to death.

"I studied dancing for thirteen years when I was young. I always wanted to be a dancer. When I decided to be an actress, I didn't study dancing anymore. I always knew I was musical—not a singer but a frustrated singer, the one who leans over the piano at parties and sings. I'm still not a singer, but I'm *musical.* . . ."

As a big hit in *Applause* and the winner of a Tony Award, she deserves to be the Broadway Woman of the Year. Her accomplishments are tremendous, especially since as a widow she could have just sat back doing nothing at all. She especially warrants the honor for becoming a distinguished stage and musical comedy star after a not particularly sensational movie career.

"How would you feel about going back to Hollywood to do movies?" I ask.

"I would be very happy to be in films on the level I feel I've earned. This is a new attitude for me because I am used to feeling grateful."

She mimics the filmmakers. "Oh, you lucky girl, we're letting you have a part, you of no talent."

What about a movie version of *Applause?*

"I would like to do it with the original company. I don't see why not. They're all talented people. But that's a couple of years away, and who the hell knows where we're all going to be two years from now?"

While Miss Bacall has been drinking some juice that I don't recognize, I have been looking around this fascinating room for the Oscar that Bogie won, for the Tony that Bacall won. Couldn't they be together here somewhere? Wouldn't that be a romantic idea? I keep looking, but I don't see them.

"When the Bogart cult started, were you aware of it?" I ask.

"No. It started in Cambridge, Massachusetts, didn't it, with the Harvard kids? I heard about it a couple of months afterward."

"Do you have his Oscar here?" I venture.

I receive a confusing answer. She says no, it's not here—not in this room—but it is here—in this apartment or in this city? She doesn't clarify her vague statement, and I have a feeling she doesn't want me to know for reasons of personal privacy.

"Do you have it with the Tony?" I ask.

"No, Earl." Her voice becomes a little low and very direct. "I can't live my whole life in the past. I don't think it's fair to anyone. I know Bogie would not have approved of it. One has to press on with one's own life. I lived enough in the past, God knows, many years after he died. I don't see any point in continuing. It's not going to help him, it's not going to help me, and it's certainly not going to help my kids."

There are sighs, as there always are on occasions such as this, and I mention that Bogart was a delightful man to interview—it is a triviality, but it is something to say to cover a difficult moment.

Lauren Bacall's face rises again, and her stately neck reminds me of some great thoroughbred's.

"Yes, Bogie's attack was always the reverse," she smiles. "His idea of having an interview was to interview the interviewer. He was very original. I don't think there has been an actor *ever* who was as good copy as he was without trying to be. Bogie was a curious mixture. He wasn't cynical. He didn't expect too much, he never realized he would leave the kind of mark he has left. He never tried to impress anyone. I've never known anyone who was so completely his own man. He could not be led in any direction unless it was the direction he chose to go."

What was his major philosophy?

"He didn't think he owed anybody anything except good work."

"He was a great man," I observe.

Lauren Bacall continues to forget her lunch. She is struck by my remark. Evidently nobody has said so much lately, although the statement has been made many times over the years.

"He *was* a great man," she agrees. There is nothing maudlin about her words. "That word greatness has been used so much. This man's great, and that's great and terrific and beautiful. But I really think *he* was, and I really believe that where he had true greatness was as a human being."

Bacall is maybe a little dreamy about him now.

"If he had chosen a political career, I think he could have gone down in history as one of the great men in political life because of the kind of man he was."

"Did he ever have any political ambition?"

"No."

I remind her of another Bogart trait. He once telegraphed Katharine Hepburn: "I went to see Christopher Fry's play. I have quit seeing Christopher Fry's plays." After I'd printed this, I saw Bogart, who said, "You know, I was going to have everybody at Western

Union fired for giving out the contents of that telegram, but Baby told me I'd had a couple of drinks and told you myself."

She nods. "That was Bogie."

Bacall and Bogart both belong to the great tradition of show business. On Sunday, September 27, 1970, Miss Bacall did *Applause* for the Actors Fund. I went to see some of it because Sean Connery, who had had supper with her the night before, told me she was apprehensive about the reaction she'd receive from her fellow professionals.

It was Standing Room Only, and the standees roared out their applause, especially when she shouted out the line, "Who said the stage is washed up? It was said by a movie producer whose office is now a parking lot."

Nervous though she may have been at the beginning, she became a paragon of confidence as she sang and danced through the first big number "But Alive."

Slim and long-legged, she swung through it furiously, kicking beautifully and being carried horizontally around the stage by "the boys," with her long legs up in the air. From the audience came shouts of "More, more!"

Bacall had come through just as Bogart had. They were quite a pair of show people!

14
Robert Mitchum: First of the Hippies

THE hippie movement, with its cry of "Make Love, Not War," was about twenty-five years in the making. It was really pioneered by the first of the Hollywood rebels, Robert Mitchum, who was arrested for marijuana possession long before it was popular to smoke pot.

Mitchum, always inclined to take everything lightly—jail included —admits with characteristic indifference that he still uses pot. In Ireland, while he was filming *Ryan's Daughter,* he took over a small hotel for his own entourage. Pointing to a small weed growing inside the living room, he maintained that it was Aztec gold—high-grade marijuana.

While he was staying at the Hotel Plaza in New York, Mitchum got into an elevator as the president of Pakistan also entered. It was during a meeting of United Nations heads of state. Four of the president's bodyguards told Mitchum to take another elevator.

A Secret Service man looked wonderingly at Mitchum's briefcase. "What have you got in the case?" he asked.

"Oh, only a little pot," Mitchum shrugged.

"O.K., as long as it's not a bomb," the Secret Service man replied.

"I've been smoking shit since 1945, and it never got to be a habit with me," Mitchum sometimes says, echoing a line attributed to Tallulah Bankhead.

Mitchum is a gifted conversationalist, though his close friends say he sometimes soars on great flights of oratory that they cannot follow. However, there are gems to be found if you can afford to wait.

He was a radio writer, among other things, when he first went to Hollywood, and he often converses like a writer today—at other times he sounds more like a convict.

"The only difference between me and other actors is that I've spent more time in jail," he once said.

Once when he was being questioned seriously by some young fans about his art as an actor, he said, "People think I have an interesting walk—like John Wayne. Hell, man, I'm just trying to hold my gut in."

Somebody inquired when he planned to write his autobiography.

"What for?" he asked. "The Los Angeles police department has it all."

That laconic remark was an oblique reference to his arrest in 1948. He was thirty-one at the time and a favorite of bobby-soxers everywhere. Thomas E. Dewey was governor of New York and about to become president—or so everybody thought. Clark Gable was dating Madeleine Carroll. Frank Erickson was bookmaker king of New York. Television was referred to as "video" in some places. Some very daring prostitutes were patroling Broadway in their new 1949 convertibles.

On the trail of marijuana smokers was a Federal Narcotics Bureau agent named George H. White. A tireless, dedicated worker, White used to spend his spare time kicking in doors of New York Chinatown dope dens before he was transferred to California. More than any officer I ever knew, he believed that every lawbreaker should be in jail. White was among those hoping to stop the use of marijuana in Hollywood.

There was a touch of humor in Mitchum's getting busted. He was scheduled to speak in observance of National Youth Month on the steps of Los Angeles City Hall; he was going to come down pretty hard on juvenile delinquency. He didn't make it, of course, because he was under arrest. His press agent said he had "laryngitis."

"It's a frameup. They didn't find a thing on me," Mitchum said at first, while signing autographs for a few fans around the court-house. But after he'd talked with celebrated lawyer Jerry Geisler, he felt better because Geisler told him that producer David Selznick, who was paying him $3,000 a week, was standing behind him.

"Yeah?" Mitchum said. "Have you ever listened to Selznick or RKO Studios when they're peeved? I think I'd rather be in jail."

The newspapers had anticipated a circus type hearing. A female star and a big producer were also expecting to be arrested. But as a show it was a disappointment. Geisler made a stirring speech for his client, stating that he would not perjure himself, that he "could not controvert the evidence." Mitchum pleaded guilty to a charge of "conspiracy to possess marijuana." The second charge, smoking marijuana, was dismissed or forgotten.

"He has a wife, mother, and two small children," Geisler stated in pleading for mercy. "The children in going to school get jibes from fellow pupils. This all brings about the realization of the wrong he has done."

"I might as well admit it, I've been smoking it since I was a kid," Mitchum was quoted as saying.

At the time he thought it was the end of his career. When he was asked in court to state his occupation, he drily replied: "Ex-actor."

Sentenced to sixty days, Mitchum was released after serving fifty days in a county penal institution called the Wayside Honor Rancho. He looked about five pounds leaner when he emerged.

"How was it inside, Bob?" a Hollywood buddy asked him.

"Just like Palm Springs—without the riff-raff, of course," he said.

Mitchum was probably not hurt by the marijuana arrest. Howard Hughes, then in movie production, sent a message that he would have film roles for Mitchum after his release and did. Mitchum may even have gained something from his arrest: it was the foundation of his becoming a Hollywood "character."

Mitchum has always been anxious to deflate Hollywood's "best people." In a few moments of frankness with Jack L. Warner, Mitchum threatened to urinate on Warner's leg, although he didn't say urinate.

When *Ryan's Daughter* was premiered at the Ziegfeld Theater, Mitchum, the hero of the evening, was interviewed by a Canadian reporter who asked how he liked the film.

"It was so goddamn long that I got cramps in my ass sitting through it," Mitchum answered.

The interviewer tried to change the subject. "What do you plan to do next?"

"I plan to join Gay Liberation as a sympathizer," Mitchum declared.

I was one of the reporters who broke the story of Mitchum's marijuana arrest. I didn't know him then. Later I came to appreciate him as a person, and I considered him my friend. Still, I had my job to do as a reporter. When I visited him at Dingle, Ireland, in 1969, I asked him what he thought about legalizing marijuana. He said he was undecided.

"I don't know," he kept repeating. "I don't know how you could control it."

I had been a guest in his living room that night. We had had some drinks. Marijuana was a sensitive subject. I wanted to quote him in an interview, but had no desire to hurt him. Therefore, after writing my interview, I took an unusual step. I airmailed him the interview and asked him to telephone me and give me his reaction.

He didn't phone. I phoned him.

"Well," I said, "how did you like the story?"

"O.K.," he answered, "but you've got me sounding awful goddamn vague about whether I think pot should be legalized. You got me saying, 'I don't know,' about six times."

"Would you like to be more specific?"

"Sure as hell would!"

"Great. That would make it better for me."

"O.K."

"Well, then," I asked, "how *do* you feel about it?"

"I don't know," Mitchum replied.

Curiously, in the many years since, Mitchum has not experienced any further trouble over pot, despite his frankness about it. His barroom fights have been headlined, but often he was tormented into taking a punch at some drunken pest.

Mitchum was anti-Establishment before the term became popular, and he was a protester before there were protests. But he was never an activist. Once I asked him, "Do you think of yourself as a successor to Humphrey Bogart?"

"Oh, come down," he said. "Bogie and I were good friends, and he gave me some good advice. He said, 'Whatever it is, be against it.' I told him, 'I've got a lot of scars already from being an againster.' He said, 'You've got a lot of scars, but you're still alive.'"

I'm sure that Mitchum enjoys his image of a one-time young rebel who is now an old rebel, still popular with young protesters. There's a certain amount of off-the-screen acting necessary to keep his image fresh and credible. Once, after he'd worked most of the night and into the early morning in Italy on the picture *Anzio*, I returned with him to his dressing room, where he launched into a blast against the producers and directors, who, he contended, didn't know what they were doing or where they were going. He also charged them with stupidity for having locked up the wine at such an early hour (it was three A.M.).

His wife Dorothy turned to him and said rather impatiently, "Oh, Robert!"

It seemed to me she meant she was aware that this was a pose and that he was overacting.

If a wife ever understood a husband, it's Dorothy Mitchum. She's a paragon of patience. She also knows, and says, when the party's over. Three overlubricated sailors once picked on him in a bar in the Caribbean. Well juiced himself he was ready to play the game when one sailor pleaded with him, "Can I take just one shot at you?"

Suspecting that the sailor's coordination wouldn't be at its maximum because of his drinking, Mitchum said, "All right, Dad."

Mitchum's chin was ready and waiting, and the sailor whopped him but didn't shake him. The sailor became annoyed and came at Mitchum with a chair.

"Hey, that ain't polite," Mitchum replied and returned the discourtesy.

Describing the carnage later, Mitchum said, "I dumped him, then looked around for his two chums."

Bob belted one of them over the railing and into a swimming pool forty feet below.

He was just working the third man over when he felt an annoying banging on his head.

"It was my wife with her shoes. She said, 'Stop it now, you're beginning to enjoy this.' I was, too."

It was my chore once to phone Dorothy about a report that one lovely actress was flying to a distant continent to terminate the threat of another lovely actress with whom Mitchum was working on a film. The latter actress was said to have confided that she would gladly be Mitchum's concubine. I would not, of course, mention such details to Dorothy Mitchum. I merely asked her whether she was planning to fly to join her husband on the picture he was making. If she were, it would mean that she knew or cared about the threat of a couple of movie ladies who were jockeying for her husband's affections.

"No, I haven't any plans to join him," Dorothy Mitchum said.

While I stammered, trying to formulate a question that would bring out the story without betraying how much I knew, she murmured gently, "I've been through this a good many times, you know."

I concluded that she knew much more about it than I did and that she wasn't alarmed in the least. And she was right, for both actresses eventually dropped out of the Mitchum sweepstakes.

These stories do get around, of course, and when Mitchum was on publicity tour for *Ryan's Daughter* in 1970, a reporter asked about his having an affair with his leading lady.

With all possible gravity, Mitchum answered, "I think you should always make out with your leading lady if you have the chance. I've discussed the subject several times at home. Unfortunately, my old lady doesn't agree."

There has always been a link between Mitchum and excitement. He speaks bluntly about his first arrest, which occurred in the South before he got into acting.

"I was hitching a ride on a freight train, and a fuzz batted me with his club," he says. "I was sentenced to a chain gang. I worked seven days repairing roads; then I took a walk and never went back."

During World War II, he got a job at Lockheed in Los Angeles, making airplane parts that he said "were obsolete before we made them. I got fired at Lockheed for throwing a clamp at the foreman. I didn't like his attitude."

Mitchum says that while working at Lockheed he got to know

a fellow toiler named James Dougherty, who annoyed him slightly because he was always so happy with life. Mitchum was silent and brooding about making plane parts that were useless, but Dougherty came in every day with his lunch, a cold egg sandwich that his "old lady" had prepared for him at home that morning. Mitchum was so moody he couldn't eat—and especially not a cold egg sandwich.

"Your old lady makes you the same sandwich every day?" Mitchum asked sourly.

"You ought to see my old lady!" Dougherty said.

"I hope she looks better than your egg sandwich," Mitch replied.

One day Dougherty brought him a snapshot. "Here's my old lady," he said.

It was one of the first nude pictures ever taken of Marilyn Monroe, standing at the garden gate, so Mitchum insisted, waiting for her husband, the same Dougherty, to come home. Mrs. Dougherty later divorced him, of course; she was still a teen-ager when she posed for that picture.

Mitchum managed to meet Dougherty's "old lady" while they were both at Lockheed, and a decade or so later they made movies together. Fate, time, or something had made stars of them both.

Going once to interview Mitchum, I found him and a press agent so deep in conversation when I arrived at his hotel suite that they ignored me and continued talking. I thought that they were being rude. I had come by invitation and by appointment to do an interview, and they had hardly looked at me.

"What the hell are you two talking about that's so fascinating?" I asked peevishly.

"Marilyn Monroe's vagina," Mitchum answered.

He demonstrated what he meant by making gestures. Marilyn was being accused of temperament, of frequently missing work in her movies, of being late or sick or just plain ornery. It was all due to Marilyn's vagina—the construction of it, Mitchum explained.

Due to its peculiar construction, he continued, in a learned fashion, Marilyn got sicker and suffered more pain and discomfort than most girls during menstruation. Not only that, she suffered cramps and bleeding frequently between menstrual periods, whenever any small crisis arrived. Marilyn might be having cramps practically the entire month. Mitchum carefully related that he knew this because he had worked with her in a film in Canada, and he had seen her suffering.

Mitchum made a bit of news at the Cannes Film Festival in 1954. I—and all the other reporters—had met an actress from England named Simone Silva. She had an especially large bosom and very little modesty. She was a favorite of the photographers that year, when the festival didn't restrict or censor photographs.

Covering the beach that April day, looking for ideas for salable photographs, the cameramen came upon Simone Silva wearing a short grass skirt and a transparent halter. Simultaneously, Robert Mitchum was leaving a hotel with his wife Dorothy for a sightseeing stroll.

Before Mitchum knew what was happening, he was posing with Simone Silva, before thirty or forty cameras, on a small cliff.

"Take off your top!" yelled one of the photographers—to Simone Silva, of course.

Miss Silva complied so swiftly that Bob couldn't have stopped her if he'd wanted to, which he probably didn't. She instantly whipped off her halter and stood smiling at Mitchum with her large bare bosom staring him in the eye.

Such was the excitement that one photographer fell off the cliff into the Mediterranean, a second broke an ankle, and a third fractured an elbow in the frenzied scramble to snap this prize picture.

Encouraged by the photographers' screams of happiness, Simone Silva went further. She threw her arms around Mitchum's neck and her overdeveloped bosom against his chest. The subsequent photographs show Mrs. Mitchum standing by, looking thoroughly annoyed.

The pictures became a *cause célèbre*. The shots went around the world, but the bare bosom photos were never published by the respectable newspapers (the warm-up pictures with the halter did get printed). However, every newspaper office received the pictures, and every self-respecting newspaperman got a look at them. Film festival officials were outraged and asked Miss Silva to depart.

"I thought if it was good for Marilyn Monroe to pose nude, it would be good for me," she said.

There was a tragic finale to the incident. Miss Silva descended upon New York, using it as a base to try to gain entry to American movies. Rejected everywhere because of the pictures snapped at Cannes, the unfortunate girl killed herself.

Although innocent in that exhibition, in other situations Mitchum often admitted he was responsible, as he eventually did in the marijuana-possession charge. He has been a rebel with charm, much of the charm stemming from his readiness to say, "Sure I did it, so what?" In that respect, he resembles the hippies and other revolutionary elements of today who view him as one of the "over fifties" who can be trusted.

Mitchum's attitude about marijuana has become bolder in recent years—and in November, 1970, a student paper, the *Chronicle*, published a story headlined: "Mitchum Heads 'Grass' Menagerie at MGM." It said that Mitchum had brought marijuana to an MGM screening room, where he was giving sort of a press conference for student journalists, and strained it for them.

"He sits down in the first row of the theater, pulls a strainer, a pan and a package the size of a brick from a monogrammed satchel," wrote Carolyn Sofia. "Soon a sound like a drizzling rain filters through the theater: the sound of clean marijuana dropping through the strainer into the precariously perched pan on Mitchum's knees.

"Because it's hard to fire questions at somebody's back, a student offers to strain the grass for him, Mitchum smiles and passes the package."

Mitchum agreed with the story in general when I checked it with him. "The shit—the marijuana—was laid on me by some cat and I told the students, 'Now I'll lay it on you.' I gave them the lot," he said.

"It was no big deal," he maintained. "Oh, a couple of them were a little stupefied. They said, 'Is that grass?' I said, 'As far as I know, it's marijuana.' Then this one boy came up and I said, 'Shake all this hamatash,' and then everybody in the crowd stepped up and took a portion. I noticed that every girl there seemed to have a glacine bag in her purse, those glacine bags that are sold just to keep narcotics in.

"So everybody got some when it was rationed out. The students taking it sort of helped me out of a spot. There was a tight security around my hotel and I didn't know what to do with it. Who gave it to me? I don't know. Some cat just laid it on me."

15
Marilyn:
Mad and Marvelous

MARILYN MONROE was the meteor of show business. There were many small, dim stars floating in the sky when the meteor streaked across the heavens. Its flash and fire blotted them into oblivion. Then suddenly the meteor was spent, plunged into darkness, and the small, dim stars could be seen floating in the sky again.

For fourteen years, I was as much a friend of Marilyn Monroe as any honest newspaperman can be of any celebrity. When I look back on the fame she achieved at the peak of her career, it seems that the cliché "meteoric" does indeed fit her. She did flash across the sky, eclipsing the other stars in the entertainment galaxies. Then she burned out and disappeared, leaving the others glowing in the wake of her passage.

Marilyn's dramatic life and death inspired several books, and I confess to having interviewed a couple of hundred of her acquaintences all over the world with the idea of writing one of my own.

But certain events were more than I wished to tackle in depth, so I abandoned the project.

For one thing, there was her mental condition. The last year of her life was heartbreaking to her friends. Some of them actually thought she should be "put away."

But these same people feared that if she were placed in a mental hospital, she would be driven to kill herself. Yet they also knew that if she were allowed to remain at home without being carefully watched, she might die of an overdose of sleeping pills and liquor. That was the problem facing Marilyn's friends in the summer of 1962.

Another subject difficult and awkward to explore was Marilyn's friendship with Bobby Kennedy.

I am convinced he should be absolved completely of responsibility for any of the events connected with Marilyn's mysterious death. It would be fairly easy, now that both are dead, to concoct a melodramatic scandal. However, in my opinion, it would be unjustified and untrue.

Marilyn in her last year was frequently seen—giggling under her black wig—boarding one of the Kennedy planes, going the Palm Springs-Las Vegas-Lake Tahoe route.

But one did not say these things about the Kennedys in print. Fred Lawrence Guiles, who wrote *Norma Jean,* a very good book about Marilyn, without ever having seen her, alluded to Marilyn's involvement with Bobby Kennedy when he said his research indicated that "Marilyn was involved with a married man."

> He wasn't in the Industry; he was an Easterner with few ties on the coast. He had come West mainly to work out the details of a film production of a literary property in which he had a hand and to escape the pressures of his work as a lawyer and public servant. He often phoned that he was back in town and asking if he could come by for a drink and maybe dinner.
>
> Or possibly it was his host who in Marilyn's view acted as a buffer between them and those forces antagonistic to their affair . . . She was beginning to see the hopelessness of her alliance; still, a phone call from him would alter whatever else she had planned for the evening, and she would go to him.

This was a dramatic way of saying that Peter Lawford had a beach house where he lived with his wife Patricia Kennedy Lawford, sister of John F. Kennedy and Robert F. Kennedy. They both visited the Lawfords at their beach house. Marilyn Monroe, who was in the circle of the Lawfords' friends, also visited them at the beach house.

Peter Lawford was a cordial host—an actor who knew Marilyn Monroe professionally as well as socially. As for Bobby Kennedy, as attorney general and brother of the president, he was a celebrity in any gathering—even among one that included such a superstar as Marilyn Monroe.

Though I did not especially treasure it then, now I value very highly my first interview with Marilyn Monroe, dated July 24, 1949.

Heading for Europe for a few weeks, I needed some "Saturday pieces" for the magazine section. They had to be written ahead of time.

I had no real desire to see her. She was an unknown. The press agents for the Shorehaven Beach Club in the Bronx, one of whom was Spencer Hare, had been trying to persuade the papers to print pictures of her in a bathing suit. When she came back to town as a starlet trying to promote a doubtful movie, I agreed to do the interview, but I was unenthusiastic: I would have preferred to interview Esther Williams or Paulette Goddard.

Still, it was a dull, drowsy summer, and I was going to Europe. There was nobody around who looked more promising than this blonde they were calling the "Mmmmmm Girl" in a buildup undertaken by Producer Lester Cowan on behalf of his film *Love Happy,* starring Groucho Marx.

Since my interview was "written ahead," I can't be sure now just when I did it. Consequently, I can't swear that I was the first New York reporter to interview her. It was either Sidney Fields, then of the *New York Mirror,* or me; we had pieces in print at about the same time. Neither of our interviews about Marilyn Monroe excited anybody very much—unless it was Marilyn Monroe who in those early days got excited about any kind of publicity. Anyway, a couple of years later when she was a big star and all the press wanted to interview her, she showed me her scrapbook with my interview pasted in it—practically in the front.

Marilyn impressed me as having a rather wooden face and a stiff, almost graceless body the first time I saw her in person. I remember

Lester Cowan taking me aside and telling me that I was not to judge her by that wooden look.

"This little dame," Cowan assured me, "could really be a big star. The minute most guys see her, they want to jump her."

Marilyn didn't especially excite me, nor did I intrigue her on that hot Saturday at the Sherry-Netherland Hotel. It was a pretty dull interview. Across the top of the newspaper spread that appeared later was a five-column picture of Marilyn, her bountiful chest overflowing the whole area. She was lying back, with her hair down to her bare shoulders. Her bust was creamy-looking against the black lace top of her negligee.

The heading was "Mmmmmm Girl."

My story ran as follows:

Over the years Hollywood has given us its "It Girl," its "Oomph Girl," its "Sweater Girl," and even "The Body"—and they've all become big movie names.

Now we get the "Mmmmmm Girl."

Miss Marilyn Monroe still wasn't quite sure what an "Mmmmmm Girl" has to do when I talked to her.

"But I'm sure none of the girls ever got hurt by being called such names," she said.

Miss Monroe is probably right. They don't get hurt, but they get mighty tired, even sick, of the tags. Miss Monroe, who is practically an unknown, is a twenty-one-year-old long-haired blonde from Van Nuys, California. She has a nice flat waist that rises to an (mmmmm!) 36 1/2" bra line. She also has long pretty legs.

"But why do they call you the 'Mmmmmm Girl'?" I asked her.

"Well," she said, "it seems it started in Detroit where they were having a sneak preview of my picture."

"But why?"

"Well," she said, doubtless remembering it just as the press agent told her to, "it seems some people couldn't whistle so they went Mmmmmm."

"Why couldn't they whistle?" I said.

"Well," she said, "some people just can't whistle."

"Maybe they couldn't whistle because they had their mouths full of popcorn," I suggested.

Personally, we think the whole thing was dreamed up by the publicist—but the fact remains that these appellations have helped to make a few girls pretty famous.

Well, to borrow a word from Miss Monroe's vocabulary as of 1949, that's about all there was to the interview except that she said she'd been working as a parachute inspector when some photographers discovered her. She was put into a Twentieth Century-Fox picture, but they cut her out. Finally, she was introduced to agent Louis Shurr, who sent her to Lester Cowan to audition for *Love Happy*. Groucho Marx liked her and told her not to worry about her acting: "You get behind me and walk like I do."

Groucho did an exaggerated girlish wiggle. Marilyn imitated him.

"You start tomorrow," Lester Cowan said.

My interview ended with Marilyn stating that she was a little starry-eyed about a young movie actor she had never met—Montgomery Clift.

"He's got tremendous talent," she said.

"And, she added, of course, 'Mmmmmmmm.'"

That was 1949—Bob Hope, George Jessel, and Martha Raye were big names then . . . Eddie Cantor was going to take over the "Take It Or Leave It" radio quiz show . . . Robert Sherwood was doing a script for Hollywood . . . Harry Richman and Martha Raye opened at the Riviera in New Jersey. Sophie Tucker was at the ringside kissing everybody . . . Paul Douglas, the radio sports announcer turned movie actor, was off to Germany to film *Two Corridors East* . . . Truman was President, and Harry Vaughn was on the hot seat . . . the Latin Quarter was giving a tryout to a "locally unknown kid performer—Joey Bishop" . . . Jack Cassidy was singing at the #1 Fifth Avenue bar . . . the Broadway joke was, "Once upon a time when a girl heard a dirty story, she blushed. Now she memorizes it."

One thing that helped Marilyn the Meteor launch into space was an interview in which she admitted that she had posed nude for a calendar picture taken by Hollywood photographer Tom Kelly. She said that she had been hungry and needed the $50 for rent. Nudity was rather scandalous at that time. The picture was not lascivious; it was simply a photograph of a naked blonde girl. It was widely displayed before Marilyn granted the interview, and still more widely displayed afterward. Marilyn subsequently gave me a copy of it with her autograph.

"I hope you like my hairdo," she wrote.

From that moment, Marilyn was *the* sex symbol. At Atlantic City she wore a dress so shockingly low-necked that she was editorially chastised by some of the newspapers.

It was then that her sense of humor became apparent. We were never sure whether she was serious or trying to make a joke. She progressed professionally in those years to the point where she got a drama coach, Natasha Lytess. Howard Hughes was then interested in Marilyn.

"Marilyn, your face is all red," Natasha said to her one day. "Have you a fever?"

"No, it's not that," Marilyn answered. "Howard hasn't shaved for four days."

Marilyn had a revulsion for wearing underpants. The director argued with her during one picture that since the camera was shooting from below and she was up high, she should wear pants.

"Ahh, pants gag me!" she grumbled.

When Marilyn championed the habit of not wearing underwear, the entire subject became controversial.

"What do you wear to bed?" she was asked.

"Just some Chanel No. 5," she replied.

"Don't you have on anything at all?" was the next question.

"Just the radio," she said.

When I heard this exchange between Marilyn and some interviewers, I credited her with some original witticisms. Later, however, in going over some joke files I discovered that versions of these jokes had been used in vaudeville. Probably some of her studio press agents had provided her with the patter to be used with reporters.

In fact, Marilyn—the better to be a successful actress—usually wore a brassiere to bed, to keep her breasts firm. She enjoyed ice-cold baths. Her masseur, Ralph Roberts, would pour ice cubes in the tub, and Marilyn would pour in Chanel No. 5.

As she grew famous and aspired to be thought cultured, Marilyn became something of a reader. Robert Mitchum once found her reading a dictionary of terms used in psychoanalysis.

"How far have you got?" Mitchum asked her.

"Just to A," she said. "I'm just up to anal eroticism. What does eroticism mean?"

Mitchum told her.

Marilyn frowned. "What does anal mean?"

Mitchum told her that, too.

Marilyn appeared to be in blooming health, yet she had spent considerable time in hospitals as an invalid. She had twice been hospitalized for appendicitis; she had had a gall bladder removed; she had had four miscarriages; she had tried to gain admission to the Menninger Clinic; she had been at Payne-Whitney Psychiatric Clinic under restraint; and she had undergone mental treatment at other hospitals. A couple of weeks before her death she asked a doctor to see what was wrong with her nose. It was badly bruised. She seemed to have fallen on it.

When Marilyn was making *The Misfits* with Clark Gable and Montgomery Clift in Reno, she went to a hospital, stopping production, and director John Huston told me later that she was under treatment for taking sleeping pills.

"I got her off of them, but she tapered off on tranquilizers," he said.

"That's a good constructive story for a change. Can I print it?" I asked him. He gave me consent.

But I decided first to ask Marilyn to give her explanation of the successful treatment. Three of her press agents came to my office to urge me not to write it after she received my request. The subject horrified Marilyn, and she, too, begged me to maintain silence. She promised that if I suppressed it she would soon give me a "good story."

I sensed that the "good story" was her approaching breakup with her husband Arthur Miller. So we made a deal, and Marilyn kept her promise. She gave me the exclusive story when she announced their divorce.

The reason for Marilyn's fear of the sleeping pill cure story was not apparent then, but it is now. She had not broken herself of the sleeping pill habit even though John Huston thought she had.

"Marilyn was always, in the later years, about two sleeping pills from eternity," one friend said.

When she was still a starlet, she was permitted to arrive late for filmings for that reason, but from this concession she developed the practice as an excuse for being late—hours late—so often.

More likely the real cause of her chronic lateness was her own fear for herself. Frequently, she would be an hour or two hours late for an interview. And all the while the interviewer was waiting, she would be sitting in her bedroom continuing to work on her makeup or merely indulging the narcissist's love of looking at herself.

Billy Wilder, who directed Marilyn in *The Seven-Year Itch* and *Some Like It Hot*, experienced so much trouble in getting her to work that he almost despaired. He felt that she wore out the other actors with her ineptness, that she may have deliberately done this to make herself look better when the others became weary and angry at her for requiring retakes.

Hearing that Marilyn was studying acting, he said she should have studied engineering—maybe she could have learned to be on time.

Marilyn once invited my wife and me to her bungalow at the Beverly Hills Hotel for a drink. I was accustomed to waiting for her while she dawdled in the next room. My wife wasn't, so she grew impatient.

After about an hour of waiting, my wife said, "Hey, Marilyn, what's keeping you?" and walked into her bedroom.

She found Marilyn fiddling around, putting on a brassiere. She came right out and served us drinks.

Just a year before her death, I had an interview with her in her New York apartment. I warned her in advance that she must not be late for this appointment. I was giving my wife a surprise birthday party, and I could not be delayed for any reason.

Marilyn was extremely proud of herself that day. She was only fifteen minutes late.

And as a birthday present, she autographed a large portrait of herself: "To Rosemary—Thanks for sharing Earl with me on your birthday." To me she explained, "I only have about six of these portraits. I am saving them for my grandchildren"—the children of the children she could never have.

Marilyn couldn't have children, so we were told, because an early lover and sponsor had persuaded her to have her Fallopian tubes tied just when she was starting out in her career as an actress. Allegedly this man told her she was going to have to go to bed with men if she wanted to be an actress and that she should take precautions against getting pregnant.

Her sex life was widely discussed. John Huston once said in an interview that Marilyn didn't really care for sex, but that must have been a private joke. Marilyn and Huston once disappeared for several days and were discovered together at the home of a socially prominent musician friend. One of Marilyn's husbands once started to his job in the morning after saying goodbye to her. Because he had forgotten something, he returned to the house a short time later and found Marilyn already in bed with another man.

Yet she rejected a European king who pleaded with her—through one of her employers at the Twentieth Century-Fox studio—to become his mistress. Marilyn laughed the suggestion off.

In Joe DiMaggio she had her most loyal husband. The torch that Joe carried for her was the brightest and hottest seen on Broadway in many years. He was in perpetual torture once their marriage headed for the rocks. When he was suffering most, he would ask my wife and me what he could do to get her back, and he would also ask other people. One night he tried to learn the number of her room in a New York hotel so that he could reach her and try to persuade her to see him.

DiMaggio always felt protective about Marilyn. I remember the night about five years before her death when Marilyn filmed a famous skirt-blowing scene in *The Seven-Year Itch.*

My wife and I were having dinner that night with Gina Lollobrigida.

"What are we going to do with Gina after dinner?" I said.

"Take her over to meet Marilyn," my wife said.

We took Gina over to the Trans-Lux Theater, where Marilyn had a dressing room. Hundreds of people were jammed around the theater. When we got inside the theater, we found that Marilyn was very nervous. She was cordial, but it was clear that she wasn't thrilled to have another sex symbol on the premises on this big night. I took some pictures of this "Big Four" meeting, as did Photographer Sam Shaw, and then we dropped Gina back at her hotel.

Back at the theater, Marilyn came out to do the skirt-blowing scene, standing over a grate in the sidewalk, her skirt billowing up around her, showing her skin-tight white panties caressing her derrière.

DiMaggio, who was stationed at a nearby street corner with Walter Winchell, watched with mounting irritation and rage as half a hundred photographers aimed their camera lenses up his wife's dress. The shooting began late and continued for most of the night. DiMaggio got angrier and angrier, and eventually he left while the photographers were still shooting away. Marilyn's and Joe's subsequent quarrel over that incident was one of the reasons for their marital breakup.

Marilyn's own torture—about her mental condition—was worse. A grandfather, grandmother, and an uncle, and her mother had been incompetents, and she would sometimes cry out to friends, "I'm sure to wind up crazy!"

That was her excuse for living fast, drinking Dom Perignon champagne, vodka, sherry, cramming everything into life while she was still stable. She was convinced that she needed sleeping pills because of nightmares that arose from guilt over her hatred of her mother for letting her be born illegitimate, and over her hatred of her father, who wouldn't acknowledge her or talk to her. Once in a wild moment she said she'd thought of disguising herself and trying to meet her father so that she could seduce *him*.

Yet Marilyn at other times possessed enormous self-assurance. If she was plagued by any fears at these times, they were under control. At a famous John F. Kennedy birthday party at Madison Square Garden in 1962, she was scheduled to sing "Happy Birthday." Producer Richard Adler was afraid Marilyn was going to sing it badly, because at rehearsal Marilyn purposely gave a bad performance—to frighten Adler. It was her idea of a good joke on him.

"How could Marilyn do it badly?" President Kennedy asked.

And after Marilyn had sung the song almost as an exotic embrace, turning the Garden into a madhouse, JFK came out and, tongue in cheek, said: "Now I can retire from politics after having had 'Happy Birthday' sung to me by such a sweet, wholesome girl as Marilyn Monroe."

The rise and fall of Marilyn as an actress is a familiar story. She began to deteriorate physically as well as mentally after she had gone through her sleeping pill illness while making *The Misfits*. She had been dejected over Yves Montand's coolness toward her: he wouldn't take her phone calls; he said she was behaving like a schoolgirl.

She was constantly gulping pills—sometimes as many as twenty a day. She was terribly confused. Was she really a good actress? She didn't know herself. One Hollywood buddy advised her, "Quit listening to that Actors Studio con and just keep shaking those things. That's what pays off."

Jane Fonda told me that she and Marilyn once discussed getting old. Jane said, "I think I'd like it. Think of the character parts you could play."

"*No, no,* it can't happen to me!" Marilyn threw her hands up to her face and shuddered.

Marilyn needed a comeback. The picture was to be *Something's Got to Give,* with Dean Martin. Even at the start, however, the studio was nervous about Marilyn because of the trouble she'd caused on *The Misfits.*

An appointment was arranged for her to lunch with producer Henry Weinstein at the studio and discuss the script. Marilyn didn't arrive. Weinstein phoned her. Marilyn talked strangely.

"Shall I come to see you?" Weinstein asked her.

"There's only one bed," she replied, probably in a sleeping pill hangover. "And drive carefully because it's raining," she added.

The fact that it was raining was a further source of puzzlement to Weinstein since it indicated a strange combination of alertness and mental divorcement in Marilyn. He found her stretched across a bed, and there were signs that she'd tried to kill herself (one of the many times). However, she recovered and went to work on the picture.

She became friendly in a sisterly way with Wally Cox, who also was in the picture. One day when she couldn't make it to the studio, she phoned him there.

In a tiny voice, Marilyn said, "Don't tell them it's me. But come over to see me."

He found her in bed, talking with hesitation—falling asleep . . . waking up again, going back to sleep . . . all the while trying to speak a sentence she never finished—and he saw no way to help her.

Later, when she was somewhat more stable, they went to a party together. When she passed out from drinking, he took her home, driving so slowly, largely to protect her, that when she woke up she said: "Wally, I'm afraid you're going to be arrested for illegal parking."

Marilyn kept missing work and finally in June, 1962, when she had missed twenty days out of thirty-two, Twentieth Century-Fox president Peter Levathes cancelled her contract and fired her. Afterward, she went into a state of collapse. After all, the picture was to have been her big comeback.

She had often made threats to kill herself—some of these apparently designed to win sympathy—and now they were renewed. She was seeing a Beverly Hills psychiatrist, Dr. Ralph Greenson, almost every day, at $50 a visit. She was also being treated by a physician, Dr. Hyman Engelberg. Dr. Greenson was trying, he said later, to get her off barbiturates, but there is evidence that Marilyn cunningly succeeded in getting pills from Dr. Engelberg while keeping it a secret from her psychiatrist.

One of her suicide crises occurred just a week before her death. She was in Lake Tahoe; the phone in her room fell off the hook, and she was subsequently found unconscious. She was also in a suicide mood the night before she actually did die. It was a hard case for the psychiatrist and the physician. Their patient was on the verge of dementia praecox. She should have been institutionalized. But if she had been, she would certainly have taken her life.

In the few weeks before she died, some of her friends tried to get her back to work, to reactivate the movie. Yet, behind these frantic efforts lurked the constant fear of the consequences if she returned, failed to report, and got fired again.

The dilemma of those around her was best pictured to me by a lawyer I know only slightly but for whom I have a great affection—Milton (Mickey) Rudin. Plump, in his early fifties now, he was an amiable pipe-smoker in a Hollywood office, which had rocks, paintings, sunshine, and smog as a decor.

A lawyer must be guided by the law. There are certain things he might feel he should do or shouldn't do, but because of the law, his activity is limited.

Marilyn was constantly talking to him about changing her will. "I avoided the subject," Rudin told me—and there was eloquence in his glance when he mentioned that there is a well-established legal principle that anybody making a will must be of sound mind.

"After all, was she of sound mind?" A terrifying thought, of course, but wasn't Marilyn Monroe already mad? If she was, then of course Mickey Rudin couldn't participate with her in making a new will.

She was angry at everybody from time to time. Somebody was always against her; somebody was no good and was hurting her. It boiled down to a dangerous persecution complex.

While Marilyn was being the happy paranoiac wanting to get rehired for the sake of her prestige but not really wanting to do the picture, Rudin was moving with caution, trying not to commit her to something she couldn't do.

"You had a girl here," Rudin told me in his office, "who feared most being institutionalized. She was obviously deeply ill. She suffered a mental disease that you would have to deny existed. She had no relatives who could say yes or no to temporary institutionalization. She didn't want to do the picture, but she needed to do the picture. If she didn't do it, it would involve a law suit, which she didn't want now. For the lawyer, there was a humane problem that was difficult to handle. Maybe she should have been in an institution, giving no thought to her work. But there was no predicting what would happen once she was signed into one of those places . . ."

Eventually, proper steps were taken to get Marilyn back to work. She appeared properly contrite, but as a face-saver the studio heads were going to say that she received some new concessions. The studio was drawing up Marilyn's new contract. Mickey Rudin wasn't in any rush to have it delivered to him because he was afraid Marilyn would never live up to her end of the agreement, anyway.

On July 4, Marilyn was back on good enough terms with Peter Levathes, who had fired her, to invite him to her house. She'd just received some pictures taken of her by *Vogue*. She spread the pictures out on the floor on the patio and asked Mr. Levathes to select a few that he liked.

Marilyn chatted with Levathes about improving her contract with the studio, and he humored her. She voiced some indignation about Darryl F. Zanuck, one of the men who she thought from time to time was persecuting her.

During the month of July, 1962, Marilyn was continuing her talk and deliberations about changing her will, and the studio was trying to get the picture reactivated. It wanted to make a big announcement about the resumption of filming with Marilyn back at work. But Rudin, still unsure of Marilyn, adopted a "be patient" attitude.

Although Marilyn had suffered one of her blackouts at Lake

Tahoe a week or so earlier, she carried on considerable normal activity in the brief interval before her death.

The day of her great despond was Saturday, August 4.

On Friday, August 3, producer-composer Jule Styne phoned Marilyn at her home from his office in New York and talked to her about doing a movie—a musical version of *A Tree Grows in Brooklyn.*

"She picked up the phone herself," Styne remembers. "Usually a secretary answered."

Styne told Marilyn his idea was to use the musical score of *Pink Tights,* which he'd written earlier. Marilyn had liked the score but not the story of the stage musical and had declined to do it as a movie—but this was different.

"You know I'm mad about the score, Jule," she said—and to prove it, she sang a few bars of one of the songs, which was "Run for Your Life." (Marilyn and Styne, incidentally, had a minor conspiracy going. At parties, he was supposed to ask her to sing, and she would respond with "Bye, Bye, Baby.")

"I'd like to get an all-star cast—Dean Martin, Frank Sinatra, Shirley MacLaine," Styne told her.

"I'm excited about it," Marilyn said. "I'm dying to work with Sinatra, anyway. I'll be in New York Thursday. We'll talk about it."

They made an appointment to talk about it the following Thursday at 2:30.

On Saturday, Marilyn also talked to columnist Sidney Skolsky about seeing some film on the next day. She said she wanted to get up early Sunday and put in a busy day.

She was doing a lot of telephoning Saturday; she was impelled by mixed moods, at times feeling happy and at other times depressed. Her friend and press agent Pat Newcomb had stayed overnight with her Friday. They had gone to dinner together. They had some difference of opinion Saturday, and Pat, who was suffering from a cold, had gone home. But before she went home, Peter Lawford had invited the two girls to his Malibu beach house for dinner Saturday night. Marilyn had accepted.

"Let's make it early. I have a busy day Sunday," Marilyn said.

She maintained that she didn't want to get into one of the all-night poker games with Peter and his guests.

They arranged to meet at seven P.M.

Marilyn was late arriving at the Lawfords, as was her usual custom. Mrs. Lawford was at Cape Cod with the Kennedys, so Peter
was the host.

At about eight P.M. when Marilyn still hadn't arrived, Lawford
phoned her.

He recalls the next hour or two vividly. Marilyn answered in a
weird, fuzzy, sleepy voice.

"Hey, Charlie"—that was the slang greeting of the day—"what's
happened to you?" he asked.

Marilyn said she was tired and wasn't going to be able to come
to dinner. From her slurred voice, Lawford recognized that she was
either drunk or nearly asleep from pills. This was, of course, not
an unusual condition for her to be in, at least it hadn't been during
the recent months.

But what Marilyn said next was unusual.

"Say goodbye to Pat, say goodbye to the president, and say goodbye to yourself, because you're a nice guy."

Her voice trailed off; the phone apparently had dropped from
her hand or she had fallen asleep.

Lawford had been through similar situations with her before, but
this one seemed different because Marilyn had said goodbye.

"When somebody says goodbye, I figure that's terminal," Lawford told me later.

Lawford immediately phoned his manager Milt Ebbins and
urged him to go with him to Marilyn's house, to get doctors, and to
do whatever was necessary.

"You can't go over there!" Ebbins protested. "You're the brother-
in-law of the president of the United States. Your wife's away. Let
me get in touch with her lawyer or doctor. They should be the ones
to go over."

Ebbins suggested that perhaps it was another one of Marilyn's
attempts to gain sympathy. Ebbins knew about the Lake Tahoe
incident when she was found naked on the floor at Cal-Neva Lodge
with the phone off the hook.

"But I'm the one who talked to her; I'm the one who should go,
and you should go with me," Lawford insisted.

"Let me call her lawyer or doctor," Ebbins insisted.

"But the girl said goodbye," Lawford argued. "She told me to say goodbye to everybody. The phone is off the hook. She may be dying."

It was now late cocktail and dinner time in Beverly Hills. Ebbins began trying to reach Rudin, the doctor, or the psychiatrist. It took several calls to reach Rudin, who was attending a cocktail party in the area.

Ebbins hastily reported Marilyn's words to Rudin. The latter quickly set about phoning Dr. Greenson. It so happened that Dr. Greenson had visited her that day and discussed her problems with her. He was trying to calm her while she uttered the usual threats. Marilyn could not be made to think logically because she could not evaluate situations any longer.

Dr. Greenson told Rudin, his brother-in-law, that he felt confident that Marilyn was all right despite the goodbye message to Peter Lawford.

Marilyn had phoned him earlier to say that she was restless and didn't want to stay in the house.

"Why don't you go with your nurse for a ride on the beach?" he had suggested.

Dr. Greenson's and Rudin's reports didn't satisfy Peter Lawford, who still wanted to go to Marilyn's house. Rudin then phoned the psychiatric nurse, Mrs. Eunice Murray, who had a separate phone, and she reported back that Marilyn seemed to be all right. Later it appeared that she had found Marilyn's door closed. Marilyn wanted privacy and resented Mrs. Murray coming uninvited into her room. So she kept the door closed. However, since there had been light on in her room, and the record player had been turned on, Mrs. Murray had assumed Marilyn was in there alive and well.

When Attorney Rudin told Ebbins of Mrs. Murray's report that Marilyn was all right, Ebbins made one more phone call to Peter Lawford.

"I want to hear it from him personally," Lawford said, still not convinced that he shouldn't go to Marilyn's house himself.

Rudin thereupon phoned Lawford and gave him Mrs. Murray's reassurances, after which Peter gave up the idea of going to Marilyn.

Probably a dozen phone calls went back and forth in response to Lawford's concern about Marilyn. Yet after she was found dead at 3:30 A.M. lying nude and face down on the bed with a phone in her hand, Lawford blamed himself, thinking that Marilyn's last phone call had been to him.

But there may have been others. Famous Hollywood hair stylist Sidney Guilaroff says she called him much later and that she told him, "I'm very depressed." The call was like many of her calls, and she didn't say goodbye to him. Guilaroff saw no reason to be alarmed.

Ralph Roberts, the masseur whom she often called when she needed help to shake off the effect of too many sleeping pills, discovered after her death that "a woman talking very weirdly" had phoned his answering service trying to contact him that night.

"I think it was Marilyn asking me for help," he said.

Even after the tragedy, mystery cloaked the exact time of Marilyn's death. Mrs. Murray saw a light under her door at midnight and was not concerned. After going to bed, the nurse got up at 3:30 and found a light still glowing under Marilyn's bedroom door, which was locked.

Mrs. Murray knocked and got no answer. She then walked out of the house to peer into the bedroom window. She saw Marilyn lying on the bed with the phone in her hand. She phoned Dr. Greenson, who arrived there within minutes, followed by Dr. Engelberg. At 3:40 Dr. Greenson broke the bedroom window and went to Marilyn, who seemed to be dead. Dr. Engelberg pronounced her dead when he arrived, estimating that she had been dead for from three to six hours. That is, she had died somewhere between ten P.M. and one A.M.

The police death certificate gave "probable suicide" as the cause of death, from "acute barbiturate poisoning, ingestion of overdose."

Joe DiMaggio's takeover of the funeral plans, even though he was neither her husband at the time nor even her last husband (Arthur Miller followed him), was big news because Joe barred all her closest Hollywood chums from the services. He blamed them for her death. Lawford and the rest of her friends were stunned by his actions. Clearly this action and his practice of continuing to send flowers to her burial place year after year proved that he had remained in love with her, that he still carried the torch.

After her death, Billy Wilder said, "Hollywood didn't kill Marilyn Monroe. It's the Marilyn Monroes who are killing Hollywood. Marilyn was mean. Terribly mean. The meanest woman I have ever met around this town. I have never met anybody as mean as Marilyn Monroe nor as utterly fabulous on the screen, and that includes Garbo."

I met Wilder at the Bistro in Hollywood in early 1971; it was almost nine years after Marilyn's death. He did not take back any of those quotes.

"But I miss her," Wilder said. "It was like going to the dentist, making a picture with her. It was hell at the time, but after it was all over, it was wonderful."

No other superstar was capable of arousing men and women to such anger and jealousy—and exhilaration. Consider that literary genius Arthur Miller married a girl who said "antidotes" when she meant "anecdotes," and once asked a friend, while she was writing a letter, "How do you spell 'were'?" Marilyn's friends forgave her for having so little information because she had so many other things.

Joe DiMaggio and Marilyn were in a Chinese restaurant one night at dinner when a man at a nearby table, entranced by her beauty, exclaimed to his wife, "Isn't she pretty?"

His wife threw a bowl of wonton soup into his face and screamed all the way to the ladies' room. Later, somewhat calmed, she returned to the table, where an Oriental waiter served her some Chinese tea.

"Gee, honey," purred her husband, "all I said was I thought she was pretty."

His wife thereupon smashed him over the head with the teapot.

16
Dino: Hard Work
Made to Look Easy

As you walk through the casino of the Las Vegas Riviera Hotel in the area where you buy newspapers and cigars, you will probably see ahead of you, with steps leading up to it, a room with a sign above it: "Dino's Den." You may have already noticed an enormous signboard out in front of the hotel that says, "DEAN MARTIN PRESENTS."

A rather select group of people is admitted to Dino's Den. They are not all millionaires; nor are they all high rollers. But it's likely that nobody who jars the nerves of Dean Martin ever gets in because that is where Dino, Mr. Ten Points Owner, relaxes between and after shows. Dino's Den seats probably no more than thirty guests, and it offers a built-in escape stairway leading to his suite, lush quarters fitting to one of America's greatest entertainers. The public thinks of Dean Martin as a loafer and a sot, but he is in his own eccentric way one of the most industrious of all the stars.

Dean's present importance in Las Vegas—and there is no other entertainer more important—is proof that the experts are often wrong. They were all ready to flush Dean Martin down the drain when he broke up his partnership with Jerry Lewis at the peak of the success of the great comedy act of Martin and Lewis. As it turned out, his drive, tenacity, and talent have made him one of the most successful and beloved stars of television.

In a way, his story is a testimonial to misspent youth. In Steubenville, Ohio, where Dean grew up, there were doubtless some boys who sold newspapers and engaged in other traditional pursuits, but there were others who went into the back of a certain store and learned to be proficient at blackjack, roulette, craps, and other such popular indoor sports.

Dino Paul Crocetti had a very short career as a fighter. Then he turned crooner, and in the 1940s—after a short stint with the Sammy Watkins band in the Midwest—he was to be found in New York City, with a nose for which there seemed little excuse.

Despite the nose, he possessed a voice with an appealing quality. He sang wherever he could, for whatever they would pay him, and he starved.

One night Hollywood producer Joe Pasternak sat in Lindy's and told me, "I'm going to get MGM to sign this kid Dean Martin for pictures."

"You think he's that good?" I asked him.

"Dean," replied Pasternak, the successful producer of several big glittery musicals, "makes the girls sweat."

Pasternak had heard Dean sing, along with several other young hopefuls, at a Leon & Eddie's Celebrity Night and was determined to cast him in a picture he was preparing, *As the Clouds Roll By*.

About a year later, I asked Pasternak, "What happened to your plans to sign Dean Martin?"

He told me a sad story. Dean was to join the MGM family, starting at $350 a week with six weeks of actor training and a $100 raise every six months. Pasternak had worked it out in detail. But Joe Schenck, one of the heads of MGM, had a different idea.

"What do you want to sign another Martin for?" Schenck asked him. "We've already got one Martin on the lot."

"Yeah, who's that?" Pasternak asked.

"Tony Martin. Why not use him?"

And so Dean's entrance to Hollywood was delayed a few years. Dean could have used the money in those days. He and his first wife

Betty were in debt, and she lived part of the time with her family in Philadelphia.

The crooner age was dawning. The Riobamba night club on East 57th Street had just racked up unexpected success with Frank Sinatra in the winter of 1943. "Bobbysoxer" had recently become part of the English language, and many actors and singers were being snapped up by the draft. One very good singer who drifted into uniform was Jack Leonard—not the comedian, Jack E. Leonard, but the singer.

The day of television lay many years in the future. The big song show on radio was "Your Hit Parade." And Lucky Strike had gone to war.

Listening to crooners became a form of sexual release for bobbysoxers, their older sisters, and their mothers as well. *Life* put skinny kid Sinatra on the cover. In the theaters, girls swooned over Frankie, though it was reported that some of them were paid to pull the fainting act by Sinatra's press agent, George Evans. Frank became known as Swoonatra. There were jokes about his being thinner than the microphone. Some people called him Frank Skinnyatra. Men got into quarrels with their wives or girl friends when they went to hear Sinatra sing. Some of the women seemed to be imagining themselves indulging in a sex act while listening to him croon. Out of pure jealousy, many men came to dislike Sinatra.

Arthur Jarwood, one of the proprietors of the Riobamba, which was cradling the crooning boom, was so overjoyed with Sinatra's hit engagement that he began scrambling to find a successor. He wasn't necessarily looking for an Italian. It just worked out that way.

The Music Corporation of America talent agency sold him this kid Crocetti out of Steubenville.

Dean Martin was no big deal at all for MCA. He owed the agency back commissions of $352.20.

Arthur Jarwood introduced Dean to a dapper little Broadway agent named Lou Perry, the discoverer of several talented performers. Lou Perry can still be seen today in the neighborhood of Broadway and 54th Street, encouraging young talent. Lou Perry saw something more in Dean Martin than MCA did at the time, and he wanted to handle him.

Dean went into the Riobamba for two weeks and stayed for seven, but a big talent agency could not be wasting time with a fellow getting $200 a week and not keeping up with his commissions.

Lou Perry discussed the problem with MCA for a couple of seasons and finally bought Dean's contract for $550—barely $200 above the commissions he owed—which was one of the most remarkable negotiations of the decade. Lou Perry still has the scrap of paper an MCA lawyer signed on October 16, 1945, throwing Dean Martin to the wolves.

A new life of a sort began for Dean Martin, though it was vastly different from the luxury that he enjoys today.

"Dean moved in with me at the Hotel Bryant," Perry remembers, referring to a small inn at Broadway and 54th Street frequented by actors and other entertainers. "Dean didn't pay a nickel for rent in four years. Sometimes I would sleep on the floor or disappear altogether so that his wife could sleep with him when she came to town from Philadelphia."

Even after he graduated from the Hotel Bryant to the London Terrace Apartments, Dean spent a good part of his free time dodging creditors. In fact, the London Terrace Apartments, which were pretty fancy for an irregularly employed singer, garnisheed $30 a week from his salary for back rent.

Next, self-conscious from the start about his nose, which was sharp and hooked, Dean decided to have his beak restyled. But a new nose had to be financed. A plastic surgeon required a down payment; he would guarantee that if you didn't like the new nose, the old nose would be cheerfully refunded. From his connections in the old days in the Steubenville back room, Dean knew a "couple of boys uptown"—bookmakers—who agreed with only a little bit of nudging to finance a new nose for him to the tune of $500.

The boys, however, required assurance that the $500 would be repaid. (Or they would take the new nose back; and they meant it.)

Would Lou Perry, the new manager, guarantee payment? He would.

The new nose was a medical triumph. A bad nose job has been known to ruin a man. But Dean's new nozzle took away his Cyrano look and made him a bit Barrymoreish. The day after the doctor took the bandages off, Dean, in one of three new Bond suits, for which he must have gone into hock, burst into Leon & Eddie's to exhibit his new profile.

A photograph we have collected from that happy afternoon shows him kissing one of the chorus girls. He looked much as he does to-day—carefree, smiling, and devilish, a little too young to be as interested as he is now in drinking. Nobody could deny that the new $500 nose was gorgeous. It was the smartest $500 he ever spent. He was almost handsome.

Yes, Dean was ready for a new life, but there were those old debts, those old bills. He was well known to the summons servers. Lou Perry fielded many of them and collected minuscule commissions (just as MCA had done before him).

Crooners were becoming kings. All the band singers, who began calling themselves crooners, were moving up. To get in on the crooning boom, the Copacabana took Perry Como (another Italian) from a Pennsylvania barbershop and made him a star and a legend because of his ability to walk in his sleep and also sing in it. Perry had been a band singer with Ted Weems, whose orchestra had broken up during World War II. One day the phone rang in the barbershop—"New York calling Mr. Como"—and a man became a millionaire.

La Martinique night club, which also was calling all crooners, hired good-looking young Dick Haymes, who'd been a band singer with Carl Huff, Freddie Martin, and Orrin Tucker. He had been in one movie and had already begun establishing a reputation as a lover.

Crooning and making love went together. When Sinatra eventually worked for the Copacabana, doubling there from the Capitol Theater stage show, he missed a couple of nights at the Copa. It was officially reported that he had laryngitis, which would have been understandable with such a heavy schedule, but the rumorologists around Broadway said he was busy romancing a beautiful singer who had an incurable weakness for crooners.

Dean evidently was romancing his wife because the children were coming along regularly and, as he said, he did pretty well, considering how seldom he was home. Strictly a singer, he worked with comedians, including Zero Mostel and Jerry Lester.

And all the while the crooners' market kept zooming and with it the prices paid by clubs and theaters to singers. Dean borrowed money from Lou Costello, who helped get him $650 a week at Loew's State. Later, Lou Perry got him $900 a week in Chicago. The fourteen weeks he worked there were marked by constant overflow crowds. Dean was becoming a big name.

One place in which Dean did well was a rumba spot on Broadway between 52nd and 53rd Streets called the Havana-Madrid. Carmen Miranda, Carmen Amaya, Desi Arnaz, and Xavier Cugat used to visit the club when they were in town and Dean Martin appeared there several times, singing to the romantically inclined night people.

Not that Dean sang in Spanish or wore any fruit on his head as Carmen Miranda did. The habitués just liked his voice.

Another performer at the Havana-Madrid was a kid named Jerry Lewis, who did what was called a "record act." On a phonograph somewhere in the back, a record would be playing, perhaps the Andrews Sisters doing their "Beer Barrel Polka." Jerry Lewis, facing the audience at a microphone, would mouth the words and make funny faces, mimicking each of the sisters. The act was as good as the impersonations. When Dean Martin returned to the Havana-Madrid as the star, Jerry Lewis preceded him on the bill as the opening act. Jerry Lewis wasn't at his best yet. He was only twenty. Dean was twenty-nine. It was 1946.

"The kid didn't have a very good act," Lou Perry—an admittedly prejudiced party—says now. "But he was pretty fresh and very eager. Jerry asked me, as Dean's manager, whether he could fool around on the floor with Dean after Dean did his full act. He just wanted to throw some funny lines at Dean.

"Dean said, 'Sure, go ahead, let the kid fool around.'

"Well, the kid was good at that, and their act became very funny. But they finished their engagements there and went their own separate ways."

Meanwhile, Jerry Lewis was having financial problems more harrowing than Dean had experienced. One day Jerry phoned Lou Perry from the Atlantic City 500 Club. He was close to tears.

"I opened here, and they cancelled me after the first show," Jerry said. "Patti's sick"—his wife was pregnant—"and I'm desperate for that $175 a week. I wonder if you'd call Irving Wolf [the operator of the club] and see if you can get him to give me another chance."

Perry found Irving Wolf chilly to the suggestion. He didn't care for Jerry's record act. Lou Perry remembered how Dean and the kid, working together, had got laughs at the Havana-Madrid. Things were slow. It was summer. Irving Wolf wanted Dean to headline at the 500. Perry countered with the proposition that Dean go in as headliner with Jerry as the opening act, but not doing his record act. Dean would get $550 a week, and Jerry would stay on at $175 a week.

"Don't let Jerry do his act, but just let him fool around with Dean on the floor because he's got some very crazy stuff," Lou Perry said. Wolf yielded.

"I called Jerry back," Lou Perry says, "and I told him the deal. I said, 'Stay where you are. Don't go near the club. Wait for Dean, and you'll work together.'"

Dean opened with Jerry as a stooge on a Saturday night, and they were a riotous combination from the first. The two caught fire. The 500 Club began doing a booming business with the pair.

However, since it was Jerry's zany stuff that was getting the laughs, the situation between the two soon was reversed. The kid was still the kid, but he was fresh and new—and something more than just a good-looking crooner. Lou Perry got some nervous calls from Irving Wolf, who said that Jerry's manager Abby Greshler was in Atlantic City, "huddling with Dean and Jerry."

They weren't a team yet, but Irving Wolf could see the possibility shaping up. Greshler might team up the $175-a-week Lewis with the $550-to-$900-a-week Martin, with himself as their manager.

"Don't worry, Dean will stick with me," Lou Perry said. "I've got a paper with him."

And so it did become "Martin and Lewis," with their price going to $1,200 a week when they went into the Latin Casino in Camden, New Jersey. Dean got most of the $1,200, but Jerry's importance was increasing. Everybody was talking about "the kid." And Abby Greshler's importance grew, too, because he represented the sensational new kid.

"How about me buying you out?" Greshler asked Lou Perry one day. Jerry was more ambitious than Dean; they were now talking motion picture and television deals, and Jerry was taking the initiative in many things—or Greshler was taking the initiative for him.

"In 1950," Lou Perry says, "I agreed to sell Abby my contract with Dean. As long as it would help Dean, I said okay. I sold it for $4,000 which was nothing."

A few years later, the same thing happened to Greshler. MCA bought out his contract with the two of them—MCA which had let Lou Perry have Dean Martin for $550.

How fresh and how hilarious they were when they began! Madman Jerry had a trick I'd never seen before: he dashed crazily among the tables on the night club floor, seemingly about to bump into everyone, but sidestepping deftly and continuing his wild and senseless tour. It was moronic enough to be funny, or so we Jerry Lewis addicts thought in those days. A wild man loose among night club tables, customers clutching their drinks, afraid he would knock over their tables, yet enjoying his temporary insanity—that was Martin and Lewis in the early 1950s. And it was mostly Jerry Lewis, the brash boy.

I went over to the Paramount stage door on West 44th Street and saw the hundreds of kid fans looking up at the dressing room window, begging the duo to throw down autographed pictures.

"Now, Oil," said Jerry, looking cross-eyed at me, "we want the whole column, see?"

"And our picture at the top, over yours. Okay?" Dean added.

They were making a personal appearance with their movie, *At War with the Army,* a smash hit produced by Hal Wallis. They'd just completed a television show, and they had to fly back to Hollywood for another movie job. They were the hottest comedy act in the country.

"Oooooh!" Jerry screamed on stage at the Paramount, pointing at Dean, "you're smoking a Camel—and you're not even a doctor!" (In those days Camel cigarettes had many doctors as spokesmen in their ads and commercials).

"I'm brown from the sun," Dean would say.

"I'm Goldberg from the *Forward,*" Jerry would answer.

Jerry, wildly playing the drums, would begin screaming. Suddenly he'd have long drumsticks stuck in each nostril so that it appeared he had either tusks or a very bad cold.

He and Dean made about $72,000 each for two weeks at the Paramount, beating the Bob Hope and Frank Sinatra records. Working six or seven shows a day, they were virtual prisoners in the theater, not leaving it for sixteen or seventeen hours.

Considering that Jerry Lewis was later to make many millions for the film companies as creator of his own special brand of comedy, and that he came to be regarded by European critics as another Charlie Chaplin, it's interesting to recall that he once said the boys in his school called him "Id" for short—"Id for Idiot."

Jerry made me laugh over things I knew were simply tributes to "Id." They were idiotic, but he somehow made them funny. I was ashamed of laughing at such nonsense, but I could not stop myself. Even mispronunciations became funny when they issued from his lips.

He had once been an usher in the Paramount. "I was a yoosher here once," he said. "Ask the mennadjer."

The kids howled. Jerry shouted at them, "You think I'm crazy—you're payin'!"

Dean wondered what song he should sing. "It's immalarial to me," Jerry would counter.

Then he pounded a straw hat to pieces, preserving the top so that it looked a little like a matzah. Holding it at the footlights, Jerry said, "Anybody want a matzah? Oh," and he went into a familiar melody, "you matzah been a beauteeefullll babe-eee-eee . . ."

Joseph Levitch—(that was Jerry's real name)—was only twenty-five then. Everybody loved him for being a nut, an idiot, "a rotten kid."

"Jerry is as great a fool as Ed Wynn," I wrote. "You'd better get used to his insanity."

Dean, who was thirty-four, was amazed at being even the minor part of a top comedy act. "Back in Steubenville," he said, "they're still bettin' six to five I get the chair. As a kid, I didn't know whether to be a card crook or a thief. Matter of fact, there wasn't much for a kid to do but work in the steel mills or steal. Why, even now when I go into a haberdashery, I always steal a tie or belt or something just to keep my hand in. I don't want to get rusty, I don't figure this thing I'm doing now can last."

When they came to their breakup in June, 1955, after eight to nine years of the most lucrative partnership in the history of comedy, Martin and Lewis astonished many people—but not those who had been observing closely the differences that had become increasingly obvious between them. Dean's loyalists had convinced him that he had to make a move to prevent himself from being eclipsed entirely by Jerry, who was becoming more and more the star of the act.

Their friendship had turned to bitterness. Off the stage and off the screen, they weren't even speaking to each other.

Utter silence between two or more professional co-workers is not unknown in show business. Abbott & Costello had reached that stage of success. In baseball, there was always the great double play combination of Tinker to Evers to Chance, who allegedly didn't talk to each other.

Dean could always be reached by telephone by a newspaper friend in those days, and I picked up one a couple of times to call him. The separation of a team that had about $20,000,000 worth of work under contract was quite a story.

"I haven't seen Jerry or talked to him for a couple of months," Dean told me. "The boy"—that was Jerry—"said he wanted to work alone, that is, not with Dean Martin. That's all right with me, but I think it's wrong for the boy to brush aside such a beautiful contract. But the funny thing is, I think we're trapped, and we've got to do it.

"The boy told Frank Freeman"—the Paramount Pictures studio head—"that he wanted to work entirely alone, meaning without Dino. Freeman flew to New York to see Barney Balaban, the Paramount chairman. Well, old Barney says there's got to be a Martin and Lewis picture or else. So now we're waiting for the boy's answer, but I think we're trapped."

Dean admitted that he'd been thinking of doing his own kind of television show—"where I can do more than two songs in an hour."

But there was a still more personal touch that rankled. Jerry had once been a busboy at Brown's Hotel at Loch Sheldrake in the Catskills. The premiere of their picture *You're Never Too Young* was set for that hotel. It was to be a sentimental trip home for Jerry on a weekend, and he expected Dean to accompany him.

Dean didn't go.

"I told Paramount three months ago I wasn't going," Dean said. "My wife and I had made plans to go to Honolulu. Well, somebody at Paramount didn't pay any attention to half of the boss of the picture, I can't help it. Don't blame me."

Dean asked why it was necessary for him to go to Brown's Hotel anyway. He'd never been a busboy there. That was Jerry's pitch.

Jerry's little group evidently thought that they'd be able to talk

Dean into going back; they didn't quite believe him when he re-fused. Paramount sent out invitations to the press for a rollicking Dean and Jerry weekend at Brown's.

Instead of yielding and getting on a train to go back with Jerry, the suddenly independent Dino met with his agents to work out a Dean Martin television show—strictly Dean.

"What does Jerry think of you doing your own show?" I asked Dean.

"Oh, I don't think anybody has ever mentioned that to him," Dean answered.

Few people realized that Dean Martin was a funny fellow, in his own way as funny as, or even funnier than, his partner. I credit myself with suspecting it because I had seen the partners together in their dressing room at the Copacabana and the Paramount The-ater. And the tall singing partner who tossed everything aside with a shrug seemed to me to be more naturally amusing than the screw-ball with the spastic walk and crossed eyes. But that was Jerry Lewis' lot in life, and he was merely working at it because, as it says somewhere in literature, he could do no other.

"The coming funnyman of our time is that one-time crooner, Dean Martin," I reported on March 9, 1958.

"Since splitting up with Jerry Lewis, Dean has taken to clowning in his own act—and has shown he can do it," I wrote after seeing him in Miami Beach.

Dean explained the switch to comedy by saying, "I've got to do it because, let's face it, I haven't got the greatest voice in the world." Comedian Joe E. Lewis, no relation, of course, to Jerry Lewis, after listening to Dino doing jokes, said, "Dino's got everybody else cheated," meaning he had topped all his competitors.

What did Dean Martin do that made for good comedy?

"I don't lie," Dean said. "A lot of performers are fakes on the floor. They play somebody other than themselves."

This was one of the most interesting and penetrating studies of comedy, under the most informal conditions I've ever known. We were having a drink in a Miami Beach saloon. Dean was honest; I have never known him to be otherwise.

"Take so-and-so." Dino named a star he regarded as a close per-sonal friend. He was celebrated for his humility, but he was not actually humble. He was truly a snob.

"He lies," Dean said. "He's not actually that humble, and I think the faking comes across to the audience. And there are a couple of women performers, so sweet butter wouldn't melt in their mouths. The audiences know they're not really that sweet, and it would be better if they would just be themselves."

Dean was always doing exactly that—just being Dean. He'd been given a reputation as a drinker by Jerry when they started together, a gimmick used by many comedy acts. Dean picked it up and made everybody believe it.

"My doctor told me to take a little nip before I go to bed," Dean said from the floor. "Do you know—I find myself going to bed nine or ten times a night?"

To make all this believable, Dean pretended he had forgotten the patter between the songs, and he may have forgotten it, at that. He would glance over at the bandleader.

"What's the next song?" That would get a snicker. The maestro would name the song. Dino would scratch his head. "What's the first word?" Then somehow Dean would bring out a stool, which Perry Como had made famous as part of his singing act—Perry the barber, said to be the most relaxed man in the world.

"Perry Como told me to relax," Dean yawned. "I was relaxed when he was learning to lather . . ."

He wasn't hilarious, but his act was relaxed, honest. It made everybody comfortable, and it made Dean Martin acceptable everywhere.

The enormous success of Dean's television show made some people wonder, "How good would it be if he *really* worked at it?"

The legend persists that he told NBC, "You can have me Sunday for about four hours and that's it." They reportedly settled for six or eight hours. Dean thinks that's overdoing it.

One day, while he was shooting one of the Matt Helm films, his daughters Deanna and Claudia were in his dressing room at Columbia Pictures, and he was explaining to me that he likes to do his show after playing eighteen holes of golf.

"I could do the show in four hours, but they won't let me," he said. "Listen, all I have to do is read some cards and sing four or five songs. If you can't do that in one day, you're stupid and don't belong in the business. *Is that clear?*" He looked with mock sternness at his daughters, who had a fancy for show business careers, as though the lecture were intended for them.

Although regarded as lazy and shiftless, Dean pointed out to me that he seldom manages to get more than two weeks' vacation.

"Last year," he said, "I did four movies, four albums, thirty TV shows, eight weeks in clubs, and about twenty-four benefits—and they say I'm lazy!"

Dean's prospects look good for at least several years more. Was he thinking of retiring? It seems absurd to consider when he is at the height of his popularity.

"I'll never retire," he said. "I'll die right on the stage singing 'Everybody Loves Somebody' at the age of ninety-six. I have to work. When I don't have anything to do, I become an old grouch, a bear. I love to work!"

Dean and Jerry feel no bitterness toward each other now. They have wished each other well personally and on television. Each has done so well alone that there is no reason to dwell on past conflicts.

Dino remains, in the mind of the average American, an easy going, liquor-loving girl-chaser. He's also pictured as a party-happy gay blade. Actually he's not fond of parties. When he was still living with his second wife Jeanne and his children were having a noisy party, he was known to pose as an irate neighbor and to phone the police to protest that there was too much noise coming from Dean Martin's house. The police would come to shush the kids, who never knew that the complaint had come from their father upstairs.

When his children's guests arrived for a party, Dean sometimes asked them, a minute or two after they came in, "When are you leaving?"

Before doing his midnight show in a night club, Dean frequently took a sleeping pill, which would make him so sleepy by the time he finished the show that he would want to go to bed rather than to gamble.

"And if I should go to sleep while doing the show," Dean said, "who'd notice it?"

Yet Dean is very much on the ball. His appearance is his life, and he's very sharp. For example, Dean went to Don Rickles' insult show, and Rickles lacerated him. Afterward, Dean stood up and thanked Rickles.

"Pally," said Dean, "I want you to know that I loved you and my Jeannie loved you and my whole family loved you."

"Gee, thanks," replied Rickles, seemingly touched.

"But don't go by me, Pally," Dean said, "because I'm drunk."

Dean's magnetism for younger girls was well known in Hollywood, and there were frequent rumors during late 1968 and early 1969 that he and Jeanne were splitting. The late Hedda Hopper once phoned Mrs. Martin about a rumor that they were breaking up over a young girl singer.

"I don't know yet," Jeanne said, a bit wearily. "Dean can't make up his mind which age group he's interested in."

Evidently he decided he was interested in a younger age group. He and Jeanne parted in the fall of 1969, after he'd been seen frequently with Gail Renshaw, a tall, blonde, statuesque twenty-two-year-old Miss World-USA from Arlington, Virginia. Dean, then fifty-two, had been displaying pictures of her, saying, "She's the girl for me."

As a beauty winner promoting the Miss World contest, Miss Renshaw visited Las Vegas. Her manager took her to the Hotel Riviera to meet and be photographed with Dean. She brought him the regards of Bob Hope, on whose television show she'd recently been a guest. All went so well with the photography that Dean had dinner with Gail, and they began seeing each other often. When Gail went to London for the contest, she was quoted as telling friends that Dean had phoned her and that they were going to be married.

Philosophical, I believe, is the word for Mrs. Martin's attitude when she was asked about it. Dean had moved to the Beverly Hills Hotel and gone from there to the Riviera.

"I haven't met her," she said, concerning Miss Renshaw. "But evidently all the children have. All I know is that he asked for a divorce —which surprised me—but I wouldn't want to live with a man who's not happy with me. I've had twenty marvelous years with him. I'm in good health, and I have no financial problems. He's been very good to me. Now he's free, which is good. Now he can hide—which is what he does best."

Dean does have a passion for privacy, but he tried to treat the situation humorously when he made an appearance at the Riviera's 14th anniversary on December 11, 1969. Gail Renshaw was in Las

Vegas too. Dean had read the stories of his breakup with his wife, and he assumed that the audience had.

"I didn't have much of a luggage problem getting over here," he grinned. "I found all of mine out on the sidewalk."

The papers were speculating about the settlement Jeanne would get. Somebody suggested $5,000,000—and their ranch.

"They say Jeanne might get the ranch," drawled Dean. "Well, that's all right. I could never find it, anyway."

The Dino and Gail romance lasted about four months. In March, 1970, it appeared that they weren't going to get married after all. In June, 1970, when he went back to the Riviera Hotel, he was often seen in the company of a leggy, blonde beauty named Kathy Hawn.

"She's no kid, you know," one of Dean's friends said describing her. "She must be twenty-four."

Dean himself took notice of his appreciation for youth at a dinner. "Well, excuse me now," he said. "I have to run along and burp my girl."

Thus we have the story of a band singer turned crooner, who, in his own words, became a comedian because he didn't have much of a voice. (This is *his* opinion. His voice hits my ear just right.)

17

Black Is Beautiful,
But It Took a Long Time

LENA HORNE was a beautiful Negro girl of twenty-nine —"probably the most beautiful girl in the world," drama critic Richard Watts had written—when she sat down with me in Lindy's one afternoon in June, 1947, and told me bluntly and with considerable bitterness how she had suffered from race prejudice in her struggle to reach the top in show business.

Lena did not use the word "black" in that interview close to a quarter of a century ago. Negroes were Negroes then, and it was difficult to be one even with Lena Horne's spectacular beauty and talent.

I remember the interview well because it cost me a paper on my syndicate list. One southern newspaper got so many protests from readers about a Negro saying those things (in print) about prejudiced whites that it dropped my column.

I was already accustomed to racism, although nobody called it that then, and important people in show business were casually aware of the situation without being moved to do anything about it. Discovering that Jack Johnson, the one-time world heavyweight champion, was working in the old 42nd Street flea circus as a sideshow attraction, I wrote about him, mentioning that I had interviewed him in a taxi riding up to his hotel in Harlem, the Theresa.

A bundle of letters came in, complaining about me, a white man, riding in the same car with a Negro.

No, we weren't very liberal in America in 1947. Negroes weren't accepted as customers or guests in most major New York hotels, although they were allowed to work there. "Give 'em Hell" Harry Truman was president, and Senator Robert A. Taft's boosters were warming up to sing "I'm Lookin' over a Four-Leaf Clover" at the 1948 convention, which would give the Republican nomination to Thomas E. Dewey. There was nothing very hopeful in that direction.

The man thought to be the world's greatest entertainer was Al Jolson, who said he was fifty-nine although *Who's Who* stated he was sixty-one. Jolie was also considered one of the richest of the show folk, and he had made most of it as a Mammy singer, working in blackface. Before him there had been the Negro Bert Williams who, along with other Negroes, "blacked up" over their own black skins, using burnt cork, and whitened their lips, to give them the caricature appearance they felt was most effective.

Lena Horne had sung her way up from the little saloons to the big saloons and was starring at the old Savoy-Plaza Hotel (where the General Motors building now stands) on Fifth Avenue. George Jessel, then in his fifties, had gone there for Lena's opening with Grace Moore, the General David Sarnoffs, and some others.

What follows is one of show business's classics as recounted by the hero himself.

After Lena finished her program of songs that night, she disappeared from the room. Jessel left his table, found her, and invited her to join his table. Lena replied that she wasn't allowed in the room except as an entertainer and wasn't permitted to sit with the guests because of her color.

"I'm a guest, and you're with me," Jessel argued, and he insisted that she come to his table.

She did go, nervously, knowing she was doing something she shouldn't be doing, according to the rules of that time.

After his first success, Jessel decided to take Lena to another forbidden place, the Stork Club. (Lena says Jessel's memory is bad; that this happened at 21 and that she never made the Stork Club.) When he and Lena arrived there, Jack Spooner, the maitre d', a kindly man but bound by the customary restrictions, gave Jessel a negative sign by shaking his head. "Drunk with power and a little champagne," Jessel pressed the matter.

"Do you have a reservation?" Spooner asked him, using the common device employed by headwaiters to keep out somebody undesirable.

"Of course I have a reservation," growled Jessel.

"Who made it for you?" Spooner asked, pretending to be looking over the reservation book to see if there was one.

"Abraham Lincoln!" thundered Jessel.

So Lena Horne was allowed in.

She was the top female Negro entertainer when I talked to her; she had top billing at the Capitol Theater and was soon to star at the Copacabana. She was under contract to MGM for pictures, but she could not get star billing there because the southern theaters—a big market—would not billboard a Negro headliner.

"They keep telling me about your romance with Lennie Hayton," I said that day, referring to the white musical director at MGM. "Are you married?"

"No, and I don't know whether I ever will be," she answered, but I saw in her thin, sensitive face a wish that she were. "How can you defy the world about marriage when other important things, such as getting a hotel room or casting a vote, are denied you because you're a Negro?

"Would you believe this? I can't even be seen *talking* to white people in pictures that are shown in the South. So," she laughed bitterly, "I can only be cast as a non-talking-to-white-people singer!"

When she appeared as a guest on Ed Gardner's popular radio program, "Duffy's Tavern," there had been a tempest about how she addressed Gardner, who was called Archie.

"People got into a group and said to Gardner, 'You can't let that Negro woman call you Archie.' They said I had to call him Mr. Archie. And this from people in show business! Ed went to the front for me, so we didn't call each other anything."

Lena was a top personality with no place to live. She asked a friend to find her a Hollywood residence. She was weary of the complaints about Negroes "ruining the neighborhood."

"Something away from the important people, where I won't offend anybody," she specified.

When she found a house in Nichols Canyon, some whites wanted to bar her by petition; but the liberals backed her, and she won.

Barred from the pleasures of life nearly every place she turned, Lena became frustrated and discouraged. However, her friend Paul Robeson urged her not to go the route of so many other Negroes, not to "join the party," not to turn Communist.

"Always," she told me, "there are people who want us to deny we're Negroes to make it easier for ourselves. They want us to say we're Indians or Mexicans or South Americans. I've worked in many hotels where they gave me a room to sit around in between shows but not to stay in or sleep in."

Later Lena came to the conclusion that a mixed marriage with Lennie Hayton (he died in 1971) would work out—her own mother had been happily married to a white man—for her and her people.

"My mother was unhappy only because of the attitude of the hotels, and she was hurt by the things she heard the maids saying about her," Lena added.

Still, when Lena and Lennie married, they kept their marriage secret for three years until people began to get accustomed to the idea. Gail Jones, her daughter by her first husband Lewis Jones, was later to marry director Sidney Lumet, who had previously been married to actress Rita Gam and socialite Gloria Vanderbilt. Therefore Lena Horne became the mother-in-law of a man who'd been married to just about the top name in New York society.

"I was constantly afraid of doing something wrong professionally that would reflect on my race," Lena said. "I'll never forget how frightened I was for Jackie Robinson when he came along in baseball. We knew that if he made the normal mistakes that baseball players make, it would reflect on Negroes. So we never forget we're Negroes. It's our burden."

While Lena was fighting her own battle—"she paid her dues," I've heard younger Negroes say—there were some night clubs on the West Side of New York City where Negroes were well treated.

A popular story illustrates the attitude of the "best people" for that section of the city. It was claimed that a rich playboy phoned his father one night from the West 54th Street police station.

"Father," the young man said, "I'm over here at the West 54th Street police station held on a charge of rape."

"Why, son," gasped his father, "what are you doing on the West Side of town?"

The Café Zanzibar, upstairs over the Winter Garden Theater on Broadway, played Negro stars and delighted in taking the money of the Negro customers. Headwaiters had orders to seat as many black customers as white customers if possible. The Zanzibar management found that the blacks were the best-paying, best-tipping patrons, and they made sure that blacks were properly treated.

On the night of the Joe Louis-Billy Conn fight in 1941, when Conn got overconfident and was knocked out in the thirteenth round after staggering Louis in the twelfth, there were 600 to 700 Negroes celebrating at the Zanzibar, most of them drinking champagne.

"It was a crowd from Detroit, and I had to borrow champagne from the other clubs to take care of them," recalls Carl Erbe, then one of the operators of the club. "The tips were enormous."

Bill Robinson ("Bojangles") was frequently a star at the Zanzibar, doing his famous stair dance—tapping up and down a few little stair steps. It was a simple routine, but it drove the crowd hysterical.

Once Bojangles was a guest at a White House correspondents' dinner attended by Franklin D. Roosevelt. As the president was riding up the ramp in his wheel chair into the hotel, he caught a glimpse of Robinson. Stopping the wheel chair, the president embraced the Negro star and told him that he was his favorite performer.

Liberalism may have been on the march, but nothing much was being done. Two of the blows struck for freedom were for the benefit of another minority, the Jews. Gentlemen's Agreement, winner of the 1947 Best Picture Oscar, exposed anti-Semitism. Dore Schary brought out Crossfire, also a serious treatment of anti-Semitism. Perhaps it was simply that life was thought to be comparatively uncomplicated in those early years after the war.

Ronald Colman was Best Actor in 1947 for A Double Life, and

Loretta Young was Best Actress for *The Farmer's Daughter.* It was also the time of the prime of Olivia de Havilland, who won Best Actress in 1946 for *To Each His Own* and again in 1949 for *The Heiress.*

It was unthinkable in those years for a Negro to try to get into the Waldorf-Astoria Empire Room or El Morocco as a customer (these places were on the East Side of town). Gradually, however, some Negro celebrities were admitted—one of the first was Congressman Adam Clayton Powell, who was at that time still married to Hazel Scott—but the management asked the columnists not to mention that one of "them" had been in their place. "Because then we'll have all of them coming . . ."

The clubs were defending their "property rights," or so they thought. If they allowed "them" in, the place would be overrun with "them," and it would soon be ruined. You could not blame any one individual or particular club owner. Nearly all felt that way. No single individual or group was responsible; rather it was the times. Perhaps some white columnist could have become a hero by crusading for the Negroes, demanding that they be treated equally, but none of us thought it was practical—or maybe we just didn't have the courage.

The major floor show night club, the Copacabana, which hired the top stars, admitted just a trickle of black customers—usually only famous or celebrated Negroes. Lena Horne, one of its stars, got increasingly furious when her black friends couldn't come in to hear her sing.

"I'm doing something about this," she promised herself.

Bill Miller, a night club operator, was running Bill Miller's Riviera across the river in New Jersey. It was a beautiful club, with a ceiling that rolled back so that the patrons could sit under the stars. In the decade before, it had been Ben Marden's Riviera, with a plush gambling casino, which the authorities never discovered.

Bill Miller was bidding for the top talent for the Riviera. Lena Horne, in the early 1950s, saw an entering wedge for her people.

"I'll work for you if you'll let the colored people in," Lena ventured.

"Sure, if they're decent people and they've got money, they can come in," Bill Miller agreed.

Lena Horne says now, "So I quit the Copa and went to the Riviera. Bill kept his word. It was Bill Miller who broke the barrier."

Sammy Davis, Jr.—"young Sammy Davis"—was coming along then with his father and uncle in the Will Mastin Trio—an act in which he wasn't even mentioned by name because he was just the kid, the unimportant one. Sammy was so vital, so energetic, and so fresh that he immediately won the respect of the café-going public and was quickly on his way to becoming "the world's greatest entertainer," as Jolson had been called before him.

We saw Sammy Davis, Jr., at Bill Miller's Riviera, too, and the blacks rushed there to enjoy the antics of the newest public member of their race. Sammy's father and uncle had confined him to dancing, drumming, and impersonations in the beginning. Even today, when Sammy is always able to draw sellout crowds to hear him sing, I think of him as a wild dancer "flying off in all directions," as Stephen Leacock once said.

Like nearly all stars, Sammy soon gathered an entourage, mostly of whites. Instantaneously popular, he was invited almost every place. He made inroads for the blacks in some of the sacrosanct areas without realizing he was doing it. He was one of the blacks El Morocco and the Waldorf were always glad to seat at choice tables. After all, Sammy was dating Kim Novak. He would eventually marry the Scandinavian blonde beauty Mai Britt after saying he didn't care what color their babies would be—"I wouldn't care if it was polka dot!"

By the middle 1950s, Sammy was at the Copacabana—it was now freely admitting Negro customers—and so was everybody else. It was the thing to do: to go to the Copa to see Sammy, who was so great at twenty-eight years old.

Marilyn Monroe might be there, or Doris Duke, Mike Todd, and his girl Evelyn Keyes, and Mike's devoted admirer and companion, Eddie Fisher (with Debbie Reynolds)—who were going to make a lot of news later. Sammy would be wearing his eyepatch—his artificial eye wasn't in working order yet—and he would be singing, dancing, blowing a cornet, and doing impersonations of the stars, including Eddie Fisher.

Thin, catlike, swift of movement, Sammy was a very happy fellow as he swept around the floor with the microphone in his hand.

Frequently there wasn't much floor—the club was so crowded—and Sammy would sing sitting atop the piano.

Pajama Game was a hit Broadway show, and redheaded Janis Paige, the star, came in to see Sammy at the midnight show. Sammy introduced her.

"Ask Janis to sing!" a voice called out.

"Oh, no, you don't," Sammy shouted back. "I went to see *Pajama Game* five times, and nobody asked me to sing."

Sammy did an impersonation of Arthur Godfrey, who had just dazzled the nation by discharging Julius La Rosa and others of his cast.

Mimicking Godfrey's voice, Sammy said, "I'd like to introduce my cast to you, but it's impossible—I've fired everybody."

Sammy was getting top money and acting like a rich man. The comedians in Las Vegas claimed that when he and his father and uncle arrived, they traveled in three Cadillacs with a Thunderbird as an outrider.

Then you just *had* to see Sammy. One night I took Groucho Marx to see him.

"Is he as great as Jolson?" I asked Groucho afterward.

"He's greater," Groucho said. "Jolson could only sing and tell stories."

When Sammy decided to marry Mai Britt in 1960, he knew that he would be criticized. I phoned him at the New Lotus Club in Washington and asked him about his reaction to some faint booing he'd received at the Democratic convention that year. Did he think he was endangering his career? Was he, in fact, already suffering from his decision?

"I've got a flash for you," he replied. "If the people of America want me to go to Europe to live because I'm going to marry Mai Britt, I'll do it. But I've got another flash for you. I just know they don't feel that way. I'm positive they're not small-minded enough to try to badger a guy into not marrying the girl he loves."

The "rumors" that he was suffering a decline in popularity had reached him, he confessed, and he had consulted his managers and agents. They had laughed and shown him the offers for his services and the confirmed bookings.

"My picture man laughed and said, 'What slacking up are you

talking about? There isn't any. I got three picture scripts for you on my desk.'

"I'm happy to tell you," Sammy said, "there's no problem, and I know there won't be."

But the marriage led to reports of a new kind—that Sammy was anti-Negro—and he took steps through his publicists to correct that false impression.

"They claim I want to be white," he said. He didn't know how the ugly rumor had started. Because he loved a white girl and had dated other white girls? Because he had many white friends? He said that if he employed a white man, some Negroes muttered that he was anti-Negro. Carefully, he pointed out that when he was on tour he took one white employee and five Negroes.

Next Sammy converted to Judaism, and this brought a wave of jokes, particularly when he refused to work on the movie *Porgy and Bess* during Yom Kippur. When Sammy told Samuel Goldwyn he didn't work on holy days, Goldwyn thought this was a night club joke.

"Mr. Goldwyn, I'm a Jew, and I don't work on Yom Kippur," Sammy declared, thrusting his jaw out defiantly.

Dorothy Dandridge was the first Negro entertainer ever nominated for an Oscar for acting in a major role (*Carmen Jones*), and she had high hopes of getting it. However, her close friend Otto Preminger sensed defeat for her, according to Earl Conrad, her biographer. He told her she wouldn't get the award.

"Why not?" she asked him.

"The time is not ripe," he answered.

The time indeed didn't ripen until 1963, when Sidney Poitier was chosen Best Actor for *Lilies of the Field*.

By 1963 Sidney Poitier, Sammy Davis, Jr., Diahann Carroll, Leslie Uggams, Harry Belafonte, Sarah Vaughan, Lena Horne, Duke Ellington, Cab Calloway, Lionel Hampton, and Louis Armstrong were welcomed everywhere—East Side or West Side. Not only welcome, they were especially invited.

One night in 1970, two black stars, Billy Daniels and Timmy Rogers, met in Danny's Hideaway and embraced. They kissed each other. Emerging from the embrace, Billy Daniels exclaimed as he looked around the expensive restaurant: "Man, we're gettin' in everywhere!"

Billy was right; they were everywhere. Flip Wilson was everybody's beloved on television following the popularity of another black comedian Bill Cosby. Diana Ross, formerly of The Supremes, sat in front of me at the Frazier-Ali fight and was unquestionably one of the prettiest, most exciting, best dressed women there. Pictures of prosperous young black men in floor-length white or beige fur coats caught your eye in the newspapers. I saw them sweeping past me in the lobby of the Hotel Americana on fight night and pulled back into a corner to stare. A beautiful black girl in yellow hot pants took my eye from the men, some of whom wore matching fur hats. I had never seen a sexier-looking girl. Yet only twenty-five years ago such a sight would have been unthinkable.

Lena Horne had complained that she hadn't been able to find a suitable Hollywood home twenty-five years before. Recently, however, I rode up to the exclusive Doheny Estates to Leslie Uggams's lavish twelve-room $100,000 home; Dionne Warwick had a home up the street. The road curved, and the tires snarled as we twisted and climbed above the fog and smog.

When we got out of the car to walk onto the patio and look down at the poor people, the young mistress of the mansion boasted, "I found it first!"

"I told Graham [her white Australian husband Graham Pratt], 'I think I've found the house.'" She was steering me about, showing me the pool, wearing a white voile blouse over a brown bikini.

"It's perfect. We're so happy, aren't we, Graham?" she said, ensconced there in the Hollywood Alps.

Changes were seen everywhere. In 1962, Diahann Carroll came to my office to protest that the producers of the movie *No Strings* were running away from the color issue and giving the leading role, which she'd originated on Broadway, to Nancy Kwan.

"There are very few roles for black girls as it is, and I feel insulted and hurt," she said. "Those of us who remain silent about these things do a disservice to our children." She then went before the House Education and Labor Committee and charged that "people in hiring positions are just not interested in working with Negroes."

It was so bad, she complained, that blacks "could not even be a summer replacement on television."

Diahann was right, at the time. The producers of *No Strings,* however, said they were looking for parts to build up Nancy Kwan, and inasmuch as they would spend $4,000,000 on the picture, "We must have a name."

The implication was that Diahann Carroll was not a name and that Nancy Kwan was. Then, of course, Diahann Carroll became "Julia" with her own television series and turned into a bigger name than Nancy Kwan. The movie wasn't made, but what an interesting reversal it would be if the producers were to make the film now and give the role to Diahann instead of Nancy "because we have to have a name."

Suddenly, it seemed, many white actors were complaining that *they* were discriminated against. The tide had turned, and some producers deemed it good politics to hire only Negro actors.

"Even for westerns," complained one shoot-'em-up white actor. "Did you ever see so many colored cowboys?"

The fight is still going on for more gains for the blacks, and Lena Horne is still battling for them a quarter of a century after she began. "The technicians, the stage crews, and the writers don't have much black representation," she told me. "We are entitled to that, too."

When Flip Wilson won a 1971 Emmy for the Best Musical Variety series, I recalled how much he moved me when he told me a couple of years before of his rough childhood living in foster homes.

"I was a bad kid in Jersey City," Flip said. "How can a kid who ran away thirteen times say he was not a bad kid?

"When I was eight, I was living in a foster home. The state was buying milk for me. I could look down through a knothole in the floor and see the lady giving my milk to her child. I was hungry and I cried when I saw her little boy drinking my milk and I ran away.

"We were never allowed out in front of the house of any of the foster homes where my brother and sister and me lived. We had to stay in the back so nobody could see us. That made me cry and I would run away again.

"They would catch me and ask me why I ran away. Then they would put me right back in the same place and I'd run away again.

"I begged them, 'Put me in the reform school.' They had put my brother and sister in the reform school and it was better than being in a foster home. In the reform school, I had my first birthday party. I got my first birthday presents—a box of Crackerjacks and a can of shoe polish so I could learn to shine shoes. I was very, very happy in the reform school."

And now Wilson is the top man in TV musical variety, the well-paid, highly respected champion in his field. That just about sums up the story of the blacks in Show Business.

18

Tin Pan Valley Town:
Johnny Cash on His Turf

"TIN PAN VALLEY . . ."

I remember hearing the words and smiling over them during a visit to Nashville many years ago.

Not Tin Pan Alley but Tin Pan *Valley*, in the mountains of Tennessee, the home of country music. The music with the wail and moan and twang, plucked out of the "gittars" by the hillbillies who, though they often couldn't read music, could make music and let it talk for them.

I don't know exactly who popularized the Tin Pan Valley expression. Abel Green of *Variety* and columnist Red O'Donnell of the Nashville scene may have coined the expression; they probably don't know either. But the fact is that in the 1950s there were prophetic people in Nashville who foresaw that the "Nashville sound" would one day be a tremendous influence in music and would win respect for Tin Pan Valley from the entire world.

Dreamers they were, haunting the little country music recording studios and the old barn-like Grand Ole Opry, grasping for the recognition, which some of them did not live to see.

Now, in the 1970s, Nashville is one of the great recording centers of the world. The top artists go there to obtain that Nashville sound as background and atmosphere.

One chilling December afternoon I found myself revisiting Nashville, deep in the Great Smokies, in Andrew Jackson country. I was going to meet Johnny Cash in person and to watch him televise a special show, which would recount the history of country and western music. Johnny Cash is a man of some mystery and considerable power, virtually inaccessible to newsmen.

"Be sure to get his picture for me," Mavis, the maid, called out to me as I left the apartment. "Make sure he puts his name on it, or nobody'll believe it."

"She wants to make her boyfriend jealous," my wife said, nodding her approval.

An icy rain struck my face on Broadway and at JFK Airport, but once we were aboard American Airlines' flight 261 to Nashville and off the ground, all went well. We were soon far above the clouds. Pleasant strips of bright sunshine made us wonder what it would be like down on the ground in the state renowned for its beauty.

The weather had made flying hazardous in New York, but in Nashville we landed twenty minutes early.

We were met by slick, suave Jeffrey Rose, director of promotion and publicity of Screen Gems' New York office, with a limousine.

I was curious about the reasons for this red carpet treatment. Obviously, Screen Gems, producer of the Johnny Cash show, was putting on the publicity pressure. I soon learned that the Cash show had suffered a tumble in the ratings—"a devastating drop" is what the *Music City News*, a local trade paper, stated in strong terms.

"And the Cash show has for one program reversed its field in great talent selection and gone to heavy emphasis on genuine country talent . . ." the paper added.

Making no effort to conceal its jealousy on behalf of its own mountain people, the publication said that the show didn't use enough country talent. And "there's strong evidence that even the great Johnny Cash can't hold an audience for more than a season or two when his product is diluted with seventy to eighty percent other stuff." Note that contemptuous reference to "other stuff." The article indicated that if the show were dropped, it couldn't be blamed on country music.

That, of course, was the reason for Johnny Cash's sudden decision to do two shows—part one and part two—of the history of country music. The big fellow with the Indian look (he's one-quarter Cherokee) from Dyess, Mississippi County, Arkansas, sixty-five miles from Memphis, was going to let the country music fanatics know that he remains loyal to the sound that made him famous and very rich.

Johnny is just about the top of the current country crop, they told me on the way into town. He has a homestead there that's been likened to the famous William Randolph Hearst ranch at San Simeon, California, though it is admittedly smaller. He has numerous corporations, the "umbrella" being The House of Cash, a name that delights Johnny and his family. Tourists clearly are as interested in Johnny Cash as they are in the celebrated Parthenon constructed in the 1890s for an exposition, or in Andrew Jackson's big white-columned residence, The Hermitage.

There we were at the handsome Ramada Inn, gathering place of the visiting country artists, where many a remarkable late night and early morning adventure could be chronicled.

Nashville, now a booming city of over half a million, has cleaned up what was once a slum and red light district and has made the area quite attractive. Gazing out of the window of a large suite they've supplied us, we saw a sign across the way: *"Bruton Snuff."*

"On a clear day, you can smell the snuff," goes a local joke.

The farmers down this way still use snuff, but the music makers around the Ramada Inn know about it from hearsay only. For music making has become modern and urbane, with nary a hillbilly to be seen. Some television staff executives from Hollywood have offices down the corridor, with pretty blonde, mini-skirted secretaries at the phones and typewriters—all part of the Johnny Cash show. Everybody was well dressed, antiseptic looking, and articulate. Sitting in the coffee shop, we heard the country artists Homer and Jethro, who are appearing on the Cash show: "I'm going to go up and get into my funny clothes," says Jethro. We assumed that he meant hillbilly attire.

"I've got funnier clothes than this," he said (he's actually normally dressed).

When we saw him later, just before the program, he and his partner were both wearing dinner jackets. It's tuxedo time for the Johnny Cash show, though not for Johnny himself. He's in boots with a frock coat that spreads over his massive shoulders, and he sports a gray sparkling silk brocade vest.

"Did you design that outfit?" I asked him.

"Me and Andrew Jackson," he answered.

"John"—as his intimates call him—said he'd see us later. The first item of business was to clear up the libel about the "gittar" players not being able to read music.

On my first visit to Tin Pan Valley—back in the days of Hank Williams, Sr., when Harry Truman was president and a longhair referred to a classical musician and not a hippie—one of the locals word-painted a quaint picture of the hillbilly musicians who came out of the brush with their jugs and their guitars and their music.

"These old guys bring their songs in here and get somebody to put them on tape or on a record," this informant said.

"They can't write it out; they can't read music. They have to get somebody else to listen to it and put it down on paper. That's how a lot of this music is born."

And, he said, when these musicians sat in an orchestra or a backup group, they just played along by ear. "They are a little suspicious of anybody who reads music. They consider it an affectation—like going to school."

True enough it was then; there's a different breed of cat around now. Some of the country singers study music at beautiful Vanderbilt University in Nashville.

And the Country Music Association's song of the year, "Sunday Mornin', Come on Down," was written by a Rhodes scholar, Kris Kristoffersen, who enjoys the Nashville sound and the Nashville scene. "Johnny Cash took him under his wing, and he's written songs for John," one gentleman states.

Even most of the unsung but not unsinging backup musicians can at least read music now, their defenders claim. The Jordonaires, the vocal group that has backed up many stars, including Elvis Presley, were a little hurt by the claim that the musicians couldn't read music. Gordon Stoker, their manager, maintained that they only give that impression because they're so relaxed during recording sessions. He insisted that three-fourths of them can take down musical notes as a secretary takes dictation.

A short ride through "Music City" seemed in order while Johnny Cash was "preparing." The first sign we saw was "Minnie Pearl's Roast Beef," over one of her restaurant franchises.

Minnie Pearl! I haven't seen her in person since she starred at the Astor Roof, when there was still an Astor Hotel. I remember talking to her once with Vice-President Alban Barkley in Washington at a big party given by Evelyn Walsh McLean. Minnie Pearl was a big country music star then and still is today. She's also on Johnny Cash's special.

A Holiday Inn loomed up. "How many are there in Nashville?" I inquire.

"Six," the driver says, "but Memphis has eleven." His tone is apologetic. "Of course, Memphis is where it started." He obviously felt better after that explanation. "You see that school building? That's Nashville's first public school. Dinah Shore and Phil Harris went there, but not at the same time."

"Indiana claims Phil Harris," I pointed out.

"He was born in Indiana, but when he was four years old, he wised up and moved to Nashville."

The driver headed for Music Row on 17th Avenue. It surprised me, for it isn't actually a row. It's a two-block residential area with some attractive new buildings and some old homes converted into offices.

ASCAP has a new building that's impressive, as does RCA. In addition, I spotted Columbia Recording Studios, Decca, Cedarwood Publishing, and several others. Then a new and different looking hexagonal glass-fronted building situated amid some trees appeared—"the Country Music Hall of Fame."

"Mama Maybelle was enshrined in there recently," Jeffrey Rose informed me.

That would be Mama Maybelle of the Carter family. And the Carter family is a country music institution. One of the three Carter daughters is June Carter, the wife of Johnny Cash and co-star of his show.

June Carter is also the girl who got Johnny Cash to quit taking pills: not narcotics but "ups and downs"—the sleepers and the stimulants. She helped Johnny to get back on his feet, and he doesn't need pills anymore. If he hadn't quit the pills, he probably wouldn't be the top of the crop with all his wealth. Johnny gives June most of the credit, though June insists that Johnny did it all by himself.

It's a rather familiar story to country music enthusiasts who know all about Johnny's past and present. June Carter is extraordinarily frank about it.

We visited the dressing room in the Grand Ole Opry Building, a one-time church, with one section labeled "Confederate Gallery." June, a shapely, busty brunette, mother of two daughters by a previous marriage and a baby son by Johnny, is sitting on a high makeup chair, seemingly in good spirits. She has the look of a happy young lady. I was puzzled when she mentioned that she had met me before.

"At the Copacabana, in a party with a lot of Tennessee people and Frank Clement," she explained. June referred to the long-time governor of the state, since killed in an auto accident when he was reportedly driving on the wrong side of the road. "It was the night that Dean Martin and Jerry Lewis did their last show together at the Copacabana," June Carter Cash says with a beautiful smile.

"I know why I was there, but why were you there?"

Though Mama Maybelle Carter and the three sisters—the Carter Family—were important in country music, June Carter had gone to New York to study dramatics with Sanford Meisner in a class that included Tom Poston, Joel Grey, Julie Wilson, and Barbara Baines. She progressed and did some television acting in New York and Hollywood.

"But I like Tennessee, so I came back."

June and Johnny Cash worked on some country shows. Both were married and breaking up.

"We both started talking seriously about getting married to each other," June says. "I had two girls, and he had four girls. Between us, we had six girls. It wasn't easy to get married. I had to see whether I could condition myself to getting married again."

June knew that 6'2" Johnny, with a scar on his chin from a cyst operation and one weak eye—"probably from measles"—was a high wheeler, lived hard and fast, and frequently took pills just because he always wanted to be awake. It worried her.

"My family had worked with Hank Williams, Sr."—who had died

from pills—"and we knew the consequences. And I said, 'Oh, my goodness, Johnny's on pills.'

"I was workin' on his show, and I just couldn't accept him takin' those pills. So I'd flush his pills down the john. I told him, 'I flushed your pills down the drain.'

"He'd be a nice Johnny Cash about it, though. He'd just buy some more.

"I went through about three or four years of that. Finally, we both began to realize that if we were going to be in love, he was going to have to get off pills, and I was going to have to get over being such an independent cuss. We had plenty of quarrels then, but I stood right up to him and fought like a tiger.

"Johnny quit the pills all by himself. He finally decided he was too good a man to treat himself the way he was doing. He took life by the tail and gave it a swing. He adjusted himself. There's nobody who can adjust you. You've got to do it yourself. A man just has to be a man, and John was."

By 1968, when Johnny was no longer taking pills, he and June decided they'd get married in June or July.

"We decided we could see our way down the road together. I told Johnny, 'Maybe I'd better tell them'"—her daughters.

"Yes, I'd love that," daughter Rosie said, but daughter Caroline went much further in her enthusiasm for the project. June had thought about having the wedding in Las Vegas, not in Nashville: the papers would make too much of a field day of it.

Meanwhile, daughter Caroline must have consulted an expert at school. "I've got it all set," she announced. "You can go to Franklin, Kentucky, and get married in one day." Caroline also advised them that there was no sense in waiting until June or July. Why not do it now?

They were eventually married in a little Methodist church in Franklin in March.

How did she know about Franklin? June murmured, "I don't know. Children know everything. As for myself, I didn't have a lick of sense the whole weekend. I burned everything I tried to cook. We lived on hamburgers."

And so it was a country music marriage that could have been material for a movie. How did they solve their problems? Was religion involved?

"No-o-o-o-o," June drawls, pausing momentarily. (She apologizes for her Nashville sound. "I took speech in New York, and the instructor almost committed suicide.") "I go to churches and pray," she nods. "Mostly I just ask for wisdom. I say a sinner's prayer telling God how I fell short of what I wanted to do. Sometimes Johnny'd say, 'Where you goin'?' I'd say, 'To church,' and he'd say, 'Could I go along?' I'd look over at him, and he'd be praying, too. I talk to God every day. Sometimes it's out in the woods."

The marriage has been enormously successful. They have a son, and Johnny and the Carter Family—mother and the three sisters—have won new fame. "I've been very happy with Johnny, and he has never let me down," says June, her face all aglow.

"Sometimes he takes the baby out walking in the woods. The baby will go out for three hours with his daddy. Johnny has a back pack, and the baby just sits down in it on his back while he walks through the woods."

Johnny Cash has frequently spoken of his baby son—and shown him on television—and of his love for June. This has led to some kidnap threats, which have made Cash more inaccessible than usual to his fans and to the press. Johnny's desire for privacy had added to the mystery and myth about him. Because he has sung in and recorded in prisons, there is a belief that he was a lifer. Those who have explored the records say he has been picked up a couple of times, once for passing out when he was going without sleep and once for picking some flowers that didn't belong to him.

The time has come to watch Johnny and talk to him.

I was up in the balcony in one of those curved wooden pews—at least they seem like pews to me. The group with me was talking about Cash, but I didn't see him yet.

"Which one's Johnny?"

"He's not there yet."

Then he strides out, taller than anybody around him. He walks with long, authoritative, heavy steps. Even if I didn't know what he looks like I would nevertheless have picked him out of the crowd as the star. The scar, the weak eye, the Cherokee ancestry, and the rather tight collar of his frock coat combine to give him a very serious appearance. The broad shoulders, wide face and forehead, and heavy stride suggest his strength. He wears the guitar around his shoulder easily; it is not an albatross around his neck like some guitars carried by other performers. Johnny Cash has the bearing of a real star.

There was the usual delay for the lighting and sound adjustments.

I was invited downstairs to observe the activity more closely. The crew was talking about the show and Johnny Cash.

"Last year was Cash's year," somebody said. "Last year Cash's LP sales exceeded anybody's in the business."

"His sales in Europe are astronomical," another mentioned. "His *Folsom Prison* album is the best seller in Denmark this week, and it came out two years ago."

"This is his sixteenth year," the first person said. "He's really sustained. Got started with 'Cry, Cry, Cry' in 1955. Got started with Presley, you know. They had the same manager, Sam Phillips, in Memphis. They even worked some dates together. Bangin' around in a beat-up old car. But Presley's momentum was much more advanced than Cash's."

The immediate objective on the stage in the Grand Ole Opry is for Cash to sing "The Prisoner's Song," which Vernon Dalhart brought out in 1924—the first country song to sell a million records. And Cash is trying. His words, "And if I had the wings of an ain-jell . . ." ring out clearly, but there's some problem with the orchestra. Johnny says very gravely to the director, "They're speedin' up on me too much."

A long pause follows. Then somebody brings up a gift box, which melts Johnny completely.

"Somebody sent me some cookies!" He grins and puts a large fist into the box, extracts a cookie, devours it, and takes another. He continued munching cookies during the rehearsal until he must have consumed a dozen. He offered cookies to grateful co-workers, who crunched contentedly.

With the delay on stage continuing, Cash moved over to the sidelines. We shook hands and recalled bits and pieces from the last time we had talked. He had been attending a tribute dinner for Bob Hope in New York, and he had split his pants in the back when he bent over to retrieve his guitar pick, which had fallen to the floor. It had made the evening memorable for him and also for those who were standing behind him.

"June said the Lord busted my pants," Johnny had reported when we discussed it. "She said I was entertainin' in high society, and the

Lord, to keep me humble and from flyin' too high in his little old sky, busted my pants."

Despite that, Johnny said that he likes New York City (so many people don't just now) and that he and June visit the city more frequently to see movies and stage shows.

"We saw *1776* the other night. It was fantastic." He ate another cookie. "I love history anyway. I was halfway through something I was writing for the three astronauts. They called and wanted some of my records for the next trip, and *1776* really sparked me to finish it. I left June up in New York and came home and did it. Just me and the guitar. I worked on it about three days. I call it 'These Are My People,' about the astronauts being trailblazers like Davy Crockett. I thought instead of giving them records, I'd write an original. I may release it as an album. It's my first totally honest work."

"What do you mean by totally honest?"

"It's the first and only take, and it's unrehearsed. I just sat down and did it."

He returned to the stage and his sister Reba, who looks after his money, was present.

"He has a lot of land, mostly around his house at Hendersonville," she informed me. "He has bought it ultimately for development. Probably a thousand acres. His idea is that they're not going to make any more land, and he's going to get all he can before they run out of it."

"How did Johnny become a country singer?"

"We always had music in our family. We would sing around the piano. John started singing in the air force and was laughed at, of course. When he graduated from school, he went to Detroit to work in the automobile plants like all the boys did. He was gone ten days. He couldn't take it, so he joined the air force.

"Our town only had a thousand people, and there was nothing else to do. He served four years—three in Germany—and worked in Intelligence. He came out in 1954 with a discharge, and in 1955 he went to Sun Records. His first record, 'Cry, Cry, Cry,' was an immediate hit. It sold 50,000 records. Tennessee Ernie Ford's song 'Sixteen Tons' was the big hit then."

There was another break in the rehearsal, and Johnny came back to the sidelines, diving in after more cookies. His wife arrived on stage, and they kissed.

"I'm fixin' to get made up," she said and left again.

"What's the biggest change you've noticed in music in the last couple of years?" I managed to ask him.

"I don't know about any change. For me the big thing's been the upsurge in record sales for me since *Folsom Prison*. I wanted that prison reaction since I appeared at San Quentin Prison in 1959. It's just that they're showin' their appreciation. They react to everything I do, whistlin' and stampin'.

"I had this song 'Folsom Prison Blues,' which I never thought of doing as a record. Well, I did two shows there in 1968. All the boys knew the song and wanted me to do it, so I recorded it in the cafeteria. That was it."

"What more do you want to do with your music?"

"I'm doin' what I want to do right now." He enjoys television. "It's a very important show."

He remembered back to 1955 when he made his first contact with Sam Phillips in Memphis. "I called him for an audition, and after I tried to get to him for six months, he finally decided to listen to me."

"Who would you say is your favorite singer?"

"Well, I like just about anybody that's got it."

Sitting around the Ramada Inn later, I talked with Jeff Rose about Johnny Cash's comeback, and I was told I should read Paul Hemphill's book *The Nashville Sound* because I haven't caught the real impact of Johnny's achievements, the greatness of his personal joust with life.

According to Hemphill, Johnny was really hooked on those pills. He spent six or seven years in a fog. In fact, he was arrested at El Paso International Airport in 1965 with 668 stimulant tablets and 475 tranquilizer pills stuffed in a sock hidden in his guitar. He was fined $1,000. Two years later the police found him stumbling around a little town in Georgia and threw him in jail. They told him he was looking so close to death that they were thinking of giving him mouth-to-mouth resuscitation.

The strange part of this story, as Hemphill points out, is that a lot of fans were afraid Johnny would be ruined by the arrest for possession of pills. Instead, it made him a martyr, a hero.

To much of Tin Pan Valley, the leader of it all is Chet Atkins— "Mr. Guitar"—who likes to say "I'm just a guitar player," although he's the head of RCA Victor in that area and has cut more than forty albums and sold better than 3,500,000 copies.

"Architect of the Nashville Sound" is one of the designations for Chet, who took his guitar with him when he left the fifty-acre farm where he was born in Union County and started out for the big city —Knoxville—twenty miles away.

Mother Maybelle Carter—of the same Carter family that took over Johnny Cash—liked his guitar playing and asked him to work with them. After that he was on his way.

Chet knocked around the radio stations in Tennessee and other states, plucking his guitar and learning the business. Eventually he made it to the Grand Ole Opry. He won respect because he was quiet but effective, and he wanted all the good musicians to go to Nashville. They liked to work with him. He was the most dogged advocate of country music. He thought it had a future even when rock 'n' roll was threatening to drive it out of business.

RCA Victor put him in charge as its Nashville vice-president in the dark days of the late 1950s. Atkins sensed that radio needed country music, and he realized that country music, in turn, needed radio. He became a successful executive and made a profit for his company.

He also adapted to the new sounds concocted by the electronic geniuses of Tin Pan Valley. He kept country music from expiring and, though he's a rich man now, he's still a guitar player.

Through it all, Chet has maintained a sense of humor. At one recording session the musicians were telling a joke about a plane trying to land when the landing gear and wheels got jammed.

The pilot, an old boy from the holy roller meeting days, knew about stomping the floor for emphasis during prayer time.

"Everybody stomp, like in meetin'," the pilot said, "and we'll stomp a hole in the floor of the plane. Then we'll stick our feet through the holes, and when we hit the ground, we'll all start runnin'."

"That's funny," Vice-President Chet Atkins said. "We'll leave that in."

19

The Talk-Talk-Talk Shows

MAYOR JOHN LINDSAY was presenting an award to Johnny Carson. "Johnny," said the mayor, "is America's midnight answer to 'No, honey, I'm too tired tonight!'" The mayor added, "We're always very glad to see Johnny when he's passing through town."

"What's Jack Paar really like?" they used to ask when Jack talked —and cried—on the "Tonight Show" on NBC. Nobody asks what Carson's really like. He's undoubtedly one of the cleverest writers on television and one of the most disciplined performers. He draws great crowds when he makes personal appearances in Las Vegas. Johnny has become rich by putting one little word after another— in conversation. He has kept up with the revolution in show business, or a little ahead of it, and surely he can stay around a few more years if he wants to. And he'll unquestionably want to, for the money and the prestige attached to his position are unmatchable.

The top man of the talkers has been mugged, robbed, divorced, and once or twice he's been denounced. The late Dorothy Kilgallen criticized him for alleged bad taste for remarks he made at the Lyndon B. Johnson inauguration.

"For Dorothy Kilgallen to criticize me for bad taste," Carson said the following night on his show, "is like being criticized by Emmett Kelly [the circus clown with all the patches on his pants] for the clothes I wear." The nighttime audience got the idea.

Figuring out that he does from 185 to 190 one and one-half hour shows in a year, Carson says he's entitled to those nights off, which the comedians and even Mayor Lindsay rib him about. Johnny has a private life that he does succeed in keeping comparatively private. I was on one midnight safari with him before he did the "Tonight Show." A young girl insisted on picking him up in Sardi's, and he allowed her to do so. He was single at the time. The girl started by writing him a fan note. The next thing we knew, she was sitting with him at his table. Johnny and the girl went with my wife and me to a couple of night clubs. When we left them, the girl was doing fine, and so was Johnny. I have often wondered whether Johnny ever learned her name.

Johnny's occasionally a cut-up when he's relaxing. I missed his most notable evening of relaxation—at singer Jerry Vale's opening at the Copacabana in September 1969—and regretted having missed it when I read columnist Dan Lewis's account in the *Bergen Record-Call.*

Not having planned to attend the opening, Johnny didn't have a reservation. He joined a table reserved by Danny Stradella, owner of Danny's Hideaway, who customarily takes thirty to forty friends to the Copa openings. Carson soon was sitting at ringside with Red Buttons, Corbett Monica, Pat Cooper, Pat Henry, Bobby Ramsen, and Bobby Shields, comedians all.

Jerry Vale was going to sing "Mala Femina" and started to explain that it meant "Bad Woman."

"It's my favorite," Carson spoke up from his table.

"At this point, anything'd be your favorite," Vale retorted.

"Jerry started the song and barely got into the lyrics when Carson, in a stage whisper loud enough to be heard up to the Copa's terrace, suggested that Jerry go forth and multiply himself," wrote Dan Lewis. "He didn't exactly say it that way . . ."

"There was a gasp. The quaint expression stopped Jerry cold for a second. He finally managed to finish the song . . ."

Carson continued talking throughout the show. But though he was loud, he wasn't always clear, and Jerry Vale, a close friend of Carson under normal conditions, had a hard time getting through the show. Red Buttons at one point said, "I think it's terrible we don't give this kid a chance to sing."

As is customary, the star introduces the celebrities at the end of the act, and Jerry Vale saluted Carson among the others.

"Johnny carefully picked himself up off the seat to acknowledge the applause, then leaned over toward Vale (squashing Mrs. William B. Williams's hairdo in the process) and once more told Jerry what he could do for himself," Dan Lewis reported.

The crowd of Jerry Vale's friends went upstairs to the Copa lounge. There Carson developed an attachment to a girl who was there with somebody else. That looked dangerous, and Carson's friends speculated about how they'd get him home.

"Tell you what, Johnny," one of them suggested, "let's all go to Jilly's, and you can play the drums."

Playing drums is one of Johnny's other passions. Off they all went to Jilly's on West 52nd Street where Johnny spent about an hour thinking he was Gene Krupa.

TV talking is a mammoth business—Carson is justifiably a rich man because NBC collects more than $30 million a year from sponsors of his show. The other big-time TV talkers, Merv Griffin and David Frost, are also comparatively wealthy, and young Dick Cavett is on his way. There's gold in all that jollying. Carson bristles when anybody applies the needle by mentioning that he's made a fortune by mugging, looking into the monitor to see how he looks, making jokes about Ed McMahon's boozing, and possessing a sturdy set of vocal cords.

"Anybody who can bring it in is entitled to a fair profit from the thing he creates," says Carson. "I remember Humphrey Bogart being asked, 'What makes you think you're worth $250,000 a picture?' back when $250,000 was a lot of money. He said, 'Because I can get it.'"

Carson can get it.

The nighttime audiences are now split between Carson, Griffin, Frost and Cavett. Occasionally a viewer says that Frost is the greatest interviewer of all time, and that Carson is too saddled with the love of his own quips. Others claim that Cavett is the only intellectual, or that Merv Griffin has been a helluva singer ever since he introduced "I've Got a Lovely Bunch of Cocoanuts."

Carson's former lawyer, Arnold Grant, started Johnny on the road to big money in 1967 in one of TV's strangest stories.

Due to certain good connections, I was on the inside of that story. It was the turning point in Carson's career, financially. Forty-one at the time, and seemingly very successful, Johnny nevertheless was frustrated, moody and unhappy. He was making a lot of money for NBC. And he didn't think his $12,500-a-week was enough. He had to pay his replacements, he was docked when sick, and he didn't have authority to raise salaries or even to change producers.

The weak efforts he made to better himself were laughed off by the mean old bosses.

"You have a contract—live up to your contract." They were blunt with him.

Carson skipped off to a Florida vacation to brood about it. While he was trying to get out of his depression, the American Federation of Radio and Television Actors went on strike. Actors weren't crossing picket lines. Unable to tape any new shows, NBC reran some old Carson programs without consulting him.

Johnny was angry because the old programs were so obviously dated. Then he started thrashing about for his contract. "They can't do that to me without my consent! They haven't lived up to their contract. Oh, have I got them over a barrel!"

He reversed the tables. "Live up to *your* contract!" he flung at them. He left the show, announced he was suing for breach of contract.

Of course he didn't want to leave the show, but this was the beautiful club he'd been looking for.

"Holdout," they called him. Just like Babe Ruth when he was trying to get more money from the New York Yankees. Carson proceeded to scare hell out of NBC. Arnold Grant was one of the best lawyers around. Grant enlisted the aid of famous trial lawyer Louis Nizer. One day these two legal giants strode into NBC with their briefcases, exuding hostility, demonstrating by their confidence that they couldn't wait to get into court. This dramatic maneuver had its desired effect. NBC crumbled. NBC President Don Durgin swept aside the lesser executives. He began yielding, personally, to Johnny's lawyers on every point. Johnny wanted to change producers. They even gave in on that. They made a new contract, which was supposed to be secret—and it was—for a few hours.

An NBC executive who was on Johnny's side, and bitter about the people who'd tried to hold the old contract over his head, leaked the details of the new document to Bob Williams, the TV columnist, and me. We broke the story before most of the brass at NBC knew that Johnny had whipped them.

"Johnny's so much in the driver's seat now that he demoted General Sarnoff to Colonel Sarnoff," somebody said.

Over three years, Johnny was to get in excess of $4 million. ("A couple of million increase," we said.) NBC would pay his replacements when he was off, allow him to raise some of his staff's salaries, switch producers as he wished, and have absolute control of his program. He would have eleven weeks off a year, plus every Monday night off.

The holdout was back in camp! But that wasn't all the drama. Having had four weeks "rest," he was to go back on the air Monday night, April 24, 1967. It was to be a spectacular return.

On the Sunday night preceding the Monday night when he would return to the air, Johnny was March of Dimes Man of the Year at the New York Hilton. As chairman of the event, I sat next to Johnny on the dais. A lot of people were boozing, but he wasn't.

"Where'd you get those figures you printed about my new contract?" he asked me.

"You know," I said. "How were they?"

"Pretty close," he grinned.

Throughout the night, the comedians there to rib Johnny, as is customary in these Man of the Year events, referred to his new contract. Toastmaster Joey Adams said, "From now on, Johnny's going to let NBC keep 10 percent of everything they make."

"NBC's had to economize since making that new deal with Johnny," claimed Henny Youngman. "The Dean Martin show has been cut down to one case a week."

When I presented the March of Dimes Man of the Year citation to Johnny on the dais, he held it up for the photographers and pretended it was his new NBC contract.

"I didn't think I'd ever be feeling sorry for NBC," he said. "I feel almost guilty about my new contract, but I'm going to learn to live with that guilt."

Everybody there, it seemed, and the whole country of nighttime TV-viewers, would be watching Johnny's return to the air the next night. As we were all thinking of this, and that we were sitting in on a slice of TV history, a friend rushed up to me with a startling piece of news.

Joey Bishop—who had started a competing show live on ABC from Hollywood—was making a bold bid against Carson. He had phoned Jack Paar, Carson's predecessor on the "Tonight Show," and asked him to appear as a guest on his show opposite Carson.

Paar had agreed. "How do you say no to an old pal?" said Paar, who was already in Hollywood.

"I don't want to make it look like I'm against Carson," Paar elaborated. "I'm not. I don't think anybody could have done a better job than Johnny has done. But I think the brave thing for me to do was to say, 'Yes,' and the cowardly thing was to say, 'Sorry.'"

As word swept through the Hilton that Bishop was going to try to steal away Carson's thunder on his return, a new excitement arose. Buddy Hackett, who was to be one of Carson's guests, told me, "Carson will murder Paar. I promise you Paar will face a black screen for the first time in his life."

And so Carson returned as Paar went on with Bishop. Carson outdrew Bishop in the ratings (with more stations, to start with). And now four years later, Bishop, having lost his program, occasionally substitutes for Carson (an old friend) and is happy doing it that way.

"Maybe I'm getting old—I'm 53—but the idea of doing anything permanent doesn't appeal to me anymore," Bishop told me recently.

Carson isn't talking about it, but today he is a very rich boy from Iowa, compared to other boys from Iowa. NBC owes him several million dollars—maybe $5 million, maybe $6 million—in deferred income, thus assuring him a rich, restful, relaxing old age if he ever wants to quit talking.

And it is still rolling in. In 1969 the lure of business seized Johnny. He became a 50-50 partner of one of the shrewdest brains in Show Business, "Sonny" Werblin, the popular one-time agent who became owner of the New York Jets and brought Joe Namath into professional football. They teamed up to go into film production, real estate development, and other business opportunities such as Johnny Carson Clothes and Johnny Carson "Here's Johnny" restaurants.

As NBC again increased his salary in his 1970-71-72 contract—the amounts are getting rather large now—Johnny found himself to be quite a financial person. He was "totally independent," as they say, with his own corporate setup, a considerable capital, and a good tax arrangement. He was investing in conservative real estate and looking for pictures to produce.

"There's nothing wrong with money," Johnny says. "I don't see why anybody resents it. The only thing, you've got to spend it. Otherwise the stuff stacks up on you."

Merv Griffin's conceivably as wealthy or wealthier than Carson. He owns a couple of TV shows on NBC and is an owner of radio stations. He's just short of being a tycoon.

Merv's had a couple of colossal disappointments. One was his failure in New York when CBS built over the Cort Theater for him, spending $2,500,000 to set him up for the Battle of the Desks and Sofas against Carson.

Though he did consistently good shows and had a big loyal following, he couldn't "dent the Carson numbers." ("The numbers" is a TV expression referring to the ratings.)

CBS considered dropping Griffin. But he asked to be moved to Hollywood. Starting out weakly there, he was again on the precipice of cancellation. But after changing the format so that he treated one subject at length, he improved his ratings.

The Cort Theater that CBS built as his playpen was closed—a white elephant that had been used little over a year. Merv said he didn't miss New York. Most of his show business friends from New York had already moved to California.

Then, in September, 1971, he announced that he was quitting and that he wanted to try syndication.

Before going to CBS, Merv was a big hit with a show for Westinghouse. He discovered that former President Eisenhower and Mamie Eisenhower were enthusiastic Griffin-watchers. Visiting their farm at Gettysburg, Griffin proposed doing an entire show there, just walking and talking with the General.

"I'll do it," Eisenhower said. "How about the fee?"

"That's up to you," Griffin said.

"Thirty thousand dollars. I want to give it to a charity," Eisenhower said.

Thirty thousand dollars! Merv gulped. His guests customarily got $265.

"O.K.," Merv said, wondering whether he could swing it. He took the breath out of Westinghouse executives when he returned and told them, but they agreed.

Dwight Eisenhower had a massive heart attack and died before Merv could ever do the show.

The enthusiasm for TV talkers David Frost and Dick Cavett is enormous and will grow. I learned this from a private poll I've taken showing that the young viewers favor Cavett for his intellectuality. Some of the middle-aged scholarly types revere Frost for his straightforward interviews, never trying to "top" the last remark of the interviewee.

Frost, after winning the 1971 Emmy for Best Talk-Variety show, found himself getting an avalanche of other honors. Johnny Carson, a candidate, shrugged, "Well, if they want to give it to a limey, it's all right with me."

"Are you a citizen of the U.S.A. now?" Frost was asked.

"No, I'm a citizen of BOAC," he said. And he was, commuting almost weekly from New York to London where he was doing another TV show there.

Repeatedly he tells about his introduction in the House of Commons. As is customary, a herald admonishes the House, "Pray, Silence for the Prime Minister." Frost alleges that the herald was so dumbstruck when he was being presented that he said, "Pray for Silence from David Frost."

When Steve Allen was the big man on the "Tonight Show," and NBC also gave him Sunday night with instructions to knock off Ed Sullivan, I phoned him to ask if I could interview him on a certain subject.

"Okay," he replied. "Come over to the apartment in about an hour."

When I arrived, Steve, without ceremony, handed me several typed pages.

"I tried to figure out what questions you would ask," he said. "Here are your answers—and also your questions."

Stunned, I looked them over. He had indeed asked almost everything I had in mind. But just so that I wouldn't look completely foolish, I quickly made up two more questions—and left with the completed interview.

"Steverino"—as they used to call him—had that kind of an orderly, time-saving brain. In these talk show days and nights of Johnny Carson, Merv Griffin, and David Frost, it's difficult to remember that it was Steve who brought the desk and the couch into television, just as Good Guy Perry Como brought the stool. Steve proved that there was an audience for mere conversation.

"He keeps more people awake nights than coffee" was first said of Steve in the middle 1950s.

The talk show format has gone onward and upward since Steve —with one exception, in which I was involved, along with several other embarrassed columnists. Late in 1956, NBC told Steve that his Sunday night experiments against Ed Sullivan had been excellent, and that starting January 1, 1957, he was to devote himself entirely to a Sunday night show.

"So all right, but I hate to give up the week-night show because I've always thought of it as my means of making a living," Steve said. He hadn't yet been exhausted by the nightly routine.

Ernie Kovacs was expected to replace Steve on "Tonight," but Dick Linkroum, who was producing the "Today," "Home," and "Tonight" shows at NBC, got an inspiration: a show conducted by columnists in New York, Chicago, and Hollywood, called "America After Dark."

A disaster from the first, it was eventually nicknamed "America in the Dark" by some of our journalistic confreres, including Jack O'Brian. They were probably right. We undertook stunts, and we tried to be different. One night I went to an all-night beauty parlor and got my hair dyed red just to show what Broadway actresses had to go through.

"Setting back journalism two hundred years," commented John Crosby in the *New York Herald Tribune.*

That was bad enough, but I was stuck with red curly hair (I also got a permanent) for several days.

The show was undertaken before taping came into use. All our gruesome mistakes were there—live—to be winced at and ridiculed by millions. On opening night Bob Considine somehow found himself in Topeka, Kansas, interviewing Alf Landon.

"If he's smart, he'll stay there and go right on interviewing Alf Landon," wrote Harriet Van Horne in the *New York World-Telegram & Sun.*

It seemed to the audience that the engineers were switching every two minutes from Jack Lescoulie, the smiling answer man in New York, to some new scene.

Switch to Irv Kupcinet landing in a helicopter on the roof of the Merchandise Mart in Chicago . . . to Paul Coates talking to a woman at a card table of a poker club in Los Angeles . . . back to New York to Hy Gardner watching a New Year's baby get born ("The baby sensibly clammed up, but Gardner didn't," one critic wrote) . . . back to Chicago to Irv Kupcinet returning to the helicopter . . . then to Hollywood where Vernon Scott was attending a party where everybody was drinking too much and talking at the same time . . . and to Jayne Mansfield disclosing how girls can increase the size of their bosoms . . . back to the Harwyn in New York where George Gobel asks me whether I sleep in pajamas, and we both ask Joan Crawford whether she sleeps in the tops or the bottoms. Totally unprepared for this question, Joan favors both of us with murderous looks.

From this distance, "America After Dark" seems to me to have been a good *idea* for a program that couldn't be mastered mechanically or coordinated, at the time. Possibly it could be today, with tape. Regardless, the enthusiasm for it at NBC was nonexistent.

"I always meant to look at that show," General David Sarnoff said, snapping his fingers over his neglect, when it was cancelled at the end of the first thirteen weeks.

All of us brave columnists began scurrying for cover when word got out that the show was dead. I developed an urgent necessity to go to South America so that I wouldn't be in town for the funeral.

Inviting Dick Linkroum to lunch to ask his permission to leave the show immediately (he was glad to oblige), I listened to his problems.

"Who are we going to get to do what Steve Allen used to do?" he asked me.

"How about Johnny Carson? He's pretty good."

"We can't get him. He's tied up with ABC." Carson was then under contract to continue the "Who Do You Trust?" show.

"Have you thought of Jack Paar?" I asked. "He's doing a CBS radio show and that's about all."

"Good thought!" exclaimed Linkroum. "We thought of him before, but he was tied up with CBS doing the "Morning Show." I'll call him when I get back to the office."

As an old friend of Paar back in the days when he did the Jack Benny summer replacements and not much else, I hurried to my own office and tried to tip him off that NBC needed him. He had always been overly protective about his private phone number, and even now, when he was working very little, it was hard to get it. His reaction, after I passed on the news, was to tell me almost plaintively how he needed something like the "Tonight Show."

"I've been about to get out of the business," he confessed.

"Don't be overanxious," I cautioned him. "Don't call them. Make them call you." Paar promised he'd take my advice.

"Linkroum said he'd call you this afternoon," I said. "You're supposed to be surprised by the whole thing."

When Linkroum returned to his "THT" (Today, Home, and Tonight) offices at NBC, he was shocked by more bad news. The "Home Show" had been cancelled. He was so overwhelmed with sudden demands to repair that situation that he didn't get around to phoning Jack Paar.

"All that time," Paar said later, "I was biting my nails at home waiting for Linkroum to call me. Several times I went to the phone to dial NBC and got my finger to the dial, but I pulled back and didn't dial because of Earl's warning."

Paar was moody and introspective and suffered from rejection because he felt nobody wanted him. Now Linkroum didn't call. Had they settled on somebody else? Was he too troublesome? He'd had a battle on the CBS "Morning Show" with rumba bandleader Pupi Campo, who sued him for derogatory remarks when Paar fired him. It was a trying afternoon and night for Paar—and the next day Linkroum didn't call, either. Jack was near nervous collapse.

The third day, Linkroum called. Controlling himself, Paar listened politely, without betraying his concern. He got the job.

Characteristically, Jack remembered my part in his deal, but he forgot it, too. Once when he was damning the newspaper columnists, especially Dorothy Kilgallen, with whom he had a feud, he included me in the pack of rats of journalism. He made amends, I felt, when he told the straight story in his book.

Six years later, when Paar had established himself as television's greatest public weeper, had made a $3 million deal for thirty live weekly shows, had bought a radio station in New Hampshire, and had given up the "Tonight Show," he delivered himself of the opinion that Johnny Carson would be a good choice to succeed him.

Laughable now is the memory of NBC's once censoring Jack Paar's "W.C." anecdote, so injuring his tender sensibilities that he wept and went on strike, rushing to Florida—where he used the time off to make some real estate deals for himself.

Until one thinks back to Jack Paar, today's Johnny Carson may seem egomaniacal or eccentric. But Johnny Carson has never burst into tears over the rejection of one of his toilet jokes.

The "W.C." joke was never actually heard by the television audience. The incredible part of it is that it was then considered shocking. In parts of England, the letters "W.C." have two meanings: "wayside chapel" and "water closet."

A weary traveler wanted to go to the powder room and came to the letters "W.C." But the door to the water closet was latched from within. He waited and waited, and as his need grew, so did his impatience. In a loud voice he shouted, "Aren't you about through in there?"

But within was a religious person praying for his soul, and he heard not . . .

Another version—published in some newspapers at the time of the controversy—concerned an English couple trying to rent a house with a water closet.

The couple stated in a letter that they wanted a W.C. The rental agent receiving the letter didn't know what W.C. meant and asked his priest, who said it stood for wayside chapel.

The agent wrote back:

"The W.C. is in the woods about nine miles from the house, and you can only use it on Tuesday and Thursday."

Suddenly, everybody was challenging Paar. His "I kid you not" expression was an easy target for the skeptics. Peter Lind Hayes mimicked that expression of Jack's on a radio show: "Hellllllllooooo, friends, this is a sincere show . . . the most sincere show I've ever been sincere about . . . sincerely yours . . . Sinceres and Roebuck."

Paar cautiously avoided joining in. "I never fight with children," he said.

Hearing that Henry Morgan had said something snide, Paar yawned. "I only hope that fellow is as funny as he thinks he is."

1959 came, and Paar wrote a piece for *Look*. It said that two years before, when he was seeking work and I called him about the possibility of his getting the "Tonight Show," he was so desperate that he was almost ready for suicide. For this article, he received $35,000. And Doubleday paid him $40,000 for a book.

Jack Paar demonstrated very early that he had heart.

Immediately after he had the NBC "Tonight Show" clinched, Paar rejected an appearance on the Steve Allen NBC Sunday night show opposing Ed Sullivan, explaining:

"You know, for a year I've been living off Ed Sullivan? When CBS dropped me a year ago, I was very low, and Ed signed me for eight shows at $5,000 a show. I don't want to appear noble, but it wouldn't appear right to run immediately to Steve when I've been depending on Ed to keep me from starving, would it?"

Paar "developed the knack of doing the wrong thing," somebody remarked.

That was the thing that made him popular. Some people were anti-Paar but were afraid not to listen. They might miss a fight, they might not see him cry or walk off. Today's teenagers hardly know Jack Paar unless they see the specials he does occasionally for NBC. But he doesn't need them. He is asked sometimes whether he'd like to go back to the nighttime routine, and he only smiles. He's had that. And anyway, it's hard to reach him to ask him anything. He still can't be reached on the phone.

One of the greatest TV talkers is personable and popular Mike Douglas, who made a reputation the hard way—by doing his show away from New York and Hollywood—first in Cleveland, then in Philadelphia. Mike has been tempted many times to move to one of the glamour centers. But he never moves, and his loyal audience seems to grow; his influence, the value of his "opinion-molding," go onward and upward.

Mike likes to play tricks. Once I got up early to get to Philadelphia by around noon. My wife got up earlier because she had an early date at the dentist's.

"Well," said Mike Douglas, when I finally was seated in his studio in Philadelphia, "they say columnists can make or break entertainers with their plugs. What do you think of that?"

"I never believed I had any influence or power," I said. "I always thought those remarks were exaggerations."

"Nevertheless," replied Mike Douglas, "here is an entertainer you more or less discovered—in fact, you created him—and you also gave him a lot of boosts." To my surprise, out came Earl Wilson, Jr., and in the audience was his mother, my wife.

20

The Great Rock Revolution

THE thing you could count on at a rock festival was a cloud of marijuana smoke floating over the unbelievable scene. And nudity and wide-open sex.

"Hey, wanta buy some acid, some mescaline?"

Adult pushers—dirty, unshaven, and unkempt—peddled their drugs to the thousands of "youth," mostly boys and girls of good families who had joined the "Revolution," to come to a remote area where they weren't sure of finding food, a place to sleep, drinking water, or toilet facilities. It was their particular thing, their mode of expression, their manifestation of relevance to contemporary life. The aim of many of them was to get stoned. Eventually, some of their more far-out and iconoclastic members would strip nude to go swimming, unless there wasn't any water, in which case they'd merely parade around the terrestrial scene in their bare skin.

"There's going to be some trouble here," the authorities—the police and the deputy sheriffs of the Establishment—were always saying. But they were hooted down because: "What did they know—the Establishment pigs?"

Then came Mick Jagger and the Rolling Stones to give a concert at Altamont, California, in 1969, during which the crowd got out of control and four people died. The stark facts cannot be denied because they are recorded on film which shows the Hell's Angels—hired to keep everything peaceful—brandishing billiard cues on the heads of people and kicking and stomping a Negro to death after stabbing him. Many thoughtful students of the contemporary scene believe that the Altamont fiasco ended the rock revolution in music.

There are others, however, who believe that the rock revolution is only beginning.

The rock concert at the anti-war demonstration in Washington in May 1971 was "another Woodstock encampment, a carnival of dope that featured the usual nudity," according to Alfred G. Aronowitz, author of the column "Pop Scene." The shaggy kids had come, he said, for music or politics or simply to take dope.

Some had apparently come for sex, and Bob Hodge of Catfish, a Detroit group, became annoyed and spoke out about it sharply.

"I came here from Detroit," he said. "I came here to be with you people for one reason. For peace. Do you hear me? You people back in the woods balling, do you hear me? There ain't no time for fucking. You got to get it together."

A medical tent was set up in the area, and the doctors and nurses on duty encountered the usual number of bad trip cases. In addition, there was a demonstration within a demonstration by some lesbians, who said, "We are women who sleep with women, and we believe sexism to be the first and most fucked-up power relationship." Police revoked the demonstrators' permit—for illegal use of drugs, among other things.

Rock, of course, has always been a little insane. It has always had links with drugs—sometimes lethal links. Janis Joplin, the goddess of rock, and Jimi Hendrix, its god, died of narcotics the same year. The Beatles, frequent proponents of drugs, wisely switched to a saner kick and broke up.

The four deaths at Altamont, recorded on film in *Gimme Shelter*, form the most convincing record of the dangers of the rock culture yet assembled. Precisely how much of the music is due to drugs is not clear. But drug and rocks go together like ham and eggs. And when several radio stations began banning "drug" tunes in 1971, claiming that some song lyrics were really a salute to narcotics, there were those in the more conservative music world who said, "It's high time," not intending to make a pun.

A defender of Mike Brewer and Tom Shipley, the authors of "One Toke over the Line," said that inasmuch as smoking marijuana is not much more serious now than drinking whiskey was during Prohibition, this song was no worse than "One More for the Road" would have been if it were sung in the 1920s.

Some rock experts contend that one of the Beatles' songs, "Lucy in the Sky with Diamonds" referred to LSD. They pointed out that the initial letters of the three principal words came out LSD. The author of the lyric, John Lennon, never secretive about his interest in LSD, denied any such intentions in writing the song, and there was never any proof.

I met the Beatles in London, at the beginning of their success, at a big benefit, "The Night of a Thousand Stars."

They were gentlemen that night, modest and humble in the presence of big stars such as Sir Laurence Olivier, Marlene Dietrich, and Judy Garland. Everybody was astonished.

"What nice young men!" we all said.

When they became a worldwide sensation in 1964, I was bold enough to say that, big as they were, Elvis Presley would outlast them. The little Beatlemaniacs, the first of the groupies, wrote me angry letters, some of them unprintable.

Despite my predictions, the Beatles had a turnout at the old Paramount Theater in August, 1964, that was wilder and bigger than any Sinatra or Presley had ever had.

Life's Tommy Thompson, a kindly man, was working on an article. Once he got located in his seat, he moved around, studying the mob. Two girls asked him if they might have his seat stubs as souvenirs. He agreed. Later, back at his seat, he was questioned by an usher as to his right to those seats.

"Do you have your stubs?" the usher asked.

He tried to explain.

"There are two girls over there"—the usher pointed to two other girls, accomplices of the first two—"who claim you're in their seats. They have the stubs to prove it."

The usher accepted Tommy's explanation; it was just one of the extreme examples of Beatlemania.

Attending a Beatles concert was akin to participating in a riot. There were the same girls one saw at the Plaza Hotel, where the Beatles lived. These girls were so desperate to be near the Beatles that some of them contrived to get themselves shipped in cartons to the singers' suites on the twelfth floor. Thus they got past the guards. But the security officers soon discovered this device and began inspecting the contents of the cartons. Other young females managed to hide in the twelfth floor exits, pounce on their idols, and hug them. It was all rather pathetic to witness.

Once in Carnegie Hall for the concert and seated, one could not hear the Beatles sing because the squirming, ecstatic girls in the audience let loose an endless, piercing shriek that drowned out the singers' voices.

The Beatles, with a keen sense of humor about the ludicrous situation, in which they were being paid to sing yet could not be heard, decided to play a private joke on the crowd.

They moved their lips, but they did not sing. They made the usual gestures, but they made no sound.

All that seems like kid stuff now—and it was kid stuff—compared to Jim Morrison of the Doors doing the masturbation scene on stage in Miami a few years later at a rock concert and getting arrested for indecent behavior.

Rock stars' conduct wasn't usually as scandalous or outrageous as that of Morrison, who was supposed to have dropped his trousers during his controversial performance.

"He didn't lower his pants at all," claimed his sidemen who testified for him at a trial at which he was convicted. "All he did was take off his shirt because it must have been 120 degrees on that stage."

"King of orgasmic rock" was the title that Morrison, the twenty-six-year-old son of a navy rear admiral, gave himself. He was sentenced to six months in jail and fined $500. The next year, Morrison was convicted of intimidating an airline stewardess—of tripping her, swearing at her, and throwing plastic drinking cups at her.

Jim Morrison was still appealing the indecent exposure conviction when he was found dead in Paris in July, 1971, evidently of a heart attack or pneumonia, at only twenty-seven. Janis Joplin and Jimi Hendrix had died barely nine months before. The huge, long-haired, heavy-bearded Morrison, who thought of himself as a poet, rather than as a pop star of the Age of Acid, was not known to be a heavy drug-user. But he would drink himself unconscious when in one of his black moods. His death was kept secret for almost a week because his friends wanted to avoid a big showy funeral.

The few times I met Jimi Hendrix and Janis Joplin, I was struck by the worshipful way their fans looked at them. The fans liked to exclaim about how Jimi could play the guitar with his teeth and how he would set guitars afire or tear them up in his frenzy. The composer of many of the songs he played, he emitted a message of freedom, liberation, and eroticism.

He might call out to a specific girl in the audience, "I want you, baby," and then play his crashing, wildly amplified music to her while leaning back almost against the floor. "Oh, come on, baby, sock it to me . . . sock it to me . . . oh, baby." His fans grieved deeply when he died at age twenty-seven and said that he was never understood, that he was years ahead of his time.

Jimi was a sensuous, exploding, dropout poet who could scream obscenities at an audience and make them think it was art. He tried all the drugs. He was constantly stoned, he tried everything, and he lost. But to his worshippers he didn't lose, he won—by dying and getting out of this crummy society.

A "drug society" is what we live in. Janis Joplin, so joyous at times and so abrasive at others, was as high as the sky one night at a party on Central Park West, where the smell of pot almost knocked us out. She was floating. Her idea of happiness was to stay stoned and stay sexy.

That about says it for rock: "Stay stoned and stay sexy."

Or perhaps we should call it "Orgasmic Society." Janis Joplin said the forty or fifty minutes she performed on stage was like going to bed with her favorite lover.

"It's like a hundred orgasms with the man you love," she told Al Aronowitz. She also told him she was going home to Port Arthur, Texas, for the tenth reunion of her high school graduating class. She was making $50,000 a night, and those high school kids who had been sure she was going to be a dropout from life were now working in gas stations.

"I'm going to jam it up their asses," Janis said.

After the tragic deaths of Jimi Hendrix and Janis Joplin and the sacrificial deaths at Altamont, the experts forecast that the rock revolution was dead.

But one man did not think it was dead, and he was an important individual.

I see him on planes; I see him checking in and out of the Beverly Hills Hotel. He's not a person I can forget. He's bald, with a black pointed beard and mustache, horn-rimmed glasses, very sharply tailored suits, and a name that sticks in the mind—Ahmet Ertegun, a Turk.

Probably the greatest merchandiser of rock records through his company, Atlantic, Ertegun now carries the imposing title: Music Division Executive Vice-President of the Kinney Group.

That's the conglomerate style description of his job. In the year of the supposed demise of rock, he gave a party at Cannes to celebrate signing a contract to distribute the Rolling Stones label. The smallest figure mentioned in the rumors about the deal was $5,000,000.

"Ertegun won't make any big money on the deal," they said in New York. "All the money will be made by the Stones."

That was Mick Jagger again. Wise in the ways of business as well as being an artist gifted with a unique sense of charisma, he had helped the Stones to record under their own label. Now there would be more wealth to toss away on the Riviera. It would mean luxurious cars, and yachts and private planes. All this for the kid who didn't feel he was in the right groove attending the London School of Economics and got the hell out.

The party was held in France because the Rolling Stones had become residents of that country. Ahmet Ertegun went from his offices in Columbus Circle, New York, to the Riviera, to give the party and arrange for the usual posing for pictures. In this case, it was the long-haired Mick Jagger posing with the bald Ahmet Ertegun.

It was smart business for Ertegun to distribute Mick Jagger and the Rolling Stones. It was also humorous because Mick Jagger was not going to get any good-conduct certificate.

Rebel, hater of the Establishment, and sex symbol, Jagger had been arrested for illegally bringing into England four pep pills that he had bought legally. There was a press furor about it, and he was placed on probation. Although the press took his side in that incident, his general reputation was hardly exemplary.

But there was promotion value in his talent and his name. The first new album, *Sticky Fingers*, was a gold record before it was released. Andy Warhol created a special sleeve for it; it featured an actual zipper on the front cover. Despite Warhol's reputation for selling sex and Jagger's for being sexy, the zipper was not, they insisted, intended to convey anything about a man or woman opening his or her fly.

"Whoever tells you rock music is dying is out of his goddamn head," Jughead Gayles, declared recently.

Jughead Gayles, also known as Juggy, is one of the most knowledgeable song promoters in America, going back to the days of song pluggers when the way to make a tune a hit was to cajole a bandleader with a small gift and persuade him to play it on his radio remote. A small gift—like an automobile.

"They're makin' so much money now on rock," says Jughead.

To him the decline of rock is a lot of fantasy. Maybe acid rock is hitting a down-curve in popularity, and the ear-splitting noise is not quite so violent—but then it couldn't get much louder. The emergence of the James Taylor sort of minstrels doesn't mean that rock is dying. What Taylor offers is another gradation of rock, nurtured in his experiences with drugs, when he was in "the zoo," the mental institution, fighting his urge for suicide. This, at least, is the way Juggy views the scene.

What is it that happens to these young people? James Taylor, son of the dean of the University of North Carolina Medical School, with all the advantages of wealth and education, takes refuge in drugs because he feels that somehow he can't live in today's society. Today's society: it's a pretty good society for him. It's not for the ghetto kids, but for the son of a wealthy southerner, it's comfortable—but he still can't take it.

He puts together some great lyrics when he straightens out, and he is acknowledged as the new pop poet of the day. He is embarrassed by all the adulation the public and the music and entertainment industry are trying to shower on a lean, long-haired, mixed-up guy in levis.

What will happen to all of them? To the Motown Sound created in Detroit by that young genius Berry Gordy, who seems to produce another group every month . . . to the Supremes and to Diana Ross, who left them to go on her own . . . to Aretha Franklin, Dionne

Warwick, Bob Dylan, the Temptations, Joan Baez, Ringo Starr, Joe Cocker, Ray Charles and all the others?

They will grow richer.

They will do shows for cassette television. They will give concerts for closed circuit television, which may even try to produce rock festivals. There will be no policing problem if a festival is handled indoors for television cameras, and the pay will be enormous. Strangely, the greatest asset in show business has always been a golden throat, but it doesn't have to be so golden anymore. For the rock stars, their sound of music will always be the sound of money.

21
Surprise—Sex
Is Here to Stay

IN writing about sex, you should start with the most shocking material you can dredge up from the least reliable sources.

Let's see . . .

Thank God for the blabbermouths. There are thousands of them who always whispered about Marilyn Monroe and Bobby Kennedy and made it the country's worst-kept secret. But the more informed blabbermouths claimed that President John F. Kennedy had considerably more than a girl watcher's interest in Marilyn.

One night in New York, Marilyn slipped out to a meeting with the President of the United States. You must remember, incidentally, that he had back trouble.

Marilyn had one confidant—a man who wasn't interested in girls. She could tell him anything. Next morning, she giggled a little as she discreetly discussed the evening. Her confidant relayed her words to me.

"I think," she said, "I made his back feel better."

JFK invited a considerably older and equally famous glamour girl to a party at the White House. Arriving there, expecting to be greeted by Jacqueline Kennedy at a small gathering, she discovered it was the old, old joke.

The party consisted of her and the president.

Not that she really minded. "The president and I slept there" were her words.

It was sex o'clock all over the world. In the same area of research, Jayne Mansfield once told me that she was always a good girl but extremely active.

A woman related to me that she had seen Jayne and her muscle-man husband Mickey Hargitay jointly enter a powder-room on a plane and remain there for a half hour while the other passengers fumed because they needed to use the room.

"Were you doing in there what I think you were doing?" I later asked Jayne.

"Of course," she said. "Doesn't everybody?"

There are some very deep thinkers who say that Kennedy and the Kennedy set brought a new sexiness to America as well as a new frontier. JFK had his eye out for a girl even the night before his inauguration. On that night he expressed to a friend of mine his appreciation of that friend's readiness to do him a big favor—lend him his apartment for a few hours.

But the new sexiness preceded the Kennedys. They just helped to make it popular.

It was taken up with vast enthusiasm by the young stars of show business. It started with the Kinsey Report on the nation's sex habits and with the discovery by women's magazines of something already known by everybody else—that there were hardly any virgins over eighteen left in the world: even most of the girls in college had been deflowered. Fornicating was going on all over the place, but nobody seemed willing to admit it.

Show folk joked about the Kinsey Report, but they were shaken up by its revelations. What secrecy surrounded it before it came out on the market! I had a friend in the publishing business who smuggled a copy to me to preview. I had to read it in a room at the Gotham Hotel and leave it there. I was sure it would not be reviewed in the nation's press. All those words such as "masturbation" and "sodomy" would surely never see print. I was wrong. And then the barriers were down, and you could say almost anything.

About that time, *Cincinnati Enquirer* columnist Ollie James printed a story that was to be repeated hundreds of times.

The telephone operator at a big company heard a voice at the other end, which asked "Do you have a Sexauer there?"

"Sex hour!" snapped the operator. "We don't even have a coffee break!"

It went on and on until in 1970 a version of "motherfucker" appeared in the *New York Post*. Freedom of the press—or whatever it was—had come quite a distance since the days when some editors didn't think you should publish the word "falsie."

On November 10, 1970, drama critic Richard Watts, Jr., wrote in the *New York Post* that the British night club comedians who protested that they weren't allowed to use words that were used by stage actors "should sympathize with drama critics."

"We aren't allowed to mention in print words we hear in virtually every play we cover," Watts said.

The next day, reviewing the movie *Where's Poppa?* Archer Winsten in the same paper wrote, "A measure of this picture's freedom from restraint lies in the name of one of its gang members, Mutha Fucka." (Executive Editor Paul Sann killed the sentence later in the day.)

A furor was stirred up by the English critic Kenneth Tynan in November, 1965, when he used a four-letter word for sexual intercourse on a BBC television program while discussing censorship. This was, of course, the same Kenneth Tynan who was later a co-producer of the nude stage show *Oh, Calcutta!* The title had nothing to do with Calcutta; the words "Oh, Calcutta!" sound like the French equivalent of "Oh, what an ass you have!"

Tynan's precise offense in England was the answer he gave while being interviewed in his capacity as literary director of the National Theater.

The moderator, Robert Robinson, asked whether he would object to his theater presenting a play in which sexual intercourse took place on stage.

"I think there are very few rational people to whom the word fuck is particularly revolting," Tynan replied, "or totally forbidden. I think anything that can be printed can also be seen."

Oldsters couldn't believe their ears. The BBC switchboards immediately became Christmas trees, and the storm began.

For one thing, the newspapers had a happy but frustrating time trying to say what Tynan had said without saying what he'd said.

"He used the four-letter word for fornication," one paper said. "He used the four-letter word for the act of love," exclaimed another, adding, "Shock waves sped across the seven seas."

There were demands that Tynan be prosecuted, but nobody knew what the precise charge should be. Attorney General Sir Elwyn Jones said his use of the word did not fall within the scope of criminal law.

Tynan, who later called himself "the thinking man's voyeur," claimed that he was delighted by a letter from a Scottish grandmother who said, "How wonderful to hear that sweet word on television."

The era of non-censorship seemed to come on us with a rush; in many ways it was hilarious.

Sir Laurence Olivier starred in a show called *The Entertainer,* which gave playgoers a quick look at the over-developed bosom of model and actress Jeri Archer. She had some blue mesh across her breasts, but she whisked the mesh away, and there she stood, barebreasted. Some censors from the New York City Licensing Department ordered her *not* to whisk the mesh away anymore, so she didn't.

That was in February, 1958. In the mid-sixties pretty actress Sue Ane Langdon got caught with her bare bottom showing when the U.S. was making nude "European version" films and covered-up "American versions."

In *The Rounders,* Sue Ane went skinny-dipping with Henry Fonda and Glenn Ford, in a trout hatchery. A game warden almost caught them. Sue Ane managed to cover her front with a waitress' apron. But it left her bare bottom exposed. The men covered that with their hats. The American version didn't show her buttocks. But the European version did. By some kind of a mix-up, the European version was shown when the film was exhibited on airlines in America. Thus, American air travelers got to see Sue Ane's bare bottom, while the stay-at-homes saw it covered. Sue Ane herself was fond of her rear view and told me, "It was cute rather than vulgar and shouldn't have been censored."

By October, 1962, the censors had faded away. I remember the shock I experienced the night Edward Albee's *Who's Afraid of*

Virginia Woolf? opened. Up there on the stage Uta Hagen, Arthur Hill, George Grizzard, and Melinda Dillon appeared to be getting drunker and drunker. Suddenly came the line, "Now we'll play the game called 'hump the hostess,'" or something close to that. (I was so astonished I could hardly make legible notes.)

I felt that Edward Albee was much too candid for the Broadway stage. The drama critics whooped with enthusiasm for the fierceness of his writing and took notice of his frank dialogue without condemning it.

The play was sufficiently controversial that two members of the Pulitzer Prize drama jury—critics John Mason Brown and John Gassner—resigned when the Pulitzer Prize advisory board rejected their recommendation that the play be given the drama award.

"I thought it was a filthy play," said W. D. Maxwell, vicepresident and editor of the *Chicago Tribune,* one of the members of the advisory board. "It's purely my personal opinion, and it's narrowminded and bigoted and anything else you want to call it."

At that time it would have been my opinion, too. The "hump the hostess" line left me shaken. And I don't think I'm a bigot, and, naturally, like all the narrowminded people in the world, I don't think I'm narrowminded.

The Pulitzer Prize advisory board voted not to make any drama award. Elizabeth Taylor and Richard Burton, of course, went on to make *Virginia Woolf* in the movies. It didn't get an Oscar, but Elizabeth Taylor did. The Oscar went to *A Man for All Seasons.* The play and the picture made an incredible amount of money for Edward Albee.

We soon became so accustomed to frank dialogue that by 1970 I wouldn't have been at all disturbed by talk about humping the hostess. But there was something did shock me in a play called *The Engagement Baby,* by Stanley Shapiro, starring Barry Nelson and Constance Towers. I would consider this the furthest that Broadway had gone in candid dialogue—up till now.

Barry Nelson had a scene with his lawyer, who is smoking marijuana.

"Well," says Nelson, "I made my first mistake. I got up with an erection."

There's a flashback. Barry Nelson is in bed with his wife Connie Towers. She's asleep, but he's extremely awake. It's seven A.M.

"What is wrong with you?" she asks sleepily.

"I have a hard-on," he says.

"What do you want?" she says, still half asleep.

"I want to fuck you," he says.

His wife wakes up and declares that she's not in the mood.

"Must you use that word in the bedroom?" she asks.

He answers that it's a fine place to use that word and that he would like to make love to her right now. Only he doesn't say "make love."

"Why don't you do what other considerate husbands do?" she says.

"What's that?" he moans.

"They jog!"

His wife is now sitting up on the bed with her head down over her knees. He is sitting on the bed behind her.

"Turn over, or, so help me," he says, "I'll do it to you just the way you are."

"That's impossible," she says.

"Not when you're desperate," he says. "Like the Man of La Mancha, I shall screw the impossible screw."

The critics unanimously demolished the show—less for the four-letter words than for the plot, which concerned the husband discovering he had a Negro son by a girl he had known many years ago, back before he decided to conceal the fact that he was Jewish. If the critics were as shocked as I was by that kind of talk, they didn't mention it. Evidently by May, 1970, just about everything was acceptable on the Broadway stage.

After that play's quick death, I saw Barry Nelson and mentioned the brave candor of that bed scene.

"You should have heard it," he said, "before we cleaned it up."

Another play with equally blunt dialogue that closed after one regular Broadway performance was *Father's Day*, by Oliver Hailey, which arrived and departed March 16, 1971.

Brenda Vaccaro played an embittered divorcée who was trying to get her ex-husband to leave his new sweetheart and return to her. Discussing the old days and the new girl, Miss Vaccaro says: "I just remember you used to look great. Now you look like shit."

"I even like your language," the ex-husband replies. "I always did."

"What language does *she* speak? No speakee fuckee?"

Then Miss Vaccaro is discussing what men want, and Marian Seldes, also playing a divorcée, gets into the conversation.

"What they all want—a fucking harem!" Miss Vaccaro says.

"A *fucking* harem!" says Miss Seldes. "Don't you think that's a bit redundant?"

Critic Richard Watts in the *New York Post* didn't find this objectionable. "Mr. Hailey has found a shrewd way of justifying his occasional use of these apparently obligatory four-letter words," he wrote. "They come from the mouth of a woman who is proud of her frank language, and they seem right for her."

The Broadway stage had "gone pubic," somebody said. They let everything hang out. Or were about to.

Oh, Calcutta! preceded *The Engagement Baby* by a year, but it was off Broadway. *Hair* had prepared us for total nudity on stage, but most of my acquaintances, at least, weren't quite ready for simulated copulation by live nude bodies right there on stage thirty or forty feet in front of us.

The fourteen *Oh, Calcutta!* sketches bore such titles as "Taking off the Robe," "Dick and Jane," "Jack and Jill," "Four in Hand," "Anybody Out There Want It?" "Delicious Indignities," and "Was It Good for You, Too?"

It had become unnecessary for a producer to tell any actress to take her clothes off when she applied for a job. She knew in advance that she'd have to strip and probably stay stripped. Producer Hillard Elkins, the husband of Claire Bloom, auditioned the bodies.

"Hilly says to hell with producing the show—he's having too much fun holding auditions," was one of the jokes.

Opening night of *Oh, Calcutta!* was particularly stimulating to women. First, as they entered the theater, they saw on the curtain a painting of a bare-derrièred lady, the derrière facing us, the derrière dominating the painting. My nearsighted wife looked up at it, puzzled, and finally decided it was a picture of the moon, which, you recall, had just been brought back to popularity by the astronauts. She was serious. Carol Channing, sitting in front of us, thought it was an enlarged picture of an apple.

The people with better eyes knew it was a lady's buttocks painted by Clovis Trouille. It was to become the symbol of the show used in all the advertising.

The female first-nighters were electrified at seeing so many naked men. For years they had trooped along with their escorts and looked at seminude or nude girls until they were quite sick of the whole idea. But now here were all these men flopping around the stage, shameless about their total nudity. And the women were looking at them in the name of art, and it was fun.

"Until tonight," Carol Channing said, "I thought all other men were built like Charles" (her husband Charles Lowe).

Carol was kidding because she was married twice before—to novelist Theodore Naidish from 1941 to 1944 and then for a time to a football star turned private eye, Alexander ("Axe") Carson.

Producer Hillard Elkins shrugged off the critics' reviews. "They were murderous," he said.

He had expected it, so he wasn't hurt. There was a part of the public that wanted to see total nudity bouncing around the stage; it wanted to see simulated copulation. Sensing that this part of the public would pay well, he raised the price of the very best seats to $25. The customers came in droves. Even though they said they were bored, they continued to come.

"I tried to get a job in *Oh, Calcutta!*" Milton Berle said, "but I couldn't pass the physical." Then he added, "Maybe I looked too Jewish."

During the early part of the run, there were some interesting reactions to all the nudity and sex. Pearl Bailey, in private life the wife of drummer Louis Belson, saw the show and watched the naked men. Afterward, she said, "All the guys in that show don't equal Louis!"

In one sketch, a girl comes on stage dressed, pulls down her panties, and bares her behind to the audience for ten minutes. After volunteering to do it and playing the role for eighteen months, she asked to be released. A friend who was a member of Women's Lib had convinced her that by baring her backside, she was demeaning womanhood.

Several close friendships developed between members of the cast. One friendly couple missed an entrance one night. The stage manager's report to Producer Elkins explained it all:

"So-and-so and so-and-so missed an entrance in Act II. They were upstairs screwing."

The swiftness of the change in the public's thinking about nudity was impressive. The idea of a man going naked on stage was considered so preposterous as to be ludicrous in March, 1967, just two years before *Oh, Calcutta!* Robert Anderson had written a short sketch about it in a series of plays *You Know I Can't Hear You When the Water's Running,* a delightful bit of comedy that the playgoers enjoyed because they thought it was so removed from reality.

George Grizzard had the part of a playwright who'd written a play about a male actor who was supposed to take his clothes off. Joe Silver portrayed a producer who just knew it was a ridiculous idea—that no man would agree to go naked. The producer set about to prove to the playwright that he was wrong by proposing it to several actors. He was sure they would all refuse.

Marty Balsam played the actor who was approached most forcefully to go naked. He immediately declined.

The producer, going ahead with his plan, said as he sat at his desk talking to Balsam, "Well, then, the only thing is, I'll call Hank." (The impression is given that he had already put the idea to another actor, maybe Hank Fonda.)

He gets Hank on the phone. "What do you think of the script?" he asks Hank. There is silence. "Oh, you liked it?"

Marty Balsam is offstage, but his voice is heard loud and strong: *"Yoo hoo, how's this?"*

He has given in, too, and is supposed to be standing naked in the wings, waiting to be applauded for his "build."

In the midst of all the laughter about this on opening night, one heard many people say, "It's hilarious, but of course it would never happen. No man would ever go nude on stage." And in only two years there were several actors showing their most private possessions on stage and dozens more who ached for the opportunity.

The rage for blatantly nude sexual shows led many voyeurs and others to go to see *The Dirtiest Show in Town,* about which somebody said, "It was." However, average playgoers didn't go to see it. Still, since some leading television and newspaper critics applauded this all-bare spectacle at the Astor Place Theater, I feared I might be missing something momentous, so I caught it in the winter of 1971, when it was about nine months old. To me it was an enormous bore, only becoming interesting when the actors got around to taking their clothes off and simulating the sex act.

"You didn't get the message that the critics got," one of the show's defenders chided me.

"There's a message?" I asked. "What is it?"

"Well, it's uhhh . . ." He said it was about pollution, environment, poverty, war, heredity, education, bad housing, the Establishment.

"It's about all that? Those naked bodies up there simulating sex? I missed that, I'm afraid. Could I see a script and fill myself in?"

"All right," he said, although nobody else had needed a script.

Reading it thoroughly to see just where I'd overlooked the important message by young playwright Tom Eyen, I found dialogue and stage directions such as this:

BILL: (The sound of African music with drums begins. He begins fucking her in tempo . . . He begins fucking hard . . . Red light flashes on his ass) I love you!

Then there's a lively passage between the girls and homosexual Cyril.

CONNIE: You shut the fuck up, you cunt-teaser, or I'll beat the shit out of you!

MONA: I'm getting out of here! There's just so much shit one person can take!

CONNIE: You can take it in all three holes, Baby!

Then Cyril the homosexual says to Rose, "Do you have any Binaca, Rose? My mouth tastes dirty."

ROSE: Dirty? Sucking big spick dicks again?

CYRIL: That was low, Rose. Just because I live on West 73rd Street and Broadway, don't give you no right to insinuate I'm orally inclined to Spanish culture!

ROSE: Shirl, there's nothing wrong in liking Spanish meat. I'm understanding.

Still not having found the message, I read on to a description of a "group grope," sort of a minor orgy, a community feel, with everybody hand-massaging everybody while piled together naked on the floor.

The group grope is getting closer. Everybody is naked. Bill asks Laura, "Why don't you put something on?"

She replies, "Why? I just took it off."

Bill says, "No, I meant put something on our beautiful new stereo."

Laura replies, "I don't like music with it, dear. I like the simplicity of animalistic human sounds."

Inasmuch as one of the stage directions has said, "Bill and Laura kneeling and kissing Ken and Lucy's asses," I guess I should have been prepared for the big scene, when bare-bottomed Laura bends backwards toward the audience, leaning on her hands, while everybody is kissing and groping. Then the girls lie down with the men on top of all of them except Jane, who sits off to the side watching as the rhythm builds faster and higher.

ALL: Beautiful Fuck! (10 times) (Last violent and then collapse) Fuck!!!

JANE: Yourself!! (Moves away from man who grabs for her)

There weren't many laughs in the show, but the homosexual Cyril's mother says, "Stop it, Cyril. Get a hold of yourself!"

"For twenty-nine years I've been getting hold of myself," he snaps back. "I want somebody else to do it for a change." He's going to get married to the man he loves.

After the group grope is over, there is another funny line.

LAURA: I think Lucy is about to say something beautiful.

LUCY: I don't want to alarm anyone, but I think I have gonorrhea.

KEN: Ridiculous, dear. It takes at least two days to get it.

LUCY: I know. I think I got it last week when we had sex with our beautiful friends from Tudor City.

JANE: You could have told us before.

LUCY: Well, I didn't remember until I heard you clap (grins idiotically).

It's unfair of me not to have mentioned that the show began against a soldier background, continued with frequent "Hup, Hup, Hup" commands and military saluting, and closed with "Stop War! Stop War! Stop War! Stop!" It was beautifully acted.

The young author, who's from Cambridge, Ohio, was celebrating the success of a song he'd written for a movie, "Ode to a Screw." It was the kind of a screw this play would have found quite in order. I never found the message in the show, but I must not forget that Tennessee Williams was considered quite daring when he started. Tom Eyen may be the Tennessee Williams of tomorrow.

While the men were doing their part to contribute to the new freedom in dirty words, the girls weren't shirking. During an otherwise prim little lunch with movie actress Ann-Margret in October, 1970, I almost dropped by fork when she related that in her picture *C.C. and Company,* with Joe Namath, "I say the funny Anglo-Saxon word—'Fuck off.'"

I blushed. She didn't.

"I would say it in real life if I were cornered as I am in this picture," she said. "I have been kidnapped by this gang. So finally after a half hour of their nonsense, I look at them and I say, 'Fuck off.'"

Her husband Roger Smith had written the scene and, of course, approved of her doing it. "That's the way people talk today," Ann-Margret said. "I have said it to Roger. I get mad about twice a year, so I guess I used it on him twice last year," she confessed with a smile. "I have been known to throw telephones at him. Not Princess phones, either. Full-sized."

By coincidence, Barbra Streisand came out the same month with the same expression in the picture *The Owl and the Pussycat.*

Playing a prostitute, Barbra encounters some characters who are as questionable as she is, and at the height of a situation, she tells them, "Fuck off."

Using these words seemed to be fast becoming a fad. *The Landlord,* produced by Norman Jewison, was considered a smash success by the *Hollywood Reporter,* but reviewer John Mahoney wrote: "The picture is not the slightest bit better or worse because it mouths 'motherfucker,' so the word hardly seems worth offending or losing a potential customer."

To show how common the expression is getting to be, the same critic reviewed another picture the same day with another reference to boldness.

The Grasshopper is about a girl (Jacqueline Bisset) hopping from bed to bed and eventually getting a boy friend—a skywriter —to spell out that popular four-letter word in the sky.

It's done as a joke in the picture. The audience wonders, when the skywriter begins by writing F, whether he's going to go through with the other three letters, and he does. Reviewer Mahoney thought it was "a desperate joke," but the laugh took one's thoughts away from the unfortunate girl. Others commented that it was a case of big boys writing dirty words not on walls but on the sky.

Katharine Hepburn was a surprising entry in the four-letter word parade. In *Coco* there is a scene at the beginning of the second act in which Coco Chanel looks over the remnants of a disastrous fashion show and, in great disgust, says, *"Shit!"*

In the original script by Alan Jay Lerner, the expletive was the French, *"Merde!"* Katharine Hepburn herself changed it. I saw some of the show at a preview and observed that the audience laughed. On opening night, December 18, 1969, when Miss Hepburn turned to them hopelessly and sang out the word, the audience not only laughed loudly but applauded. Nobody could remember any other Broadway actress tossing off that word so blithely and resoundingly, so Miss Hepburn had perpetrated a Broadway "first."

When Richard Rodgers's *Two by Two* came along about a year later, Danny Kaye, as Noah, had an exchange with his daughter-in-law about the ark's being loaded with brickettes made of manure, which were to be sold.

"Is that the way you want to start the new world—with a ton of shit?" Noah asks.

Critic Clive Barnes of the *New York Times* objected, pointing out that in the play, *The Flowering Peach*, on which the musical was based, Menasha Skulnick had merely said the word "manure."

But then morals had changed tremendously since the Clifford Odets play was brought to Broadway in 1954. In many ways, in fact, morals and codes seemed to have been reversed.

American tourists strolling around London fifteen years ago were amazed at seeing two or three street-walkers loitering at so many street corners in Berkeley Square, Mayfair (and perhaps in other areas I didn't visit). We were so unaccustomed to public display of prostitution that at first we were a little shocked. We went back to the neighborhood on our next visit to see if the same sorts of girls were still doing business at the same corner. They always were. Thank God, we always said, shuddering slightly at the thought, there was nothing like that in New York City.

The prostitutes were quite possessive about their street corners, as though they had exclusive rights to solicit there. An American woman who happened to stroll through that area one afternoon, doing some leisurely sightseeing, aroused the anger of some of the street-walkers, who considered her an interloper.

They warned her to get out in salty language. One of the girls was impressed with her fur coat. "One of them French whores," she sneered.

The tourists from New York were especially startled that the prostitutes solicited in daylight—in the afternoon! Somehow that made it extraordinarily immoral.

Then England began enforcing a ban on soliciting, and the girls were driven off the streets and indoors. If a man came into a brothel or a prostitute's apartment and wished to sample her wares, that seemed not to be illegal.

So the London street corners were purified, and the American tourists no longer saw girls selling sin.

One afternoon in 1970, a friend of mine who had lived in New York most of his life but had been in Las Vegas for a couple of years spoke to me in astonishment about the change in New York.

"I just walked from 42nd Street up Broadway to 52nd Street," he said, "and I'll bet I saw two hundred whores."

They lingered in doorways, and they bounced up and down the streets. They were younger and brassier than the girls we used to see in London—and they were much more numerous. It was sickening to see that New York had picked up where London had left off.

"Hooker" has become the American word for prostitute, and one restaurant at 52nd Street and Broadway, a ham and eggery now under new ownership, was referred to as "The Hookerama." In one block on Broadway between 52nd and 53rd Streets, I once counted seventeen hookers. Nearly every night there was a loud screaming, cursing battle between the girls over business matters. True to the popular picture of pimps, nearly all the "business managers" wore expensive, flashy clothes and drove Cadillacs, which they parked near the Hookerama.

Mayor John Lindsay cleaned them out from time to time, but the city had a problem: there wasn't enough room in jail for all of them. Besides, after a few days of incarceration they would be free and back in business.

Prostitution, of course, is a matter of "dirty sexiness." At the same time, there is another group of individuals who think of sex as being beautiful. To these people, while it has nothing to do with love, sex is something that should be enjoyed by all. An extreme faction of this group feels that sex should be freely passed around and shared without restriction.

If a copulation scene were to be performed on stage, does it have to be simulated? Why couldn't it be the real thing? If an actor thought that he should play a drunk scene really drunk—as some actors have indeed said—then why shouldn't he be actually copulating instead of simulating?

It raised all sorts of marvelous questions, which Actors Equity had to consider carefully. Should an actor be paid extra, for example, for going naked? A theoretical question was: if an actor really had to copulate instead of simulate, how many performances did he have to give in a week, and did he have to do a matinée?

Madeline Le Roux, an actress in the off-Broadway *The Dirtiest Show in Town,* who played the hostess of a love-in, said that she couldn't understand the public's being so curious about nudity. She complained that people trained binoculars on her to get a better view even though the theater was so small and intimate.

And Claudia Jennings of *Dark of the Moon* prophesied that by 1975, nudity in public would not be unusual. For some situations, she forecast, it would be normal.

A Broadwayite named Hal Stone ran an agency that supplied nude models. I said jokingly to him one day, "Why don't you supply nude secretaries?"

A few days later, a pretty Scandinavian blonde came to my office, took off her raincoat, kicked off her shoes, and stood before me completely naked. Without hesitation she went to a typewriter, sat down, and began typing. I nervously suggested that she'd better leave, fearing somebody might come in and, not knowing the background, misunderstand. She left, and I went to the typewriter to see whether she could type. She had typed that well known four-letter word several times—nothing more. She was the first and last topless secretary I have seen.

One of the most frank actresses, Sylvia Miles, who was a Best Supporting Actress Oscar nominee for *Midnight Cowboy,* told me in 1970 that a lovemaking scene she had with Jon Voight (she played a fading prostitute) must have been good because some actresses thought the part was actually played by a genuine prostitute.

"Julie Harris called Maureen Stapleton," Miss Miles informed me, "and said, 'Well, this proves you don't have to be an actress anymore. They found this hooker, and she played the part better than any actress could.'"

Actually, Sylvia Miles had been in twenty off-Broadway shows and five previous movies.

"How were you able to be so realistic?" I asked her. "Did you make a study of prostitutes?"

"There's a little bit of hooker in every woman," she answered. "A little bit of hooker and a little bit of God." Miss Miles was disturbed that she had become, as she said, "Everybody's favorite hooker," and there was no future for her but to grow older and become "Everybody's favorite madam."

How did she prepare for the lovemaking scene?

She had worried about the part, she admitted. First, she hadn't wanted to do it. Deciding that she would—that she was going to play the prostitute and perform the sex act—she didn't want any nonsense. She didn't want to have to be interrupted with a lot of dropping her robe and putting it back on and dropping it again for the scene in bed. The best course was just to forget the robe and stay naked.

Therefore she made a little speech to the crew.

"I'm coming out in the raw and I'm going to stay that way, and if you fellows don't look at me or pay me any special attention, we'll get the work done and get the hell out," she told them.

The lovemaking scene was to be filmed starting in the morning— "Very early for sex, maybe too early, although playing opposite Jon Voight a girl doesn't really have any trouble," she said.

There they were, in bed without clothes, and what does the director say?

"Action" is the word, as the whole world knows, but according to Sylvia, the director didn't use that word.

"Fuck her, Jon, fuck her. Do it to her!" were his words, according to Miss Miles.

"It started out wrong," she admitted. "We landed on the bed in the wrong place and had to work ourselves around."

In fact, she claimed, Jon Voight was off target and was about to try to penetrate her knee when she shouted, "Jon, you're raping my knee!"

He got back on target quickly. They wound up with Sylvia on

top. The scene took seventeen minutes but was cut to less than eight minutes.

The crew cooperated and didn't give her any trouble with undue staring. Miss Miles conceded that maybe they had cooperated too much and were non-responsive. "I knew I looked pretty good nude, and I got to wondering what was wrong that there wasn't any commotion."

"Suppose you were asked to do a movie in which you actually had to copulate—not simulate—would you do it?" I asked.

"Perhaps," she laughed, "if I could do my own casting."

A short time after this, Miss Miles gave a magazine interview in which she called a fellow actress a "prunt," that being a combination of two vulgar words. She also posed nude with six naked men for the article. She said there really wasn't much reason for her to pose nude with the six men "except that it's about me, and that's where I'm at."

Over on the night club circuit comedians were getting so risqué that the veteran comic, B. S. Pully, complained they were making him vomit.

B. S.—the initials, he said, stood for "Bernard Shaw"—was using what he also called his "venereal material" for ten or fifteen years before Lenny Bruce began offending some people—and delighting others—with his sacrilegious jokes in Greenwich Village and at the old Blue Angel.

A huge, boisterous fellow with a roaring voice, Pully dealt out his bathroom laughs from little strip joints in Miami Beach where one could go for a last drink at three or four in the morning or from places of dubious ownership on 52nd Street in New York.

"Wit' one line, I can turn dis jernt into a bowlin' alley," he would boast.

He was correct in calling his material venereal. His act was replete with discourses on good friends of his "that got the clap."

"I am very selective with muh material," Pully would wheeze at you. "I would never use a word like privy when crapper would do."

Pully got his laughs from the shock value of his material. You could not believe this man was uttering those words. Pully played Big Julie in *Guys and Dolls* on Broadway and then got into *Myra Breckinridge*. He found the latter shocking even for him.

"Buddy Hackett and Don Rickles come along and put me outa work," he said. "I gotta dirty up my act to compete with them. Pardon my English but dey drove me right into the shithouse."

While Pully's fans adored him, they were mostly late night drunks, and he never got "high class" like Lenny Bruce, who, some café customers thought, was a premature genius. I will ask their pardon for putting Bruce in the same paragraph with B. S. Pully. They will consider that as sacrilegious as he was.

Lenny Bruce repelled me at the Blue Angel when he made some jokes alluding to Jesus Christ and homosexuality. That offended my Bible Belt upbringing and prejudiced me against him forever. I was relieved when his act was finished and I could walk out into what we thought then was the pure New York air. I regret that I wasn't big enough to give him another chance to amuse me and demonstrate his genius, if such it was, but I never could.

The Lenny Bruce admirers said after his death that he was a moral satirist "in the tradition of Swift, Rabelais, and Twain," and that he was a brilliant, courageous, sweet, and beautiful man.

John Cohen brought out an "uncut and uncensored" written record of his work, *The Essential Lenny Bruce,* which showed that he was a heavy user of the words "motherfucker," "cunt," "cocksucker," "bullshit," "asshole," "prick," and "tits," and—especially— "schmuck." He said that police thought of him as "Dirty Lenny" but that they, of course, missed the point of his social satire.

Lenny Bruce especially infuriated Catholics—and probably pleased some of them, too—by kidding the clergy. In one sketch, he imagined a priest saying he was weary of hearing the same tired old confessions over and over. One of the congregation was always confessing month after month that he smelled bloomers.

"These bastards come in like they think they got some new stories all the time," the priest moaned. "It's a lot of horseshit." He pictured the priest as longing for a good "horny" confession some time.

The name Pope Pius was, to Bruce, as ludicrous as "Rock Hudson" or "Rip Torn." He said that Cardinal Spellman looked like Shirley Temple—and that a priest told him so. In one amazing sketch, he had Christ and Moses standing in the back of St. Patrick's Cathedral, having descended from heaven and come down to Fifth Avenue by way of Spanish Harlem, where Christ wondered why fifty Puerto Ricans were living in one room.

"Why weren't the Puerto Ricans living here? That was the purpose of the church—for the people."

Bruce then imagines a conversation between Bishop Fulton J. Sheen and Cardinal Spellman:

SHEEN: Psst! I gotta talk to you! They're here!

SPELLMAN: Get back to the blackboard, dum-dum, and stop bugging me.

SHEEN: Dum-dum, your ass. You better get down here.

SPELLMAN: O.K. Put the choir on for ten minutes.

SHEEN (gasping): They're here!

SPELLMAN: Who's here?

SHEEN: Christ and Moses, schmuck, that's who's here.

SPELLMAN: Oh, bullshit! Are you putting me on now? Where? Which ones are they?

SHEEN: The one that's glowing. *Hoo!* Glowing!

SPELLMAN: Are you sure it's them?

SHEEN: I've just seen 'em in pictures, but I'm pretty sure. Moses is a ringer for Charlton Heston.

SPELLMAN: We're in for it now, goddamnit! Did Christ bring the family with him? What's the mother's name?

Spellman tries to get Pope John on the phone for instructions—but he's interrupted. The lepers are trying to come in the front door. He advised them "to split."

SPELLMAN: You're waiting for St. Francis? Look, I'm gonna level with you right now. That's a bullshit story.

He has Pope John on the horn! "Yes, him, yeah . . . yes, he brought an attractive Jewish boy with him . . . Excuse me . . ." The reporters from *Life* are inquiring if it's really them.

SPELLMAN: Sonny, will you get off of my hem? Yes, that is them—.

The Cardinal is back on the phone with Pope John.

SPELLMAN: Of course they're white! Look, all I know's that I'm up to my ass in crutches and wheel chairs here!

In another sketch that shocked some of the liberals, Bruce said, "Eleanor Roosevelt had nice tits. She really did. A friend of mine saw them and said they were terrific. He walked into the bedroom and—"

Bruce defended his act by claiming it was satire, although there were always people who thought it was better categorized with one of the vulgarisms he loved so passionately. He dealt, in my opinion, in shock. He talked about snot in one sketch. He heard people walking out on him, saying, "He's disgusting," and he enjoyed that in some masochistic way. One night at Basin Street East, a busload of 120 people walked out on him without even waiting for the bus. He was a martyr to his brilliance and his wit.

Bruce was considered an original by some admirers. He replied, "The only way I would truly say I was an original is if I created the English language. I did, man, but they don't believe me."

He did, if the English language consists of the dozen words that he used to shock people.

A play about Bruce, *Lenny*, by Julian Barry, opened at the Brooks Atkinson Theater in May, 1971, with a brilliant performance by Cliff Gorman, the only Broadway actor to be born on a freighter in the South Pacific. The show had all the familiar four-letter, ten-letter and twelve-letter Lennyisms. It presented Lenny Bruce sympathetically and was a smash hit.

In the second act, Lenny is on trial for obscenity. Throughout the play he is lecturing to us that he is not obscene.

He reflects out loud that in some San Francisco schools there were homosexual teachers, and that one kid came home and said, "Today I learned five minutes of geography and ten minutes of cocksucking."

He asks, "Why didn't they fire those teachers? Maybe because they were good teachers."

He preaches additionally that the show business attractions are really "tits and ass . . . tits and ass . . . tits and ass." He says that *Life* Magazine devoted three pages to tits and ass right next to articles by Billy Graham and Norman Vincent Peale. That brings him around to discussing "the stroke magazines" (reading to masturbate by.)

Commenting on the nude pull-out girl pictures, Lenny says, "Actually, it would take the seriousness out of things like the Bay of Pigs or the Cuban Missile crisis if you could just imagine JFK in the back of the bathroom door whacking it to Miss July once in a while."

Later, a peace officer who's taken Lenny into court tries to recall what Lenny's said that was objectionable, and quotes him:

"President Kennedy jacked off during the Cuban Missile crisis . . . then his wife hauled ass to save her ass."

Buddy Hackett, I always felt, was about as close to genius as you can find in night club or personal appearance comedy. With his little fat boy smile, he could toss out the word "ass" from the stage at the Palace Theater and shock the audience but in a gentle way. After all, he made us feel, ass was not the worst word in the language. He claimed that almost everybody had one and that almost everybody used the word from time to time.

"And people smile when I say it, so it must not be offensive," Buddy told people who asserted it was vulgar. "How offended are you when I say it? Are you so offended that you won't smile?"

From the word ass, the jokes went to other areas with some of the comedians. Comedian Don Rickles, for example, would scratch his private parts and make comments about that. He was so popular with the night club crowd that people lined up to get tables hours before he was due to perform.

I raised the question in 1968 as to whether Buddy Hackett was doing some serious pioneering in the area of dirty words. Accustomed as we were to hearing him use the word ass, we somehow didn't expect he'd say it on stage at the new Lincoln Center Philharmonic Hall.

It was one of those dressy evenings at the Philharmonic, with Alan King raising money for the Alan King Medical Center in Jerusalem. King introduced Buddy as "the nut of our age." Buddy proceeded not only to use a couple of the words but to defend the use of them. Ass, he claimed, was a medical abbreviation, though it wasn't in any medical dictionary I could find.

When Buddy, looking like a cherub, stood up there and tossed those words out into that swank atmosphere, I was stunned and glanced around to see if others were shocked. They weren't. They were rocking with laughter.

"One wonders whether he isn't pioneering," I wrote the next day, "whether all entertainers aren't going to have to sound like best-selling novels or European movies to hold their crowds."

(Notice that I said European movies; in 1968, American movies hadn't really gotten dirty.)

Making an appearance at a Broadway theater benefit, Buddy said that since he was in a legitimate theater, he supposed he had to use the same language they used on the stage. He said his language was mild compared with that of Tennessee Williams.

"I'm funny, not dirty," Buddy said frequently. "When a man's funny, he's not dirty, and when he's dirty, he's not funny."

There was no question about Buddy being funny. In 1967, when Johnny Carson was returning to the air after a salary disagreement, his opposition, Joey Bishop, secured Jack Paar as a guest for the night. Talking to me at a banquet, Buddy prophesied that Carson would "murder" them in the ratings and demanded that I print his forecast. I did.

The next day Buddy phoned me angrily and asked why I printed those things.

"Because you said them," I said.

"I said them, but why did you *print* that I said them?"

"Because you asked me to," I said.

"Then why," he shouted, *"did you listen to me?"*

Hackett has a fondness for nudity—not nude girls, especially; a nude Buddy Hackett. Once while playing golf, he hit a ball into the tall grass, went looking for it, and came back onto the course with his clothes off. "Damned locusts!" he shouted.

When roly-poly Buddy became vice-president of the Sahara-Nevada Corporation, supervising four hotels in Nevada, he said his job was to be talent consultant. That didn't make him any more serious. When he opened at the new Kings Castle Hotel near Lake Tahoe, he came out looking as if he had on nothing but a gentleman's G-string. It was actually a few medallions that had been issued to guests at the opening, hanging from a coverlet over his pelvic area. The shocked audience once more howled with laughter.

Young people seem to like the move toward sexual provocation and frank speech in entertainment. Older people are often puzzled. Yet by May, 1970, Milton Berle was flinging out gags that he'd have kept for stag audiences ten years before. I wondered if he wasn't influenced by the younger comedians.

One night at the Americana Royal Box, Berle seemed to be tugging at the microphone to lower it.

"Here's a switch," he said, "now I can't get it down."

When the females laughed as knowingly as the males, Berle knew he was in the right room.

"Sinatra was supposed to be here, but he's in Rome," Berle said.

"The Pope's making him a cardinal. From now on we only have to kiss his ring." He went on to speak of *Oh, Calcutta!* reporting that there was one sexy little actress in it—"she turns out to be another Dyke Van Dick." And closed with a verse: "They're not having guys like me this year. Wish I was queer, wish I was queer."

It was happening all over town. When Ella Fitzgerald opened at the Waldorf's Empire Room, Louis Armstrong was at the ringside almost dozing. He seemed about to be falling out of his chair. Ella decided after her opening song to introduce the celebrities present, and when she called out the name "Satchmo," Louis came awake instantly and rushed right up onto the stage—to the great discomfort of Ella, who didn't want anybody to interfere with her carefully prepared act.

But sleepy Satchmo had heard his name, and, in his drowsy state, he evidently thought he should say something so as not to let Ella down.

While Ella waited nervously for him to get off, Louis began reminiscing.

"'Member, Ella, when we used to work up at the Apollo? There was that wonderful place we got hamburgers. And that pretty waitress tried to get me off eatin' so many. Well, one night I go up there same as usual, and she's gonna tell me, there's no more hamburgers. So this waitress says, 'Louis, sorry to tell you, I scratched your favorite thing.' I says to her, 'That's all right, honey, go wash your hands and get me a hamburger.'"

Truly, things were loosening up everywhere. I even heard one day that in 1969 Bob Hope had told an objectionable story at a White House Party given by President Nixon.

Upon checking out the item, I found the story concerned a nun whose car ran out of gas. Leaving her car, she walked to a gas station, where the attendant regretfully informed her that he had no gasoline cans. The only possible receptacle he could offer her was a chamber pot. Back at the car, the nun was just pouring the gasoline from chamber pot into the gas tank when a rowdy crowd drove by.

"Sister, have you got faith!" somebody yelled.

Aristotle Onassis and Jacqueline Kennedy figured in many folk tales of the period. Some were crude and ribald; many were borrowed from burlesque.

One of the stories was about a rich Greek friend asking Onassis why he married Jackie.

"Look, you know I'm rich enough to get almost any dame I want," Onassis purportedly answered. "Jackie's not the sexiest, she is not the most beautiful, she's not the most pleasant woman in the world."

"Then why?"

"I'm getting along in years. I'm not going to last forever. And you've got to admit this dame throws a hell of a funeral."

I couldn't find anybody, not even a priest—I didn't ask any nuns —who considered the chamber pot story objectionable, nor the Onassis story either. Even I, though I felt they were in questionable taste, thought them printable. In fact, when I saw four-letter words popping out at me in the *Village Voice* and some other journals, I began to wonder just what wasn't printable these days. Would the four-letter copulation verb ever become commonplace in the "All the News That's Fit to Print" *New York Times*, I wondered?

Always I'd thought of the *Times* as a yardstick of good taste. It was "carefully edited." It wouldn't stoop to anything that wasn't mannerly. After all, even in its crime stories, it frequently referred to the prisoner as "Mr."

Then its Sunday drama section began saying in interviews that certain actors and actresses were living together without being married. One interview with Jacqueline Bisset and Michael Sarrazin reported that they found it convenient to set up housekeeping, as it was called long ago.

The masterpiece of a headline said: *"A Good Roommate Is Hard to Find."*

Zsa Zsa Gabor had a nice sense of delicacy about it when explaining her arrangement with George Sanders, to whom she had once been married. Shortly before Sanders married her sister Magda— who divorced him not long afterward—Zsa Zsa said that she was staying at the Waldorf Towers and "George is my houseguest."

Interviewing Vanessa Redgrave one day in 1969, I choked a little on the tea she was serving me when she said, yes, it was true, she and Franco Nero were expecting a baby in September and had no plans to get married now or ever.

"I don't believe marriage would make me a very nice person to live with. I had to make too many plans to get out of my first marriage to get into marriage again." She said this in a soft voice while she looked at me through her tinted glasses and twirled a room key on a chain.

"But you will live together?"

"Oh, we won't live together. I'll live with my children in London and he'll live wherever he's working." With similar calm, she added that she didn't know whose name the baby would have, hadn't thought about that. Well, they had the baby, a boy, and gave it its father's name. And, as Vanessa said, they don't live together.

That extraordinarily voluptuous singer and actress Lainie Kazan let it be known before she began a singing engagement at the Plaza Hotel that she and her musical director and accompanist Peter Daniels were expecting a baby but doubted whether they'd get married. "I'm not sure whether marriage is the right thing to do today," Lainie explained.

They did have the baby; they did have some kind of a ceremony, which they maintain wasn't specifically a marriage. Miss Kazan joked about it from the floor when she sang and said, "I'd do a dance if I weren't with child."

People wondered why she made the announcement of her pregnancy. "Probably didn't want everybody to say, 'Isn't she getting terribly fat?'" somebody said.

Paralleling the liberalization of sex was a more open attitude to race. Racial jokes could go as far as the comedians wished, with nobody stopping them. The singer Steve Rossi got together with the black comedian Slappy White as the first big integrated team.

"Oh, we get along fine, and we have no problem getting rooms," the Italian singer Rossi assured café crowds. "I always get the presidential suite at any hotel, and Slappy gets the best room at the YMCA."

This moved Slappy to offer a comment about his wife.

"She's a wonderful girl, but she's always complainin'," Slappy said.

"Is she a nagger?" asked Steve.

"No," replied Slappy. "She's a Mexican girl."

There were scores of Polish jokes ("What are 37 and 95?" . . . "Adjoining rooms in a Polish hotel."), but I didn't hear about any

Poles protesting. Curiously, the Gay Activists were the only organized group to object to jokes about themselves.

"A fellow in Greenwich Village said he had a very unhappy childhood. There was only one homosexual in his little home town—and it was him." That was one that was going around.

"The Gay Crowd plans to call its annual reunion Old Homo Week" was another one.

When I printed those, the attorney for the Gay Activists warned me that if I persisted in such behavior, they would picket me.

Rather than have that happen, I desisted.

Gradually, we grew accustomed to the liberalization of language and attitudes, if that's what it was. The husband and wife team of Sonny and Cher opened at the Waldorf's Empire Room in 1970. At one point Cher, a charming, attractively gowned girl, burst into laughter as she stood beside her husband, looking down at his feet.

"What are you laughing about?" he asked.

"You've got patent leather shoes on," she said, "and I can see up your pants leg."

The rough language was increasing on television and it was getting to be a problem.

DIRTY WORDS DOG TV, said a headline in the Newark, New Jersey *Evening News* October 21, 1970, in a column by Tom Mackin.

Amusingly, one of the debates about word choice involved Federal Communications Commissioner Nicholas Johnson, who used a questionable word and defended his use of it.

Speaking out against television commercials claiming that certain products will make one more sexually desirable, Johnson used a not generally acceptable expression.

"They tell a woman that if she looks sexy by using their product, she's going to get laid," he said.

One station, an NBC affiliate, blipped out that part of the speech. Angered at the censorship, the commissioner protested that the expression was a common one in the streets.

NBC replied that it was not beaming its programs at street corners.

Here was a strange situation, in which a federal official was employing a "dirty word" instead of censuring a station for using one.

Well aware that they could lose their licenses for repeated use of material of questionable taste, the stations and networks try to be on their guard, but sometimes they suffer an accident or two.

Two bad ones occurred on football fields. In an NBC Thanksgiving broadcast of a Detroit-Oakland game, millions of viewers saw an Oakland player sweeping around end for a gain. One of the Detroit Lions was heard shouting, "We'll get you, you cocksucker!"

Covering the traditional Ohio State-Michigan game, famous for its bitterness, ABC moved its cameras to catch crowd scenes. The cameramen weren't fast enough to avoid a big sign held up by some Michigan student. It said: "FUCK OHIO STATE!"

"Let's be more careful, fellows," the networks advised their crews afterward.

Governor Ronald Reagan openly called a member of the California Board of Regents "a lying son of a bitch." What was television supposed to do about that? Blip out "bitch"?

"There are those who feel the news media, both electronic and print, are rather hypocritical and just a little bit ridiculous in maintaining a puritanical stance at a time when ribald books ride the best seller lists, and smutty movies are the only ones filling the theaters," wrote Tom Mackin. "Who is being protected? And from what? A growing number of free spirits holds that the only dirty words are 'nigger,' 'kike,' 'wop,' and 'polack,' and that words writers since Chaucer have employed to describe bodily functions and lovemaking, are merely vulgar at worst."

Shelley Berman, always controversial, got into the debate over what was dirty and what was decent when he did a bathroom routine at the Americana Royal Box. His sketch made some of the reviewers question his taste.

"My toilet routine," Shelley called it, and it concerned going to the toilet. The hotel management asked him to launder it. He refused. Furthermore, he called the New Yorkers a bunch of hicks for taking exception to material that had been well received in San Francisco, Dallas, Chicago, and Oklahoma City.

"I'm not cutting it just because some columnists in New York knock it," he declared in defiant tones.

Pointing out that the Broadway stage was not criticized for using similar material, he asked, "If you're surrounded by the exalted proscenium of the theater, does that make it okay? Jean Kerr's *Mary, Mary* had such jokes. Some of the critics of the night clubs are just stiffnecks. They just can't face themselves if they use the word toilet for toilet."

Bob Tisch, head of the Tisch-Loew's hotel chain, personally objected to Berman's references to President Lyndon B. Johnson going to the toilet.

"We all tried to get Shelley, who is a brilliant comedian, to modify it, but he wouldn't," said Eddie Risman, the talent booker for the hotels.

In using President Johnson's name, Berman said, "The man goes to the toilet. They say he went to the bathroom. He didn't go to take a bath. He went to the toilet. They call it bathroom tissue. It's not bathroom tissue. It's toilet paper. President Johnson goes to the toilet the same as we do. There's no other way to do it."

Berman was "expressing his art," Risman said, "with his 'terlet routine,' but the question is, 'Is terlet art?'"

Certainly it became ludicrous at times. Carol Burnett had a discussion about nudism on her program.

"How do people dance at a nudist camp?" a nudist was asked.

"Very carefully," it said in the script.

The censor—the protector, "the vice-president in charge of program practices"—objected to that answer. He ruminated about it and finally suggested seriously what he thought was a clean way of handling it.

His answer was: "Cheek to cheek."

22
Now Nudity

A Broadway photographer named Dave Workman once told me the facts of life about girls posing nude.

"Used to be," he said, "you couldn't get none of 'em no way, unless, of course, it was some tramp. I'm speakin' about nice girls. Then, maybe ten years ago, some girls wanted the pictures either for themselves or their boy friends . . . or . . ."—he smiled wisely as he added—"their girl friends. Then suddenly they all wanted you to shoot 'em raw. They hardly got in your studio before they had their clothes off."

Part of this change can be attributed to the new sexual permissiveness, the revolution in morals, but some of it derived purely from monetary considerations. Girls with beautiful bodies learn things faster than other girls. They learned that Hugh Hefner of *Playboy* was paying $1,500, sometimes as much as $3,000, for pictures of girls who could become centerfold playmates. Often this was more than the girl, or even her father, might earn for half a year's work. It also opened doors to rich men's penthouse apartments, to gay, glamorous night clubs, and even to the movies.

Hedy Lamarr had been rather daring with that flash of nakedness in *Ecstasy*. Now, Americans found that their little sisters were bouncing around nude for weeks at a time in a photographer's studio doing "test shots," hoping they'd look sexy enough for Hugh to consider them for that pullout section that would enable millions of men to drool over them.

Then came the term "Beautiful People," and the young began taking it more seriously than the old. They believed it. (To some sophisticates, it meant old, ugly, rich people.)

I'd had an appointment to interview an extremely handsome young actor, Michael Blodgett. But a mixup occurred in the schedule, and I found myself forced to board a plane to cover a special story.

"Listen, we'll ride to the airport with you," Blodgett said. "I want you to meet my girl. She got fixed up special."

As they climbed into the car at their hotel, he (a really beautiful man—muscular, curly-haired, and blue-eyed,—a true Adonis) introduced his girl, Cynthia Myers, as "the hottest playmate in the history of *Playboy* magazine."

Immediately Michael Blodgett began filling me in on all the exciting details of Cynthia's nubile charms but, in addition, he began whipping out pictures of her in the nude. They were mostly *Playboy* test shots. And while he was showing me photographs of her in "total nudity," he was happily telling me that he was going to marry her.

I was an old-fashioned fellow, and it seemed to me that a prospective bridegroom did not normally exhibit photographs that showed his fiancée in all her lovely nakedness. But I was probably wrong, for he continued to exhibit them, and his fiancée was seemingly happy for me to be enjoying the views of her.

While he sat snuggling up to Cynthia, discussing their forthcoming marriage and shuffling out more nude pictures, I learned that Cynthia was in her early twenties and that she comes from Toledo. As that was not far from my home town, Rockford, Ohio, I felt I might have something in common with her. But I fear I was wrong again.

"How did you get to be such a hot playmate?" I asked her.

"Remember that Nietzsche said, 'Audacity is essential to greatness'?" Cynthia queried.

It had been years since I'd heard anybody quote Nietzsche. Cynthia, nevertheless, had read Nietzsche in Woodward High in Toledo when she was sixteen, and she had resolved to be audacious because she wanted greatness.

"I wrote a letter to Hugh Hefner," Cynthia said. "I told him in effect, that I had a beautiful body and that he should see it."

Michael Blodgett looked at his girl and marveled. "Talk about an aggressive chick!"

Cynthia dimpled at the compliment. "So while the other girls my age were trying out for cheerleader, I was writing to *Playboy*. Mr. Hefner said he would like to see my body, so I went to Chicago and began posing for the magazine."

"Let's push our wedding date up a couple of months!" Michael Blodgett said.

"What did your mother say about your nude pictures?" I asked.

"I was an only child and spoiled, I guess. I usually get my own way. My mother said, 'Oh, isn't that nice?' Girls don't wear white gloves anymore, you know. Women are more pragmatic than men. She thought it was all right if it was what I wanted to do."

And thus, in a way, Nietzsche was responsible for getting one girl to cast off her clothes and pose nude for the world to see. Well, he's been blamed for a lot, so I suppose one more thing . . .

Men started playing their part in the nudity revolution in the middle 1960s. Ian Richardson was a brief sensation in *Marat Sade* at the Martin Beck Theater when he got out of a bathtub with his bare bottom clearly exposed to the audience. The front row seats, incidentally, became more than usually precious.

Time went to photograph him and his bare bottom one night in January, 1966. Julie Christie, who had been nominated for the 1965 Best Actress Oscar, which she won for *Darling*, started to go backstage with her escort, Don Bessent. The stage manager stepped forward.

"I'm afraid," he said, "it might be embarrassing for you to pay Mr. Richardson a visit at this moment. He's completely nude and likely to be so for some time. You know how these photographers are. Always asking for one more shot. But if you don't mind, I don't imagine he will."

Miss Christie looked to her escort for a sign. He gave one—of disapproval. So they left and missed a close look at the Richardson rear.

Although the Richardson backside is sort of a milestone in the now nudity, exposing simply that part of one's anatomy is small beer today.

It has become commonplace for some actors to receive backstage guests totally naked. One of them, Keith Baxter, the gifted young Welshman who co-starred with Anthony Quayle in *Sleuth,* said that he liked to let his body "breathe" after doing a performance, so he walks around unencumbered by clothes while resting.

Press agent Dorothy Ross took me backstage at the Music Box. Baxter was just disrobing. He went around bare for a few minutes; then he put on some shorts and a robe—out of deference to me. He seemed to think it might interfere with my interview if he stayed naked.

"I know Dorothy won't mind," he said.

"Oh, no, not me. I've seen him naked several times," Miss Ross shrugged.

"I really never think anything about it," Baxter said. "If Anthony Quayle and his wife come in here—people I know like that—I sit around naked if I happen to be naked already. If you and your beautiful wife were outside and I heard about it, I'd probably put on something."

But nakedness as a business decoy makes him angry. "I went down to see *The Dirtiest Show in Town,*" he related. "And to think that to see all those bodies in that so-called orgy scene, I had to pay $1.50 more than I would have to see a hit show uptown!"

The bare-chested Ballets Africains threatened to upset our morals way back in 1960. To force those bouncing black ballerinas to wear brassieres seemed criminal, and License Commissioner Bernard O'Connell approved their bareness.

In the pre-Mayor La Guardia days, bare-bosomed girls had been allowed to appear in shows provided they stood statue-still. But to move about—and especially to bounce—was forbidden.

The girls at the Latin Quarter got offended. They had to wear pasties! Well, they wouldn't do it! They'd have a topless strike! Picket line of bare bosoms; how would they like that?

When the Folies Bergère girls, with the tiniest pasties in history, were showing in New York in 1964, a peeping Tom was thrown out by a stagehand.

"I was just looking for a friend," the peeping Tom said.

"Let your friend do his own looking," the stagehand suggested.

As might be expected, the French led the trend for nakedness, and in St. Tropez I found that even the "nice" girls went about topless. Brigitte Bardot and the other beauties would merely shuck off their bikini tops or forget to put them on. It was quite scandalous for a few weeks, but there was a nudist colony nearby. That seemed to make it all right.

"If they're nudists and go nude, that's accepted, but if they're not nudists and go nude, that's not accepted," a French newspaper endeavored to explain.

There was a fat, funny, middle-aged stripper named Carrie Finnell who, on behalf of America, offered a special nude art form to connoisseurs. She was a "tassel-tosser." She wore tassels on her breasts. By careful study she had learned over the years to make her breasts rotate either clockwise, counterclockwise, or both. The spectator saw a considerable portion of the two breasts but even more of the tassels swinging through the air. Carrie Finnell appeared in some New York cafés and in a Broadway show. One night I found her sipping a drink in a Paris sidewalk café. This American *artiste* was teaching the French some new tricks that could be accomplished by *la belle poitrine*.

Kim Novak was an excellent and beautiful example of the change in the attitudes about girls posing for nude or seminude pictures.

Mark Twain said every man was entitled to his favorite brand of insanity, and mine for a while was taking pictures of girls. I was leaving for Hollywood in the fall of 1954 accompanied by my wife and a couple of cameras to do some Hollywood columns. Photographer Gary Wagner said to me, "There's a new girl out there named Kim Novak. Why don't you get some cheesecake of her?"

Kim was narcissistic. She loved being photographed. But Harry Cohn, the czar boss of Columbia Pictures, kept a woman press agent with her to assure that pictures taken of her were decent and had a modicum of dignity. But Kim adored the way her bare body was revealed in pictures and was willing, even eager, to cheat a little so that there'd be more than a flash of her bosom.

I photographed her on a Saturday with the woman press agent watching over her protectively.

"Maybe," Kim said, in an aside to me, "I could come around to-morrow when *she* [the press agent] won't be here, and we can do some different shots."

That was the same as saying she wanted to pose for some cheese-cake. And on Sunday she visited our suite. My wife lent her some fur pieces, slips, etc., and Kim stripped to seminude. We put her in the bathtub, which was common then, and took some pictures that were pretty daring for that year. They mostly showed Kim's shoulders and breasts peeking over the top of the tub.

Kim claimed to love those pictures more than any ever taken of her. Later, she sent me some Christmas cookies along with a tender note signed: "Kimmie."

Harry Cohn exploded when my pictures of chesty Kim started appearing in the girlie magazines.

"Have this photographer barred from the lot!" he commanded, not knowing that the culprit was a columnist conspiring with Kim, who claimed she was hoarding all the clippings showing her semi-nude self and loving them.

After a couple of years of studio buildup to establish that she was a dramatic actress, Kim wearied of the pictures and wrote me a note that hurt.

"Don't you think you should take those horrid pictures of me off the market?" she demanded.

I reminded her that she'd once loved them. "But we're both older now," she replied.

Accepting this slap on the wrist, I withdrew the pictures.

Nine years passed. In the interval she became a big star and, like many similar celebrities, unpredictable. I never knew whether she felt kindly toward me. In March, 1963, my wife and I were in Dub-lin watching her and Laurence Harvey in *Of Human Bondage*. On St. Patrick's night we attended a dinner where I sat on the dais with Kim and talked to her about two nude scenes she was going to do as Mildred in the Somerset Maugham classic.

Kim bubbled over with happiness at the opportunity to go naked.

"At first," she told me, "I thought I should wear some sort of night dress. But now I've decided that nothing should come between me and my audience!"

In fact, when it had been suggested that a "body double" should do the naked scene for her, Kim protested, "Wait a minute! Why should I use a double? Who's got a better body than I have?"

"You've changed your attitude about nudity, haven't you?" I asked her.

"I certainly have!" she said with a laugh that was apologetic and self-accusing. "Say, Earl, why don't you start selling those cheesecake pictures of me again?"

I never did.

Kim was only seminude in my pictures of her. But there were *nude* photographs of her around from the movie.

Diving into the nudity swim about the same time—probably enough months ahead to make her the first and the pioneer—was Carroll Baker, a most unusual girl and one of the first of the movie stars to wear nothing but a smile in a *Playboy* layout. Brought up in Greensburg, Pennsylvania, and St. Petersburg, Florida, she started in show business as a baby-fat brunette teenage magician who called herself "Karol Carroll." She had met "The Great Volta," he had taught her magic, and she had gone on tour with him, acclaimed in the advance publicity as "the Southland's prize-winning beauty." Then came the movies.

After *Giant* and *Baby Doll* in which she played a young wife who sleeps in a crib to avoid her husband—and sucks her thumb a lot—Carroll became known as a sex symbol and became emphatic about the right of a girl to go naked in a picture.

There was a wave of excitement about Carroll being one of the "Three Bares" and remarks about movies being barer than ever. Carroll was in *The Carpetbaggers, Station 7 Sahara,* and *Harlow—* and her opinion about acting in the nude was considered worth printing.

For the first time we heard actresses defending their nakedness by declaring it was "in the context of the story." It became the standard defense.

"I approved the nude scenes each time in the scripts," Carroll said, "because they were in the context of the story. For actresses to do supposed nude scenes and actually wear some kind of flesh-colored tape is ridiculous! Every author—John O'Hara and the rest —are depicting love realistically. Why shouldn't actresses do it?"

Carroll at this time—in 1963—had hopes of succeeding Marilyn Monroe as *the* sex symbol. Her second husband Jack Garfein, who had been her drama coach, was directing her career, and he approved of her nude pictures. But she barred him from the set, she claimed, when she emoted in the nude, fearing his presence would make her nervous.

Carroll Baker was a startlingly beautiful girl up close. Once I went to talk to her in her big apartment on Central Park West. She was wearing lavender slacks of silk jersey and a flowered blouse, and she impressed me with her delicate beauty as well as her hospitality because she had thoughtfully iced some champagne and set out some caviar.

She lectured me gently about "the male propaganda" that alleged that girls were becoming wilder and looser.

"What about the belief that leading men and leading women do better acting if they have a love affair while they're making the film?" I asked her.

"Oh, boy, I call that male propaganda! I don't go along with that at all!"

It seemed very strange a few years later to hear men saying—as the girls had said before them—that *they* would not work nude in a film unless it was "in the context of the story."

But still more remarkable was the new male sex symbol, Frank Langella, fighting off the efforts of a female magazine editor to persuade him to be the first man ever to pose nude for a center spread.

"Girls don't react to pictures of nude men, and I can't think of one reason I should do it," Langella told me.

He was thirty, 6′3″, a bachelor, dark-eyed, with semilong hair, and he excited all excitable girls, portraying a cruel lover in *Diary of a Mad Housewife*. Women started calling him for dates. They were calling him "the sexiest man ever in pictures," and he was rather bored with it all.

"He can't turn down being the first man to do a center spread for a woman's magazine," some of the agents said. "Think of all the publicity."

But he did decline. He also declared he was never going to get married. He'd had an affair with a woman for five years, but he didn't like that arrangement. Women were now just like men.

"They call you, they chase you, they catch you, and then they tell you, 'I don't want you anymore.' Anybody in my business has a lot of men as well as women, crazy about him. What do I do about that? I smile a lot. What can I do?"

Other sex symbols were having their own nudity problems. Kirk Douglas was dressed principally in a belt and gun holster in a western picture, with his buttocks showing.

"What about doing an all-nude western?" we asked Glenn Ford.

"Oh, I'm afraid not," he shuddered. "What about that cactus and climbing over fences? And a cowboy can't be completely naked. A cowboy's got to have on his boots!"

French sex symbol Alain Delon and Maximilian Schell, the Viennese bachelor, were both holding to the line that they'd do it "within the context of the story"—but both sided with Frank Langella in insisting that they'd never marry in today's mixed-up sexual world.

"I can't be stuck with somebody twenty-four hours a day; I can't stand being with the same person all the time," Delon said. "I tell a girl, 'That's the way it is.'"

Max Schell said he simply warned girls ahead of time that he had no intention of getting married; moreover, he has never had a romance with a girl with whom he worked. He might have a romance with her after the picture was completed but never while it was being produced.

"You can wait," he said quite firmly.

In 1970 a new development occurred. Girl dancers came out in the bars on the Hollywood Strip with their pubic hair showing.

They "danced" for lunch and through the cocktail hour. Their dance was just a few wiggles and tosses while they stood there allowing men to ogle their total nudity.

I'd been a girl watcher for several years, but this news stunned me when I heard it. But, if it happened in *Hair* and *Oh, Calcutta!*, why not in bars and bistros?

My wife and I stopped at one such place, "Carolina Lanes," near the Los Angeles International Airport, while en route to catch a night plane. We entered a brightly lit restaurant with all the charm of a cafeteria. Immediately a waiter zoomed over to us with two drinks for each of us at $1.50 a drink. That was our $3 per person minimum charge. And so far we hadn't seen anything. Then we were handed a "souvenir copy" sheet explaining the policy.

"Nude entertainment has been found to be one of our legal rights under the framework of our constitution; it is considered to be a freedom of expression," said a statement on one side of the sheet. "Write to your Councilman or State Senator . . ."

I began wondering where the show was I had come to see.

I began looking at the small stage. Yes, those people definitely had clothes on! But pretty soon those people on stage—the girls—weren't wearing a stitch. They were naked to their shoetops, except that they weren't wearing shoes, either. They were, even with their wiggling and their pubic displays, rather dull. When you've seen one of those girls, you've seen them all. That, I suppose, is a terrible cliché, but like most clichés, it is true. After a certain amount of displaying their naked nooks and crannies, they became sad creatures whom nobody cared to admire.

Then I glanced at the other side of the leaflet . . .

"The only choreographed show in southern California," it said.

And then on to the questions most answered by the nude girls . . .

"Why do the girls do it? For the money. Approximately $50 is average for a four-hour night."

There were some silly questions and answers: "Where do the girls go at night? In the employees' bathroom." "Do all the topless dancers have silicone injections? No, but all the floor men do." "Are the girls married? No, but they are not against practicing." "Why don't the dancers converse with customers? Because most of our customers use the Braille system." "How does one apply for a job as topless or nude? Look for a dirty old man with a lecherous facial expression and ask him for work. If he commences to drool, the job is yours. Warning! Stay out of arm's reach." And so on.

In one of the total nudity bars on the Hollywood Strip, I suddenly felt enormously sorry for the girl who was jiggling listlessly to the music while displaying her pudendum to the audience of seven men.

Three men sat drinking beer at a table near the dancer; three sat at a bar; and then there was me. The three men at the bar observed her sexy gyrations. But the three near her—in fact, only three or four feet from her—were not even looking at her. They were deeply immersed in conversation about something more exciting, and their faces were turned away from her as she went through her erotic contortions.

"This poor girl," I thought, "must have endured mental torture before deciding whether she should make a living by letting men look at her naked body and all its private parts. No matter how sophisticated she has become, she must have given it deep, conscientious thought. And then to stand totally exposed before them—and have them not even look at her—how sad and frustrated she must feel!"

(She probably didn't feel a thing.)

The showing of pubic hair in girls' pictures didn't greatly horrify the girls who discussed it. "They were always putting a fish bowl or an apple in front of it to hide it, and that only drew attention to it," Playmate of the Year Claudia Jennings said. "They felt they had to hide it with something. They got letters from readers saying it wasn't natural not to show the hair, and 'Show the hair!' Now they get letters saying 'Don't show the hair!' The way I feel is, if they can stand up there with their boobs flapping, why not show pubic hair?"

Miss Jennings was much more excited when I told her that the *New Woman* had published a center-spread picture of a nude male model, but hadn't employed "total frontal nudity."

"Well, just tell me," she said, "did they cover it with a big fish bowl or a little fish bowl?"

Recently, too, we have, for the first time, begun to hear talk about the "endowments" of male actors.

Always the term had applied to a bosomy actress but now it could refer to a virile-looking man. A nude play, *Grin and Bare It*, was in rehearsal. The producer, Barry Plaxen, took the cast to a New Jersey nudist camp to get accustomed to walking around naked. It helped make the cast "feel free." One stalwart and also robust actor, James Burgen, attracted the attention of a fellow performer, who said to him:

"I'm going to a costume ball tonight, Jim. Can I borrow your costume?"

(He was looking straight at his "costume" at the time.)

"Sorry," Burgen said, "I never let it out of my sight."

Press agent Mary Bryant issued a "photo call"—the cast members were to pose for pictures.

"I never thought," Miss Bryant reported later, "that I'd have to say to an actor, 'Please cover up your penis.'"

It's all part of the show business revolution. All photographers were warned by the press agents, "Remember, no vaginas and no penises!" The warning was given for good reason. No above-ground newspapers would print pictures with penises and vaginas showing. For most photographers, it was no problem, but for one very good photographer from *Life* magazine, it was impossible. His hand trembled, his camera shook, and he shot the subjects too low, in three different attempts.

They called another photographer to replace Mr. Nervous.

23

The Porno Era, or There's Nowhere to Go But Up

A breasty twenty-one-year-old topless dancer who was also an underground film actress came bouncing into my office to brag how she chased the stars of the rock singing groups right into bed with her.

"You're a groupie?" I asked her.

She threw out her breasts indignantly. (She was wearing a very thin blouse.) "Mr. Wilson, I'm a super groupie! I'm the best ball in town. I've got a great body, and I'm funny. I can go as far as Liz Taylor did in the movies because I've got the same thing she has."

"What's that?"

"Big tits!"

I was a little taken aback at such candor from a youngster and appalled at what seems to be happening to actresses. She was one of those tigresses of the slimy seventies who throw their bodies at rock heroes and then tell the other groupies—as the camp-followers are called—just how titanic or disappointing the gentlemen are in bed.

They are daughters of the bobby-soxers of the forties and a wild modern version of that cult. They are part of the porno, or permissive, period, a product of the sex revolution that is going God knows where. Once it was young men—called wolves or studs—who rampaged about, flouting their carnal exploits. But today's girls— the now girls—are hunting sex in packs, trying more shamelessly to get "celebrity-fucked" than the studs ever did.

Because this sexually precocious youngster's blatant actions may portend the future of many of the nation's modern females, I am going to tell more about her than perhaps I should.

"Gerri," as she called herself, had already achieved some status. She was playing in an underground movie featuring a scene in which she performed fellatio upon an impotent homosexual. She had been praised for the realism of her performance, which she attributed to the fact that she "acted natural."

It occurred to me that she might be a nymphomaniac and therefore not a proper scientific exhibit in this informal study.

"You mean how many guys did I ball?" Her brow creased. "Do you want to count them?" Laughing she produced a telegram from a great soul singer professing his love for her and suggesting their next meeting place. Then she proudly mentioned fifteen or twenty others. "When I watched one television show, I realized I had balled everyone on it . . . No, not all at once!" she hastened to say.

"If I see a cute guy, I want to ball him the same as a guy wants to ball a chick." She paused, licked her sultry lower lip, then added pertly, "Oh, I don't ball anyone—just the ones I like."

"How did you get started?" I asked, becoming more and more astonished by her recital.

She lay back in the comfortable chair in my office and smiled as she recalled with seeming relish some gamy incidents from her past. "I was still little. I started with the high school football star. He asked me to be his girl. He said he couldn't fuck me, and he started to cry. So I helped him and got him to ball me, so I wasn't a virgin anymore. But he was too old-fashioned. I needed somebody more intelligent."

Then she got intoxicated over pursuing the singing stars.

"Last night I was balling Freddie when Jimmy called me," she went on with a kind of relentless and fatalistic glee. "I didn't want to talk to him, so I took the phone off the hook. Well, Jimmy hung on the phone and heard me balling Freddie. He called me back and said, 'How could you? You were saying the same thing to him you said to me.' I always tell them, 'Hey, you're terrific. You're the greatest.' That's what they all want to hear: how good they are.

"Oh, I got it made," Gerri continued, "because I ball good, and I make them breakfast. I have a red spotlight over my bed that makes me look pretty and stuffed animals and a bubble gum machine. Some guys don't like the red light. They tell me to turn it off because it turns them off."

Miss Gerri was so graphic in her descriptions of her sexual gymnastics that I found myself quite shaken. One of her girl friends was pretty snobbish, she thought. This girl didn't like some of the English rock singers and said, "All they want is a good fuck."

"That's all I want, too, a good fuck," Miss Gerri said right back.

But she didn't want to be thought undiscriminating. She made a distinction between those she balled and those for whom she practiced fellatio, depending on what language you're using.

"Who did I ball and who did I blow?" was the way she said it. "Let's see now, who did I ball and who did I blow? I didn't ball just anyone. Just the ones I liked. The ones I didn't like, I just blew." One singer, she said, had taught her to ball, and one had taught her to blow, and she had added certain artistic fine points that drove them wild about Gerri.

Gerri appeared in an Andy Warhol movie that had been not unfavorably reviewed by the *New York Times,* and she was very proud of her part. "You must let me take you to see my movie, Mr. Wilson," Gerri kept saying. I passed up the invitation.

One night on the way to the De Mille Theater on Seventh Avenue, I noticed Gerri's picture on the window display at the Metropole on Broadway and went in. Gerri was on the raised runway above the bar, topless, thrusting out her pelvis in bumps and jerks that suggested copulation. She also shot out her hand several times from her pubic area in a gesture that could only indicate masturbation.

Standing at the bar, I gazed up at her. As her eyes swept the bar crowd, she discovered me, pointed me out, giggled, and threw in several special jerks and bumps. The management bought me a drink. Gerri called down to me that I must go see her picture. I swallowed my drink speedily and fled in embarrassment.

Subsequently, Gerri had some new nude pictures taken. She

thought her naked body photographed well, but she didn't care for her new hairdo.

One of the rock singers wanted one of the pictures.

"I'll let you have one if you promise when you look at it, you won't look at my hair," Gerri said.

He promised.

Gerri excelled at her specialties in the era of the plaster-casters, two groupies who hung around the rock stars' dressing rooms trying to get their idols to insert their penises in plaster so that the girls could have permanent casts of them for their walls or dressing tables.

These incredible girls succeeded in getting some of the most famous rock stars to agree. They took photographs of the plaster penises, and the photographs were published, along with the owners' names, in some underground magazines. The plaster-casters were very proud of their very special art and were angry about other girls competing.

Who were the owners of the penises? Usually the best known American rock singers. Never the Beatles, Tom Jones, nor Engelbert Humperdinck because the plaster-casters probably couldn't get through the security to reach them. But there were certain big rock stars—one of whom was arrested for indecently exposing himself on stage—on their list. The girls simply hung around their dressing rooms at television studios until the stars got the message: that this dumb girl wanted to get into bed with him, and give him a few minutes' pleasure, and make a casting of his organ.

"Man, that's a new kick!" He'd yield, then throw her out when he'd finished with her.

Times Square—and even 42nd Street—will be beautiful some day. "Slime Square," *Variety* aptly called it.

It's a stomach-turner now. But when our sex revolution and era of permissiveness have dwindled away, the porno shops will be replaced by handsome skyscrapers with beautiful theaters visited by attractive people. The old New York will have been succeeded by a new New York composed of sophisticates who fly to Europe in a couple of hours.

But Times Square today—well, that's another story.

Stepping out of my office recently into that area of mental and emotional pollution a few blocks south, I set out to investigate a yellow leaflet handed to me on the street by a man with a lascivious leer. Leaflets from men with lascivious leers intrigue me.

SWINGING FUN CITY, 252 West 46th Street . . .
Model studios are all over the city. And like all of them, we too have Beautiful Models available for Body Painting, Sketching, Nude Photography, and a delightful, relaxing Body Rub. And our Nude Models are truly beautiful. It is a whole new concept. There are continuous LIVE SHOWS from Noon and a special 10:30 performance every evening.

On this yellow leaflet there was a line drawing of a nude model—with the closing line: "Bring this in for a $1.00 discount."

A $1 discount! For what? Well, whatever it is, a $1 discount is a $1 discount—and I rushed pell mell toward Swinging Fun City to get my $1 discount.

"Slime Square" had become a big sex fair. Everywhere I looked were signs, "Mature Adults Only," overhanging the small Broadway and Seventh Avenue theaters showing the skin flicks, the hard-core pornos.

"*The Deviates* in color" shrieked the sign on the Lido, where the Latin Quarter once lured tired businessmen in because it had leg shows. "*Ginger* . . . Her weapon is her body," announced a nude girl poster at the Astor. The World Theater offered *Sexual Freedom Permissiveness in America*—Incredible Keyhole Look at Pornography."

Virgin Runaway and *Balls in Action* . . . *Pillow Party* . . . "Live —The Love Show." *The Sex Machine* at the Circus Cinema . . . "Big 3-Unit Sex Show," "Peep Show," "Sex Show," "Live Nude Models," "Sex Show."

You can get tired of sex shows, even live sex shows.

On the corner of Broadway and 43rd Street, once the location of the Paramount Theater entrance where the bobby-soxers waited during the cold nights for their crooner heroes, is now the New York Bank for Savings.

But show business has not deserted 43rd Street. Eastward between Broadway and Sixth is the once celebrated Henry Miller Theater, named for producer Henry Miller, not the sex author by the same name.

What is there now?

"Male Film Festival—First Run: *Night of Submissions*. Also Male Shorts."

A smaller sign alongside the box office says: "Only for mature adults over twenty-one *who are not easily offended*."

I never got my $1 discount at Swinging Fun City. I walked over there, but it looked too tacky; besides, it was near Dinty Moore's restaurant, and I was afraid some of its celebrity customers whom I know might see me going upstairs to get a body rub from a beautiful nude model or to give a body rub to a beautiful live model, or whatever it is they do there in their "whole new concept."

The porno industry (*porno* is from the Greek and refers to harlots) is involved with show business in that it gives work to actors including some men who are supposed to be having intercourse publicly four or five times a day with a dancing partner who gets as worn out the fourth or fifth time as he does.

The truth is that they're both pretending—or acting—and the happier part is that they get well paid for it—after all, it is acting.

Girls become especially disenchanted with this kind of acting and want to withdraw from it, but some of them reason that it is not much different from burlesque (which keeps coming back into respectability).

You can see these topless, bottomless performers in the so-called live sex shows in sleazy joints where they sometimes pretend to be making a movie.

A fellow with a camera runs around, going through the motions of filming a couple in the act of fornication.

"Hey, Fuzzy," he says to the naked girl—he's supposed to be the director and cameraman as well—"blow some my way," and she turns her writhing body toward him and makes with a bump.

"Yeah, yeah, he's making a movie," laughs one member of the audience scornfully. He knows it's just an excuse to show a couple of people copulating. And just as has always been the case in burlesque houses, there are men sitting around with newspapers over their laps, enjoying themselves in their own way.

"Hey, Pussycat," the director calls to the naked girl—this gets a big laugh—"bring your pussycat over here. I want to stroke your pussycat."

"There's an uncover charge to stroke my pussycat," she says.

The ensuing dialogue is even worse. Shows with such talk as this are featured in the "live sex" emporia. One wild place, the Club Orgy in Greenwich Village, was closed by police after a newspaper undertook to review its acts with complete candor.

In the Broadway burlesque houses, the strippers no longer wear G-strings—and it seems a disservice has been done somehow to stripping.

For all those years girl stopped just short of showing their dearest possession to men, and now they show it. And it doesn't seem so dear anymore.

Total nudity hurt their business—that and those peep-show machines and live sex shows that made stripping thoroughly passe.

The Don Rickles comedy show at the Copacabana in April, 1971, was the most physical, the sexiest, and the dirtiest, that I had ever seen in a night club of standing. However, bad taste has now become quite popular, and Rickles did a huge business. He himself probably thought he had cleaned up the show because he no longer publicly scratched himself and hardly ever goosed people, especially women.

"Oh, I gotta get a broad so bad," he would say as he roamed the floor. Then he would get racial and refer to some Italian singer "with oil on his ass," not forgetting the Poles, the Irish, and "the spooks."

He would induce two men to come from the audience and insist that they participate with him in an imaginary football huddle.

"Signals!" he would call out. Then there would be a suggestion of sodomy in the backfield, with him as the sodomist.

"You got a fever, for Christ's sake," he would tell one of the bent-over men. Then he would continue the imaginary anal attack, finally shouting, "You better get some water, we're locked!"

Enemas were gag material to Rickles. And, describing how various nationalities would behave in time of a military attack, he pictured a Mexican saying, "I don't care who's attackin', I'm goin' to the toilet." Some Chinese sat in the mezzanine. "You enjoyin' the show, Chink?" he asked. "Go back there and eat the egg rolls and get the runs like I did."

CBS President Robert Wood, who was giving Rickles a chance on television after he'd lost out at ABC, was singled out for special attention.

"Not too many asses I kiss," Rickles said, "but I'm gonna kiss his till I find out I'm not on, and then he can do the job himself."

One wondered when some gallant male escort was going to punch him for implying that his girl friend was ugly. "You're very pretty," he would say to a ringside female. Then, shaking his head, he would add, "Must have been a head-on crash."

"You gotta be Jewish," he would say. "A mink coat on and it's 105 in here."

Continuing his policy of offering something to alienate everybody, he mentioned religion. The Jews' God, he said, would never be riding on any donkey. He's come up in a Rolls-Royce. He'd say to his wife, "Hi, Mary. Is the kid in?"

Rickles came up with approximately two printable jokes in an hour of material.

"Kirk Douglas couldn't be here," he said. "He's in Washington introducing himself to anybody." And he claimed to have had a note from Frank Sinatra, Jr. "We're gonna kidnap the old man." Rickles also dwelt upon an alleged sexual experience with his wife that impressed me as being both revolting and unfunny. However, Don Rickles liked it.

Red Buttons, when introduced, was not satisfied to merely be introduced. He complimented Rickles on using the word *ass* so effectively. "Buddy Hackett tried it," Buttons said. "But you're so much better. When you say, 'Kiss my ass,' you can almost taste it."

Everybody was talking about free speech and more freedom of expression in 1971—but they didn't refer to the startling language tossed lightly across dinner tables or over cocktail glasses when the Beautiful People gathered. That language had been free as a bird for some time. For one who remembered when whore was a word no nice girl used, it was a shock to hear a teenaged or early twentyish dinner companion rip off a Lenny Bruceism. And, whereas males shrank from using such expressions, girls in show business especially dropped words like prick, cunt and cocksucker quite freely in normal conversation.

Gwen Davis in her novel *The Pretenders* word-painted a scene at a dinner party where the guests discovered that there were several people under the table ready to make oral love to them while *they* had dinner.

The dinner party stories in 1970 and 1971 included one about a man about to have sex with his wife, going into a bathroom to put on a contraceptive. His small son followed and observed.

"What are you doing, Daddy?" the boy asked.

Flustered pater said, "I'm going to catch a mouse."

"What are you going to do with it, Daddy? Fuck it?"

Where do we go from here in this crazy revolution, this sick era of permissiveness? The overturning of the traditional has been so drastic and swift (in show business as in all other areas) that one hesitates to predict.

It seems as if it was only last week that we were shocked to read about wife-swapping in novels. When *Screw* magazine left the underground and came above ground, we saved a few copies, convinced that they would be collectors' items because the periodical would be banned, and everybody connected with it would land in jail. But the rag got bolder, its "spread shots" introduced new slang, and some of the more acceptable "literary" magazines decided that if *Screw* could show pubic hair, they could too. Where do we go from here? What hasn't been shown?

In the movies, the "tits and sand" pictures were once thought daring, but now the "sex and sadism" productions make them seem like Bible treatises.

The Bang Bang Gang was reviewed in *Variety*, August 26, 1970, and showed just what can be accomplished if you try:

> Brutal stuff . . . This cheapie is a graphic, sado-sexual orgy in a barn . . . Edward Blessington shoots Michael Kirkwood in both hands, then strips and spread eagles Revel Quinn across a car and beats her buttocks bloody with a leather strap . . . Next in front of his gang and hers, he forces her to perform fellatio on him and when she hesitates, pumps a bullet into her boy friend, Mark Griffin.
>
> Blessington rapes the dazed girl, and stabs her to get her to writhe orgiastically. Bambi Allen ties Jae Miller to the wall and performs the standard lesbian sequence. It is the type of project that the producer-director-actor-writer Van Guylder, the actors and actresses, technicians and distributors and exhibitors, can always be ashamed of.

The film producers are claiming that the pendulum has swung back and that sex pictures will vanish. There's been a backlash against permissiveness and pornography. The public has had too much "dirty" movie fare and is ignoring the X-rated pictures, show-ing a preference for simple, sweet, straightforward stories. A little sex is all right, but not just sex for sex's sake, is what the producers are saying.

But I do not believe the forecasts that the era of sexy movies is over. At the 1971 Cannes Film Festival, Mrs. Mike Frankovich, actress Binnie Barnes, a lady not easily shocked, showed me a bro-chure and exclaimed, "Look what Denmark's trying to sell us!"

The brochure extolled a documentary film titled *Why* in which a girl from the farm fondles a horse's penis and frolics with other beasts of the field in what's clinically called bestiality.

The film was shown on four different days and was offered for distribution in America and elsewhere. It was one of the few films that's gone beyond the American-made sex shockers. As *Variety* says:

"The time is now at hand when European audiences are looking for a U.S. label on pix to insure titillation, much as U.S. sensation seekers sought out the Danish, Swedish, Italian features a few years back."

America—the land of the free and the home of dirty movies! Puri-tan America had become Prurient America. If you didn't get a glimpse of some pudenda in a movie, you could ask for your money back. And it wasn't just "cheapies" and "skin flicks" either (although on Broadway, the only movies getting $5 admission, beside *Wood-stock*, were the pornographics).

Lana Turner told me as she went on stage for the first time in *40 Carats* that she took the chance because of Hollywood's sex trend.

"I was so tired of turning down that Hollywood junk they kept offering me," she said. "The last one I read had a father who was a degenerate and a mother who would play with anything that would hold still. A real American love story for the whole family!"

In England, too, voices were lifted against "the tidal wave of obscenity," as the Bishop of Coventry, the Rt. Rev. Cuthbert Bardsley, called it when he attacked the avant-garde for encouraging dirty films and plays.

Labeling the obscenity-pornography wave "the disease of perver-sion and depravity," the bishop said—correctly, in my opinion—"The paradox is that the purveyors of the disease are represented as the fighters for freedom and those who oppose them as the enemies of progress."

Yes, there were those claiming there was a reformation starting.
But the theater is not cleaning itself up. The night club acts are
still sex-oriented. Rather, the shows and movies and skits seem to
be getting racier, spicier, and bluer. The revolution in show business
sweeps right ahead in those areas. Some day, however, the theater
and night club audiences will return to simpler, saner, more pleasant fare. That will be a happy time for the moralists. But I suppose
it will also be a rather dull time, compared to the wild and wicked
show business that we're living through today.

Index

N